AF335275

THE PSYCHOLOGY
OF LEARNING AND MOTIVATION

Advances in Research and Theory

VOLUME 46

THE PSYCHOLOGY OF LEARNING AND MOTIVATION

Advances in Research and Theory

EDITED BY BRIAN H. ROSS

BECKMAN INSTITUTE AND
DEPARTMENT OF PSYCHOLOGY
UNIVERSITY OF ILLINOIS AT URBANA-CHAMPAIGN
URBANA, ILLINOIS

Volume 46

AMSTERDAM • BOSTON • HEIDELBERG • LONDON
NEW YORK • OXFORD • PARIS • SAN DIEGO
SAN FRANCISCO • SINGAPORE • SYDNEY • TOKYO
Academic Press is an imprint of Elsevier

Academic Press is an imprint of Elsevier
525 B Street, Suite 1900, San Diego, California 92101-4495, USA
84 Theobald's Road, London WC1X 8RR, UK

This book is printed on acid-free paper. ∞

For information on all Elsevier Academic Press publications
visit our Web site at www.books.elsevier.com

ISBN-13: 978-0-12-543346-4
ISBN-10: 0-12-543346-8

PRINTED IN THE UNITED STATES OF AMERICA
06 07 08 09 9 8 7 6 5 4 3 2 1

CONTENTS

CONCEPTS AS PROTOTYPES

James A. Hampton

AN ANALYSIS OF PROSPECTIVE MEMORY

Richard L. Marsh, Gabriel I. Cook, and Jason L. Hicks

ACCESSING RECENT EVENTS

Brian McElree

SIMPLE: FURTHER APPLICATIONS OF A LOCAL DISTINCTIVENESS MODEL OF MEMORY

Ian Neath and Gordon D. A. Brown

WHAT IS MUSICAL PROSODY?

Caroline Palmer and Sean Hutchins

CONTRIBUTORS

Numbers in parentheses indicate the pages on which the authors' contributions begin.

F. Gregory Ashby (1), Department of Psychology, University of California, Santa Barbara, Santa Barbara, California 93106

Gordon D. A. Brown (201), Department of Psychology, University of Warwick, Coventry CV4 7AL, United Kingdom

Gabriel I. Cook (115), Department of Psychology, Claremont McKenna College, Claremont, California 91711

John M. Ennis (1), Department of Psychology, University of California, Santa Barbara, Santa Barbara, California 93106

James Hampton (79), Department of Psychology, City University, London EC1V 0HB, United Kingdom

Brett K. Hayes (37), School of Psychology, University of New South Wales, Sydney, New South Wales, Australia

Jason L. Hicks (115), Department of Psychology, Louisiana State University, Baton Rouge, Louisiana 70803

Sean Hutchins (245), Department of Psychology, McGill University, Montreal, QC H3A 1B1, Canada

Richard L. Marsh (115), Department of Psychology, University of Georgia, Athens, Georgia 30605

Brian McElree (155), Department of Psychology, New York University, New York, New York 10003

Ian Neath (201), Department of Psychological Sciences, Purdue University, West Lafayette, Indiana 47907-2081

Caroline Palmer (245), Department of Psychology, McGill University, Montreal, QC H3A 1B1, Canada

THE ROLE OF THE BASAL GANGLIA IN CATEGORY LEARNING

F. Gregory Ashby and John M. Ennis

I. Introduction

Categorization is the act of responding differently to objects or events in separate classes or categories. It is a vitally important skill that allows us to approach friend and escape foe, to find food and avoid toxin. Every organism must have some categorization ability. Even bacteria categorize. For example, the bacterium *Escherichia coli* tumbles randomly until it encounters a substance that it categorizes as a nutrient. It then suppresses its tumbling behavior and swims up the concentration gradient in search of the nutrient's source.

The scientific study of human category learning has a long history. For most of this time, the focus was on the cognitive processes that mediate categorization. Within the past decade, however, considerable attention has shifted to the study of the neural basis of category learning. Categorization is an ancient skill, so we should expect to find some categorization abilities in phylogenetically older parts of the human brain. In fact, this research indicates that among the most important brain areas in human category learning are the basal ganglia, a prominent collection of subcortical structures that have been implicated in procedural learning.

Squire (1992) was perhaps the first to propose that the basal ganglia might play some role in human categorization. The first theory of category learning that assigned a major role to the basal ganglia was COmpetition between

THE PSYCHOLOGY OF LEARNING
AND MOTIVATION VOL. 46
DOI: 10.1016/S0079-7421(06)46001-1

Verbal and Implicit Systems (COVIS) (Ashby, Alfonso-Reese, Turken, & Waldron, 1998). Briefly, COVIS postulates that human category learning is mediated by multiple systems, with two hypothesized systems that assign a key role to the basal ganglia—a logical-reasoning system and a procedural-learning system. The past few years have seen many results that link the basal ganglia to category learning. These new data were collected using a wide variety of methodologies, including animal lesions, single-cell recording, functional neuroimaging, traditional cognitive testing, and a diverse set of research subjects, including animals, healthy humans, and various neuropsychological patient groups.

This chapter reviews evidence that the basal ganglia play various important roles in category learning. We begin with an overview of the functional neuroanatomy of the basal ganglia, including its relatively unique neural plasticity. We then review the behavioral neuroscience studies that originally called attention to this brain region as a possible important locus of category learning. Next we describe the most important category-learning tasks that are used with human subjects. Section V reviews the relevant neuropsychological patient data, with a focus on patients with basal ganglia disease, while Section VI reviews the existing neuroimaging data. Section VII describes the COVIS theory in more detail, and Section VIII considers some tests of this theory. Section IX discusses some possible future extensions of the model, and in Section X we close with some general comments and observations.

II.   Functional Neuroanatomy of the Basal Ganglia

This section reviews the functional neuroanatomy of the basal ganglia, with special emphasis on features that are relevant to category learning. For more details, see Gerfen and Wilson (1996). The basal ganglia, which are an important collection of subcortical structures, include input structures, output structures, and collections of cells that produce the neurotransmitter dopamine. A schematic illustrating the functional anatomy of the basal ganglia is shown in Fig. 1.

The input structures include the caudate nucleus, the putamen, and the nucleus accumbens. The caudate nucleus and putamen together are often referred to as the neostriatum, and when the nucleus accumbens is added, the entire set is called the striatum. For category learning (at least with visual or auditory stimuli), the caudate nucleus is the most important of these three structures.

The striatum receives numerous prominent inputs. For category learning, the most important of these are from cortex. In humans, all areas of cortex

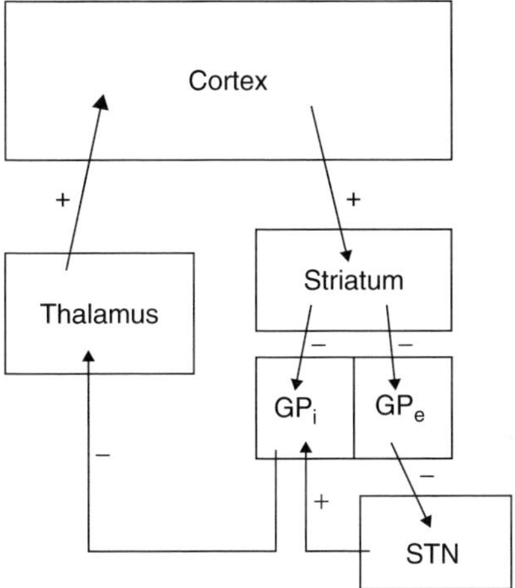

Fig. 1.　Schematic illustrating major structures and primary projections of the basal ganglia (GP$_i$: internal segment of the globus pallidus, GP$_e$: external segment of the globus pallidus, STN: subthalamic nucleus).

(except V1) send direct excitatory projections to the striatum. The putamen receives input from somatasensory and motor areas, the caudate receives input from visual and auditory association areas and frontal cortex, and the nucleus accumbens receives input from orbitofrontal cortex and anterior cingulate (Heimer, 1995). The projections from cortex to the striatum are characterized by massive convergence. In fact, it has been estimated that the convergence ratio from cortex to the striatum is approximately 10,000:1 (Wilson, 1995). Thus, the striatum is in a unique position in the human brain, since it receives direct but highly compressed input from virtually the entire cortex.

Compared to cortex, the structure of the striatum is extremely simple. It contains a single layer composed of medium spiny cells. The dendrites of these cells receive input from the axons of cortical pyramidal cells, and the medium spiny cell axons project out of the striatum to the basal ganglia output structures—primarily the globus pallidus and substantia nigra pars reticulata. The medium spiny cells are gabaergic and hence inhibitory, with a low spontaneous firing rate.

The output structures of the basal ganglia include the globus pallidus, the substantia nigra pars reticulata, and the subthalamic nucleus. There are two primary output pathways from the striatum to cortex, called the direct and indirect pathways. In this section, we focus on the direct pathway, which is the more relevant pathway to current theories of category learning. The indirect pathway is discussed in Section IX.

In the direct pathway, the medium spiny cells project from the striatum to the internal segment of the globus pallidus or the substantia nigra pars reticulata.[1] These gabaergic cells then project to the thalamus, which in turn, sends excitatory projections to cortex. Spontaneous activity in the globus pallidus is high (Wilson, 1995), and the globus pallidus tonically inhibits the thalamus. Cortical activation of the striatum, however, causes the striatal medium spiny cells to inhibit the pallidal cells, thereby releasing the thalamus from its tonic inhibition. Because of this functional architecture, the basal ganglia are frequently described as applying a brake on cortex because they tonically prevent the thalamus from stimulating cortex. Cortex can release the brake by stimulating the striatum.

Dopamine-producing cells originate in the ventral tegmental area (VTA) and the substantia nigra pars compacta (SN_{PC}). The VTA dopamine cells project to frontal cortex (primarily orbitofrontal, prefrontal, and anterior cingulate cortices) and structures in the limbic system (primarily amygdala and nucleus accumbens). These dopamine pathways constitute the mesocorticolimbic dopamine system. Dopamine cells in the SN_{PC} project to all input and output structures of the basal ganglia and form the nigrostriatal dopamine system (Heimer, 1995).

The axons of dopamine cells display many characteristic varicosities that each contains a high density of synaptic vesicles. Stimulation of a single dopamine cell therefore causes dopamine release at a wide number of target sites. For this reason, dopamine is often classified as a neuromodulator rather than as a neurotransmitter. Within the striatum, the varicosities tend to be localized in the vicinity of the dendritic spines that characterize the medium spiny cells. These same spines are the terminal projection sites of the axons of glutamatergic pyramidal cells from cortex (DiFiglia, Pasik, & Pasik, 1978; Freund, Powell, & Smith, 1984; Graybiel, 1990; Smiley, Levey, Ciliax, & Goldman-Rakic, 1994).

There is good evidence that dopamine modulates the effects of presynaptic glutamate release into medium spiny cell synapses in two separate ways. First, it increases postsynaptic signal-to-noise ratio and second, it promotes long-term potentiation (LTP), which effectively strengthens the synapse. Both of these actions are thought to be dependent on exactly which postsynaptic glutamate receptors are activated. The role of dopamine in striatal LTP is a critical feature of current neurobiological theories of category

---

[1] The internal segment of the globus pallidus and the substantia nigra pars reticulata are functionally similar. Figure 1 depicts only the former of these structures.

learning. The ability of LTP to increase signal-to-noise ratio plays a central role in a number of current neurobiological models of executive function, but this property has not yet been incorporated into models of category learning. Thus, in this section we focus on the role of dopamine in LTP, and we briefly consider how dopamine affects signal-to-noise ratio in Section IX.

There are a number of different glutamate receptors, but for our purposes the two most important are the NMDA and AMPA receptors. The AMPA receptor becomes active when small amounts of glutamate are presynaptically released. However, the NMDA receptor has a high threshold for activation because when the postsynaptic cell is hyperpolarized, the NMDA receptor is blocked by a magnesium plug. This plug dissociates from the receptor after the cell is partially depolarized. Thus, a strong presynaptic glutamate signal is required to activate postsynaptic NMDA receptors (Cooper, Bloom, & Roth, 1991).

Dopamine plays a key role in learning and memory within the basal ganglia. Many years ago, Donald Hebb (1949) proposed that memories are encoded as changes in the strengths of synapses across widely distributed neural networks. Much evidence suggests that the empirical signatures of such changes are long-term potentiation (LTP) and long-term depression (LTD) (Grimwood, Martin, & Morris, 2001), which refer to persistent increases and decreases, respectively, in synaptic efficiency that are observed under certain laboratory conditions. One of the conditions that are necessary for LTP to occur is NMDA receptor activation (Bliss & Collingridge, 1993; Malenka, 1995). Within the neostriatum, a second necessary condition is dopamine receptor activation (Centonze, Picconi, Gubellini, Bernardi, & Calabresi, 2001; Kerr & Wickens, 2001). These discoveries have led to proposals that learning in the striatum (i.e., synapse strengthening) requires three factors: (1) strong presynaptic activation, (2) strong postsynaptic (i.e., NMDA receptor) activation, and (3) dopamine release (Arbuthnott, Ingham, & Wickens, 2000; Calabresi, Pisani, Centonze, & Bernardi, 1996; Nairn, Hemmings, Walaas, & Greengard, 1998; Pessin et al., 1994; Wickens, 1990, 1993). Together, these factors constitute the "three-factor learning."

The first two factors should occur if the cortical input is coming from cells representing the signal. For example, in the case of sensory association cortex, cells that are maximally tuned to the presented stimulus will fire strongly and therefore will likely activate postsynaptic NMDA receptors in striatum. In contrast, cortical noise will tend to activate striatal medium spiny cells only weakly. Therefore, according to the three-factor learning rule, noise is most likely to cause LTD. Assuming then that some relevant signal is represented in cortex, the three-factor learning rule predicts that learning will occur in the striatum if and only if dopamine is released shortly after NMDA receptor activation occurs. Thus, to develop a theory of the conditions under which striatal learning can occur, we need only study the conditions under which striatal dopamine release is likely.

A review of the voluminous dopamine literature is beyond the scope of this article. Briefly, however, dopamine cells have been shown to fire to *any* unexpected salient stimulus, including unexpected rewards (Mirenowicz & Schultz, 1994), stressful or noxious stimuli (Imperato, Puglisi-Allegra, Casolini, & Angelucci, 1991; Sorg & Kalivas, 1993), and even to random light flashes and tones that are not associated with either reward or punishment (Horvitz, Stewart, & Jacobs, 1997). These results have led to proposals that dopamine serves as a learning signal (Beninger, 1983; Miller, Sanghera, & German, 1981; Montague, Dayan, & Sejnowski, 1996; Schultz, 1998; Sutton & Beninger, 1999; White, 1989; Wickens, 1993), and also that it plays a prominent role in motivational processes (Robbins & Everitt, 1996; Salamone & Correa, 2002; Wise, 2002). Satoh, Nakai, Sato, and Kimura (2003) reported evidence that dopamine can play both roles—in particular, that dopamine release to a stimulus is primarily motivational, whereas dopamine release to feedback that follows a response serves as a learning signal.

Many studies have shown that dopamine release to a feedback signal increases with the difference between the obtained reward and the expected reward—that is, dopamine release increases when the outcome is unexpectedly good, dopamine levels remain at baseline if the outcome is as expected, and dopamine levels are depressed if the outcome is worse than expected (Schultz, 1998; Schultz, Dayan, & Montague, 1997). So if LTP occurs in the basal ganglia only when dopamine levels are elevated, we can expect LTP in the basal ganglia during category learning on trials when the subject receives feedback that his or her response was correct but only before categorization expertise develops (i.e., so that the positive feedback is unexpected) and only at synapses from cortical cells strongly tuned to the presented stimulus (so NMDA receptors are activated). In all other cases, we expect either no change in synaptic strength or LTD.

This three-factor model of LTP is appealing, but a serious timing problem must be solved before it can operate effectively. The problem is that shortly after the stimulus is presented, the (visual) cortical-striatal synapse (i.e., in the tail of the caudate) will be activated, but the dopamine release must necessarily occur several seconds later. This is because dopamine release follows reward, which follows the response, which follows the stimulus presentation. Without an additional mechanism, there will be no record of which synapse was responsible for the decision, so that there is no possibility for the correct synapse to be strengthened. Evolution has produced an ingenious solution to this problem. NMDA receptor activation causes an influx of free Ca^{2+} into the spines of the striatal medium spiny cells. This Ca^{2+} triggers a number of chemical reactions, some of which have the effect of depolarizing the cell and eventually causing it to fire. After the cell fires, a natural hyperpolarization process is triggered that resets its membrane potential. The result is that by the time the dopamine is released, the depolarization produced by the presynaptic glutamate release has been erased from the major compartments of the medium spiny cell. However, because the spines are physically separated from the bulk of the intracellular medium, the mechanisms that reset the membrane potential operate more slowly in the spines than in the main cellular compartments. In fact, it turns out that free Ca^{2+} persists in the spines for several seconds after entering the cell (Gamble & Koch, 1987; MacDermott, Mayer, Westbrook, Smith, & Barker, 1986). Thus, so long as the reward is delivered within a few seconds of the response, a trace will still exist in the critical spines that were responsible for eliciting the behavior that earned the reward, and the correct synapses will be strengthened (i.e., via LTP). One should note that an obvious and exceptionally strong prediction of this model is that category learning mediated by the striatum should be severely impaired if the feedback is delayed more than a few seconds after the response. We describe a successful test of this prediction in Section VIII.

Other brain areas, most notably hippocampus and cortex, appear to require only two factors for learning to occur, namely strong pre- and postsynaptic activation (Malenka & Siegelbaum, 2001). Thus, such learning is not reward mediated but instead simply requires mere stimulus presentation. For example, we typically have episodic recall of neutral events that happen during the day as well as those associated with reward. Although dopamine is released into frontal cortex (from the VTA), dopamine reuptake in cortex is much slower than in the striatum, and dopaminergic effects in prefrontal cortex (PFC) have been observed for many minutes after brief phasic firing of VTA dopamine cells (Scatton, Dubois, Dubocovich, Zahniser, & Fage, 1985). As a result, if cortical dopamine promotes LTP, then one might expect LTP to occur not only at synapses that were active just before reward but also at synapses that are active many seconds or minutes after reward. Reward-mediated learning requires temporal specificity—that is, it is critical to strengthen only those synapses that were responsible for eliciting the reward. As a result, PFC might be a poor candidate for reward-mediated learning. If so, then we should expect category learning that is mediated by hippocampus or PFC to be flexible with respect to the timing and nature of feedback.

III.   Behavioral Neuroscience Studies

The first behavioral neuroscience evidence that the basal ganglia might play an important role in category learning came from lesion studies in rats and monkeys showing that the tail of the caudate[2] is both necessary *and* sufficient for visual discrimination learning. Many studies showed that lesions of the tail of the caudate nucleus impair the ability of animals to learn visual discriminations (McDonald & White, 1993, 1994; Packard, Hirsch, & White, 1989; Packard & McGaugh, 1992). For example, in one study, rats with lesions in the tail of the caudate could not learn to discriminate between safe and unsafe platforms in the Morris water maze when the unsafe platform was marked with vertical lines and the safe platform was marked with horizontal lines (Packard & McGaugh, 1992). However, the same animals learned normally when the cues signaling which platform was safe were spatial. This normal performance and their intact visual cortex suggest that the visual discrimination learning deficit of these animals was not perceptual in nature. Rather, it appears that their difficulty was in learning to associate an appropriate response with each stimulus alternative, and in fact, many researchers have hypothesized that this is the primary role of the neostriatum (Rolls, 1994; Wickens, 1993). Technically, such visual discrimination tasks are categorization tasks with one exemplar per category, so these caudate lesion studies support the hypothesis that the caudate contributes to normal category learning.

The sufficiency of the caudate nucleus for visual discrimination learning was shown in a series of studies in which all pathways out of visual cortex were lesioned except those into the tail of the caudate, [e.g., projections into PFC were lesioned by Eacott and Gaffan (1991) and Gaffan and Eacott (1995); projections to the hippocampus and amygdala were lesioned by Gaffan and Harrison (1987)]. None of these lesions affected visual discrimination learning. Another related line of work showed that visual discrimination learning is not mediated by medial temporal lobe structures (McDonald & White, 1993, 1994; Packard et al., 1989).

Single unit recording studies confirm the neostriatal contribution to category learning. For example, Romo and his colleagues taught monkeys to classify a vibrotactile stimulus (i.e., a rod vibrating against the monkey's finger) as either "low speed" or "high speed" (Merchant, Zainos, Hernandez, Salinas, & Romo, 1997; Romo, Merchant, Ruiz, Crespo, & Zainos, 1995). A large number of cells in the putamen showed learning-related changes in their firing properties. For example, after training, many cells fired to any vibrational frequency in the low-speed category but not to frequencies in the high-speed category (and vice/versa). These neurons were not active during passive experience with the stimuli or during a control

---

[2] In rats, the caudate and putamen are not distinct. So in the rat studies, the lesions were to an area of the striatum homologous to the primate tail of the caudate.

motor task. Furthermore, the activity of these neurons predicted the behavior of the monkeys.

A separate line of research implicates the dorsal striatum (e.g., head of the caudate nucleus) in another skill that could be important in many forms of category learning—namely, task and rule switching. This evidence is reviewed in part A of Section VII.

IV. Category-Learning Tasks Used with Human Subjects

Until only a few years ago, little attention was paid to the specific categorization task used in human studies. This led to considerable confusion and disagreement in the literature. For example, some studies showed that Parkinson's disease patients were profoundly impaired in category learning, some showed that they were only mildly impaired, and some reported normal performance for this group. Ashby and Ell (2001) identified four types of category-learning tasks and showed that most of these discrepancies disappear when the data are partitioned according to the type of task used. Ashby and O'Brien (2005) argued that this scheme for classifying category-learning tasks is successful because the four different tasks primarily load on different memory systems. There is substantial evidence that the basal ganglia help mediate procedural memory (Mishkin, Malamut, & Bachevalier, 1984; Saint-Cyr, Taylor, & Lang, 1988; Willingham, 1998) and working memory (Ashby, Ell, Valentin, & Casale, 2005; Hikosaka, Sakamoto, & Sadanari, 1989; Janahashi et al., 2002; Schultz & Romo, 1992), so according to the Ashby and O'Brien (2005) hypothesis category-learning tasks that depend on either of these two memory systems should show sensitivity to basal ganglia function. The four category-learning tasks identified by Ashby and O'Brien (2005) are rule-based tasks, information-integration tasks, unstructured tasks, and prototype-distortion tasks. We briefly describe these tasks in the remainder of this section. For more details, see Ashby and Maddox (2005) or Ashby and O'Brien (2005). In later sections, we review evidence that, of these tasks, rule-based and information-integration tasks are most dependent on basal ganglia function.

A. Rule-Based Tasks

In rule-based tasks, the categories can be learned via some explicit reasoning process. In most cases the rule that maximizes accuracy is easy to describe verbally (Ashby et al., 1998). In the simplest applications, only one stimulus dimension is relevant, and the subject's task is to discover this relevant dimension and then to map the different dimensional values to the relevant categories. More difficult rule-based tasks require attention to two or more dimensions. For example, the correct rule might be a conjunction of the type: "the stimulus is in category A if it is large and bright." The key requirement is that the correct categorization rule in rule-based tasks is one that can be discovered by an explicit reasoning process.

Virtually all category-learning tasks used in neuropsychological assessment are rule based, including the widely known Wisconsin Card Sorting Test (Heaton, 1981). Stimuli in this test are cards containing geometric patterns that vary in color, shape, and symbol number, and in all cases the correct categorization rule is one-dimensional and easy to describe verbally. Perseverative errors on the Wisconsin Card Sorting Test are a classic symptom of frontal dysfunction (Kimberg, D'Esposito, & Farah, 1997).

Ashby and O'Brien (2005) argued that learning in rule-based tasks is mediated primarily by declarative memory systems. The idea is that working memory is used to store hypotheses about category membership during their testing and medial temporal lobe memory systems are used for the long-term storage and consolidation of these rules.

B.   INFORMATION-INTEGRATION TASKS

In information-integration category-learning tasks, accuracy is maximized only if information from two or more stimulus dimensions is integrated at some predecisional stage. Typically, the optimal strategy in information-integration tasks is difficult or impossible to describe verbally (Ashby et al., 1998). An example is shown in Fig. 2. Each stimulus in this experiment is a circular sine-wave grating that varies across trials in the width of the dark and light bars, and in the orientation of these bars. The category boundary is denoted by the broken diagonal line. In this case, because of the incommensurable nature of the two stimulus dimensions, this bound is difficult (or impossible) to describe verbally. Even so, healthy young adults can reliably learn such categories (Ashby & Maddox, 1992).

Real-world examples of information-integration tasks are common. For example, deciding whether an x-ray shows a tumor requires years of training, and expert radiologists are only partially successful at describing their categorization strategies. In part B of Section VIII, we will describe evidence that information-integration tasks frequently activate procedural memory.

One information-integration task that has been popular historically is the weather prediction task (Knowlton, Squire, & Gluck, 1994) in which subjects are required to classify constellations of one, two, or three tarot cards into one of two categories ("rain" or "sun") based on a probabilistic relationship among the cues displayed on each card. Although many experiments have been performed using the weather prediction task, it is difficult to

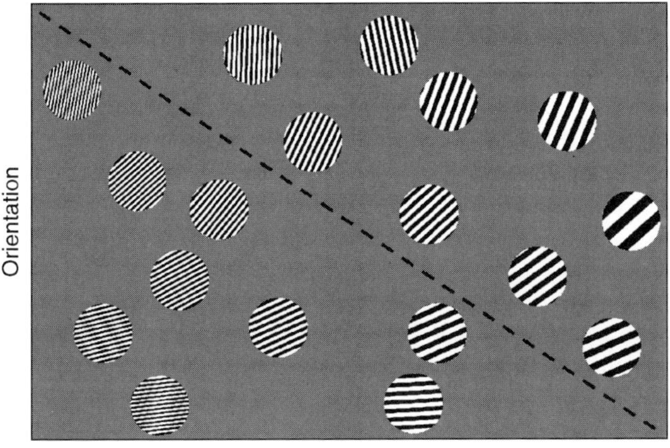

Fig. 2.   Stimuli and category structure of an information-integration category-learning task.

draw strong inferences from data collected with this task because near optimal performance can be achieved by a variety of different strategies (e.g., information-integration, rule-based, explicit memorization). In fact, an analysis of the strategies used by subjects in this task suggests most either memorize responses to single-cue stimuli and otherwise guess or else they apply simple single-cue rules (Ashby & Maddox, 2005; Gluck, Shohamy, & Myers, 2002).

C.   Unstructured Tasks

In unstructured category-learning tasks, the exemplars of each category lack any coherent structure that could be discovered, for example, via logical reasoning. For example, it seems likely that unstructured categories, such as "my personal numbers" (e.g., phone numbers, zip code, and social security number), are learned via explicit memorization that depends on the medial temporal lobes.

D.   Prototype-Distortion Tasks

In a fourth type of category-learning task, a category is created by first defining a category prototype and then by randomly distorting the prototype to create the other category members. In the most popular version, the prototype is a constellation of dots and the category exemplars are created by randomly perturbing the location of each dot in the prototype pattern (Posner & Keele, 1968, 1970). In the (A, not A) prototype-distortion task, there is a single prototype. Stimuli not belonging to the category that results from distortions of this prototype are random patterns. It has been proposed that the perceptual representation memory system mediates much of the learning that occurs in the (A, not A) prototype-distortion task (Ashby & Casale, 2002; Ashby & O'Brien, 2005; Reber & Squire, 1999).

V. Neuropsychological Patient Data

The basal ganglia are affected in a number of neuropsychological diseases, but the two for which there is the most category-learning data are Parkinson's disease and Huntington's disease. Parkinson's disease is a neurodegenerative disorder in which the brain's dopamine-producing cells die. The loss of dopamine causes abnormal functioning in areas that are targets of dopamine release. All of the dopamine-producing areas are affected, although typically the cells in the SN_{PC} are the first to die. Thus, the striatum is typically the first target area affected. There is considerable individual difference in Parkinson's disease with respect to the locus of greatest effect. However, postmortem autopsy reveals that, within the caudate nucleus, the greatest and earliest damage is predominantly within the head (van Domburg & ten Donkelaar, 1991).

Huntington's disease is a rare (1 in 18,000) and fatal genetic disorder that kills the medium spiny cells in the caudate and putamen. Symptoms typically appear between the ages of 30 and 50, and the disease has a time course of between 10 and 20 years. Frontal dementia appears early in the disease, so patients with advanced Huntington's disease are impaired in many cognitive tasks. For this reason, research into the role of the basal ganglia in category learning must focus on patients in early stages of the disease. There is evidence that the tail of the caudate is the first area affected by the disease (Gomez-Tortosa et al., 2001; Vonsattel & DiFiglia, 1998; Vonsattel et al., 1985), although this hypothesis remains controversial.

A. Parkinson's Disease

1. Rule-Based Tasks

Many studies have shown that Parkinson's disease patients are impaired on the Wisconsin Card Sorting Test (Brown & Marsden, 1988; Cools, van den Bercken, Horstink, van Spaendonck, & Berger, 1984; Downes et al., 1989). Several studies have examined the learning ability of Parkinson's disease patients in more traditional rule-based category-learning tasks. First, Ashby, Noble, Filoteo, Waldron, and Ell (2003) tested Parkinson's patients and both young and age-matched controls on one-dimensional rule-based tasks with stimuli that varied across trials on four binary-valued dimensions (16 total stimuli). The patients were massively impaired relative to both control groups, with half of them failing to learn (i.e., achieve 10 correct responses in a row) in 200 trials.

Filoteo, Maddox, Ing, Zizak, and Song (2005a) examined the effects of the number of dimensions with irrelevant variation on the performance of Parkinson's patients in one-dimensional rule-based category learning. In the Ashby et al. (2003) rule-based tasks, there were always three irrelevant dimensions that varied across trials. Filoteo et al. (2005a) used similar binary-valued stimuli and allowed irrelevant variation on 0, 1, 2, or 3 dimensions. When 2 or 3 irrelevant dimensions varied, Parkinson's patients were impaired relative to age-matched controls (replicating Ashby et al., 2003), but with irrelevant variation in 0 or 1 dimension the patients' performance was essentially normal. This result suggests that the role of the striatum in rule-based category learning may be to filter out irrelevant stimulus information or to facilitate switching among alternative categorization rules.

2. Information-Integration Tasks

In addition to the rule-based task described previously, subjects in the Ashby et al. (2003) study also attempted to learn several information-integration category structures created from the same four binary-valued stimulus dimensions. In the information-integration conditions, three stimulus dimensions were relevant, one was irrelevant, and the correct categorization rule was difficult to describe verbally. For both the younger and age-matched controls, the information-integration categories were much more difficult to learn than the rule-based categories. However, although the Parkinson's patients were severely impaired on the rule-based task, they were no worse than the age-matched control group on the information-integration categories. In addition, performance with the rule-based categories was a poor predictor of performance with the information-integration categories, which is further evidence for the existence of distinct learning systems used in these tasks.

Filoteo, Maddox, Salmon, and Song (2005b) trained Parkinson's and control subjects on two information-integration tasks that varied in difficulty. In the easier task, the categories were linearly separable (i.e., a linear decision bound was optimal), whereas the categories were nonlinearly separable in the more difficult condition (a quadratic bound was optimal). The Parkinson's patients were impaired only on the more difficult task. They learned the linearly separable categories as well as the control subjects. The information-integration categories used by Ashby et al. (2003) were linearly separable, so the Filoteo et al. (2005b) study replicates and extends these earlier results. Together, the results of these two studies suggest that

Parkinson's disease patients may be impaired in information-integration category learning but only when the category structures are complex.

A number of studies with Parkinson's disease patients have used the weather prediction task. Parkinson's patients are impaired in this task (Knowlton, Mangels, & Squire, 1996; Sage et al., 2003; Shohamy, Myers, Onlaor, & Gluck, 2004; Witt, Nuhsman, & Deuschl, 2002). Even so, because a variety of alternative strategies are all about equally effective (as noted earlier), it is difficult to interpret this result. Strategy analyses suggest that Parkinson's patients persist in using inferior single-cue strategies in the weather prediction task, whereas control subjects eventually adopt multiple-cue strategies (Shohamy et al., 2004).

A surgical intervention that is sometimes used to treat the motor slowing often seen in Parkinson's disease (i.e., bradykinesia) is to lesion part of the globus pallidus. The theory is that this reduces the inhibition on the thalamus, thereby increasing excitation of the motor cortex (Fig. 1). Sage et al. (2003) reported that pallidotomy patients were more impaired than untreated Parkinson's patients on the weather prediction task, especially on the cues that only weakly signal category membership.

3. Prototype-Distortion Tasks

Reber and Squire (1999) reported normal (A, not A) prototype-distortion learning in Parkinson's disease patients.

B. Huntington's Disease

1. Rule-Based Tasks

Huntington's disease patients are impaired on the Wisconsin Card Sorting Test (Snowden, Craufurd, Griffiths, Thompson, & Neary, 2001). This is expected later in the disease, when frontal dementia is common. Fewer studies have tested presymptomatic subjects, who carry the gene for Huntington's disease but do not yet show motor symptoms. At least one study reported that presymptomatic Huntington's disease subjects are not impaired on the Wisconsin Card Sorting Test relative to age-matched controls (Snowden, Craufurd, Thompson, & Neary, 2002). On the other hand, Lawrence et al. (1998) reported a deficit of presymptomatic Huntington's subjects in a task that required switching from one explicit rule to another (an extradimensional shift) but not when the same rule required a switch to a new response criterion (an intradimensional shift).

2. Information-Integration Tasks

Filoteo, Maddox, and Davis (2001a) compared the performance of Huntington's disease patients and matched controls on their ability to learn linearly and nonlinearly separable category structures. The Huntington's patients were impaired in both conditions, and their deficit was greater with the more difficult nonlinearly separable categories. An earlier study reported a similar Huntington's deficit in the weather prediction task (Knowlton et al., 1996). There are no published studies that examine the ability of subjects with presymptomatic Huntington's disease in information-integration tasks.

C. OTHER DISORDERS

1. Cerebellar Damage

The best-known role of the basal ganglia is in motor skill acquisition. Another brain area known to be critical for motor skill learning is the cerebellum. Two studies tested whether the primary role of the basal ganglia in category learning is motor skill acquisition by comparing the category-learning performance of Parkinson's disease patients against patients with cerebellar damage.

Maddox, Aparicio, Marchant, and Ivry (2005) compared the two groups in two different rule-based tasks. In both cases, the Parkinson's patients were impaired, whereas the cerebellar patients performed as well as healthy controls. Witt et al. (2002) reported a similar dissociation on the weather prediction task—that is, impaired performance by Parkinson's patients but not by patients with cerebellar damage. Thus, the role of the basal ganglia in category learning appears to not be simply motor. Instead, a cognitive contribution is likely.

2. Amnesia

Another important group to consider is patients with anterograde amnesia—that is, deficits on tests that depend on recent declarative memories. The most theoretically important of these patients have medial temporal lobe damage and, especially, damage to the hippocampus. A widely held view is that such patients have difficulty consolidating new episodic memories (Squire, Stark, & Clark, 2004). Most category-learning studies on amnesiacs, however, have used patients whose amnesia is from a variety of different etiologies, including medial temporal lobe damage and Korsakoff's syndrome.

Procedural memory is nondeclarative, and anterograde amnesiacs frequently have normal working memory. Furthermore, the basal ganglia are not thought to play a critical role in either episodic or semantic memory consolidation. Thus, if the basal ganglia participate in category learning then the performance of amnesiacs in category-learning tasks should be quite different from the performance of patients with basal ganglia disease. In fact, there is good evidence supporting this prediction.

Several studies have shown that amnesiacs are normal in rule-based tasks such as the Wisconsin Card Sorting Test (Janowsky, Shimamura, Kritchevsky, & Squire, 1989; Leng & Parkin, 1988). Filoteo, Maddox and Davis (2001b) reported normal performance by amnesiacs in a difficult information-integration task with nonlinearly separable categories that required hundreds of training trials. In fact, in the Filoteo et al. (2001b) study, one (medial temporal lobe) amnesiac and one control subject completed a second day of testing. Despite any explicit memory of the previous session, the amnesic patient and the control again showed equivalent performance on the second day. In fact, the amnesic patient performed slightly better than the control on the first block of day 2. One should note that this result rules out the possibility that amnesic performance is normal in category learning because amnesiacs resort to using working memory to learn the categories.

Evidence also exists that amnesic patients perform normally on the weather prediction task for the first 50 trials, although after that time an amnesic deficit is observed (Hopkins, Myers, Shohamy, Grossman, & Gluck, 2004; Knowlton et al., 1994). In contrast, as described previously, several studies have reported impaired performance by basal ganglia disease patients during the first 50 trials of the weather prediction task.

D.   SUMMARY OF PATIENT RESULTS

Parkinson's disease patients are impaired on rule-based tasks in which irrelevant stimulus dimensions must be ignored. They perform no worse than controls on simple information-integration tasks, but they are impaired on complex information-integration tasks. Huntington's disease patients are significantly impaired on both rule-based and information-integration tasks. As a contrast, amnesic patients are either normal in these tasks or else only mildly impaired.

VI.   Neuroimaging Data

A number of neuroimaging studies have used the Wisconsin Card Sorting Test or a similar rule-based task. All of these have reported task-related activation in PFC, most have reported activation in the head of the caudate nucleus, and at least one also reported task-related activation in the anterior cingulate (Konishi et al., 1999; Lombardi et al., 1999; Rao et al., 1997; Rogers, Andrews, Grasby, Brooks, & Robbins, 2000; Volz et al., 1997).

A few neuroimaging studies have used information-integration tasks. Seger and Cincotta (2002) trained subjects in an information-integration task before scanning and reported significant striatal and lateral occipital activation during performance of the task. Neuroimaging studies of the weather prediction task indicate that the medial temporal lobes are active early in learning and gradually become deactivated as learning progresses (Poldrack et al., 2001). This deactivation is mirrored by a simultaneous activation of the basal ganglia. Specifically, early in learning the basal ganglia are inactive and gradually become more active as learning progresses.

Using an event-related design, Seger and Cincotta (2005) reported that successful learning in a version of the weather prediction task was positively correlated with activation in the body and tail of the caudate nucleus and negatively correlated with hippocampal activation. In contrast, activation in the head of the caudate and in the nucleus accumbens was associated with feedback processing.

A variety of other fMRI studies of category learning have used prototype-distortion tasks (Aizenstein et al., 2000; Little, Klein, Shobat, McClure, & Thulborn, 2004; Reber, Gitelman, Parrish, & Mesulam, 2003; Reber, Stark, & Squire, 1998; Reber, Wong, & Buxton, 2002). None of these reported significant striatal activation.

Many more neuroimaging studies of category learning are needed, but the existing data support the hypothesis that the basal ganglia play important roles in rule-based and information-integration categorization tasks, and perhaps that they are not critical in prototype-distortion tasks.

VII.   COVIS

The only theory of category learning that assigns a role to the basal ganglia is called COVIS (Ashby et al., 1998). COVIS proposes that human category learning is mediated by multiple functionally distinct systems. The theory focuses on two of these systems—an explicit system that depends on working memory and executive attention, and a procedural-learning system. The explicit system is best suited for quickly optimizing performance in rule-based category learning, whereas optimal performance in information-integration tasks can only be obtained by using the procedural system.

A.   The COVIS Explicit System

The COVIS explicit system assumes subjects generate and test hypotheses about category membership. For example, with the circular disk stimuli from Fig. 2, the initial hypothesis may be "Respond A if the grating is tilted up, otherwise respond B." This candidate rule is held in working memory while it is tested. If the candidate rule is incorrect, feedback eventually indicates this to the subject, and an alternative hypothesis is selected. At this point executive attention must be switched from the old rule to the new rule.

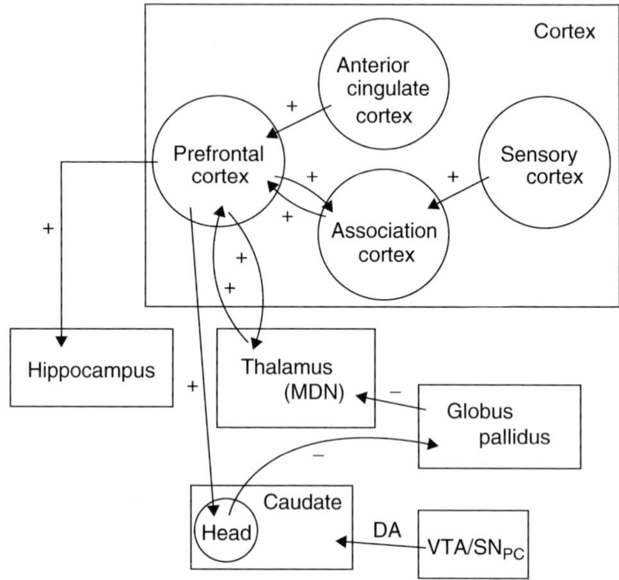

Fig. 3. Schematic showing the major structures and pathways of the COVIS explicit system (MDN: medial dorsal nucleus, VTA: ventral tegmental area, SN_{PC}: substantia nigra pars compacta).

This selection, switching, and testing process continues until performance stabilizes.

Figure 3 shows the neural mechanisms that mediate performance in the COVIS explicit system. The key structures are the anterior cingulate, the PFC, the hippocampus, and the head of the caudate nucleus. There are two main subnetworks in this model; one that generates or selects new candidate hypotheses and one that maintains candidate rules in working memory during the testing process and that mediates the switch from one rule to another. COVIS assumes that these selection and switching operations are mediated by separate neural processes.

The process of generating new candidate hypotheses is clearly complex and is not directly modeled by COVIS. Instead, COVIS assumes only that this process is mediated by some cortical network that includes the PFC and anterior cingulate.

The working memory maintenance and attentional switching network includes all the structures in Fig. 3, except the anterior cingulate. This portion of the model is essentially equivalent to the FROST model of working memory (Ashby et al., 2005). Briefly, the long-term representation of each possible salient rule is encoded in some neural network in sensory association cortex. These cortical units send excitatory signals to working memory units in lateral PFC, which send recurrent excitatory signals back to the same cortical units, thereby forming a reverberating loop. At the same time, the PFC is part of a second excitatory reverberating loop through the medial dorsal nucleus of the thalamus (Alexander, Delong, & Strick, 1986). These double reverberating loops maintain activation in the PFC working memory units during the hypothesis testing procedure.

As described previously, the globus pallidus tonically inhibits the thalamus. FROST predicts that during periods of high working memory demand, the PFC excites the head of the caudate nucleus, which inhibits the pallidal cells and allows reverberation in the cortical-thalamic working memory loops. Thus, according to COVIS, one of the key roles of the basal ganglia in rule-based category learning is to maintain candidate rules in working memory until they can be accepted or rejected.

When feedback convinces a subject that the current rule is incorrect, then a new rule must be selected and executive attention switched from the old rule to this new one. Once a new rule is selected, its representation is maintained in its own set of reverberating loops. The subject must then switch attention to the loop encoding this new rule. In COVIS, a volitional switch of attention from an old rule to a new rule is mediated by a reduction in the PFC excitatory input to the head of the caudate nucleus. The consequent deactivation in the head of the caudate allows activation in the globus pallidus to return to its high-baseline levels, which in turn inhibits the thalamus. As a result, the cortical-thalamic loop is broken, and the rejected rule is no longer the focus of executive attention. Thus, a second role that COVIS assigns to the basal ganglia in rule-based category learning is to facilitate switching executive attention from one rule to another.

Although COVIS assumes that the signal for switching executive attention from one rule to another originates in the PFC, the switching itself is mediated within the basal ganglia. A variety of evidence supports this hypothesis. First, injections of a glutamate agonist directly into the striatum increase the frequency with which cats switch between motor activities (Jaspers, de Vries, & Cools, 1990a,b). Second, lesioning the dopamine fibers that project from the VTA into the PFC improves the performance of monkeys in an analog of the Wisconsin Card Sorting Test (Roberts et al., 1994). Such lesions increase dopamine release into the basal ganglia (Roberts et al., 1994), so this result established that decreasing PFC dopamine levels and increasing levels in the basal ganglia improves performance in a task that depends heavily on cognitive switching. Third, van Golf Racht-Delatour and El Massioui (1999) reported that rats with lesions to the dorsal striatum had no deficits in learning which arm of a radial arm maze was initially baited, but they did have deficits when the position of the baited arm was successively switched according to a simple rule. Finally, there are well-known switching deficits in individuals with caudate dysfunction. For example, as mentioned previously, numerous studies have shown that Parkinson's disease patients, who have abnormally low levels of dopamine in the striatum, have a greater tendency to perseverate on the Wisconsin Card Sorting Test (Brown & Marsden, 1988).

B.   THE COVIS PROCEDURAL-LEARNING SYSTEM

Figure 4 shows the COVIS procedural-learning system (Ashby & Waldron, 1999; Ashby et al., 1998). The key structure is the caudate nucleus. In primates, all of extrastriate visual cortex projects directly to the tail of the caudate nucleus, with about 10,000 visual cortical cells converging on a single caudate cell (Wilson, 1995). COVIS assumes that, through a procedural learning process, each caudate unit associates an abstract motor program with the large group of visual cortical cells that project to it. These associations are assumed to be established by the dopamine-mediated three-factor learning rule described earlier in this chapter.

The medium spiny cells in the tail of the caudate send projections to a variety of prefrontal and premotor cortical areas. There are two synapses on this pathway (Fig. 1). The first synapse on the principal path is in the globus pallidus and the second synapse is in the thalamus, primarily in the ventral

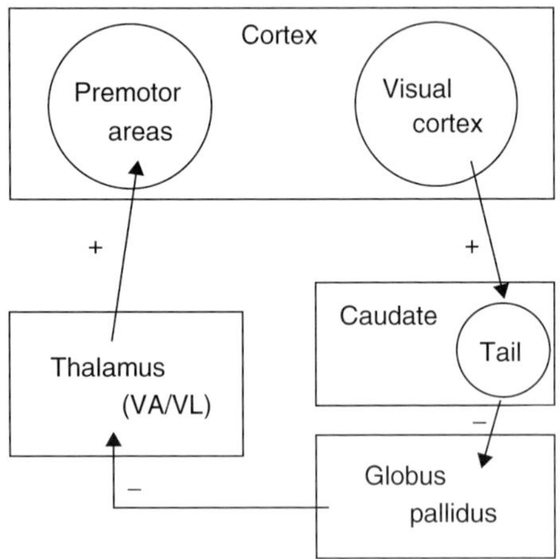

Fig. 4.   Schematic showing the major structures and pathways of the COVIS procedural-learning system.

anterior nucleus, par magnocellualaris (VAmc). The primary cortical projection is to Brodmann Area 8 and the supplementary eye fields (Shook, Schlag-Rey, & Schlag, 1991).

Although this description of the COVIS procedural system focuses on the learning of visual categories, it is feasible that a similar model exists for other modalities because they almost all also project directly to the basal ganglia and then indirectly to frontal cortical areas via the thalamus and either the substantia nigra pars reticulata or the globus pallidus (Chudler, Sugiyama, & Dong, 1995). The main difference is where within the basal ganglia they initially project. For example, auditory cortex projects directly to the body of the caudate rather than to the tail (Arnalud, Jeantet, Arsaut, & Demotes-Mainard, 1996).

VIII. Tests of COVIS

A. TESTS WITH NEUROPSYCHOLOGICAL PATIENTS

COVIS accounts for virtually all of the neuropsychological data reviewed previously. First, it correctly predicts that basal ganglia disease patients should be impaired on rule-based tasks because it predicts that damage to the head of the caudate nucleus impairs working memory and the ability to flexibly shift executive attention among candidate rules. Second, it correctly predicts that these same patient groups should be impaired in information-integration tasks because of damage to the tail of the caudate nucleus (i.e., with visual categories). And if one accepts that as a group, Parkinson's disease patients tend to have more damage to the head of the caudate than to the tail, then it also correctly predicts that Parkinson's patients should be more impaired in rule-based tasks than in information-integration tasks. Third, it also predicts that patients with no basal ganglia damage should perform almost normally in information-integration tasks. This prediction has not been extensively tested, although there is some supporting evidence from patients with amnesia (Filoteo et al., 2001b; Knowlton et al., 1994).

B. COGNITIVE BEHAVIORAL TESTS OF COVIS

COVIS makes a number of strong and somewhat nonintuitive predictions about the performance of healthy young adults in rule-based and information-integration tasks. Many of these have now been thoroughly tested. The predictions arise from two properties of COVIS—first, that the explicit system dominates performance in rule-based tasks and the procedural-learning system dominates in information-integration tasks and second, that these two COVIS systems are characterized by a number of qualitative differences. The published tests focus on three important differences: (1) how sensitive the two systems are to the nature and timing of feedback, (2) how closely linked they are to specific motor responses, and (3) whether they require access to executive attention.

1.   *Sensitivity to the Nature and Timing of Feedback*

COVIS predicts that, since the explicit system has access to working memory and executive attention, learning in rule-based tasks should be robust to changes in the nature and timing of feedback. However, because it depends on the three-factor learning rule, the procedural system requires feedback to be delivered immediately following the subject's response. Otherwise, as explained earlier, the synapses responsible for eliciting the correct response will not be strengthened. A number of studies confirm these predictions. First, Ashby, Queller, and Berretty (1999) showed that subjects can learn some rule-based categories in the absence of any feedback, whereas there is no evidence that information-integration categories can be learned without feedback.

Second, even when feedback is provided after every response, information-integration category learning is impaired if the feedback is delayed by as little as 2.5 s after the response. In contrast, delays as long as 10 s have no effect on rule-based category learning (Maddox, Ashby, & Bohil, 2003). These results hold when there are two contrasting categories, and the correct rule in the rule-based task is one-dimensional (Maddox et al., 2003) and when there are four contrasting categories and a conjunction rule is optimal in the rule-based task (Maddox, Ashby, Ing, & Pickering, 2004a).

Another study compared observational and feedback training. With observational training, subjects are shown an exemplar on each trial along with its category label, and they then press the appropriate response key. In feedback training, an exemplar is shown, subjects assign it to a category by pressing the appropriate response key, and then they receive feedback about the accuracy of their response. Ashby, Maddox, and Bohil (2002) found that with rule-based categories observational training was as effective as feedback training, but with information-integration categories, feedback training was significantly more effective than observational training.

2.   *Links to Motor Responses*

A second group of studies investigated how closely linked the two systems are to specific motor responses. The idea is that if procedural learning mediates performance in information-integration tasks but not in rule-based tasks then there should be evidence of some motor learning in information-integration tasks. To test this prediction, Ashby, Ell and Waldron (2003) had subjects learn either rule-based or information-integration categories using traditional feedback training. Next, some subjects continued as before, some switched their hands on the response keys, and for some the location of the response keys was switched. For subjects who had learned rule-based categories, there were no differences among any of these transfer conditions, suggesting that abstract category labels had been learned. In contrast, among the subjects who had learned information-integration categories, switching hands on the response keys caused no interference, but switching the location of the response keys caused a significant decrease in accuracy. Thus, it seems that response locations, not specific motor programs, are learned in information-integration category learning. This observation is consistent with some premotor area of cortex being the terminal projection of the COVIS procedural system. These information-integration results essentially replicate results found with traditional procedural-learning tasks (Willingham, Wells, Farrell, & Stemwedel, 2000).

In a similar study, subjects learned either rule-based or information-integration categories using either standard feedback training or YES–NO training (Maddox, Bohil, & Ing, 2004b). In the latter conditions, a stimulus would appear and then either the query "Is this stimulus a member of Category A?" or "Is this stimulus a member of Category B?" In either case, the subject responded by pressing either a YES or NO response key. One should note that in YES–NO training, there is no consistent association of a response position with a category. As one might predict from the button-switch interference observed by Ashby et al. (2003), with the rule-based categories both training procedures were equally effective, whereas feedback training was significantly more effective than YES–NO training with information-integration categories (Maddox et al., 2004b). These studies represent the first direct evidence that perceptual categorization is sometimes mediated by a procedural-learning system.

3. *Access to Executive Attention*

A third set of studies tested the COVIS prediction that the explicit system requires working memory and executive attention, whereas these resources are not critical to the procedural-learning system. First, Waldron and Ashby (2001) had subjects learn rule-based and information-integration categories either under typical single task conditions or while simultaneously performing a secondary task that required working memory and executive attention. The dual task had a massive detrimental effect on the ability of subjects to learn the rule-based categories, but it had no significant effect on the ability of subjects to learn the information-integration categories. If all category learning were mediated by a single system then this result would be counterintuitive because, under control (i.e., single task) conditions, the information-integration task was considerably more difficult than the rule-based task, and we typically expect a dual task to interfere more strongly with the more difficult task. Zeithamova and Maddox (in press) replicated this result with continuous-valued stimuli and with rule-based categories in which a conjunction rule was optimal—that is, the dual task interfered more strongly with learning of the conjunction rule than learning of the information-integration categories.

Second, Maddox et al. (2004a) tested the assumption that feedback processing requires executive attention in rule-based tasks but not in information-integration tasks. The idea is that if feedback indicates that a response is incorrect then the explicit system might decide that the current rule is incorrect, select a new rule, and then switch attention from the old rule to the new rule. These operations require attention and time. As a result, if subjects have limited time to process the feedback signal then explicit system learning should be impaired. In contrast, learning in the procedural system is automatic. If a correct response is emitted and feedback is given quickly after the response then dopamine is released and the appropriate synapses are automatically strengthened. To test this hypothesis, Maddox et al. (2004a) had subjects alternate trials of category learning with trials of the classic Sternberg (1966) memory scanning task. Two conditions were identical except for the durations of the intertrial intervals (ITI). In one condition, a short ITI followed categorization and a long ITI followed memory scanning, whereas these delays were reversed in the second condition. Information-integration category learning was the same in both conditions, but rule-based category learning was significantly impaired when subjects had the short ITI followed categorization.

4. *Implications for Training*

All of these results have significant implications for the proper format in which to teach various categories. Traditional lecture-based instruction in the classroom makes heavy use of observational training. Feedback training is typically used only when students take exams, and in these cases feedback is usually delayed for many hours or days. The results described in this section indicate that such training will be effective for rule-based learning but almost completely ineffective for procedural learning.

To become expert at many real world difficult categorization tasks probably requires both explicit and procedural learning. For example, medical school provides much explicit instruction on how to detect tumors in x-rays. But radiologists continue to improve their skills long after leaving medical school by making thousands of diagnoses. Some of this additional skill might be imparted more quickly in medical school if some observational instruction was replaced with feedback training accompanied by rapid feedback.

IX. Future Theoretical Extensions

In Section II, the neuroantomy of the basal ganglia was reviewed, which was needed to understand neurobiological models of category learning (e.g., COVIS). However, future models are likely to be considerably more general than COVIS and to rely on neuroanatomical details that we did not review. In this section, we describe some possible future extensions of COVIS and briefly review the neuroanatomy of the basal ganglia that could help drive these extensions.

In Section II, we mentioned that there are two prominent output pathways from the striatum—the direct pathway and the indirect pathway. COVIS assigns a role only to the direct pathway, and although the function of the indirect pathway is a topic of intense current debate, it seems likely that future generalizations of COVIS are likely to assign some functional role to both pathways.

As described in Section II (and in Fig. 1), in the direct pathway, the medium spiny cells project from the striatum to the internal segment of the globus pallidus or to the substantia nigra pars reticulata.[3] These gabaergic cells then project to the thalamus, which in turn, sends excitatory projections to cortex. Spontaneous activity in the globus pallidus is high (Wilson, 1995), and the globus pallidus tonically inhibits the thalamus. Cortical activation of the striatum, however, causes the striatal medium spiny cells to inhibit the pallidal cells, thereby releasing the thalamus from its tonic inhibition. Thus, the striatum excites the thalamus via the direct pathway.

On the other hand, the indirect pathway passes from the striatum to gabaergic cells in the external segment of the globus pallidus (Fig. 1). These cells then project to excitatory cells in the subthalamic nucleus, which in turn, project to the internal segment of the globus pallidus. Stimulation of the subthalamic nucleus increases pallidal inhibition of the thalamus. Activation of the indirect pathway releases the subthalamic nucleus from tonic pallidal inhibition and thereby serves to increase thalamic inhibition so that the direct and indirect pathways have opposing effects on the thalamus.

Several proposals for the function of the indirect pathway have relevance for models of category learning. Berns and Sejnowski (1996) proposed that the indirect pathway serves as a gate to the direct pathway that allows the

---

[3] The internal segment of the globus pallidus and the substantia nigra pars reticulata are functionally similar. Figure 1 depicts only the former of these structures.

basal ganglia to select among competing alternatives. The idea is that the alternative with strongest striatal activation will propagate fastest down both the direct and indirect pathways. But the indirect path is slower because of the extra synapse. Thus, the favored alternative will excite cortex first (via the direct path) and shortly thereafter it will traverse the indirect path, which shuts the gate to cortex (i.e., by inhibiting thalamus), thereby preventing access to the weaker alternatives. This could be a mechanism via which competition is resolved between the explicit and procedural-learning systems of COVIS.

Frank (2005) proposed an alternative interpretation of the function of the indirect pathway. According to Frank (2005), the direct and indirect pathways mediate the learning of GO and NO GO responses, respectively. The idea is that trials, when a correct response is made, increase the probability that the response will be repeated under the same stimulus conditions (a GO response) by facilitating LTP on the direct path. In contrast, error trials increase the probability that the response will be avoided (a NO GO response) by facilitating LTP on the indirect pathway. According to this model, during categorization training, subjects learn which response to make on trials when their response is correct and which response not to make on error trials.

Another important neuroanatomical feature overlooked by COVIS is that dopamine not only facilitates striatal LTP but it also effectively increases signal-to-noise ratio carried by presynaptic glutamate signals. In fact, a variety of evidence suggests that dopamine potentiates the glutamate response through the NMDA receptor (Cepeda, Radisavlijevic, Peacock, Levine, & Buchwald, 1992; Cepeda et al., 1999; Hemmings, Walaas, Ouimet, & Greengard, 1987; Pessin et al., 1994; Wickens, 1990, 1993) and depresses the glutamate response through AMPA (i.e., non-NMDA) receptors (Cepeda et al., 1992, 1999; Del Arco & Mora, 2002; Gao, Krimer, & Goldman-Rakic, 2001). Because a signal will tend to cause greater presynaptic activation than noise, the signal will be more likely to activate post-synaptic NMDA receptors, whereas noise will be more likely to activate only AMPA receptors. As a result, the presence of dopamine will tend to increase signal-to-noise ratio. Several quantitative models of these effects have been proposed (Ashby & Casale, 2003; Cohen & Servan-Schreiber, 1992). Ashby et al. (1999) proposed that dopamine-mediated increases in signal-to-noise ratio in frontal cortex might play an important role in rule-based category learning, especially in facilitating the process of rule selection.

A third neuroanatomical feature of the basal ganglia not mentioned in Section II, which could play an important role in future neurobiological theories of category learning, is that the medium spiny cells of the striatum are segregated into two cytoarchitecturally distinct compartments, called the patch and matrix (Graybiel, 1983). The matrix compartments receive cortical input, as described earlier, and project to the basal ganglia output structures. The patch compartments primarily receive input from limbic structures— including the amygdala and hippocampus and project to dopamine-producing areas in the SN_{PC} and the VTA (Graybiel, Aosaki, Flaherty, & Kimura, 1994). The striatal cells in COVIS are all assumed to be from the matrix. The limbic input to the striatal patch compartments represent a promising vehicle via which affective and motivational factors could influence category learning (e.g., by controlling the amount of dopamine released).

X. Conclusions

We have reviewed extensive evidence that the basal ganglia play important roles in both rule-based and information-integration category learning. Furthermore, although hardly conclusive, there is now considerable evidence that the role of the basal ganglia in these two types of tasks is qualitatively different. In particular, the evidence suggests that the striatum is the primary locus of learning in information-integration tasks, whereas in rule-based tasks the striatum appears to contribute primarily to executive functions, especially to working memory maintenance and the switching of executive attention.

The evidence for basal ganglia involvement in information-integration tasks includes single-cell recording data (Merchant et al., 1997; Romo et al., 1995), neuropsychological patient data (i.e., Parkinson's and Huntington's disease patients are both impaired), neuroimaging data (Seger & Cincotta, 2002, 2005), and cognitive behavioral data (Ashby et al., 2003). In addition, information-integration learning is only minimally dependent on executive function (Waldron & Ashby, 2001), and feedback processing requires little attention or effort (Maddox et al., 2004a). For these reasons, the contributions of the basal ganglia to information-integration category learning are not likely to be executive in nature. Finally, information-integration learning is extremely sensitive to the nature and timing of feedback. In particular, effective learning requires feedback immediately after the response (Ashby et al., 1999, 2003; Maddox et al., 2003). This result is characteristic of three-factor learning, which is thought to be a signature of the striatum. Thus, in information-integration category learning, evidence suggests that the striatum is the site at which synapses that mediated the selection of the correct response are strengthened—in other words, the locus of primary learning.

We also reviewed extensive neuropsychological and neuroimaging evidence that the basal ganglia contribute to rule-based category learning. Even so, the role of the basal ganglia in rule-based learning appears to be quite different than in information-integration learning. First, rule-based learning depends heavily on executive function, both for selecting a response (Waldron & Ashby, 2001) and feedback processing (Maddox et al., 2004a). There is also strong evidence that the basal ganglia (i.e., head of the caudate) participate in executive functions, including working memory (for a review, see, Ashby et al., 2005) and attentional switching. Second, rule-based learning is not especially sensitive to the nature and timing of feedback, which suggests that the three-factor learning thought to be characteristic of the basal ganglia does not mediate rule-based learning. Thus, the basal ganglia are not likely to be the primary locus of rule-based learning. Instead, their contribution is likely to be primarily in their participation in executive function.

Finally, evidence also suggests that the basal ganglia are not critical to all forms of category learning. For example, in the (A, not A) prototype-distortion task, basal ganglia disease patients perform normally (Reber & Squire, 1999), and neuroimaging studies report no task-related striatal activation (Aizenstein et al., 2000; Reber et al., 1998). Thus, it appears that the basal ganglia are not part of some general-purpose category-learning module. Instead, the evidence suggests that they have some specific features that make them well suited to facilitate learning certain particular types of category structures.

We believe that the results reviewed in this article constitute strong evidence that the basal ganglia play important roles in category learning. Moreover, these results are beginning to paint a detailed picture of the specific nature of some of these various roles. Even so, there remain some important unanswered questions for which there are almost no current data. For example, we know almost nothing about how the various category-learning systems interact during the course of a single categorization trial or during the much longer course of learning. We also know little about the transition from novice to expert. For example, basal ganglia disease patients are impaired in learning new categories, but they apparently do not lose old familiar categories, so it appears that at some point during the learning process the role of the basal ganglia changes. These questions are likely to be the focus of intense research efforts during the coming years.

ACKNOWLEDGMENTS

This research was supported in part by Public Health Service Grant MH3760. We thank Vince Filoteo for his helpful suggestions. Correspondence concerning this article should be addressed to F. Gregory Ashby, Department of Psychology, University of California, Santa Barbara, CA 93106, USA. E-mail: ashby@psych.ucsb.edu.

REFERENCES

Aizenstein, H. J., MacDonald, A. W., Stenger, V. A., Nebes, R. D., Larson, J. K., Ursu, S., & Carter, C. S. (2000). Complementary category learning systems identified using event-related functional MRI. *Journal of Cognitive Neuroscience, 12*, 977–987.

Alexander, G. E., DeLong, M. R., & Strick, P. L. (1986). Parallel organization of functionally segregated circuits linking basal ganglia and cortex. *Annual Review of Neuroscience, 9*, 357–381.

Arbuthnott, G. W., Ingham, C. A., & Wickens, J. R. (2000). Dopamine and synaptic plasticity in the neostriatum. *Journal of Anatomy, 196*, 587–596.

Arnalud, E., Jeantet, Y., Arsaut, J., & Demotes-Mainard, J. (1996). Involvement of the caudal striatum in auditory processing: C-Fos response to cortical application of picrotoxin and to auditory stimulation. *Brain Research: Molecular Brain Research, 41*, 27–35.

Ashby, F. G., Alfonso-Reese, L. A., Turken, A. U., & Waldron, E. M. (1998). A neuropsychological theory of multiple systems in category learning. *Psychological Review, 105*, 442–481.

Ashby, F. G., & Casale, M. B. (2002). The cognitive neuroscience of implicit category learning. In L. Jiménez (Ed.), *Attention and implicit learning* (pp. 109–141). Philadelphia: John Benjamins Publishing Company.

Ashby, F. G., & Casale, M. B. (2003). A model of dopamine modulated cortical activation. *Neural Networks, 16*, 973–984.

Ashby, F. G., & Ell, S. W. (2001). The neurobiology of category learning. *Trends in Cognitive Sciences, 5*, 204–210.

Ashby, F. G., Ell, S. W., Valentin, V. V., & Casale, M. B. (2005). FROST: A distributed neurocomputational model of working memory maintenance. *Journal of Cognitive Neuroscience, 17*, 1728–1743.

Ashby, F. G., Ell, S. W., & Waldron, E. M. (2003). Procedural learning in perceptual categorization. *Memory & Cognition, 31*, 1114–1125.

Ashby, F. G., & Maddox, W. T. (1992). Complex decision rules in categorization: Contrasting novice and experienced performance. *Journal of Experimental Psychology: Human Perception and Performance, 18*, 50–71.

Ashby, F. G., & Maddox, W. T. (2005). Human category learning. *Annual Review of Psychology, 56*, 149–178.

Ashby, F. G., Maddox, W. T., & Bohil, C. J. (2002). Observational versus feedback training in rule-based and information-integration category learning. *Memory & Cognition, 30*, 666–677.

Ashby, F. G., Noble, S., Filoteo, J., Waldron, E. M., & Ell, S. W. (2003). Category learning deficits in Parkinson's disease. *Neuropsychology, 17*, 115–124.

Ashby, F. G., & O'Brien, J. B. (2005). Category learning and multiple memory systems. *Trends in Cognitive Sciences, 9*, 83–89.

Ashby, F. G., Queller, S., & Berretty, P. M. (1999). On the dominance of unidimensional rules in unsupervised categorization. *Perception & Psychophysics, 61*, 1178–1199.

Ashby, F. G., & Waldron, E. M. (1999). On the nature of implicit categorization. *Psychonomic Bulletin & Review, 6*, 363–378.

Beninger, R. J. (1983). The role of dopamine in locomotor activity and learning. *Brain Research, 287*, 173–196.

Berns, G. S., & Sejnowski, T. J. (1996). How the basal ganglia make decisions. In A. Damasio, H. Damasio, and Y. Christen (Eds.), *The neurobiology of decision-making* (pp. 101–113). New York: Springer-Verlag.

Bliss, T. V. P., & Collingridge, G. L. (1993). A synaptic model of memory: Long-term potentiation in the hippocampus. *Nature, 361*, 31–39.

Brown, R. G., & Marsden, C. D. (1988). Internal versus external cues and the control of attention in Parkinson's disease. *Brain, 111*, 323–345.

Calabresi, P., Pisani, A., Centonze, D., & Bernardi, G. (1996). Role of Ca^{2+} in striatal LTD and LTP. *Seminars in the Neurosciences, 8*, 321–328.

Centonze, D., Picconi, B., Gubellini, P., Bernardi, G., & Calabresi, P. (2001). Dopaminergic control of synaptic plasticity in the dorsal striatum. *European Journal of Neuroscience, 13*, 1071–1077.

Cepeda, C., Li, Z., Cromwell, H. C., Altemus, K. L., Crawford, C. A., Nansen, E. A., Ariano, M. A., Sibley, D. R., Peacock, W. J., Bathern, G. W., & Levine, M. S. (1999). Electrophysiological and morphological analyses of cortical neurons obtained from children with catastrophic epilepsy: Dopamine receptor modulation of glutamatergic responses. *Developmental Neuroscience, 21*, 223–235.

Cepeda, C., Radisavljevic, Z., Peacock, W., Levine, M. S., & Buchwald, N. A. (1992). Differential modulation by dopamine of responses evoked by excitatory amino acids in human cortex. *Synapse, 11*, 330–341.

Chudler, E. H., Sugiyama, K., & Dong, W. K. (1995). Multisensory convergence and integration in the neostriatum and globus pallidus of the rat. *Brain Research, 674*, 33–45.

Cohen, J. D., & Servan-Schreiber, D. (1992). Context, cortex, and dopamine: A connectionist approach to behavior and biology in schizophrenia. *Psychological Review, 99*, 45–77.

Cools, A. R., van den Bercken, J. H. L., Horstink, M. W. I., van Spaendonck, K. P. M., & Berger, H. J. C. (1984). Cognitive and motor shifting aptitude disorder in Parkinson's disease. *Journal of Neurology, Neurosurgery, and Psychiatry, 47*, 443–453.

Cooper, J. R., Bloom, F. E., & Roth, R. H. (1991). *The biochemical basis of neuropharmacology* (6th ed.). New York: Oxford University Press.

Del Arco, A., & Mora, F. (2002). NMDA and AMPA/kainate glutamatergic agonists increase the extracellular concentrations of GABA in the prefrontal cortex of freely moving rat: Modulation by endogenous dopmamine. *Brain Research Bulletin, 57*, 623–630.

DiFiglia, M., Pasik, T., & Pasik, P. (1978). A Golgi study of afferent fibers in the neostriatum of monkeys. *Brain Research, 152*, 341–347.

Downes, J. J., Roberts, A. C., Sahakian, B. J., Evenden, J. L., Morris, R. G., & Robbins, T. W. (1989). Impaired extra-dimensional shift performance in medicated and unmedicated Parkinson's disease: Evidence for a specific attentional dysfunction. *Neuropsychologia, 27*, 1329–1343.

Eacott, M. J., & Gaffan, D. (1991). The role of monkey inferior parietal cortex in visual discrimination of identity and orientation of shapes. *Behavioural Brain Research, 46*, 95–98.

Filoteo, J. V., Maddox, W. T., & Davis, J. D. (2001a). A possible role of the striatum in linear and nonlinear categorization rule learning: Evidence from patients with Huntington's disease. *Behavioral Neuroscience, 115*, 786–798.

Filoteo, J. V., Maddox, W. T., & Davis, J. D. (2001b). Quantitative modeling of category learning in amnesic patients. *Journal of the International Neuropsychological Society, 7*, 1–19.

Filoteo, J. V., Maddox, W. T., Ing, A. D., Zizak, V., & Song, D. D. (2005a). The impact of irrelevant dimensional variation on rule-based category learning in patients with Parkinson's disease. *Journal of the International Neuropsychological Society, 11*, 503–513.

Filoteo, J. V., Maddox, W. T., Salmon, D. P., & Song, D. D. (2005b). Information-integration category learning in patients with striatal dysfunction. *Neuropsychology, 19*, 212–222.

Frank, M. J. (2005). Dynamic dopamine modulation in the basal ganglia: A neurocomputational account of cognitive deficits in medicated and nonmedicated parkinsonism. *Journal of Cognitive Neuroscience, 17*, 51–72.

Freund, T. F., Powell, J. F., & Smith, A. D. (1984). Tyrosine hydroxylase-immunoreactive boutons in synaptic contact with identified striatonigral neurons, with particular reference to dendritic spines. *Neuroscience, 13*, 1189–1215.

Gaffan, D., & Eacott, M. J. (1995). Visual learning for an auditory secondary reinforcer by macaques is intact after uncinate fascicle section: Indirect evidence for the involvement of the corpus striatum. *European Journal of Neuroscience, 7*, 1866–1871.

Gaffan, D., & Harrison, S. (1987). Amygdalectomy and disconnection in visual learning for auditory secondary reinforcement by monkeys. *Journal of Neuroscience, 7*, 2285–2292.

Gamble, E., & Koch, C. (1987). The dynamics of free calcium in dendritic spines in response to repetitive synaptic input. *Science, 236*, 1311–1315.

Gao, W.-J., Krimer, L. S., & Goldman-Rakic, P. S. (2001). Presynaptic regulation of recurrent excitation by D1 receptors in prefrontal circuits. *Proceedings of the National Academy of Sciences of the United States of America, 98*, 295–300.

Gerfen, C. R., & Wilson, C. J. (1996). The basal ganglia. In T. Hokfelt and L. W. Swanson (Eds.), *Handbook of chemical neuroanatomy* (pp. 365–462). New York: Elsevier.

Gluck, M. A., Shohamy, D., & Myers, C. (2002). How do people solve the "weather prediction" task?: Individual variability in strategies for probabilistic category learning. *Learning & Memory, 9*, 408–418.

Gomez-Tortosa, E., MacDonald, M. E., Friend, J. C., Taylor, S. A., Weiler, L. J., Cupples, L. A., Srinidhi, J., Gusella, J. F., Bird, E. D., Vonsattel, J. P., & Myers, R. H. (2001). Quantitative neuropathological changes in presymptomatic Huntington's disease. *Annals of Neurology, 49*, 29–34.

Graybiel, A. M. (1983). Compartmental organization of the mammalian striatum. In J. P. Changeau (Ed.), *Progress in brain research: Molecular and cellular interactions underlying higher Brain function*, (Vol. 58, pp. 247–256). Amsterdam: Elsevier.

Graybiel, A. M. (1990). Neurotransmitters and neuromodulators in the basal ganglia. *Trends in Neurosciences, 13*, 244–254.

Graybiel, A. M., Aosaki, T., Flaherty, A. W., & Kimura, M. (1994). The basal ganglia and adaptive motor control. *Science (New York), 265*, 1826–1831.

Grimwood, P. D., Martin, S. J., & Morris, R. G. M. (2001). Synaptic plasticity and memory. In W. M. Cowan, T. C. Südhof, and C. F. Stevens (Eds.), *Synapses* (pp. 519–570). Baltimore, MD: Johns Hopkins Press.

Heaton, R. K. (1981). *A manual for the Wisconsin Card Sorting Test*. Odessa, FL: Psychological Assessment Resources.

Hebb, D. O. (1949). *The organization of behavior*. New York: Wiley.

Heimer, L. (1995). *The human brain and spinal cord* (2nd ed.). New York: Springer-Verlag.

Hemmings, H. C., Walaas, S. I., Ouimet, C. C., & Greengard, P. (1987). Dopaminergic regulation of protein phosphorylation in the striatum: DARRP-32. *Trends in Neuroscience, 10*, 377–383.

Hikosaka, O., Sakamoto, M., & Sadanari, U. (1989). Functional properties of monkey caudate neurons III. Activities related to expectation of target and reward. *Journal of Neurophysiology, 61*, 814–831.

Hopkins, R. O., Myers, C. E., Shohamy, D., Grossman, S., & Gluck, M. (2004). Impaired probabilistic category learning in hypoxic subjects with hippocampal damage. *Neuropsychologia, 42*, 524–535.

Horvitz, J. C., Stewart, T., & Jacobs, B. L. (1997). Burst activity of ventral tegmental dopamine neurons is elicited by sensory stimuli in the awake cat. *Brain Research, 759*, 251–258.

Imperato, A., Puglisi-Allegra, S., Casolini, P., & Angelucci, L. (1991). Changes in brain dopamine and acetylcholine release during and following stress are independent of the pituitary-adrenocortical axis. *Brain Research, 538*, 111–117.

Janahashi, M., Rowe, J., Saleem, T., Brown, R., Limousin-Dowsey, P., Rothwell, J., Thomas, D., & Quinn, N. (2002). Striatal contribution to cognition: Working memory and executive function in Parkinson's Disease before and after unilateral posteroventral pallidotomy. *Journal of Cognitive Neuroscience, 142*, 298–310.

Janowsky, J. S., Shimamura, A. P., Kritchevsky, M., & Squire, L. R. (1989). Cognitive impairment following frontal lobe damage and its relevance to human amnesia. *Behavioral Neuroscience, 103*, 548–560.

Jaspers, R. M. A., de Vries, T. J., & Cools, A. R. (1990a). Effect of intrastriatal apomorphine on changes in switching behaviour induced by the glutamate agonist AMPA injected into the cat caudate nucleus. *Behavioral Brain Research, 37*, 247–254.

Jaspers, R. M. A., de Vries, T. J., & Cools, A. R. (1990b). Enhancement in switching motor patterns following local application of the glutamate agonist AMPA into the cat caudate nucleus. *Behavioral Brain Research, 37*, 237–246.

Kerr, J. N., & Wickens, J. R. (2001). Dopamine D-1/D-5 receptor activation is required for long-term potentiation in the rat neostriatum *in vitro*. *Journal of Neurophysiology, 85*, 117–124.

Kimberg, D. Y., D'Esposito, M., & Farah, M. J. (1997). Frontal lobes: Neuropsychological aspects. In T. E. Feinberg and M. J. Farah (Eds.), *Behavioral neurology and neuropsychology* (pp. 409–418). New York: McGraw-Hill.

Knowlton, B. J., Mangels, J. A., & Squire, L. R. (1996). A neostriatal habit learning system in humans. *Science, 273*, 1399–1402.

Knowlton, B. J., Squire, L. R., & Gluck, M. A. (1994). Probabilistic classification learning in amnesia. *Learning & Memory, 1*, 106–120.

Knowlton, B. J., Squire, L. R., Paulsen, J. S., Swerdlow, N. R., Swenson, M., & Butters, N. (1996). Dissociations within nondeclarative memory in Huntington's disease. *Neuropsychology, 10*, 538–548.

Konishi, S., Karwazu, M., Uchida, I., Kikyo, H., Asakura, I., & Miyashita, Y. (1999). Contribution of working memory to transient activation in human inferior prefrontal cortex during performance of the Wisconsin Card Sorting Test. *Cerebral Cortex, 9*, 745–753.

Lawrence, A. D., Hodges, J. R., Rosser, A. E., Kershaw, A., ffrench-Constant, C., Rubinsztein, D. C., Robbins, R. W., & Sahakian, B. J. (1998). Evidence for specific cognitive deficits in preclinical Huntington's disease. *Brain, 121*, 1329–1341.

Leng, N. R., & Parkin, A. J. (1988). Double dissociation of frontal dysfunction in organic amnesia. *British Journal of Clinical Psychology, 27*, 359–362.

Little, D. M., Klein, R., Shobat, D. M., McClure, E. D., & Thulborn, K. R. (2004). Changing patterns of brain activation during category learning revealed by functional MRI. *Cognitive Brain Research, 22*, 84–93.

Lombardi, W. J., Andreason, P. J., Sirocco, K. Y., Rio, D. E., Gross, R. E., Umhau, J. C., & Hommer, D. W. (1999). Wisconsin Card Sorting Test performance following head injury: Dorsolateral fronto-striatal circuit activity predicts perseveration. *Journal of Clinical and Experimental Neuropsychology, 21*, 2–16.

MacDermott, A. B., Mayer, M. L., Westbrook, G. L., Smith, S. J., & Barker, J. L. (1986). NMDA-receptor activation increases cytoplasmic calcium concentration in cultured spinal cord neurons. *Nature, 321*, 519–522. Erratum in: *Nature, 321*, 888.

Maddox, W. T., Aparicio, P., Marchant, N. L., & Ivry, R. B. (2005). Rule-based category learning is impaired in patients with Parkinson's disease but not in patients with cerebellar disorders. *Journal of Cognitive Neuroscience, 17*, 707–723.

Maddox, W. T., Ashby, F. G., & Bohil, C. J. (2003). Delayed feedback effects on rule-based and information-integration category learning. *Journal of Experimental Psychology: Learning, Memory and Cognition, 29*, 650–662.

Maddox, W. T., Ashby, F. G., Ing, A. D., & Pickering, A. D. (2004a). Disrupting feedback processing interferes with rule-based but not information-integration category learning. *Memory & Cognition, 32*, 582–591.

Maddox, W. T., Bohil, C. J., & Ing, A. D. (2004b). Evidence for a procedural learning-based system in perceptual category learning. *Psychonomic Bulletin & Review, 11*, 945–952.

Malenka, R. C. (1995). LTP and LTD: Dynamic and interactive processes of synaptic plasticity. *The Neuroscientist, 1*, 35–42.

Malenka, R. C., & Siegelbaum, S. A. (2001). Synaptic plasticity. In W. M. Cowan, T. C. Südhof, and C. F. Stevens (Eds.), *Synapses* (pp. 393–453). Baltimore, MD: Johns Hopkins Press.

McDonald, R. J., & White, N. M. (1993). A triple dissociation of memory systems: Hippocampus, amygdala, and dorsal striatum. *Behavioral Neuroscience, 107*, 322.

McDonald, R. J., & White, N. M. (1994). Parallel information processing in the water maze: Evidence for independent memory systems involving dorsal striatum and hippocampus. *Behavioral and Neural Biology, 61*, 260–270.

Merchant, H., Zainos, A., Hernandez, A., Salinas, E., & Romo, R. (1997). Functional properties of the primate putamen neurons during the categorization of tactile stimuli. *Journal of Neuroscience, 10*, 3032–3044.

Miller, J. D., Sanghera, M. K., & German, D. C. (1981). Mesencephalic dopaminergic unit activity in the behaviorally conditioned rat. *Life Sciences, 29*, 1255–1263.

Mirenowicz, J., & Schultz, W. (1994). Importance of unpredictability for reward responses in primate dopamine neurons. *Journal of Neurophysiology, 72*, 1024–1027.

Mishkin, M., Malamut, B., & Bachevalier, J. (1984). Memories and habits: Two neural systems. In G. Lynch, J. L. McGaugh, and N. M. Weinberger (Eds.), *Neurobiology of human learning and memory* (pp. 65–77). New York: Guilford.

Montague, P. R., Dayan, P., & Sejnowski, T. J. (1996). A framework for mesencephalic dopamine systems based on predictive Hebbian learning. *Journal of Neuroscience, 16*, 1936–1947.

Nairn, A. C., Hemmings, H. C., Jr., Walaas, S. I., & Greengard, P. (1998). DARPP-32 and phosphatase inhibitor-1, two structurally related inhibitors of protein phosphatase-1, are both present in striatonigral neurons. *Journal of Neurochemistry, 50*, 257–262.

Packard, M. G., Hirsh, R., & White, N. M. (1989). Differential effects of fornix and caudate nucleus lesions on two radial maze tasks: Evidence for multiple memory systems. *Journal of Neuroscience, 9*, 1465–1472.

Packard, M. G., & McGaugh, J. L. (1992). Double dissociation of fornix and caudate nucleus lesions on acquisition of two water maze tasks: Further evidence for multiple memory systems. *Behavioral Neuroscience, 106*, 439–446.

Pessin, M. S., Snyder, G. L., Halpain, S., Girault, J.-A., Aperia, A., & Greengard, P. (1994). DARPP-32/protein phosphatase-1/Na+/K+ ATPase system: A mechanism for bidirectional control of cell function. In K. Fuxe, L. F. Agnati, B. Bjelke, and D. Ottoson (Eds.), *Trophic regulation of basal ganglia* (pp. 43–57). New York: Elsevier.

Poldrack, R. A., Clark, J., Pare-Blagoev, E. J., Shohamy, D., Moyano, J. C., Myers, C., & Gluck, M. A. (2001). Interactive memory systems in the human brain. *Nature, 414*, 546–550.

Posner, M. I., & Keele, S. W. (1968). On the genesis of abstract ideas. *Journal of Experimental Psychology, 77*, 353–363.

Posner, M. I., & Keele, S. W. (1970). Retention of abstract ideas. *Journal of Experimental Psychology, 83,* 304–308.

Rao, S. M., Bobholz, J. A., Hammeke, T. A., Tosen, A. C., Woodley, S. J., Cunningham, J. M., Cox, R. W., Stein, E. A., & Binder, J. R. (1997). Functional MRI evidence for subcortical participation in conceptual reasoning skills. *Neuroreport, 8,* 1987–1993.

Reber, P. J., Gitelman, D. R., Parrish, T. B., & Mesulam, M. M. (2003). Dissociating explicit and implicit category knowledge with fMRI. *Journal of Cognitive Neuroscience, 15,* 574–583.

Reber, P. J., & Squire, L. R. (1999). Intact learning of artificial grammars and intact category learning by patients with Parkinson's disease. *Behavioral Neuroscience, 113,* 235–242.

Reber, P. J., Stark, C. E. L., & Squire, L. R. (1998). Contrasting cortical activity associated with category memory and recognition memory. *Learning & Memory, 5,* 420–428.

Reber, P. J., Wong, E. C., & Buxton, R. B. (2002). Comparing the brain areas supporting nondeclarative categorization and recognition memory. *Cognitive Brain Research, 14,* 245–257.

Robbins, T. W., & Everitt, B. J. (1996). Neurobiological mechanisms of reward and motivation. *Current Opinion in Neurobiology, 6,* 228–236.

Roberts, A. C., De Salvia, M. A., Wilkinson, L. S., Collins, P., Muir, J. L., Everitt, B. J., & Robbins, T. W. (1994). 6-Hydroxydopamine lesions of the prefrontal cortex in monkeys enhance performance on an analog of the Wisconsin card sort test: Possible interactions with subcortical dopamine. *The Journal of Neuroscience, 14,* 2531–2544.

Rogers, R. D., Andrews, T. C., Grasby, P. M., Brooks, D. J., & Robbins, T. W. (2000). Contrasting cortical and subcortical activations produced by attentional-set shifting and reversal learning in humans. *Journal of Cognitive Neuroscience, 12,* 142–162.

Rolls, E. T. (1994). Neurophysiology and cognitive functions of the striatum. *Revue Neurologique, 150,* 648–660.

Romo, R., Merchant, H., Ruiz, S., Crespo, P., & Zainos, A. (1995). Neuronal activity of primate putamen during categorical perception of somaesthetic stimuli. *Neuroreport, 6,* 1013–1017.

Sage, J. R., Anagnostaras, S. G., Mitchell, S., Bronstein, J. M., De Salles, A., Masterman, D., & Knowlton, B. J. (2003). Analysis of probabilistic classification learning in patients with Parkinson's disease before and after pallidolomy surgery. *Learning & Memory, 10,* 226–236.

Saint-Cyr, J. A., Taylor, A. E., & Lang, A. E. (1988). Procedural learning and neostriatal dysfunction in man. *Brain, 111,* 941–959.

Salamone, J. D., & Correa, M. (2002). Motivational views of reinforcement: Implications for understanding the behavioral functions of nucleus accumbens dopamine. *Behavioral Brain Research, 137,* 3–25.

Satoh, T., Nakai, S., Sato, T., & Kimura, M. (2003). Correlated coding of motivation and outcome of decision by dopamine neurons. *The Journal of Neuroscience, 23,* 9913–9923.

Scatton, B., Dubois, A., Dubocovich, M. L., Zahniser, N. R., & Fage, D. (1985). Quantitative autoradiography of [^{3}H]nomifensine binding sites in rat brain. *Life Sciences, 36,* 815–822.

Schultz, W. (1998). Predictive reward signal of dopamine neurons. *Journal of Neurophysiology, 80,* 1–27.

Schultz, W., Dayan, P., & Montague, P. R. (1997). A neural substrate of prediction and reward. *Science, 275,* 1593–1599.

Schultz, W., & Romo, R. (1992). Role of primate basal ganglia and frontal cortex in the internal generation of movements. I. Preparatory activity in the anterior striatum. *Experimental Brain Research, 91,* 363–384.

Seger, C. A., & Cincotta, C. M. (2002). Striatal activity in concept learning. *Cognitive, Affective & Behavioral Neuroscience, 2,* 149–161.

Seger, C. A., & Cincotta, C. M. (2005). The roles of the caudate nucleus in human classification learning. *Journal of Neuroscience, 25*, 2941–2951.

Shohamy, D., Myers, C. E., Onlaor, S., & Gluck, M. A. (2004). Role of the basal ganglia in category learning: How do patients with Parkinson's disease learn?. *Behavioral Neuroscience, 118*, 676–686.

Shook, B. L., Schlag-Rey, M., & Schlag, J. (1991). Primate supplementary eye field. II Comparative aspects of connections with the thalamus, corpus striatum, and related forebrain nuclei. *Journal of Comparative Neurology, 307*, 562–583.

Smiley, J. F., Levey, A. I., Ciliax, B. J., & Goldman-Rakic, P. S. (1994). D_1 dopamine receptor immunoreactivity in human and monkey cerebral cortex: Predominant and extrasynaptic localization in dendritic spines. *Proceedings of the National Academy of Sciences, 91*, 5720–5724.

Snowden, J. S., Craufurd, D., Griffiths, H., Thompson, J., & Neary, D. (2001). Longitudinal evaluation of cognitive disorder in Huntington's disease. *Journal of the International Neuropsychological Society, 7*, 33–44.

Snowden, J. S., Craufurd, D., Thompson, J., & Neary, D. (2002). Psychomotor, executive, and memory function in preclinical Huntington's disease. *Journal of Experimental and Clinical Neuropsychology, 24*, 133–145.

Sorg, B. A., & Kalivas, P. W. (1993). Effects of cocaine and footshock stress on extracellular dopamine levels in the medial prefrontal cortex. *Neuroscience, 53*, 695–703.

Squire, L. R. (1992). Memory and the hippocampus: A synthesis from findings with rats, monkeys, and humans. *Psychological Review, 99*, 195–231.

Squire, L. R., Stark, C. E. L., & Clark, R. E. (2004). The medial temporal lobe. *Annual Review of Neuroscience, 27*, 279–306.

Sternberg, S. (1966). High-speed scanning in human memory. *Science, 153*, 652–654.

Sutton, M. A., & Beninger, R. J. (1999). Psychopharmacology of conditioned reward: Evidence for a rewarding signal at D_1–like dopamine receptors. *Psychopharmacology, 144*, 95–110.

van Domburg, P. H. M. F., & ten Donkelaar, H. J. (1991). *The human substantia nigra and ventral tegmental area.* Berlin: Springer-Verlag.

van Golf Racht-Delatour, B., & El Massioui, N. (1999). Rule-based learning impairment in rats with lesions to the dorsal striatum. *Neurobiology of Learning & Memory, 72*, 47–61.

Volz, H.-P., Gaser, C., Haeger, F., Rzanny, R., Mentzel, H.-J., Kreitschmann-Andermahr, I., Alois Kaiser, W., & Sauer, H. (1997). Brain activation during cognitive stimulation with the Wisconsin Card Sorting Test–A functional MRI study on healthy volunteers and schizophrenics. *Psychiatry Research: Neuroimaging, 75*, 45–157.

Vonsattel, J. P., & DiFiglia, M. (1998). Huntington disease. *Journal of Neuropathology and Experimental Neurology, 57*, 369–384.

Vonsattel, J. P., Myers, R. H., Stevens, T. J., Ferrante, R. J., Bird, E. D., & Richardson, E. P., Jr. (1985). Neuropathological classification of Huntington's disease. *Journal of Neuropathology and Experimental Neurology, 44*, 559–577.

Waldron, E. M., & Ashby, F. G. (2001). The effects of concurrent task interference on category learning: Evidence for multiple category learning systems. *Psychonomic Bulletin & Review, 8*, 168–176.

White, N. M. (1989). A functional hypothesis concerning the striatal matrix and patches: Mediation of S-R memory and reward. *Life Sciences, 45*, 1943–1957.

Wickens, J. R. (1990). Striatal dopamine in motor activation and reward-mediated learning: Steps towards a unifying model. *Journal of Neural Transmission, 80*, 9–31.

Wickens, J. (1993). *A theory of the striatum.* New York: Pergamon Press.

Willingham, D. B. (1998). A neuropsychological theory of motor skill learning. *Psychological Review, 105*, 558–584.

Willingham, D. B., Wells, L. A., Farrell, J. M., & Stemwedel, M. E. (2000). Implicit motor sequence learning is represented in response locations. *Memory & Cognition, 28*, 366–375.

Wilson, C. J. (1995). The contribution of cortical neurons to the firing pattern of striatal spiny neurons. In J. C. Houk, J. L. Davis, and D. G. Beiser (Eds.), *Models of information processing in the basal ganglia* (pp. 29–50). Cambridge, MA: Bradford.

Wise, R. A. (2002). Brain reward circuitry: Insights from unsensed incentives. *Neuron, 36*, 229–240.

Witt, K., Nuhsman, A., & Deuschl, G. (2002). Dissociation of habit-learning in Parkinson's and cerebellar disease. *Journal of Cognitive Neuroscience, 14*, 493–499.

Zeithamova, D., & Maddox, W. T. (in press). Dual task interference in perceptual category learning. *Memory & Cognition.*

KNOWLEDGE, DEVELOPMENT, AND CATEGORY LEARNING

Brett K. Hayes

I. Introduction

It now seems uncontroversial to assert that "prior knowledge" or naïve theories play a key role in adult categorization. Twenty years ago, Murphy and Medin (1985) published a seminal paper arguing that most concepts are acquired in the context of larger "theory-like" knowledge structures. Since then a wealth of data has accumulated documenting the effects of prior knowledge on adult categorization (Ahn & Luhmann, 2005; Heit, 1997; Murphy, 2002), and a variety of formal models have been developed to explain these effects (Heit, Briggs, & Bott, 2004; Rehder & Murphy, 2003).

In the case of category learning by infants and young children, however, there remains intense debate about how background knowledge may (or may not) affect concept acquisition and development. At one extreme, some view children's concepts as informed by broader knowledge structures or theories from an early point in development (Gelman, 2003; Keil, Smith, Simons, & Levins, 1998). Background knowledge or naïve theories are seen as providing important constraints on the way that children encode new exemplar information and make decisions about category membership. Age-related changes in children's knowledge or theories therefore affect the way that they categorize (Carey, 1985; Vosniadou & Brewer, 1992). This will be referred to as the "knowledge-based" approach to early category learning.

THE PSYCHOLOGY OF LEARNING
AND MOTIVATION VOL. 46
DOI: 10.1016/S0079-7421(06)46002-3

Many, however, remain skeptical about the impact of such theories on early categories, insisting that these are acquired from the "bottom-up," through the learning of the perceptual and statistical regularities present in category exemplars (Jones & Smith, 1993; Quinn, 2002; Rakison & Hahn, 2004; Sloutsky & Fisher, 2004). Such approaches include applications of seasoned theories of adult category acquisition involving either the abstraction of prototypes from experience with category members (Hayes & Taplin, 1993; Younger, 1990) or the encoding and retrieval of specific exemplars (Boswell & Green, 1982; Hayne, 1996). According to this "similarity-based" approach, naïve theories are the products of rather than contributors to conceptual development.

One reason why this debate has proven difficult to resolve is a lack of consensus as to just what constitutes a "theory" or "knowledge" in early categorization. A second problem is that proponents of the knowledge-based approach have often been vague about how knowledge interacts with more fundamental categorization processes such as exemplar encoding or prototype abstraction.

In this chapter, the aim is to deal with these issues by proposing a rapprochement between knowledge-based and similarity-based views of children's categorization. The central argument is that from an early point in development, prior knowledge and statistical learning processes are closely integrated and interdependent. Prior knowledge suggests which features are most relevant during category learning and influences how similarity is computed during categorization. However, the effects of prior knowledge are not static. Increasing experience with the members of a new category can lead children to incorporate into their concept representation features that were not predicted by prior knowledge. Experience with instances that violate expectations can also lead children to revise their general beliefs about a category domain.

This analysis suggests that there are three routes to developmental change in children's concepts. The first route is via domain-general changes in the efficiency with which children process the regularities in observed exemplars. The second involves age-related changes in the accrual and reorganization of domain knowledge. Finally, there may be developmental change in the interaction between these two sources. With age we may see changes in how children integrate their new experiences with their knowledge to produce conceptual representations. In this chapter, I will review evidence bearing on the first two of these routes, suggesting that each has a role to play in shaping children's concepts. I will also present data suggesting that the third route is particularly important for understanding conceptual development.

To make this case I will first review the arguments for a role of background knowledge in children's categorization and examine the various ways that "knowledge" has been defined. I will then review the empirical evidence illustrating the many different ways that background knowledge can affect children's encoding of new exemplars, decisions about category membership, memory for instances, and category-based inferences. I will then describe an explicit theory of how prior knowledge and exemplar information are integrated during category learning and examine how this theory can be applied to children's concept learning and conceptual development. In the final sections, I will examine the challenges that remain for theories that assume that early categorization is driven by an interaction between knowledge and experience with novel category exemplars.

II. The Case for Prior Knowledge in Children's Categorization

A. THEORETICAL ARGUMENTS

Consider a child learning about *zebras* for the first time. According to similarity-based approaches learning this category involves encoding information about the similarities between category members and noting how they differ from the members of other categories. So after observing several instances at the zoo a child's zebra concept might include features like "has black and white stripes," "has four legs," "has hooves," and so on. In the future when the child sees something that may be a zebra, their category membership decision will be determined by the similarity between these features and those of the target. In many respects this seems entirely reasonable. As well as being intuitively appealing there is a wealth of data suggesting that featural similarity does influence children's classification decisions (Farah & Kosslyn, 1982; Murphy, 2002) as well as related conceptual functions like inductive inference (Sloutsky & Fisher, 2004).

Similarity-based models, however, fail to explain some crucial aspects of the process of category acquisition and transfer. In the earlier example it is not at all clear how a child would know just what features they should be comparing as they encounter zebras and nonzebras. As Murphy and Medin (1985) point out, any two objects could be compared in an infinite number of ways. Some of the ways that zebras are similar to one another seem relevant to learning the concept (e.g., body shape and color, habitat, diet), while other similarities are specious (e.g., they live on the planet Earth, they are larger than mice, they cannot fly). A related complexity is that it is not always clear just what object parts should count as features. For example, is the zebra's mane best treated as a separate feature or as part of the animal's head? It may be possible to narrow this feature space through extended experience with category members and nonmembers.[1] But this does not seem to be the way that concept learning works. Children aged between 18 months and 6 years learn new language concepts very rapidly, often recognizing the meaning of a word after exposure to only one or two referents (Carey, 1978; Macario, Shipley, & Billman, 1990).

One way to explain such prodigious learning is that children's prior knowledge constrains their learning of new concepts. Prior knowledge or beliefs about the domain in which a target concept is located can help to define and direct attention toward the features that are most relevant features for similarity comparisons. On first inspection of a zebra, a child might note that it has many features in common with familiar animals. Hence, the child might make a starting assumption that observable features, like body shape and covering, as well as unobservable features, like internal physical structure, will be important in distinguishing zebras from other things. Other characteristics, like the exact size of observed zebras and their position and orientation in the zoo enclosure, are unlikely to be considered because such features were not predictive of membership in known animal categories.

In addition to facilitating the learning of new category exemplars, prior knowledge can have a direct effect on categorization decisions. If I was to paint a zebra black and ask a 4-year old whether this object is still a zebra, then the chances are that they would answer confidently in the affirmative (Keil, 1989). Since the child is unlikely to have ever encountered a black zebra their response would not be guided by any information encoded during category learning. In this case the child's categorization decision looks more like an inference derived from some general beliefs about the principles governing biological categories (e.g., that internal structure is more important than external appearance).

Another way that knowledge could affect children's categorization is through making certain instances more memorable. The effects of background knowledge on memory in both adults and children have long been recognized (Bartlett, 1932; Pressley & Schneider, 1997). In particular, from at least 2 years of age children show effects of memory "schemata"; when they recall information relating to a familiar situation, children report a mixture of presented details and details inferred from background knowledge (Schneider & Bjorklund, 1998). Recall of events that conflict with canonical knowledge will often be distorted so that children report expected

---

[1] The encoding of some features may also be constrained by the operation of our perceptual system and by the process of comparison. These constraints alone, however, are unlikely to be sufficient to explain the range of prior knowledge effects reviewed here (Goldstone, 1994; Murphy, 2002).

details or event sequences rather than those presented (Bauer & Thal, 1990). This suggests that prior knowledge will affect the way that category exemplars or exemplar features are stored. Features that are consistent with a child's expectations about a category might be retained over longer periods and, hence, have a greater effect on categorization decisions, than unexpected features.[2]

Finally, knowledge could affect children's inferences about category properties. If a child has some beliefs about the principles that underlie the concept of *animals*, for example, then this will affect the way they generalize the properties of category members. Once they have learned that a zebra is a kind of animal then, without further learning, they may infer that zebras share many of the nonobvious features of other animals (e.g., that zebras have internal organs) regardless of the surface similarity between these instances.

To summarize, prior knowledge may affect children's categorization processes in at least four ways: (1) specifying the features that are relevant for similarity comparisons and thereby facilitating category learning; (2) providing a basis for decisions about category membership; (3) making particular features or instances more or less memorable, and (4) influencing patterns of inductive generalization. This list is not meant to be exhaustive. Prior knowledge could also conceivably affect the way that children combine concepts (Johnson & Keil, 2000) and use concepts to communicate when solving problems (Markman & Makin, 1998). In the following review I will concentrate on existing developmental work that bears on the first four issues. Before examining this work in detail, however, it would be useful to have a clearer idea of just what is meant by the term "prior knowledge." Such an analysis is important because different kinds of prior knowledge may affect category acquisition in very different ways.

B. VARIETIES OF "PRIOR KNOWLEDGE"

Although the importance of knowledge effects in categorization has been widely discussed over the past two decades, there is still no agreement on what constitutes such knowledge, either in adults or in children. At least three kinds of knowledge have been identified as having a possible influence on early categorization.

1. *Specific knowledge*: This includes children's specific beliefs or expectations about features and feature structure. This may involve a belief that individual features are more strongly associated with certain kinds of categories (e.g., that features like "wearing pink" and "liking ballet"

---

[2] It is also possible to argue for a reverse effect of prior knowledge so that instances that violate expectations will be better remembered. This possibility is discussed in Section IV.

are more characteristic of girls than boys). It may also involve beliefs about the relationships between features (e.g., things with feathers and wings may nest in trees). In its broadest sense the term "specific knowledge" could be applied to any relevant expectations about category structure that are in place before a person encounters the members of a new category. It encompasses beliefs about causal relations, thematic and script-based links between categories, features, or events (Murphy, 2002). This kind of knowledge does not have to be particularly complete or coherent (Mills & Keil, 2004; Rozenblit & Keil, 2002), and for that reason it is probably misleading to refer to it as a "theory." Nevertheless, even minimal levels of knowledge can affect the way that new categories are learned. Kaplan and Murphy (2000), for example, found that having some prior knowledge about just one of the six features present in individual exemplars facilitated category learning by adults.

Specific forms of background knowledge are likely to be involved in all of the effects on category processing discussed earlier. Children acquire a larger and better-organized base of specific knowledge as they get older. Findings like those of Kaplan and Murphy (2002), however, suggest that even the very modest levels of specific knowledge held by young children may influence their category acquisition.

2. *Framework theories:* These are broader kinds of beliefs about the causal mechanisms that operate in different ontological domains (Carey, 1985; Wellman & Gelman, 1998). The central argument is that at some point in development children recognize that different kinds of causal mechanisms apply to material inanimate objects, such as rocks and balls, biological kinds, like animals and plants, and sentient kinds capable of psychological states like emotions and beliefs. Knowing (or at least suspecting) that something is a living thing, for example, implies that it will be capable of self-generated motion, growth, and reproduction. If the same object were thought to be inanimate then it would be expected to move only if external force was applied. Framework theories are thought to arise from a belief in psychological essentialism or that category members share core properties that explain their superficial similarities (Gelman, 2003; Hirschfeld, 1995; Medin & Ortony, 1989).

Such theories provide general intuitions about the kinds of causal relations that might operate within a broad domain but do not predict the properties of specific categories or category members. This implies that framework theories may have a stronger impact at the earliest stages of category learning. Knowing something is an animal allows you to make some general inferences about an object's properties. But more specific knowledge and/or experience with category members will be necessary to learn basic-level categories like dog, horse, or canary.

3. *Domain-general biases*: The third kind of "knowledge" that may influence the early development of categorization involves domain-general biases or implicit assumptions about the way that categories are organized. Psychological essentialism, described earlier, is an example of an implicit belief that leads children to go beyond similarity-based information in classification.[3] Another example is the "causal status hypothesis" (Ahn & Kim, 2000). According to this view, people regard causal features (i.e., those believed to give rise to other features) as more fundamental to category membership than "effect" features (i.e., those which are causally dependent on other features). In other words, this approach suggests that certain kinds of specific knowledge or beliefs (i.e., involving causal relations between features) are central to classification and induction.

III. Experimental Evidence for Prior Knowledge Effects on Children's Categorization

A. Feature Weighting in Category Learning

Much of the existing work on feature weighting effects in children's category learning has examined the role of specific kinds of knowledge. This work has focused mainly on how knowledge can facilitate category learning by highlighting features that are relevant to the discrimination between alternative categories. The effect of children's social knowledge was examined by Hayes and Taplin (1992), who taught 6- and 11-year olds to discriminate between two artificial social categories. These categories had a family resemblance structure such that certain features occurred more frequently in one category than the contrast category, but no feature was necessary and sufficient for category membership. Category members were made up of descriptive statements relevant to the type of education they had received, their place of work, preferred type of holiday, and favorite leisure activities, together with photographs illustrating these features. During training, some were given category labels designed to activate children's social knowledge ("doctors" or secretaries"; "indoor people" or "outdoor people"). The control group was simply told that the categories represented the members of two different families. Children in both age groups given the more meaningful category labels learned the categories more quickly than the controls. Moreover, children in the different label conditions focused on different kinds of

---

[3] There is some debate, however, about just how domain general this assumption is (Gelman, 2003; Sloman & Malt, 2003).

features when asked to classify learned and novel test items. Those given the occupational labels classified mainly on the basis of features relating to place of work and education, while those given the "indoor–outdoor" labels directed their attention to the features relevant to recreation.

A related effect of specific knowledge was demonstrated in 5-year-old children by Krascum and Andrews (1998). Children learned to discriminate between two family resemblance categories made up of instances that varied across a number of feature dimensions. During learning, some children were given a theme that linked all of the features (e.g., category members had horns, armor, and claws because they were "fighters"). Other children were given information about the function of each feature, but the features were not linked by a common theme (e.g., horns were for picking up leaves, claws were for digging in the ground to find food) or were given no information about feature function at all. Children who were given the linking theme learned the family resemblance structure better than the other groups, showing more accurate classification of individual category features.

As well as directing attention to feature-category associations, prior knowledge can also help children to identify and learn relationships between features. An important characteristic of our understanding of everyday categories is that we recognize that certain features are correlated. At some point in learning about *fish,* for example, we become aware that features like having fins, scaly skin, and gills tend to co-occur and that the presence of one of these features can be used to predict the others. In laboratory experiments examining category learning, however, even adults often find it difficult to detect feature correlations (Chin-Parker & Ross, 2002; Murphy & Wisniewski, 1989). Having relevant background knowledge about a category domain can direct attention to these correlations and make them easier to learn. This point was illustrated by Barrett, Abdi, Murphy, and Gallagher (1993) who taught 6- and 9-year olds to discriminate between two artificial bird categories. Two sets of correlated features were embedded within these categories. One set contained features that children could link via their background knowledge of biology (e.g., having a "big and complicated brain" was correlated with having a good memory). The other contained features that were individually meaningful but which were not linked by prior knowledge (e.g., "has a two-part heart" and "has a rounded beak"). After being familiarized with these categories both age groups correctly classified test items that contained the knowledge-based correlated features more frequently than those containing the knowledge-neutral features. They also viewed items containing the knowledge-based correlated features as more typical category members. So children as young as six attended to feature correlations and incorporated these into their category representations but only when the correlations were consistent with their background knowledge.

These studies show that prior knowledge can assist children's learning of novel categories by directing their attention to feature-category associations or important connections between features. One question that arises from such work is whether having knowledge about some aspects of a category causes children to ignore features that are not directly connected with that knowledge. Hayes and Taplin (1992) found that this was not the case. Although having familiar labels like "doctor" or "secretary" increased children's attention to features connected with these occupations, 6-year olds still noticed and learned about the other "knowledge-neutral" features. Moreover, children used these knowledge-neutral features when classifying novel transfer items. This is an important result as it shows that the effects of prior knowledge on children's category learning can coexist with the "similarity-based" tabulation of feature structure embodied in more traditional prototype and exemplar categorization models (Kaplan & Murphy, 2000).

B. USING BACKGROUND KNOWLEDGE TO DETERMINE CATEGORY MEMBERSHIP

In the previous section, we saw that background knowledge affects children's category learning by directing their attention toward or away from certain features. Knowledge, however, may have a more direct affect on children's categorization by changing the criteria that children use to determine category membership. In a widely cited study, Keil (1989) asked children to decide whether the identity of animals would be changed when various transformations were made to their external appearance. For example, they were told that a raccoon was dyed to look like a skunk and surgically altered so that it emitted a skunk odor. By 7 years of age children judged that such superficial changes did not alter an animal's identity. In contrast when artifacts were transformed in ways that altered their intended function (e.g., a coffeepot was altered to make it look like a bird feeder), children of all ages accepted that the identity of the object had changed. This suggests that children believe that internal structural features are more central in determining membership in biological categories, whereas function (either intended or current) is central for artifacts. Supporting this argument is the finding that preschoolers believe that an animal's identity is more strongly determined by its "insides" than by its "outsides" (Gelman & Wellman, 1991; Shipley, 2000). They also generalize novel animal but not artifact names based on information about internal parts (Diesendruck, Gelman, & Lebowitz, 1998). In contrast, objects that are perceptually dissimilar but share a common function are often judged to be members of the same lexical category by children as young as 2 years of age (Diesendruck, Markson, & Bloom, 2003; Kemler-Nelson, Russell, Duke, & Jones, 2000).

Providing background knowledge about an object can significantly alter the kinds of features that young children use to determine category membership and to extend category labels. Keil (1995) found that when preschoolers were shown a novel object and told it was a "frog," they extended the label to objects with a similar shape, disregarding color and surface markings. When the same object was labeled a "rock," color and surface markings affected label extension (Macario, 1991).

One limitation of Keil's (1995) study is that the use of familiar labels like "frog" may have simply caused children to retrieve exemplars of the category and generalize labels to test items based on similarity to these exemplars. An effect of knowledge on children's extension of *novel* labels was reported by Booth and Waxman (2002). Three-year-old children were shown a three-dimensional wooden model of an abstract object that was given a novel label such as "dax." The target was presented together with a cover story that implied that it was animate (e.g., a dax is usually very hungry) or that it was an artifact (e.g., a dax is used to fix something). Children generalized the novel name differently depending on their beliefs about animacy. Those in the animate condition used both shape and texture to guide name extension, while those in the artifact condition only used shape. Information about ontology was also found to override salient perceptual cues in guiding name extension. Previous studies have shown that the addition of a feature, like "eyes," which is frequently associated with animacy leads children to generalize names on the basis of shape and texture (Jones, Smith, & Landau, 1991). Booth and Waxman (2002), however, found that when eyes were added to the target but the cover story implied that it was a kind of tool, children treated the target as a tool (i.e., generalized the label on the basis of shape alone).

Two final examples suggest that, as predicted by the causal status hypothesis, beliefs about causal mechanisms are given special weight in decisions about category membership. Ahn, Gelman, Amsterlaw, Hohenstein, and Kalish (2000) taught children aged 7–9 years about a fictitious animal category composed of three features (e.g., *Pizers* have promicin in the nerves, thick bones, and large eyes). Children in an experimental condition were given information about the causal relations between features (e.g., promicin causes thick bones and large eyes) while controls were simply given a second exposure to the features. When children were asked to decide whether stimuli made up of two features belonged to the same category, those in the experimental group were more likely to accept items containing the causal feature.

Gopnik and Sobel (2000) demonstrated children's use of shared causal powers as a basis for classification and naming. Children aged between 2 and 4 years were shown a colored block with a novel name (e.g., "blicket") that appeared to cause a machine (a "blicket detector") to light up and play music. Children subsequently extended the novel name to blocks that displayed similar causal powers regardless of differences in noncausal features like shape or color. In other words, 2-year olds classified objects on the basis of shared causal powers even when these conflicted with perceptual characteristics.

These studies suggest that background knowledge in the form of general assumptions about the features that are most central to a domain or cues that imply membership of a certain domain can alter the way that young children make categorization decisions about novel items. Beliefs about internal structure or object function frequently override perceptual similarity when these cues are placed in conflict.

Such studies provide convincing demonstrations of the impact of knowledge on categorization. However, they shed little light on how knowledge interacts with similarity-based information. Believing that the members of animal categories share similar insides may be a useful starting point for children learning to distinguish living things from other kinds of objects. But in order to distinguish more specific categories, like *rabbit* and *mouse* or *trout* and *cod*, information about shared internal structures needs to be combined with features relating to surface appearance, habitat, and so on. Again what is needed is a principled account of how initial beliefs about the features that are relevant for categorization are combined with new information that is not predicted by a naïve theory.

C.   CATEGORIZATION AND MEMORY

To date relatively few studies have focused on the way that prior knowledge might affect children's memory for category information. Indirect evidence for such effects, however, comes from studies of children's memory of instances that do or do not conform to social stereotypes. Stereotypes are entrenched beliefs about the kinds of behaviors and traits associated with members of different social, racial, or ethnic groups. In this respect, they function like powerful forms of prior knowledge that can affect the way we process information about individuals (Wittenbrink, Hilton, & Gist, 1998). By 2–3 years of age most children have formed stereotypical beliefs about gender-appropriate traits and behaviors (Signorella, Bigler, & Liben, 1993). These beliefs have a profound influence on children's memory for gender stereotype-consistent or inconsistent information (Signorella, et al., 1997; Stangor & McMillan, 1992). Liben and Signorella (1993), for example, presented children aged between 5 and 10 years with photographs of males and females performing either gender-consistent or gender-inconsistent activities. In all age groups recognition and recall was superior for the gender-consistent items. This effect was found even when the link between the study stimuli and gender categories was deemphasized by providing unique labels for each photograph.

D. INDUCTION

Children's background knowledge has been shown to affect their inductive inferences in a number of ways (Hayes, in press). Children's projection of properties from one category to another is governed by their beliefs about the taxonomic and causal relations between the categories. As children's knowledge about the relationship between the categories develops, we see significant changes in their patterns of property generalization. Carey (1985) found that preschool children judged that a biological property of people (e.g., "has a spleen inside it") was reasonably likely to generalize to dogs. When this property was attributed to dogs, however, preschoolers were unlikely to generalize it to people. Ten-year olds and adults, who presumably have a better understanding of the underlying biological similarities be- tween humans and other mammals, were less likely to show these inductive asymmetries (Medin & Waxman, in press).

Children's inductive inferences are also affected by their knowledge about the properties that are to be generalized. In one case, preschool children were shown a target instance (e.g., a triceratops), which was given a familiar category label ("dinosaur") and asked to generalize either a biological prop- erty ("has cold blood") or a physical property ("weighs 1 ton") to other animals (Gelman & Markman, 1987). Preschoolers were more likely to gen- eralize the biological property to other dinosaurs (e.g., a brontosaurus) but generalized physical properties to animals that were similar in appearance to the target (e.g., a rhinoceros). Such findings suggest that even young children are sensitive to the causal mechanisms that underlie different kinds of proper- ties. Models of induction that rely primarily on assessments of the similarity between target and test categories (Osherson, Smith, Wilkie, Lopez, & Shafir, 1990; Sloman, 1993; Sloutsky & Fisher, 2004) are therefore incomplete. Once again, however, we should remember that although more abstract knowledge can sometime override featural similarity as a basis for inductive projection both knowledge *and* similarity contribute to children's inductive inferences. Florian (1994), for example, showed that both shared category membership and the perceptual similarity between target and test items contribute to preschooler's inferences.

E. SUMMARY

This review has highlighted the ways that having background knowledge can affect children's category learning, decisions about category membership, memory for category members, and inductive generalization. It is clear from this work that even when children have relevant knowledge about a category domain, the application of this knowledge during learning does not suppress the operation of more domain-general mechanisms that focus on the similarities and differences between observed exemplars. Such mechanisms are necessary since the skeletal theories and beliefs of children are unlikely to predict the precise structure of the members of any domain. We have also seen a number of examples of how background knowledge and similarity-based processes are interdependent. Knowledge can assist in the parsing of objects into relevant features and determining feature weights (Hayes & Taplin, 1992; Krascum & Andrews, 1998). Once this process is completed, the relevant features can act as input to similarity-based learning processes. The next section will explore this interaction between similarity-based learning and children's background knowledge in greater depth.

IV. Integrating Prior Knowledge and Exemplar Learning

The work reviewed so far suggests that many forms of background knowledge play an important role in determining children's categorization judgments and category-based inferences. In most cases, such knowledge works by modifying or supplementing domain-general processes that involve encoding of the statistical regularities within a category (e.g., by directing attention toward relevant features).

An important goal therefore is to explain how the effects of prior knowledge might be reconciled with similarity-based categorization processes. One way of tackling this problem is to argue that one kind of information typically has a general priority over the other during category learning; it is possible that the detection of similarities between exemplars may initiate the use of prior knowledge, which in turn leads to the formation of a new concept. Developmentally, such a *"similarity-first"* approach implies that young children initially construct categories based on similarity alone and that the use of prior knowledge emerges later in development (Jones & Smith, 1993). Such an approach would have difficulty in explaining many of the results reviewed earlier, which suggest that from at least 2 years of age children's background knowledge or beliefs about causal relations play a central role in category acquisition (Gopnik & Sobell, 2000). Alternately, prior knowledge about categories may have general priority in categorization and override observed category structure when these two forms of information are placed in conflict (Ahn & Kim, 2000). Some of the findings reviewed earlier are consistent with this view (Barrett et al., 1993; Booth & Waxman, 2002). We have shown, however, that in many cases similarity-based processes still have an important role to play in domains in which children can apply their background knowledge (Florian, 1994; Hayes & Taplin, 1992).

An approach that is more likely to be successful is one that assumes a dynamic and ongoing relationship between children's prior knowledge and their encounters with novel category members. Wisniewski and Medin (1994) argue that knowledge and similarity-based processes are "tightly-coupled." Background knowledge directs our attention to certain features during category construction. Encounters with exemplars that do not fit our expectations, however, can cause us to change the way that we apply this knowledge. This interactive process was illustrated by Wisniewski and Medin (1994), who presented adults with categories of ambiguous drawings and asked them to construct rules for differentiating the categories. The rules generated were affected by different kinds of background knowledge (e.g., being told that the drawings were done by "creative" or "noncreative" children or by "city" or "farm" children). After receiving disconfirming feedback though adults changed the way they applied their knowledge to the stimuli. For example, one subject started with the belief that use of exact body proportions in a drawing was evidence that it was done by a creative child. Following negative feedback about category membership the subject decided that this same feature was actually evidence of a lack of creativity.

A.   THE INTEGRATION MODEL

A more explicit account of how expected and observed information are combined in category learning, the integration model, was proposed by Heit (1994). Adopting many of the general assumptions of information integration theory (Anderson, 1981), the model views categorization as jointly determined by similarity to observed category members *and* exemplars recruited from prior knowledge. These two sources of information are combined using a Bayesian algorithm. An important feature of the model is that prior knowledge is conceived of in terms of the recruitment of exemplars from known categories that resemble the new instances that are being learned. This allows the model to incorporate many of the general processing assumptions of exemplar-based categorization models (Nosofsky, 1988). So when a child learns about a new category, like *zebras*, their representation of the category will be influenced by both observed exemplars of the category as well as specific exemplars from known categories like *horses* and *donkeys*.

One of the most important implications of the integration model is that the relative influence of prior knowledge on categorization will change during the course of category learning. In the early stages, when only a few exemplars of the new category have been encountered, the conceptual representation will be strongly influenced by prior knowledge in the form of exemplars from related categories. So when learning about the members of a new animal category a child might begin with expectation that features like "covered in wool" and "lives in snowy mountains" will be found together because many familiar animals have both of these features. As learning continues, however, the ratio of observed exemplars to known exemplars will increase, and the category representation will be increasingly dominated by the features of observed category members. After exposure to many instances that violate knowledge-based expectations (e.g., animals covered in wool but live in a hot climate) children may be more likely to classify new items on the basis of this observed feature structure rather than on prior knowledge.

Carmichael and Hayes (2001) examined evidence for such integration in category learning by 4-, 6-, and 10-year-old children. Children in the "knowledge" training conditions learned about novel animal, social or artifact categories made up of exemplars containing pairs of features. In the no-knowledge control features were not linked by prior knowledge (e.g., "has a curly tail and big eyes") so that feature covariation within the category could only be learned by encoding training exemplars.

In the knowledge conditions, feature covariation was either congruent (e.g., "woolly and lives in snowy mountains") or incongruent (e.g., "woolly and lives in sunny deserts") with prior knowledge.[4] The proportion of congruent instances per category was varied from 25% to 75%. In other words, for some training categories the majority of instances were congruent with children's knowledge while for others most instances were incongruent with this knowledge. After viewing all the members of a given category children were shown individual exemplar features (e.g., "is woolly") and asked to judge whether each one was more likely to be found together with a knowledge-congruent or incongruent feature.

Across age and category domain, children in the knowledge training conditions were more likely to choose congruent responses at test than those in the no-knowledge group. Children of all ages were also sensitive to the level of feature covariation observed during training. When the majority of training exemplars were incongruent with prior knowledge, children were less likely to choose a knowledge-congruent response at test. So, as predicted by the integration model, categorization judgments were jointly influenced by prior knowledge *and* observed feature covariation.

These findings were extended by Hayes, Foster, and Gadd (2003), who found that both prior knowledge and observed feature covariation could

---

[4] In the no-knowledge condition certain feature pairs were arbitrarily selected as "congruent" or "incongruent," and the frequency with which these features covaried during training was manipulated in the same way as in the knowledge condition.

influence children's judgments about transfer features that were expected on the basis of prior knowledge but were not presented during category learning. These results reinforce the view that background knowledge can facilitate children's learning of exemplars that are related in some way to that knowledge, but this does not suppress the learning of the similarity-based aspects of the category (Hayes & Taplin, 1992; Kaplan & Murphy, 2000).

To test the integration model predictions about changes in the influence of knowledge during the course of category learning Carmichael and Hayes (2001) and Hayes et al. (2003) also varied number of training exemplars (e.g., 8 or 24 exemplars per category). The effects of increasing category exposure are illustrated in Fig. 1. As children were exposed to more training instances per category, the influence of prior knowledge on subsequent categorization judgments declined. Conversely, with more training instances sensitivity to observed covariation increased. This is an important result as it shows that the effects of prior knowledge on category learning are not static. With additional experience with the members of novel categories children incorporate new features into their category representations. Many of these features will not be predicted by existing knowledge or may even run contrary to such knowledge.

Having said that it is also important to remember that the effect of prior knowledge on children's categorization never disappeared completely. Even after extended experience with category members children never classified test items only on the basis of the statistical regularities observed during training. Children trained with categories containing a majority of knowledge-incongruent exemplars were conservative in their updating of category representations, showing a smaller but still measurable influence of prior knowledge after extended learning.

B.   DEVELOPMENTAL CHANGE IN THE INTEGRATION PROCESS

With age there are likely to be increases in both the depth and organization of children's knowledge (Carey, 1985; Keil et al., 1998), as well as in the efficiency with which they encode information about new exemplars (Boswell & Green, 1982; Hayes & Taplin, 1993). The methods used by Carmichael and Hayes (2001) and Hayes et al. (2003) made it possible to track developmental changes in the influences of these two information sources. Although the older children studied by Carmichael and Hayes (2001) undoubtedly knew more about animals, artifacts, and social groups than the 4-year olds, all age groups used their knowledge in category learning. A more marked developmental change was found in sensitivity to observed covariation. As illustrated in Fig. 2., older children were more likely than younger children

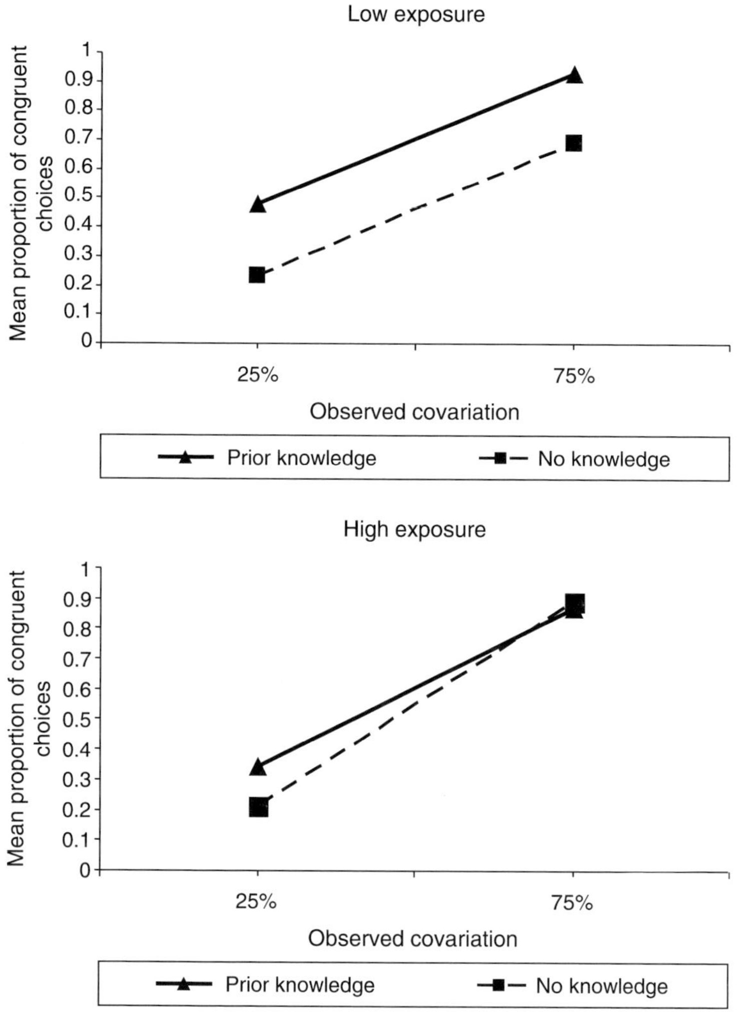

Fig. 1.   The effects of category exposure on children's use of prior knowledge in categorization (adapted from Carmichael & Hayes, 2001, Experiment 2 with permission from the Society for Research in Child Development).

to vary their responding according to the levels of feature covariation that they had observed during training.

This result may reflect two underlying developmental changes. First, older children are better able to encode and remember the features of observed exemplars (Kail, 1990). This is indicated by the fact that older children are

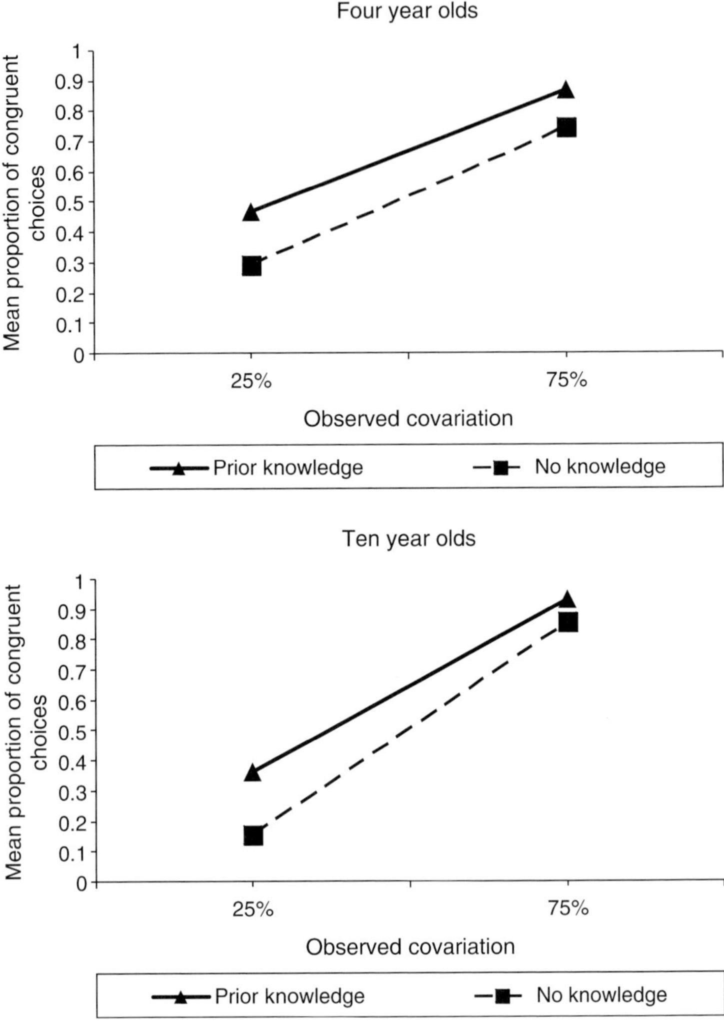

Fig. 2.   Developmental change in children's use of prior knowledge and observed covariation (adapted from Carmichael & Hayes, 2001, Experiment 2 with permission from the Society for Research in Child Development).

more sensitive to observed covariation in the neutral control conditions as well as the knowledge condition. Second, older children may be more efficient at incorporating unexpected or incongruent information into their category representations. This is suggested by the fact that, in the knowledge conditions, older children were more likely than younger children to change their level of congruent responding after observing a large proportion of knowledge-incongruent items. Older children appear to be not only better at tabulating the statistical regularities in observed categories but more likely to incorporate this information into their categories when it conflicts with their existing knowledge.

This conclusion accords with social developmental data suggesting that older children are more aware of the variability in social categories and are more likely to accept exemplars that violate stereotypical expectations (Bigler & Liben, 1992; Levy, Taylor, & Gelman, 1995). The developmental trends that we observed are also consistent with the view that from early to late childhood there is substantial improvement in the ability to coordinate new evidence with background beliefs and expectations (Kuhn, 2002; Zimmerman, 2000).

C. INTEGRATION AND SELECTIVE WEIGHTING

The findings of Carmichael and Hayes (2001) and Hayes et al. (2003) support a number of the key predictions of Heit's (1994) integration model. This model therefore seems like a useful starting point in the development of a more comprehensive account of how prior knowledge interacts with exemplar observation in children's categorization. This section examines in greater depth how well other assumptions made by the model fit the data on knowledge effects in children's category learning.

One aspect of the integration model that requires further investigation is the extent to which children selectively weight exemplars that do or do not fit their background knowledge during category learning. In the original instantiation of the integration model Heit (1994) argued that the effects of prior knowledge on category learning could be largely explained via the combination of exemplars from known categories with new category members. In this integration process equal weight is given to exemplars or features that are congruent or incongruent with prior knowledge. This assumption was later revised in the light of data suggesting that adults gave extra weight to knowledge-incongruent items when given more encoding time (Heit, 1998; Heit et al., 2004). The studies reviewed in Section II also suggest that one of the key effects of prior knowledge in children's categorization involves the selective weighting of particular features or exemplars.

To further examine the role of selective weighting in children's categorization, three versions of the integration model were fitted to the test phase data from Carmichael and Hayes (2001). Equations (1) and (2) were derived from Heit (1998) and describe the probability that a child given a feature of the training category will pair this with a congruent feature x at test.

Equation (1) describes a model in which more weight is given to congruent exemplars. Equation (2) describes a model in which more weight is given to incongruent exemplars.

$$p(x) = \frac{WNp + Gq}{WNp + N(1-p) + G} \qquad \text{integration + congruent weighting} \qquad (1)$$

$$p(x) = \frac{Np + Gq}{Np + WN(1-p) + G} \qquad \text{integration + congruent weighting} \qquad (2)$$

Parameters p and N represent the proportion of congruent covariation observed during training and the total number of exemplars in the category, respectively. The contribution of prior knowledge is represented by q, children's prior belief in the covariation between congruent features, and G that can be interpreted either as the number of relevant instances recruited from memory or a measure of confidence in the belief represented by q. In this case, the value of q for each age group and category domain was derived from the pretest data of Carmichael and Hayes (2001). This value was set at the proportion of congruent responses made by children in each age group before training with the novel category commenced. The selective weighting of exemplars is represented by the value of the parameter W. When the value of W is set to one, Eqs. (1) and (2) are equivalent, with equal weight given to congruent and incongruent observations.

The two integration plus selective weighting models and the integration model without weighting model were fitted to test data from the knowledge conditions of Carmichael and Hayes (2001, Experiment 3). In this experiment, children were exposed to four levels of congruent feature covariation (20%, 40%, 60%, and 80%) during training. Training and test items were drawn from animal or social domains. The integration (no weighting), integration + congruent weighting, and integration + incongruent weighting models were fitted to data for each domain separately in each of the three age groups. Fixed and estimated parameter values and goodness-of-fit measures are given in Table I. In every case the values of the free parameters estimated by the integration + incongruent weighting model did not differ from those generated by the integration model without selective weighting so only the former are reported.

In most cases, each model produced a reasonable fit to the data (with RMSEs = 0.16). The most important result, however, was that in both animal and social domains the version of the integration model, which allowed for selective weighting of *congruent* exemplars, provided a significantly better fit

TABLE I

SUMMARY OF MODEL FITS FOR CARMICHAEL AND HAYES
(2001, EXPERIMENT 3)

Age (year)	Model	Weighting ratio (W)	Pretest prior knowledge estimate (q)	Prior strength (G)	Root mean square error (RMSE)
Animal categories					
	Integration + con. wtg.	1.65:1	0.67	3.0	0.0227*
4	Integration + incon. wtg.	1.0:1	0.67	3.0	0.0918
	Integration + con. wtg	3.99:1	0.78	1.0	0.0888*
6	Integration + incon. wtg.	1.0:1	0.78	3.0	0.2497
	Integration + con. wtg.	1.8:1	0.94	1.0	0.0688
10	Integration + incon. wtg.	1.0:1	0.94	3.0	0.1097
Social categories					
	Integration + con. wtg.	2.5:1	0.80	3.0	0.0372*
4	Integration + incon. wtg.	1.0:1	0.80	3.0	0.1581
	Integration + con. wtg	2.5:1	0.82	1.0	0.0654*
6	Integration + incon. wtg.	1.0:1	0.82	3.0	0.1639
	Integration + con. wtg.	1.2:1	0.97	1.0	0.0850
10	Integration + incon. wtg.	1.0:1	0.97	1.5	0.0929

Note: The weighting ratio (W) represents the ratio of Congruent:Incongruent items for the integration + congruent weighting model. This ratio is reversed for the Integration + Incongruent weighting model. All models were fitted to 4 values of observed covariation, $p = 0.2, 0.4, 0.6,$ and 0.8. $N = 10$ for each level of covariation. In this model fit only W and G were free parameters. Fitted values of W ranged between 1 and 5. Fitted values of G ranged between 1 and 3.

The symbol (*) indicates that fit was significantly better than integration model with no weighting.

to the data from 4- and 6-year olds than either of the other models.[5] For the 10-year olds the integration model without a selective weighting parameter produced a reasonable fit to the data (with RMSE below 0.11 in each domain). For these older children the addition of a selective weighting parameter for congruent items did not significantly improve model fit.

This suggests that for younger children prior knowledge affected category learning in two ways. First, knowledge was integrated with observed exemplars in the manner described by Heit (1994). Second, exemplars that were consistent with children's knowledge were given more weight in their

---

[5] The fit of the two integration + weighting models was compared with that of the integration model with no weighting using the technique for comparing nested models described by Borowiak (1989) and Heit (1998).

category representations. By contrast, for 10-year olds only the integration process was needed to explain the effects of knowledge on categorization.

This developmental trend is interesting because it is inconsistent with a "similarity-first" account. Prior knowledge had a more complex and far-reaching effect on the category learning of 4- and 6-year olds than was the case for older children. Young children's weighting of knowledge-congruent information may be adaptive in the light of their more limited attentional and memory capabilities. As we have seen previously, exemplars that are consistent with prior knowledge are often easier for young children to encode and retrieve from memory. Paying attention to these items makes the task of learning a new category easier for younger children. Young children may also selectively attend to congruent items because they find it hard to accept items that violate their background knowledge or beliefs (Kuhn, 2002; Levy et al., 1995). An interesting goal for future work will be to explain the shift from young children's preference for encoding knowledge-congruent items to the selective encoding of incongruent exemplars that seems more common among adult learners (Heit, 1998; Heit et al., 2004).

V.   Integrating Different Kinds of Knowledge

A.   BACKGROUND AND METHODOLOGY

So far the focus has been on how specific knowledge about category features is integrated with information derived from observations of category members. Section II , however, identified several different kinds of "knowledge," which impact on children's categories. In this section, I examine whether the processes for combining knowledge and exemplar learning are the same for different kinds of knowledge.

One distinction that is likely to be particularly important in this regard is between knowledge based only on previous observations and knowledge based on beliefs about causal mechanism. Children are much more likely to impute causal relationships between events if they have some understanding of the mechanism that links them (Ahn et al., 2000; Bullock, Gelman & Baillargeon, 1982; Shultz, Fisher, Pratt, & Ruff, 1986). In the absence of such mechanistic beliefs, children may not impute causal relations even when the target events are strongly correlated (Gopnik & Sobel, 2000).

Such results suggest that causal knowledge and knowledge based on observed correlations will be subject to different kinds of integration processes. Feature correlations that are based on some known causal mechanism may be perceived as highly stable across category members. Such causal knowledge therefore is more likely to be used as a basis for category decisions than knowledge based only on previous observation of empirical relationships between features.

A second implication of the difference between these two kinds of knowledge is that children may be more reluctant to incorporate instances that violate beliefs about causal mechanism into category representations. The features "has wings" and "lives underwater," for example, seems like an implausible pairing not only because it does not fit with any known exemplars but because it violates our causal beliefs about the functions of wings. By contrast, for most children the pairing of features, like "does not have hair" and "meows" (as found in Mexican Hairless cats), would also be highly novel. However, children may be more likely to incorporate this instance into their concept of *cats* because it does not violate any causal principles. In this respect, children's category learning may parallel patterns of causal induction shown by scientists (Dunbar & Fugelsang, 2005) and lay adults (Fugelsang & Thompson, 2000; White, 1995), who are more skeptical about exceptions to previously experienced correlations when these also violate beliefs about causal mechanisms.

Kellie Bragg and I tested these predictions about the effects of different kinds of knowledge on children's category learning using a paradigm adapted from Carmichael and Hayes (2001) and Hayes et al. (2003). As in these earlier studies children in the knowledge conditions learned about exemplars containing feature pairs that they did or did not expect to covary. In the causal knowledge condition, children expected features to covary and were able to explain why the features were connected. In the covariation-knowledge condition, children expected features to covary but could not articulate a mechanism that linked them. Critically, items were selected so that the strength of belief in feature covariation before training was equated across the covariation- and causal-knowledge conditions. This meant that any differences obtained between the two knowledge conditions would be due to the presence or absence of beliefs about causal mechanisms rather than overall differences in the expected level of feature covariation.

To construct these stimuli we ran a pretest with twenty 7-year olds who were presented with a variety of animal features that could plausibly covary. For each item we verbally and pictorially described a target feature (e.g., "has long legs"). Children then had to choose which of two test features was most likely to be found with the target. Congruent features were those likely to be linked to the target on the basis of background knowledge (e.g., "moves very fast"). Incongruent alternatives were those which we expected to have a negative association with the target (e.g., "moves very slowly"). After children chose a test feature they were asked to explain *why* it went with the target. Responses to this question were transcribed and scored as "causal," "noncausal," or "other." To be accepted as causal, the explanation had to include the appropriate use of words, like "because," to link the features or equivalent causal expressions (e.g., "having long legs makes you able to run faster"). Noncausal responses usually involved an affirmation of the empirical relationship between the features (e.g., "They just go together") or a reference to a familiar exemplar ("they go because it's a kind of horse").

This pretest yielded the eight feature sets (four causal knowledge, four covariation knowledge) in Table II. The causal and covariation sets showed similar levels of expected congruent covariation (93% in each case). The sets differed substantially, however, in the proportion of items for which children generated causal explanations (causal sets $M = 0.90$; noncausal sets $M = 0.22$).

The pretest was followed by the main category learning study in which stimuli drawn from either the causal or covariation sets were presented as exemplars of a novel category of extraterrestrial animals. As in Carmichael and Hayes (2001) and Hayes et al. (2003) observed covariation between the features of the new categories was manipulated during training (20% versus 80%). The categorization performance of the causal and covariation

TABLE II

FEATURE SETS FROM HAYES AND BRAGG (2003)

Set	Causal features	Noncausal (covariation-only) features
A	1. Lives in a tree	1. Barks
	2. Lives on the ground	2. Hisses
	3. Climbs	3. Lives in a kennel
	4. Runs	4. Lives in the bush
B	1. Has no legs	1. Has humps
	2. Has long legs	2. Has feathers
	3. Moves slow	3. Lives in the desert
	4. Moves fast	4. Lives in trees
C	1. Eats fish	1. Furry
	2. Eats plants	2. Scaly
	3. Lives in the ocean	3. Has whiskers
	4. Lives in the forest	4. Has gills
D	1. Flies	1. Makes a "moo" sound
	2. Swims	2. Makes a "baa" sound
	3. Has wings	3. Covered in hair
	4. Has webbed feet	4. Covered in wool

Note: For each feature set "congruent" exemplars were generated by pairing features 1 and 3, and features 2 and 4. "Incongruent" exemplars were generated by pairing features 1 and 4, and features 2 and 3.

knowledge groups was also compared with a no-knowledge control in which children had no prior expectations about feature covariation.

Forty-eight children aged between 7 and 8 years ($M = 7$ years, 2 months), who did not participate in the pretest, were randomly allocated to either the causal, covariation or no-knowledge training group. All children were taught about two different categories of extraterrestrials in successive training-test blocks. Each training category contained 10 instances. For the causal and noncausal knowledge conditions exemplars were constructed by combining the first or second feature from the relevant set in Table I with the third or fourth feature. In one of the training categories (80% congruent condition), eight exemplars were congruent with prior knowledge (e.g., "furry and has whiskers") and two were incongruent (e.g., "furry and has gills"). In the other category (20% congruent condition) these proportions were reversed. Each exemplar was described verbally and pictorially. After all exemplars for a given category were presented twice children were given four test items. For each test item a target feature from the training category was presented and children had to choose whether that feature was likely to be found together with a congruent or incongruent feature. The order in which the training-test sequences were presented for the 20% and 80% congruent conditions was counterbalanced across subjects. The procedure for the no-knowledge training condition was identical except that the stimuli were drawn from the no-knowledge animal feature sets developed by Carmichael and Hayes (2001). In this condition feature pairs were arbitrarily deemed to be "congruent" or "incongruent." The only way that children in this condition could learn the structure of the training categories was for them to encode the observed covariation between features.

B. RESULTS AND DISCUSSION

The proportion of congruent test choices for each group is given in Fig. 3. Planned contrast testing revealed that, overall, children in the knowledge conditions made more congruent choices at test than those in the no-knowledge condition. Critically, however, children in the causal knowledge condition made more congruent responses than those in the covariation condition. There was also a significant effect of observed covariation with children in all three training groups showing a higher level of congruent responding following training with a majority of congruent exemplars. No interactions between these factors were found.

So like Carmichael and Hayes (2001) and Hayes et al. (2003), this study found that the categorization responses of children in the knowledge conditions were affected by both observed covariation and prior beliefs. The novel finding was that the impact of prior knowledge on categorization was greater

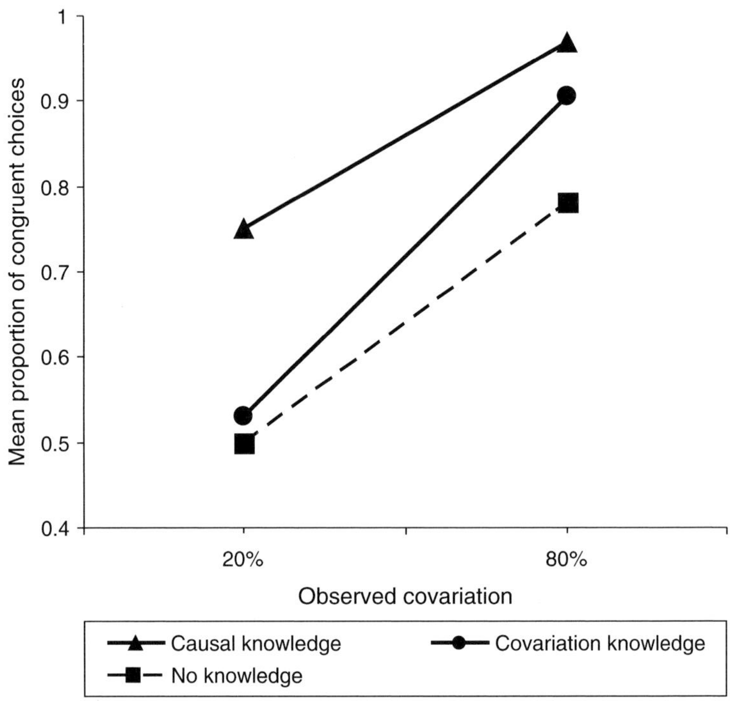

Fig. 3. Effects of causal and covariation knowledge on category learning by 7-year olds.

when this knowledge was based on beliefs about causal mechanisms rather than on prior experience with related exemplars. This is despite the fact that prior to training children showed similar levels of expected covariation for features in the causal knowledge and covariation knowledge conditions. Inspection of Fig. 3 suggests that the most important difference between the causal and covariation knowledge conditions was in the way they responded to categories composed of a majority of exemplars that challenged prior beliefs. Although both knowledge conditions showed a significant reduction in congruent responding at test relative to pretraining levels (92% in each condition), the reduction was much greater for the covariation knowledge group. In other words, although both knowledge conditions commenced training with similar expectations about feature covariation, those in the covariation condition were more likely to revise these beliefs after observing many incongruent exemplars.

These results show that the kind of knowledge one has about feature relationships is important. Seven-year olds were less likely to incorporate new exemplars into their category representations when these challenged causal beliefs. Those who expected features to covary but had no causal theory about this relationship were more likely to combine observed information with their prior beliefs when learning a new category.

It remains an open question whether, given sufficient experience with incongruent exemplars, there would be further change in the impact of causal beliefs on children's categorization. In speculating about this issue it is important to note that in the 20% congruent condition children in the causal knowledge group did show a measurable impact of observed information. Having causal beliefs slowed the rate with which children incorporated incongruent information into their categories but did not block the encoding of this information completely. Hence, further learning could lead to the formation of categories that more closely resemble observed exemplars [see Fugelsang and Thompson (2000) for analogous findings in studies of adult causal learning].

Overall, the data support the contention of causal status theory (Ahn & Kim, 2000) and related theoretical approaches (White, 1995) that prior beliefs based on causal relations will be treated differently to those based only on knowledge about empirical covariation. Knowledge about feature relations based on experience with past exemplars and knowledge based on beliefs about causal mechanisms were combined with new exemplars in different ways.

This is a novel and provocative finding, which suggests that in future work on children's integration of knowledge and exemplar learning it will be important to specify just what kind of knowledge is being targeted. Nevertheless, it may be possible to address the effects of these different kinds of knowledge within the general framework of the integration model. One approach would be to assume that causal- and covariation-based knowledge may give rise to similar prior estimates of observed covariation (as captured by the q parameter) with confidence in these estimates (represented by G) greater in the causal case. Alternately, these results may be explained by the integration plus weighting model considered in Section IV by assuming that more weight is given to exemplars that are consistent with causal expectations than to those which are simply consistent with previously observed exemplars.

VI. Limitations and Extensions of the Integration Model

The previous sections suggest that a modified integration model incorporating a selective weighting component offers the prospect of explaining a considerable amount of developmental data concerning the effects of prior knowledge on categorization. Nevertheless, there remain a number of significant challenges for this model. So far we have mainly applied the model to children's learning of single categories containing relatively simple exemplars (i.e., made up of only two or three features). An important objective therefore is to apply the model to the more conventional category learning task in which children have to discriminate between the members of two or more categories, with exemplars that may differ across several dimensions (Heit, 2001).

A number of assumptions of the integration model also require further clarification. Heit (1994, 1998) characterizes "prior knowledge" as exemplars of known categories that are retrieved and combined with observed exemplars during the learning of a new category. This may, however, be an overly narrow definition of prior knowledge. Many kinds of prior knowledge (e.g., predicting that an object made of paper will be unsuitable for storing liquid) may be hard to reduce to known examples. Even though a 4-year old has never encountered such an object she is highly likely to be able to make this prediction based on her background knowledge about the properties of these materials.

This kind of challenge to the integration model, however, may be relatively easy to respond to. With minor modifications, it should be possible to incorporate this more general sort of knowledge into the integration model. The first model parameter representing prior knowledge (q) indicates children's prior belief in covariation between exemplar features. This expectation could be derived from prior exemplars as suggested by Heit (1994) but could equally come from more abstract category knowledge, including culturally transmitted beliefs about biological, artifact, or social kinds. Similarly, if the G parameter is interpreted as a measure of confidence in prior beliefs about feature covariation, this could also be derived from sources other than direct experience with related categories. In short, as long as knowledge leads to specific beliefs about feature covariation, the source of this knowledge (specific exemplars, cultural beliefs, information acquired in school, or through the media) is not critical to the operation of the integration model.

A more contentious issue is the integration model assumption about the incremental effects of exposure to new category members. According to the model, each time a knowledge-congruent or incongruent exemplar is encountered one's category representation is incrementally shifted in the direction of the observed exemplar. This assumption is similar to those made by "bookkeeping" models of social perception and stereotyping in which stereotypes are modified each time an individual who conforms or violates stereotypical expectations is encountered (Rothbart, 1981).

This approach predicts that if a child is exposed to enough exemplars that contradict their knowledge or beliefs they will inevitably revise those beliefs.

We have already seen, however, that younger children may be slower to incorporate knowledge-incongruent information into their categories than older children. It is also not too hard to think of cases, such as racial and gender stereotypes, in which even extended exposure to counter-stereotypical instances often produces little change in the stereotype (Hilton & von Hippel, 1996).

Such exceptions to the integration model were highlighted by Hayes et al. (2003), who presented 5- and 10-year olds with instances of a novel social category ("children from a foreign school") that contained feature pairings that were congruent (e.g., "wears stockings and likes to play tea parties") or incongruent (e.g., "wears stockings and likes to play car races") with children's gender stereotypes. In the critical "knowledge-subtyping" condition a feature was added to each exemplar, which made the congruent and incongruent items more discriminable (e.g., all the congruent instances had "blue eyes," "all the incongruent instances had brown eyes"). Children in the "knowledge standard" condition also saw the added feature during training, but it was uncorrelated with the congruent/incongruent status of the item. At test children in the knowledge-subtyping group were more likely than controls to make categorization judgments on the basis of gender stereotypes and showed less sensitivity to observed levels of feature covariation. Making the congruent and incongruent items more discriminable promoted "subtyping" of the incongruent items. Children in this training condition were more likely to treat these items as if they were members of a different subgroup with the consequence that the counter-stereotypical instances had less impact on children's representations of the novel category (Kunda & Oleson, 1995).

This subtyping phenomenon suggests that in certain contexts children may discard category information that does not fit with their existing knowledge or beliefs. This phenomenon poses problems for the integration model, which assumes that people do not filter out incongruent information during category learning.

Further research is needed to investigate the conditions under which subtyping occurs in children's categorization. Research on stereotyping in social categories suggests people may be more likely to subtype when the information that contradicts expectations is concentrated in only a small number of exemplars (Hewstone, 1994) or when those exemplars are perceived to be atypical of the category (Hantzi, 1995). We also need to establish whether this subtyping occurs in nonsocial domains. It is important to remember that subtyping represents a rather extreme exception to the general processes governing how children combine knowledge with new exemplars. Hayes et al. (2003) found that, in general, the integration model gave a good account of the data on the learning of social categories, even when children had very strong stereotypical beliefs about these categories (before training, the mean expected covariation for stereotype-congruent features exceeded 80% for each age group). Subtyping was only found when these strong beliefs were combined with exemplars that contained the added feature, which made the incongruent exemplars more discriminable.

The final limitation of the integration model is one that applies to pretty much all existing accounts of how knowledge affects categorization. This is the problem of knowledge selection. When children come to learn about a new category how do they know which aspects of their knowledge are relevant? In laboratory studies children are usually given category labels that make it clear what knowledge is relevant (Krascum & Andrews, 1998) or learn about exemplars with familiar features designed to prime a particular kind of knowledge (Carmichael & Hayes, 2001). Learning about categories in the real world is considerably more complicated. When a young child sees something that looks like a kind of flying animal how do they know what kind of knowledge is relevant in learning about the category to which the animal belongs? Perceptual features suggesting that it can fly might activate the child's existing knowledge about birds. But this could be misleading. The animal could actually be an insect or bat-like mammal. There are a number of ways that knowledge selection could work in this case. If an initial inspection suggests that the animal is most likely to be a bird then perhaps knowledge about birds is activated and applied to the learning of subsequent exemplars. Other possibilities are not considered unless ongoing experience disconfirms the initial bird hypothesis (e.g., the child notices that none of the exemplars have feathers). An alternative is that early in learning a number of potentially relevant pools of knowledge (i.e., about birds, insects, etc.) are activated. The relative weight given to each of these kinds of knowledge will then be adjusted during learning depending on how well each predicts subsequent exemplar features.

We are only just beginning to understand the process of knowledge selection in category learning. Heit et al. (2004), for example, have shown how a connectionist model that allows for the activation of multiple pools of relevant knowledge can explain adults' learning of knowledge-congruent and incongruent exemplars. One of the most interesting ideas to emerge from this work is that the interaction between knowledge and exemplar learning may be even more complex than suggested by the integration model. We saw earlier that following extended experience with category members children's representations are more strongly influenced by their observations than their prior knowledge. The work on knowledge selection, however, suggests that in the course of learning a new category the knowledge-exemplar relationship may pass through a number of cycles. Consider our child who is trying to learn about the ambiguous flying animal. To get some idea of just what kind of thing this is the child will have to extract some data from the exemplars that they observe. So, in the very first couple of learning trials the child may be guided mainly by the features of the exemplar. This information will be used to select the relevant knowledge domain (or domains) for the task. Once these domains are activated they are likely to shape the learning of many subsequent exemplars. With extended experience, however, it will be apparent that not all the features of the new animal can be predicted from existing knowledge and observed exemplars will begin to dominate the category representation. In other words, the time course of knowledge effects may follow an inverted "U" function with the strongest effects of knowledge found at intermediate stages of learning.

Evaluating this more complex model of children's category learning is no trivial matter. Among other things it requires a microgenetic study of category acquisition from the presentation of initial instances through to extended exposure to category members and nonmembers (see Clapper & Bower, 2002; Heit et al., 2004 for methods that might be adapted for this purpose). However, the payoff from such studies in terms of the development of a more comprehensive theory of knowledge effects in concept acquisition and development would be considerable.

VII. Prior Knowledge in Infant Categorization

A. Empirical Evidence

Another important goal for future work is to examine the developmental links between the integration of prior knowledge and exemplar learning by preschoolers and older children and category acquisition by young infants. Studies with infants less than 12 months of age have shown that they are capable of categorizing stimuli from a variety of domains, including human faces (Cohen & Strauss, 1979), furniture (Quinn, 2002), and animals (Pauen, 2002). Moreover, there are many similarities between the processes involved in infant categorization and those involved in category learning by older children and adults. Infants are able to form prototypes (Bomba & Siqueland, 1983), retrieve specific exemplars to classify new objects (Hayne, 1996), and can detect correlations among exemplar features (Younger, 2003).

We have shown that by at least 2 years of age prior knowledge plays a crucial role in category formation. Many researchers, however, have argued that categorization by young infants is best explained by focusing on how they extract featural (usually perceptual) information that is predictive of category membership (Rakison & Hahn, 2004; Quinn & Eimas, 2000). Such approaches often reject the notion that infants access more general knowledge about objects or events when categorizing.

The empirical work bearing on infants' use of background knowledge in categorization has produced a mixed set of findings. In an influential series of studies, Mandler and others used an object examination procedure to assess categorization in infants less than 12 months (Mandler & McDonough, 1993, 1998; Pauen, 2002). In this procedure, infants manually examine scale models of exemplars drawn from a broad target category like *animals*. They are then given a model from a contrast category (e.g., *vehicles*). If the infant spends more time examining this new item than the target instances it is concluded that they can discriminate between the categories.

Using this procedure, it was found that infants as young as 7 months discriminated between models of animals, vehicles, and furniture, even when the models from different superordinate categories were perceptually similar (e.g., birds with outstretched wings and aircraft). Infants failed to differentiate between instances of more subordinate animal categories that differed markedly in appearance (e.g., dogs and fish). It was concluded that by 7 months infants have acquired an understanding of that superordinate kinds like animals and vehicles represent "different kinds of things" and use this knowledge as a basis for classification and induction.

Rakison and Butterworth (1998) offer an alternative interpretation of this research, arguing that although the members of superordinate groupings, like animals, are perceptually diverse, they may share some critical perceptual features (e.g., legs), which distinguish them from other global categories. When Rakison and Butterworth (1998) removed these critical features or added them to models of both animals and vehicles they found that even 22-month-old infants did not reliably distinguish between members of the global category. Similarly in studies of induction 14-month-old infants have been shown to generalize the actions of a target item to other items from the same superordinate category *only* when these share structural features that are relevant to the modeled action (Rakison & Hahn, 2004; Rakison & Poulin-Dubois, 2002). For example, infants who saw a cat walking a nonlinear path imitated the action with model dogs but not dolphins. They also generalized the modeled action to inanimate test items that had motion-relevant features (e.g., a bed with legs).

These results undermine the view that preverbal infants use their abstract knowledge about superordinate categories as a basis for categorization and induction. They do suggest, however, that infants are sensitive to the functional properties of object parts and to the significance of these parts in object categorization. Further evidence of this kind of knowledge use during infancy comes from work by Madole and Cohen (1995). They presented 14- and 18-month olds with novel objects in which a particular object part was shown to be correlated with a specific function. In the "within-parts" condition these form–function relations were consistent with those that might be observed in more familiar objects (e.g., the presence of black rubber wheels was associated with the object moving). In the "between-parts" condition the form–function correlations did not correspond to the causal relations observed in other objects (e.g., the presence of black wheels was associated with the object making a whistling sound). After being habituated to these objects the infants were shown items in which the previous form–function relationships were violated. The 18-month olds showed an increase in their visual fixation to test items that violated within-part correlations but not to those that violated between-part correlations. The 14-month olds showed dishabituation to both sets of test items. These results suggest that by 18 months of age infants have some knowledge about the characteristic functions of object parts, like wheels, and that this knowledge constrains their encoding of form–function relations in new objects (Horst, Oakes, & Madole, 2005; McCarrell & Callanan, 1995).

B. THE ORIGINS OF EARLY KNOWLEDGE

By at least 18 months of age there is a close relationship between an infant's knowledge about the appearance and canonical function of category features. The origins of such knowledge are yet to be determined. One possibility is that infants are innately endowed with modules for learning about causal relations (Leslie, 1995) or have innate knowledge of some basic ontological principles like the distinction between animate and inanimate kinds (Carey & Spelke, 1994; Gelman, 1990). This innate knowledge could generate expectations about the kinds of features and feature combinations that are likely to be encountered in a given domain. These expectations are then combined with the features of observed instances to produce early category representations.

Alternately, infants' expectations about correlated features may themselves be the product of learning. Rogers and McClelland (2004), for example, suggest that young children's expectations about feature correlations reflect the statistical regularities or "coherent covariation" between features in the environment. Because wings and feathers are causally related to being able to fly, for example, these properties are highly likely to covary across instances. The argument is that even infants possess relatively sophisticated learning mechanisms that can pick up these patterns of coherent covariation. There is no need therefore to posit innate knowledge structures (see Jones & Smith, 1993; Mareschal, 2003; Rakison & Hahn, 2004; Sloutsky & Fisher, 2004 for related approaches). Support for this approach comes from demonstrations that certain connectionist architectures that have no a priori "knowledge" about features can learn to attend to the kinds of nonobvious causal features in children's categorization of animals (Mareschal, 2003;

Rogers & McClelland, 2004). Like children some of these networks can also learn to generalize properties differently depending on the type of category and property.

The integration model makes no hard assumptions about the origins of children's expectations about feature relationships. Expectations could be given (via innate constraints or, in older children, direct transmission of verbal knowledge) or learned through the sorts of mechanisms described above. In some respects, the integration model seems compatible with learning accounts like that of Rogers and McClelland (2004). Both kinds of accounts, for example, suggest that the effects of prior knowledge on categorization will not remain static during learning but will be revised in the light of exemplar experience.

It remains unclear, however, how connectionist and dynamic learning accounts of knowledge effects would explain the special role of beliefs about causal mechanism and causal centrality in children's categorization. In particular, a theory of category learning based on the encoding of coherent feature covariation could not explain the Hayes and Bragg (2003) finding that features linked by a belief about causal mechanism have more influence on category learning than noncausal features with equal levels of expected covariation. More generally, it is not clear how statistical learning accounts would explain how knowledge alters young children's interpretation of exemplar features (Booth & Waxman, 2002). Such evidence suggests that even sophisticated learning accounts like those of Rogers and McClelland (2004) will fail to explain the early development of categorization unless they incorporate mechanisms that allow for more abstract knowledge like feature function to be combined with novel observations during the course of learning.

VIII. Conclusions

Throughout this chapter, I have argued that categorization involves an ongoing interaction between knowledge-based expectations about category structure and the features of observed category members. Neither of these sources of information is seen as primary. Rather I have tried to demonstrate a number of ways in which they may be seen as interdependent. Accounts that rely exclusively on the extraction of statistical regularities from category exemplars or naive theories fail to explain the way that children categorize and many of the important developmental changes in categorization.

One of the most common criticisms of the knowledge-based approach to categorization is that it lacks the precision and explicit assumptions of similarity-based approaches (Rogers & McClelland, 2004; Sloutsky & Fisher, 2004). The application of the integration model to children's categorization addresses this problem by providing an explicit mechanism for combining knowledge and exemplar information. This account explains how children's category decisions are influenced by prior knowledge in the form of relevant information retrieved from memory early in learning and the selective weighting of new instances that fit this knowledge. It also emphasizes the dynamic nature of learning with increasing exemplar exposure leading to category representations that are more strongly influenced by observed rather than expected features.

The use of more explicit models of the interaction between prior knowledge and exemplar learning also leads to new insights into developmental change in categorization. We have shown that, in addition to changes in the sophistication of children's background knowledge, there are important age changes in the efficiency with which new similarity-based information is incorporated into children's concepts. Preschool children seem just as likely as older children and adults to make use of their background knowledge in learning new categories. They differ from older children, however, in the flexibility with which this knowledge is applied and the rate at which it is revised during learning.

A final positive feature of applying approaches like the integration model to children's category learning, is that it offers an opportunity for exploring the processing implications of changes in the *content* of prior knowledge. We have shown that knowledge about the causal mechanisms that link features affects category learning in a different way than knowledge based only on past experience of feature correlations. Both kinds of effects can be explained within the framework of the integration model. Future work might examine how children integrate other kinds of knowledge structures, such as thematic associations or script-based knowledge, with their learning of new category members (Lin & Murphy, 2001; Waxman & Namy, 1997).

The integration model was originally devised to explain the interaction between knowledge and exemplar learning by adults. On reflection it is not that surprising that a model that has had considerable success in explaining adult categorization can be usefully applied to category learning by young children. Although this chapter has highlighted a number of developmental issues, it is clear that there are important continuities in the way that adults, children, and possibly infants process categorical material. Like Madole and Oakes (1999), I acknowledge that the content of children's beliefs and knowledge changes with age but see many of the essential processes involved in categorization as developmentally stable. In particular, it is clear that from at least 4 years of age children readily combine their prior knowledge with exemplar information to form new concepts. The rate at which this process operates may accelerate with age, but the fundamental architecture of the process seems to remain unchanged.

ACKNOWLEDGMENTS

I would like to thank Evan Heit for comments on an earlier draft of this chapter, Kevin Brooks for advice on mathematical modeling, and Tamara Cavenett for her assistance in preparation of the manuscript. This work was supported by Australian Research Council Discovery Grant DP0344436. Correspondence should be addressed to Brett K. Hayes, School of Psychology, University of New South Wales, Sydney, NSW 2052, Australia. E-mail: B. Hayes@unsw.edu.au.

REFERENCES

Ahn, W., & Kim, N. S. (2000). The causal status effect in categorization: An overview. In D. L. Medin (Ed.), *The psychology of learning and motivation* (Vol. 40, pp. 23–65). New York: Academic Press.

Ahn, W., & Luhmann, C. C. (2005). Demystifying theory-based categorization. In L. Gershkoff-Stowe and D. Rakison (Eds.), *Building object categories in developmental time: 32nd Carnegie Symposium on Cognition* (pp. 33–62). Mahwah, NJ: Erlbaum.

Ahn, W., Gelman, S. A., Amsterlaw, J. A., Hohenstein, J., & Kalish, C. W. (2000). Causal status effect in children's categorization. *Cognition, 76*, B35–B43.

Anderson, N. H. (1981). *Foundations of information integration theory.* New York: Academic Press.

Barrett, S. E., Abdi, H., Murphy, G. L., & Gallagher, J. M. (1993). Theory-based correlations and their role in children's concepts. *Child Development, 64*, 1595–1616.

Bartlett, F. C. (1932). *Remembering: A study in experimental and social psychology.* Cambridge: Cambridge University Press.

Bauer, P. J., & Thal, D. J. (1990). Scripts or scraps: Reconsidering the development of sequential understanding. *Journal of Experimental Child Psychology, 50*, 287–304.

Bigler, R. S., & Liben, L. S. (1992). Cognitive mechanisms in children's gender stereotyping: Theoretical and educational implications of a cognitive-based intervention. *Child Development, 63*, 1351–1363.

Bomba, P. C., & Siqueland, E. R. (1983). The nature and structure of infant form categories. *Journal of Experimental Child Psychology, 35*, 294–328.

Booth, A. E., & Waxman, S. R. (2002). Word learning is "smart": Evidence that conceptual information affects preschoolers' extension of novel words. *Cognition, 84*, B11–B22.

Borowiak, D. S. (1989). *Model discrimination for nonlinear regression models.* New York: Marcel Dekker.

Boswell, D. A., & Green, H. F. (1982). The abstraction and recognition of prototypes by children and adults. *Child Development, 53*, 1028–1037.

Bullock, M., Gelman, R., & Baillargeon, R. (1982). The development of causal reasoning. In W. J. Friedman (Ed.), *The developmental psychology of time* (pp. 209–254). New York: Academic Press.

Carey, S. (1978). The child as word learner. In M. Halle, G. Miller, and J. Bresnan (Eds.), *Linguistic theory and psychological reality* (pp. 264–293). Cambridge, MA: MIT Press.

Carey, S. (1985). *Conceptual change in childhood.* Cambridge, MA: MIT Press.

Carey, S., & Spelke, E. (1994). Domain-specific knowledge and conceptual change. In L. A. Hirschfeld and S. A. Gelman (Eds.), *Mapping the mind: Domain specificity in cognition and culture* (pp. 169–200). New York: Cambridge University Press.

Carmichael, C., & Hayes, B. K. (2001). Prior knowledge and exemplar encoding in children's concept acquisition. *Child Development, 72*, 1071–1090.

Chin-Parker, S., & Ross, B. H. (2002). The effect of category learning on sensitivity to within-category correlations. *Memory & Cognition, 30*, 353–362.

Clapper, J. P., & Bower, G. H. (2002). Adaptive categorization in unsupervised learning. *Journal of Experimental Psychology: Learning, Memory, and Cognition, 28*, 908–923.

Cohen, L. B., & Strauss, M. S. (1979). Concept acquisition in the human infant. *Child Development, 50*, 419–424.

Diesendruck, G., Gelman, S. A., & Lebowitz, K. (1998). Conceptual and linguistic biases in children's word learning. *Developmental Psychology, 34*, 823–839.

Diesendruck, G., Markson, L., & Bloom, P. (2003). Children's reliance on creator's intent in extending names for artifacts. *Psychological Science, 14*, 164–168.

Dunbar, K. N., & Fugelsang, J. A. (2005). Causal thinking in science: How scientists and students interpret the unexpected. In M. E. Gorman, R. D. Tweney, D. C. Gooding, and A. P. Kincannon (Eds.), *Scientific and technological thinking* (pp. 57–79). Mahwah, NJ: Lawrence Erlbaum Associates.

Farah, M. J., & Kosslyn, S. M. (1982). Concept development. *Advances in Child Development and Behavior, 16*, 125–167.

Florian, J. E. (1994). Stripes do not a zebra make, or do they? Conceptual and perceptual information in inductive inference. *Developmental Psychology, 30*, 88–101.

Fugelsang, J. A., & Thompson, V. A. (2000). Strategy selection in causal reasoning: When beliefs and covariation collide. *Canadian Journal of Experimental Psychology, 54*, 15–32.

Gelman, R. (1990). First principles organize attention to and learning about relevant data: Number and the animate-inanimate distinction as examples. *Cognitive Science, 14*, 79–106.

Gelman, S. A. (2003). *The essential child.* New York: Oxford University Press.

Gelman, S. A., & Markman, E. M. (1987). Young children's inductions from natural kinds: The role of categories and appearance. *Child Development, 58*, 1532–1541.

Gelman, S. A., & Wellman, H. M. (1991). Insides and essence: Early understandings of the non-obvious. *Cognition, 38*, 213–244.

Goldstone, R. L. (1994). The role of similarity in categorization: Providing a groundwork. *Cognition, 52*, 125–157.

Gopnik, A., & Sobel, D. (2000). Detecting blickets: How young children use information about novel causal powers in categorization and induction. *Child Development, 71*, 1205–1222.

Hantzi, A. (1995). Change in stereotypic perceptions of familiar and unfamiliar groups: The pervasiveness of the subtyping model. *British Journal of Social Psychology, 34*, 463–477.

Hayes, B. K. (in press). The development of inductive reasoning. In A. Feeney and E. Heit (Eds.), *Inductive reasoning: Cognitive, mathematical, and neuroscientific approaches.* London: Cambridge University Press.

Hayes, B. K., & Bragg, K. (2003). *Concept learning in children: The roles of causal and associative knowledge.* Paper presented at the 13th Biennial Conference of the Australasian Human Development Association. Auckland, NZ.

Hayes, B. K., & Taplin, J. E. (1992). Developmental changes in categorization processes: Knowledge and similarity-based models of categorization. *Journal of Experimental Child Psychology, 54*, 188–212.

Hayes, B. K., & Taplin, J. E. (1993). Developmental differences in the use of prototype and exemplar-specific information. *Journal of Experimental Child Psychology, 55*, 329–352.

Hayes, B. K., Foster, K., & Gadd, N. (2003). Prior knowledge and subtyping effects in children's category learning. *Cognition, 88*, 171–199.

Hayne, H. (1996). Categorization in infancy. In C. Rovee-Collier and L. P. Lipsitt (Eds.), *Advances in infancy research* (Vol. 10, pp. 79–120). Norwood, NJ: Ablex.

Heit, E. (1994). Models of the effects of prior knowledge on category learning. *Journal Experimental Psychology: Learning, Memory, and Cognition, 20*, 1264–1282.

Heit, E. (1997). Knowledge and concept learning. In K. Lamberts and D. Shanks (Eds.), *Knowledge, concepts, and categories* (pp. 7–41). Hove, UK: Psychology Press.

Heit, E. (1998). Influences of prior knowledge on selective weighting of category members. *Journal of Experimental Psychology: Learning, Memory and Cognition, 24*, 712–731.

Heit, E. (2001). Background knowledge in models of categorization. In U. Hahn and M. Ramscar (Eds.), *Similarity and categorization* (pp. 155–178). Oxford: Oxford University Press.

Heit, E., Briggs, J., & Bott, L. (2004). Modeling the effects of prior knowledge on learning incongruent features of category members. *Journal of Experimental Psychology, 30*, 1065–1081.

Hewstone, M. (1994). Revision and change of stereotypic beliefs. In W. Stroebe and M. Hewstone (Eds.), *European review of social psychology* (Vol. 5, pp. 69–109). Chichester, UK: Wiley.

Hilton, J. L., & von Hippel, W. (1996). Stereotypes. *Annual Review of Psychology, 47*, 237–271.

Hirschfeld, L. A. (1995). Do children have a theory of race? *Cognition, 54*, 209–252.

Horst, J. S., Oakes, L. M., & Madole, K. L. (2005). What does it look like and what can it do? Category structure influences how infants categorize. *Child Development, 76*, 614.

Johnson, C., & Keil, F. C. (2000). Explanatory understanding and conceptual combination. In F. C. Keil and R. A. Wilson (Eds.), *Explanation and cognition* (pp. 328–359). Cambridge, MA: MIT Press.

Jones, S., & Smith, L. B. (1993). The place of perception in children's concepts. *Cognitive Development, 8*, 113–139.

Jones, S., Smith, L. B., & Landau, B. (1991). Object properties and knowledge in early lexical learning. *Child Development, 62*, 499–516.

Kail, R. (1990). *The development of memory in children* (3rd ed.). New York: W. H. Freeman.

Kaplan, A. S., & Murphy, G. L. (2000). Category learning with minimal prior knowledge. *Journal of Experimental Psychology: Learning, Memory, and Cognition, 26*, 829–846.

Keil, F. C. (1989). *Concepts, kinds, and cognitive development*. Cambridge, MA: MIT Press.

Keil, F. C. (1995). The growth of causal understandings of natural kinds. In D. Sperber, D. Premack, and A. J. Premack (Eds.), *Causal cognition: A multidisciplinary approach* (pp. 234–262). Oxford: Clarendon Press.

Keil, F. C., Smith, W. C., Simons, D. J., & Levin, D. T. (1998). Two dogmas of conceptual empiricism: Implications for hybrid models of the structure of knowledge. *Cognition, 65*, 103–135.

Kemler-Nelson, D. G., Russell, R., Duke, N., & Jones, K. (2000). Two-year-olds will name artifacts by their functions. *Child Development, 71*, 1271–1288.

Krascum, R. M., & Andrews, S. (1998). The effects of theories on children's acquisition of family-resemblance categories. *Child Development, 69*, 333–346.

Kunda, Z., & Oleson, K. C. (1995). Maintaining stereotypes in the face of disconfirmation: Constructing grounds for subtyping deviants. *Journal of Personality and Social Psychology, 68*, 565–579.

Kuhn, D. (2002). What is scientific thinking, and how does it develop? In V. Goswami (Ed.), *Blackwell handbook of childhood cognitive development* (pp. 371–393). Malden, MA: Blackwell Publishing.

Leslie, A. M. (1995). A theory of agency. In D. Sperber, D. Premack, and A. J. Premack (Eds.), *Causal Cognition: A multidisciplinary debate* (pp. 121–141). Oxford: Clarendon Press.

Levy, G. D., Taylor, M. G., & Gelman, S. A. (1995). Traditional and evaluative aspects of flexibility in gender roles, social conventions, moral rules, and physical laws. *Child Development, 66*, 515–531.

Liben, L. S., & Signorella, M. L. (1993). Gender-schematic processing in children: The role of initial interpretations of stimuli. *Developmental Psychology, 29*, 141–149.

Lin, E. L., & Murphy, G. L. (2001). Thematic relations in adults' concepts. *Journal of Experimental Psychology: General, 130*, 3–28.

Macario, J. F. (1991). Young children's use of color in classification: Foods and canonically colored objects. *Cognitive Development, 6*, 17–46.

Macario, J. F., Shipley, E. F., & Billman, D. O. (1990). Induction from a single instance: Formation of a novel category. *Journal of Experimental Child Psychology, 50*, 179–199.

Madole, K., & Oakes, L. (1999). Making sense of infant categorization: Stable processes and changing representations. *Developmental Review, 19*, 263–296.

Madole, K., & Cohen, L. (1995). The role of object parts in infants' attention to form-function correlations. *Developmental Psychology, 31*, 637–648.

Mandler, J. M., & McDonough, L. (1998). On developing a knowledge base in infancy. *Developmental Psychology, 34*, 1274–1288.

Mandler, J., & McDonough, L. (1993). Concept formation in infancy. *Cognitive Development, 8*, 291–318.

Mareschal, D. (2003). The acquisition of use of implicit categories in early development. In D. H. Rakison and L. M., Oakes (Eds.), *Early category and concept development: Making sense of the blooming, buzzing confusion* (pp. 360–383). London: Oxford University Press.

Markman, A. B., & Makin, V. S. (1998). Referential communication and category acquisition. *Journal of Experimental Psychology: General, 127*, 331–354.

McCarrell, N. S., & Callanan, M. A. (1995). Form-function correspondences in children's inference. *Child Development, 66*, 532–546.

Medin, D. L., & Ortony, A. (1989). Psychological essentialism. In S. Vosniadou and A. Ortony (Eds.), *Similarity and analogical reasoning* (pp. 179–195). Cambridge, MA: Cambridge University Press.

Medin, D. L., & Waxman, S. (in press). Interpreting asymmetries of projection in children's inductive reasoning. In A. Feeney and E. Heit (Eds.), *Inductive reasoning: Cognitive, mathematical, and neuroscientific approaches.* London: Cambridge University Press.

Mills, C. M., & Keil, F. C. (2004). Knowing the limits of one's understanding: The development of an awareness of an illusion of explanatory depth. *Journal of Experimental Child Psychology, 87*, 1–32.

Murphy, G. L. (2002). *The big book of concepts.* Cambridge, MA: MIT Press.

Murphy, G. L., & Medin, D. L. (1985). The role of theories in conceptual coherence. *Psychological Review, 92*, 289–316.

Murphy, G. L., & Wisniewski, E. J. (1989). Feature correlations in conceptual representations. In G. Tiberghien (Ed.), *Advances in cognitive science* (pp. 23–45). Chichester, UK: Ellis Horwood.

Nosofsky, R. M. (1988). Exemplar-based accounts of relations between classification, recognition, and typicality. *Journal of Experimental Psychology: Learning, Memory, and Cognition, 14*, 700–708.

Osherson, D. N., Smith, E. E., Wilkie, O., Lopez, A., & Shafir, E. (1990). Category-based induction. *Psychological Review, 101*, 5397.

Pauen, S. (2002). Evidence for knowledge-based category discrimination in infancy. *Child Development, 73*, 1016–1033.

Pressley, M., & Schneider, W. (1997). *Introduction to memory development during childhood and adolescence*. Mahwah, NJ: Erlbaum.

Quinn, P. C., & Eimas, P. D. (2000). The emergence of category representations in infancy: Are separate perceptual and conceptual processes required? *Journal of Cognition and Development, 1*, 55–61.

Quinn, P. C. (2002). Early categorization: A new synthesis. In U. Goswami (Ed.), *Blackwell handbook of childhood cognitive development* (pp. 84–101). Oxford: Blackwell Publishers.

Rakison, D. H., & Butterworth, G. E. (1998). Infants' use of object parts in early categorization. *Developmental Psychology, 34*, 49–62.

Rakison, D. H., & Poulin-Dubois, D. (2002). The developmental origin of the animate-inanimate distinction. *Psychological Bulletin, 127*, 209–228.

Rakison, D. H., & Hahn, E. (2004). The mechanisms of early categorization and induction: Smart or dumb infants? In R. Kail (Ed.), *Advances in child development and behavior* (Vol. 32, pp. 281–322). New York: Academic Press.

Rehder, B., & Murphy, G. L. (2003). A knowledge-resonance (KRES) model of category learning. *Psychonomic Bulletin & Review, 10*, 759–784.

Rogers, T. T., & McClelland, J. L. (2004). *Semantic cognition: A parallel distributed processing approach*. Cambridge, MA: MIT Press.

Rothbart, M. (1981). Memory processes and social beliefs. In D. L. Hamilton (Ed.), *Cognitive processes in stereotyping and intergroup behaviour* (pp. 145–181). Hillsdale, NJ: Erlbaum.

Rozenblit, L., & Keil, F. (2002). The misunderstood limits of folk science: An illusion of explanatory depth. *Cognitive Science, 26*, 521–562.

Schneider, W., & Bjorklund, D .F. (1998). Memory. In W. Damon, (Series Ed.), D. Kuhn, and R. Siegler (Vol. Eds.), *Handbook of child psychology: Cognition, perception and language* (5th ed., pp. 467–522). New York: Wiley.

Shipley, E. F. (2000). Children's categorization of objects: The relevance of behavior, surface appearance, and insides. In B. Landau, J. Sabini, J. Jonides, and E. Newport (Eds.), *Perception, cognition, and language: Essays in honor of Henry and Lila Gleitman* (pp. 69–85). Cambridge, MA: The MIT Press.

Shultz, T., Fisher, G., Pratt, C., & Ruff, S. (1986). Selection of causal rules. *Child Development, 57*, 143–152.

Signorella, M. L., Bigler, R. S., & Liben, L. S. (1993). Developmental differences in children's gender *schemata* about others: A meta-analytic review. *Developmental Review, 13*, 147–183.

Signorella, M., Bigler, R., & Liben, L. (1997). A meta-analysis of children's memories for own-sex and other-sex information. *Journal of Applied Developmental Psychology, 18*, 429–445.

Sloman, S. A., & Malt, B. C. (2003). Artifacts are not ascribed essences, nor are they treated as belonging to kinds. *Language and Cognitive Processes, 18*, 563–582.

Sloutsky, V. M., & Fisher, A. V. (2004). Induction and categorization in young children: A similarity-based model. *Journal of Experimental Psychology: General, 133*, 166–188.

Sloman, S. A. (1993). Feature-based induction. *Cognitive Psychology, 25*, 231–280.

Stangor, C., & McMillan, D. (1992). Memory for expectancy-congruent and expectancy incongruent information: A review of the social and social developmental literatures. *Psychological Bulletin, 111*, 42–61.

Vosniadou, S., & Brewer, W. F. (1992). Mental models of the earth: A study of conceptual change in childhood. *Cognitive Psychology, 24*, 535–558.

Waxman, S. R., & Namy, L. L. (1997). Challenging the notion of a thematic preference in young children. *Developmental Psychology, 55*, 555–567.

Wellman, H. M., & Gelman, S. A. (1998). Knowledge acquisition in foundational domains. In D. Kuhn and R. S. Siegler (Eds.), *Handbook of child psychology: Cognition, perception and language* (5th ed., pp. 523–573). New York: Wiley.

White, P. A. (1995). *The understanding of causation and the production of action: From infancy to adulthood.* Hillsdale, NJ: Erlbaum.

Wisniewski, E. J., & Medin, D. L. (1994). On the interaction of theory and data in concept learning. *Cognitive Science, 18*, 221–281.

Wittenbrink, B., Hilton, J. L., & Gist, P. L. (1998). In search of similarity: Stereotypes as naive theories in social categorization. *Social Cognition, 16*, 31–55.

Younger, B. A. (1990). Infant categorization: Memory for category level and specific item information. *Journal of Experimental Child Psychology, 50*, 131–155.

Younger, B. A. (2003). Parsing objects into categories: Infants' perception and use of correlated attributes. In D. H. Rakison and L. M. Oakes (Eds.), *Early category and concept development: Making sense of the blooming, buzzing confusion* (pp. 77–102). London: Oxford University Press.

Zimmerman, C. (2000). The development of scientific reasoning skills. *Developmental Review, 20*, 99–149.

CONCEPTS AS PROTOTYPES

James A. Hampton

"... whatever vagueness is to be found in my words must be attributed to our ancestors for not having been predominantly interested in logic."

(Bertrand Russell, 1923).

I. Introduction

The Prototype Theory of conceptual representation in large part owes its beginnings to Rosch and Mervis (1975), who, in the space of a couple of years, published a string of major papers laying out the empirical basis for the theory. The motivation for the theory came from a perceived crisis in philosophy and linguistics to do with defining the meaning of words. To the lay person, who has never worried too much about such things, the meaning of words is just given in the dictionary. The trouble is that most dictionary definitions are really only approximate or partial. The word "red," for example, is not defined by a fixed interval of the color spectrum but is the name for an imprecisely defined region with vague edges. The word "chair" could perhaps be defined as a movable object made for sitting on that stands on the floor and has a back. However, once again the actual use of the word tends in practice to allow for vagueness—designers continually create new objects for sitting on and new contexts in which to sit, so that it is often unclear whether they should be counted as chairs or not. The central insight of Prototype Theory is that word meanings and the conceptual classes

THE PSYCHOLOGY OF LEARNING
AND MOTIVATION VOL. 46
DOI: 10.1016/S0079-7421(06)46003-5

that the words name are distinguished one from another not in terms of an explicit definition but in terms of similarity to a generic or best example. The concept red is the class of colors that are centered around a particular point on the spectrum that everyone tends to agree is the *prototype* red. Berlin and Kay (1969) reported that there was better agreement about the *best* examples of color terms than there was about the boundary between one color and another (e.g., between red and orange). The category of red things is therefore the category of things whose color is sufficiently similar to a prototypical red (and dissimilar from other prototypes). Similarly, there are concept representations for "chair" and "stool" and "bench" and "sofa," each of which is associated with a prototype example of the class. Objects are then classified on the basis of which prototype they are most similar to.

Rosch, Simpson and Miller (1976) showed that people could readily learn novel categories based around prototypes (a point already demonstrated by Posner & Keele, 1968), and Rosch and Mervis (1975) analyzed a number of semantic categories, such as fruit, sport, or vehicle, to show that what members of the category had in common was not some set of defining features but a sufficient degree of resemblance to each other. In some of their writings, it is implied that the *best example* of the category, whatever that might be, would be the prototype. However, it quickly became clear that the prototype should better be considered as a more abstract, generic concept that was constituted from the different ways in which the category members resembled each other and differed from nonmembers. Unlike a best example, an abstract prototype allows for the representation of different possible values of relevant features such as that apples can be red, green, brown, or yellow or that furniture can be sat on, slept on, used for storing things, or provide a surface for supporting things. An apple that had *all* these colors or a piece of furniture that served *all* these functions would not necessarily be prototypical.

Prototypes then are the centers of clusters of similar objects and prototype concepts form similarity-based categories. The center of the cluster is well established and agreed upon, but the boundary between one category and another may be subject to vagueness and disagreement. Talk of clusters with centers implies a spatial metaphor, and prototypes have often been discussed as points in *similarity space*. A mathematical exploration of the implications of this approach can be found in Gärdenfors (2000), and Osherson and Smith (1981) included a similarity space as part of their formalization of Prototype Theory. Spaces, however, have additional structural properties, which impose unnecessarily strict constraints on prototypes. Verbeemen, Storms, and Verguts (2004) have explored the degree to which natural categories can be represented in spaces (through multidimensional scaling) and concluded that at least for some semantic domains, a nonspatial similarity model provides a better fit.

Following its introduction into cognitive psychology, Prototype Theory was also taken up enthusiastically by cognitive linguists, such as Ross (1973) and Lakoff (1987), and anthropologists such as Kempton (1978) and Randall (1976). Ross (1973), for example, proposed that the syntactic class NOUN in English is based around a prototype. He suggested a scale of "nouniness" associated with a hierarchy of syntactic acceptability in different contexts. The more nouny a word or phrase was, then the more contexts in which it would behave like a noun. A useful source of different views on the value of prototypes in linguistic theory can be found in Aarts, Denison, Keizer, and Popova (2004).

While Rosch and Mervis provided overwhelming evidence for widespread prototype effects in semantic concepts and category learning, the development of the theory in psychology subsequently remained relatively underspecified. In one of the last chapters in the series, Eleanor Rosch (1978) discussed the theoretical underpinning of the data and warned that a distinction should be made between the empirical phenomena of prototype effects and any theoretical model that concepts are actually represented by prototypes. In fact, she doubted that the latter was the case.

The purpose of this chapter will be to reexamine Prototype Theory and the evidence with which it is associated. One of the major difficulties with the theory may be that, with the early withdrawal of Rosch from the field, it has lacked a champion to develop and refine a working model of prototype representations, as new empirical results have been discovered. Thus, at various times, the theory has been criticized in many ways. For example, it is claimed that the theory lacks any way to represent the variability allowed on different dimensions within a category (e.g., the range of possible sizes of apples rather than just their average size). The theory is said not to be able to account for some categories having wider or more flexible boundaries than others [and, hence, is unable to explain why a sphere half-way in size between a basketball and a watermelon is more likely to be a watermelon than a basketball; (Rips, 1989)]. The theory is said to rely too heavily on statistical cue validity to determine feature weights (i.e., on the relative frequency of the feature for members and nonmembers of the category) and so to ignore causal dependencies among features such as that birds need their wings in order to fly. The theory is said to be circular in that no account is offered of why our attention is drawn to particular sets of features or particular sets of objects in the first place.

In every case, the criticisms may be well-founded, but what has been lacking is a coordinated attempt to modernize the theory to incorporate mechanisms to deal with the failures. It is, of course, easy to find data that a model has no way of explaining, if the model was not created with those data in mind. However, one is then faced with a choice of discarding the model altogether or of adapting the model to fit the data.

A notable exception to the lack of development of Prototype Theory has been the work on category learning of Don Homa and colleagues (Homa, 1984; Homa, Sterling, & Trepel, 1981) and Smith and Minda (2000). Both of these groups of researchers have generated valuable evidence that in classification learning paradigms, there are conditions under which abstraction of prototypes does occur. They have also developed precise quantitative models of how prototypes develop and are used in such learning situations. The question remains, however, whether the original aim of Prototype Theory— to provide an account of the natural concepts that we use to understand our everyday world and that serve to support the meanings of common nouns in natural language—can be met satisfactorily.

The chapter therefore will focus on the original evidence on which Prototype Theory was based and will discuss which aspects of that evidence should be retained as central to the theory and which aspects may be less crucial. I will also use this opportunity to present new results relating to prototype effects and to reflect on some of the theoretical debates that surround the model. There is a nice irony here, in that the theory as applied to itself would suggest quite plausibly that "Prototype Theory" as a concept is itself a family of related concepts in which different importance might be attached to different assumptions of the theory. A prototype of Prototype Theory might be that presented by Rosch and Mervis, or that described in Hampton (1995), but other characterizations have been offered (Osherson & Smith, 1981). Leaving this irony aside, it is important first to try to capture the more essential characteristics of a prototype model, in order to consider how the central insights of the approach can be made consistent with evidence on the nature of conceptual representation.

II.   The Origins of Prototype Theory

Prototype Theory enjoyed rapid and considerable success in the years following Rosch and Mervis. Researchers were quick to apply the general notion of a prototype to a wide range of domains such as clinical diagnosis and social stereotypes. The theory and its applications have been described in detail elsewhere (Hampton, 1997c; Murphy, 2002), so what follows will be a brief sketch. In general, the way in which prototype structure was demonstrated for a domain was to establish one or more of four key phenomena about categories in that domain.

a. *Vagueness:* Categorization of items could be vague or "fuzzy." That is to say, there exist cases whose membership in a category is uncertain, not because of lack of knowledge but because of the lack of a clear rule for categorization that applies to every case.

b. *Typicality:* Within a category, items differ reliably in their "goodness-of-example" or typicality.

c. *Genericity:* When asked to define or describe the meaning of a concept term, people tend to generate descriptions that are generically true of the class, although not true of all members.

d. *Opacity:* When asked for a rule that might be used to determine category membership, people are generally unable to come up with such a rule, and even professional linguists typically find it an unrewarding goal (Wierzbicka, 1985). That is to say that the basis of categorization is not transparent to the speaker (as it would be when applying an explicit rule)—it is opaque.

These four phenomena are well documented, and they constituted the basis on which domains as different as syntactical word classes, phonetic categories, speech perception, speech acts, psychiatric diagnosis, and personality perception were given a prototype treatment. For example, in recognition of the fact that psychiatric disorders most typically have borderline cases, typical and atypical cases, symptoms that are commonly but not universally present in cases, and rely on a pattern of symptoms, rather than a set of necessary and sufficient criteria, the Diagnostic and Statistical Manual of Mental Disorders-Fourth Edition (DSM-IV), published by the American Psychiatric Association in 1994 explicitly adopted prototype definitions for mental disorder categories. A person might be classifiable in a category providing that N out of M symptoms have been present for some given period of time.

The first two of the prototype phenomena relate to the "extensional structure" of a category—the way in which individuals and subclasses relate to the category. The second two relate to the "intension" of the category concept—the beliefs that a person holds that constitute the "narrow content" of the concept. Following Frege, *Descriptivist* theories of concepts, of which Prototype Theory is an example, argue that the two kinds of information are intimately related. In some direct way, category extensions are determined through comparing an object or class with the intensional information constituting the concept. To decide what should be put in the category "bird" or "tool," any putative case is compared to the stored conceptual representation for that category, and a decision is computed based on the relation between what is known about the case and what is known about the category. Thus, according to descriptivist theories, intensions determine extensions. Although many philosophers (Fodor, 1998; Millikan, 1998; Rey, 1983) have identified major difficulties with descriptivism, preferring to fix conceptual contents in terms of extensions (an *Externalist* theory of concept individuation), the large majority of cognitive psychologists still subscribe to this basic descriptivist position.

For Prototype Theory the determination of extension is achieved by specifying a measure of the match between the representation of an object or class and the prototype representing the category. If the degree of match is above some criterion, then the object is included in the category. If it is close to the criterion then it may be a borderline case, thus giving rise to Vagueness, and the further above criterion it is, the more typical a category member the item becomes, hence leading to the phenomenon of Typicality. The phenomena of Genericity and Opacity are found because a partial match to the prototype may yet be sufficient to be clearly included in the category—descriptive attributes that form a part of the representation may not be matched by all category members, and there may be no simple Boolean logical formula for devising a rule for categorization. (One should note, however, that the similarity-to-prototype rule would correspond to a number of equivalent complex Boolean expressions and that under certain circumstances it does in fact correspond to disjunctive or conjunctive rules; Hampton, 1995.)

Since these four phenomena are key to the proposal that a concept has prototype structure, the chapter will proceed by taking each in turn, reviewing what is known about each phenomenon, and examining the validity of the arguments relating each effect to its supposed explanation. Alternative explanations offered by other theories of concepts (where they exist) will also be considered as appropriate.

III. Vagueness

A. EXPLANATION WITHIN PSYCHOLOGICAL MODELS

The existence of borderline cases for categories was first demonstrated systematically by McCloskey and Glucksberg (1978). They provided people with lists of items and asked them to classify them as members or nonmembers of a category. Their participants then repeated this exercise some weeks later. The finding was that for items that were independently rated as atypical of the category there was considerable disagreement about whether they should count as category members or not, and also considerable inconsistency across occasions, with people changing their minds as much as 25% of the time from one occasion to the next. It was also important to note that these items were not just unfamiliar. In a follow-up study, Hampton (1998) showed that while a small number of McCloskey and Glucksberg's borderline items were unfamiliar (is euglena an animal?), others were highly familiar (is a woman an animal?). With some few notable exceptions, Hampton (1998) found that for the majority of borderline cases, the probability of being placed in the category was directly predictable from judgments of how typical or representative the items were of the category prototype. It seems then that, at least in terms of empirical evidence, Prototype Theory is best placed to account for vagueness. Providing there is some randomness in the prototype representation or in the way that it is used, then we can expect probabilistic responding at the borderline, leading to disagreement and inconsistency in categorization.

Other psychological models can also explain vagueness. Exemplar models (Medin & Shaffer, 1978; Nosofsky, 1988) propose that concepts are similarity clusters very much like prototypes, with the exception that there is no central abstracted representation of the prototype. Instead there is a memory store containing a selection of actually encountered exemplars (items that have previously been categorized as falling under the concept). An item is categorized into the class to which it has maximum average similarity, the average being calculated across all stored exemplars. However, categorization is explicitly probabilistic, with relative similarity to different categories determining the likelihood of being placed in one category rather than another. It is only once categories have been very well learned (or where the categories are very distinct from each other) that responding becomes all-or-none, and disagreement or inconsistency disappears.

The other class of models, theory-based or knowledge-based models, have in fact little to say about vagueness, but being Descriptivist, the same story can be given as for prototype and exemplar models. These models (Murphy & Medin, 1985; Rips, 1989, 2001) propose that concepts are individuated in terms of the role that they play in naïve theories that we use to explain our world. When this idea is cashed out into actual proposals for what is represented mentally, then concepts actually look very much like prototypes again but with an important difference. Like a prototype representation there are different features or attributes involved; degree of membership depends on the features that a potential item may have; and typicality will depend on how closely an item resembles the paradigmatic case of a category member. The crucial difference is that similarity-to-prototype is not a simple function of matching attributes but involves deeper causal information. One way to think of this is to suppose that in addition to having a set of features, a theory-based prototype has a set of information about the *relations* between those features. If an item has the features but does not have them in the right relations to each other (which will include causal dependencies), then its similarity to the prototype will be poor. Authors of these theories of concepts may well resent the appropriation of their ideas into a form of prototype account, yet if they are to explain probabilistic responding, and residual effects of surface similarity in their data, (to say nothing of typicality effects) they are left with little alternative.

Taken more broadly, borderline cases are in fact an instance of a much more general problem—the problem of vagueness in natural language. Interest in vagueness goes back at least as far as the Ancient Greek philosopher Eubulides of Megara, who devised the Sorites Paradox to illustrate the problem. Sorites means a heap in Greek, and the paradox involves asking how many grains of sand are needed to constitute a heap of sand. It appears, for example, that removing a single grain from a heap could not of itself turn a heap into a nonheap. Yet repeating the action will eventually leave no sand left at all, so that at some point the heap must cease to be a heap. In fact, this must presumably happen before the number of grains reaches some (again unspecified) small number. The paradox can be run in the opposite direction as well, by starting with a single grain (not a heap) and then asking if addition of one grain could turn the collection of grains into a heap.

B. PHILOSOPHICAL ACCOUNTS OF VAGUENESS

Resolution of the problem of vagueness remains a current goal in philosophy, logic, and psychology (Hampton, 2005; Kamp & Partee, 1995; Keefe & Smith, 1997; Osherson & Smith, 1997). A notable attempt to resolve the issue is to relate vagueness to epistemological uncertainty. Williamson (1994) has developed an epistemological account of vagueness in which it is claimed that the meaning of terms is actually precise, but we all have different partial understanding of what that meaning may be. Because the true meaning may be highly complex and does not correspond to any simple definitional rule, the average language user learns to approximate to that meaning. This approach is an example of the Externalist view of concepts/ meaning, described previously. A concept is something external to the thinker that we come to represent in our minds more or less accurately as the case may be. Concepts and the meaning of terms that name them are constituted by the existence of a particular class in the external world. Our representation of that class may therefore show signs of inaccuracy and vagueness. Hence, disagreement and inconsistency are to be expected, just as if one asked people to rank order a set of rivers in terms of their length or historical events in terms of their chronological order. Different people will know the answer with different degrees of accuracy and reliability. It is, of course, also possible that the true meaning is not a class in the external world but a type of language use sanctioned by the social structure of the language group. In both cases, however, the definition of a term is external to the individual, and so vagueness could reflect a partial grasp of that definition.

This is clearly a defensible position if one takes an Externalist view of what a concept is—namely an entity that exists in external reality rather than in our heads. The position is also (perhaps paradoxically) quite consistent with the existence of prototypes in our minds—as Fodor (1998) has made quite clear. It may be the case that the concept of an X is clearly delineated in the real world but that my understanding of it is sufficiently partial that I am unable to decide clearly whether a particular sample is actually an X. My understanding of the concept could in fact be a descriptivist prototype, acquired from experience with typical cases of X, which has led me to form an internal representation of beliefs about Xs.

There is a sensible view, expressed by Bertrand Russell (1923), which says that vagueness is inherent in the relation between a representation and the world. There is no vagueness in the world itself. As he wrote: "things are what they are, and there is an end of it. Nothing is more or less what it is, or to a certain extent possessed of the properties which it possesses." The challenge for the Externalist view of concepts is then to find anything at all to say about the properties of concept classes, given that the very act of describing those properties introduces a symbolic representation, which must on all accounts involve vagueness. In fact, one would have liked to ask Russell what possible candidate "properties" he had in mind. It would be a trick question of course, since he could only answer in language in which by necessity the property in question would be vague, and so a thing might possess it to only a certain extent. Perhaps it is better to think of things being what they are and not of "having properties" at all (Quine, 1948; Mellor & Oliver, 1997). Perhaps the very notion of ascribing a property to a thing is to create the logical problem of potential vagueness.

C.   FURTHER STUDIES OF VAGUENESS

What do people say about the vagueness of their categories? In a study (Hampton, 2004), I presented people with eight category lists that included borderline cases and nonmembers and first asked them to rate each word with one of three responses "definitely in the category" "intermediate," and "definitely not in the category." Once people had given their ratings, they were then asked to go through the booklet once more and indicate which of a number of possible reasons they might have for giving an "intermediate" response. The most common reasons chosen were variability of criterion ("because it depends on whether you take the category in a broad or in a narrow sense"), 31%, and epistemological uncertainty about the item ("because I do not know enough about the item to say"), 25%. Two other reasons that reached double figure percentages were category polysemy ("because it depends on how you define the category"), 15%, and item polysemy ("because it depends on how you define the item"), 11%. So it seems that people's intuitions about vagueness do include the possibility that they did not know enough about an item, but at the same time they see the category terms as being vague in the sense of having broader and narrower senses and having different ways of being defined. Both of the latter reasons are consistent with prototype representations with variable dimensional weights and variable criterion placement. They are not, however, consistent with the idea that all vagueness is caused by ignorance.

A follow-up to this study considered the question of stability of category decisions over time. One particular suggestion for handling vagueness in logic, supervaluation theory (Kamp & Partee, 1995), proposes that there is a given region of vagueness at the boundary of a category. It should therefore be the case that if people were given three response choices in categorization—"definitely yes," "possibly," and "definitely no,"—then there should be less inconsistency in a test–retest measure. The idea is that people may not know how to categorize the "possible" items and so may shift their decisions about this subset of vague borderline cases, responding in a probabilistic way depending on their current whim. Yet they may have a much clearer idea of what is definitely in the category and what is definitely not in the category.

The study conducted with my student Bayo Aina involved two groups of participants. One group categorized the same lists of category items using a traditional "yes"/"no" decision, while the second group had three options as outlined in the previous paragraph. Both groups returned a week later to make the decision again. The proportion of responses remaining the same on the second occasion was 83% in the two-choice condition and only 73% in the three-choice condition. So there was clearly no well-defined boundary region that people could easily discriminate. Why was there a *drop* in consistency given the three options? One possibility is that with three options there are more opportunities to change your mind than with just two. We therefore reanalyzed the data, collapsing the three options into two by either comparing definitely yes with the other two or comparing definitely no with the other two. Is it perhaps the case that we can consistently judge what is "definitely" in a category but find it harder to judge what is definitely not? When the boundary between "definitely yes" and the other options was examined, 84% of responses remained the same, and exactly the same degree of stability was observed between "definitely no" and the other two options. The results therefore supported the view that instability due to vagueness is the same across the category scale. No matter whether the criterion is set high ("definitely yes" versus "not definitely yes"), in the middle ("yes" versus "no") or low ("definitely not" versus "not definitely not"), the same degree of inconsistency in responding was observed. A final note about this study: over 5% of responses were changed from "definitely yes" to "definitely no" or vice versa, and only 1 of 28 participants failed to make any radical changes of this kind. Requiring a high level of confidence in a response was no protection against at least some degree of vagueness.

In the remaining part of this section, I turn in more detail to the question of how Prototype Theory actually accounts for the empirical behavioral phenomena of vagueness and instability in categorization. I will consider three of these—the disagreement among individuals on what should be included in a category, the instability of categorization judgments over time within the same individual, and the question of what type of logic can be applied to vague category propositions.

D. ACCOUNTING FOR THE DATA

1. Between-Person Disagreement in Categorization

The fact that disagreement among individuals is generally higher than the level of inconsistency within individuals (Barsalou, 1987) should probably be put down to the socially mediated nature of conceptual contents. Words in a language represent not a single meaning but a family of possible meanings that will naturally drift and evolve over time. Each individual keeps track of how others are using words, and so there is an approximate convergence in meaning within a given linguistic community. In this case, the observed probability of categorizing a word in a given category reflects the frequency of that belief/practice within the sample of people tested. Clearly, any theory of conceptual representation would need to subscribe to a similar account to explain the existence of disagreement. However, it is important to note how readily the prototype representation allows for families of closely related meanings. In fact, similarity-based categorization is the only theory that explains how variation in meaning appears to be *continuous* rather than discrete.

If concepts were based on definitions or on theories of causal determination, it is likely that different meanings would be discrete, and hence more easily differentiated—as when we notice partial translation between languages (the French word *"fruit"* does not include nuts whereas for many English speakers the equivalent English word "fruit" does). There is no evidence that individual variation in conceptual representation shows clusters that might correspond to some small number of different meanings possessed by different groups of individuals (although to be fair few attempts have been made to look for such evidence). Having a prototype with continuously variable dimensional weights captures this nondiscrete nature of conceptual variation very neatly.

2. *Within-Individual Inconsistency in Categorization*

Within-individual inconsistency itself requires some external or random process to be at work. After all, any determinate system for using intensional information to perform categorization will always be perfectly consistent, whether it is based on a simple definitional rule or based on similarity computed across multiple dimensions. One suggestion for the source of the inconsistency (Braisby, 1993) has been that participants may recruit different contexts or perspectives in responding on each occasion. If a person's representation of a category varies according to factors, such as the communicative context or the implicit contrast category, then failing to control such influences would contribute to inconsistency. There is, however, little or no evidence that within-individual inconsistency is due to failure to specify the context. At least one study failed to show any change in inconsistency when context was added. Hampton, Dubois, and Yeh (2006) provided people with two strongly different purposes for providing a classification of common everyday category items. In one condition they were asked to classify pragmatically—placing items in the category in which they thought that most people would expect to find them. In a different condition, they were asked to classify in a quasi-legal context—for example, classifying artifacts as tools or furniture so that import tax regulations would be fairly applied, or classifying different academic pursuits as science or not so that a science funding agency would know how wide to draw the remit of their activities. Neither condition showed any reduction in individual inconsistency compared with a no-context control condition, and in fact all three conditions showed high levels of correlation between likelihood of categorizing an item and context-free judgments of its typicality in the category.

In the absence of evidence to the contrary, inconsistency is more likely to reflect random variation in processing. Barsalou (1987) suggested that experiences and random influences on memory retrieval probably lead to different conceptual representations being constructed in working memory on each occasion prior to the categorization. Requiring the intermediate stage of constructing the conceptual representation in working memory means, of course, that we have less direct evidence about the structure of the long-term store from which the information is retrieved. It is therefore difficult to judge to what extent the randomness occurs in the process of information retrieval, as opposed to in the permanent semantic memory store itself.

3. *Prototypes and Logic*

The final issue arising from category vagueness concerns the mapping of sentences in natural language onto logic. We commonly like to think that when we make assertions then the things that we say may be true or false.

Nothing could be plainer. However, it turns out that within every statement there is a sometimes uneasy trade-off between the truth or falsity of the statement and the interpretation of the words within it (Bill Clinton's narrow legal definition of "sex" in the Monica Lewinksi scandal is a good case in point). If there are borderline cases of category membership, then how does one handle the truth of statements that involve such cases? The problem lies in the famous dictum of the Law of the Excluded Middle. As Frege (1903–1970) puts it:

> A concept that is not sharply defined is wrongly termed a concept. Such quasi-conceptual constructions cannot be recognized as concepts by logic; it is impossible to lay down precise laws for them. The law of excluded middle is really just another form of the requirement that the concept should have a sharp boundary ... Has the question "Are we still Christians?" really got a sense, if it is indeterminate whom the predicate "Christian" can truly be asserted of, and who must be refused it?

Early attempts to rescue the situation with Zadeh's fuzzy set logic (Zadeh, 1965) came to grief as it was quickly noticed that while (probably) a consistent logic in itself, with useful applications in control engineering, the logic made the wrong predictions about behavioral data such as judgments of typicality or categorization in complex concepts (Osherson & Smith, 1981, 1982; Roth & Mervis, 1983). Hampton (1997b) reviewed a series of studies I conducted on this question from which it is clear that when people form conjunctions (Sports that are also Games), disjunctions (Fruits or Vegetables), or complement conjunctions (Dwellings that are not Buildings) they do not respect the constraints of set logic—fuzzy or otherwise. As a brief example, people say that chess is a sport that is a game but that it is not a sport, they say that a mushroom is not a fruit and that it is not a vegetable but that it *is* one or the other, and they say that a tent is not a dwelling but that it *is* a dwelling that is not a building. These studies and others (Cohen & Murphy, 1984) strongly suggest that people form quasi-logical combinations of nouns using the natural language conjunctives "and" "or," and "not," not by forming Boolean set intersections, unions, or complements but by combining the *prototypes* of the concepts in question (Hampton, 1987). As a further example, Hampton (1996) showed that judgments of membership in a conjunction showed *compensation*. The more typical an item was as a member of class A, then the less similar it needed to be to B, to be counted as a member of the conjunction A^B. For example, if judging whether faces are those of a "happy child," the more typically childish an already clearly childish face became, the less happy the child needed to look in order to still count in the category. Logical conjunction just does not work this way.

The discovery of this nonlogical system for combining concepts is one of the key factors supporting prototype representations, since it flies in the face of grounding the meaning of terms in extensionally delineated classes in the world and of grounding complex concepts in set logic. It is not then surprising to find the whole process of conceptual combination becoming one of the major battlegrounds in the debate between externalist and descriptivist theories of concepts. In a number of books and papers, Fodor (Fodor & Lepore, 1994) has presented the case that concepts cannot be prototypes as follows (I paraphrase):

a. It is a fundamental tenet of the representational theory of mind that thought is compositional—that is, the meaning of a complex thought is solely made up from the meaning of its component parts and the syntactical function of the linguistic structure that links them together.
b. Concepts are the component parts from which complex thoughts are created.
c. Therefore concepts must compose in the way stated.
d. Prototypes do not compose in this way; therefore, concepts cannot be prototypes.

Fodor does not claim that concepts do not *have* prototypes, just that they are not themselves prototypes. So, terminological tussles aside, what we have is the suggestion that the entities that psychologists study and like to call concepts are not in fact concepts and might better be called conceptions or prototypes. A different level of mental representation contains our concepts. These concepts are atomistic symbols (cannot be further analyzed into simpler terms such as descriptions) and have the requisite properties of composing according to Boolean logic. It is possession of these concepts that explains the compositional properties of our thought.

It will be interesting to see if this proposal can be cashed out into empirical predictions about those circumstances in which concepts "proper" are involved in thinking and those in which we rely instead on our prototypes. One possible way forward may be in differentiating rule-based and similarity-based systems of thinking (Smith & Sloman, 1994). Ashby, Alfonso-Reese, Turken, and Waldron (1998) have intriguing data that in category learning there are two independent systems that learn through either hypothesis testing of rules or through accumulation of associative similarity-based links and that these are associated with different brain regions. There is also assorted evidence emerging that individuals differ systematically in whether they use similarity or rules in solving conceptual problems (Hampton & Estes, 2000; Winman, Wneerholm, Juslin, & Shanks, 2005).

The issue of how to marry our ability to think in logical terms with the flexibility and adaptability of our conceptual system is a key issue for cognitive science. Clearly, if we went around thinking that something could be an A that is a B but at the same time not an A, then we would be continually falling into reasoning errors. In fact, when faced with logical arguments dressed up in real-world situations, it would appear that most people find it very hard to judge the logical validity of arguments (Henle & Michael, 1956). My guess is that thinking in terms of set logic and compositional concepts is a relatively late cultural acquisition that arose with the development of civilizations involving technology, economic accounting, and mathematics in the last few thousand years. To use language for logical thinking requires that we *stipulate* and then hold constant the meaning of words in the given context so that Frege's dictum of sharp boundaries can be respected. For example, we could answer Frege's question, "Are we still Christians?" in one of two ways. Following Frege, we could stipulate (for example) that a Christian is one who is baptized into some closed set of recognized churches—hence, everyone on the planet is either a Christian or not a Christian. If we then stipulate who Frege is referring to by "we," we can check whether the set defined by "we" is included within the set defined by "Christian." QED. Alternatively, we can take the question in a nonlogical way, as asking (perhaps even rhetorically) whether the current trends in our religious beliefs and practices have taken us away from the original "true" notion of Christianity. This way of answering the question requires a discussion about the true meaning of Christianity—it becomes no longer a question about sets of entities and their set relations but a question about concepts and how they should be defined. Having identified the fundamental core beliefs and values that we want the term "Christian" to imply, we can then come to some broad judgment about the *degree* to which such values are prevalent within the group of people defined by "we" (which in turn may not be well defined as a group but admit of clear and borderline members).

This example illustrates the problem that we have. When we use language we may be either referring to sets in the world or alternatively asserting the meaning of our words. I suspect that sentences, such as "the cat is on the mat," with literal interpretations and straightforward truth evaluation are quite rare in our daily discourse.

4.   *Conclusions about Vagueness*

In sum, category vagueness provides support for prototype representations given an additional assumption that the representation itself or the processes that utilize that representation are subject to random or contextual noise. It is interesting that other psychological accounts of concepts, such as the theory-based view (Murphy & Medin, 1985), have little to contribute to the discussion about vagueness. It seems that disagreement and inconsistency of categorization of familiar items and the close link between probability of categorization and similarity to the category are key pieces of evidence in favor of the prototype view. Exemplar models, however, make much the same predictions, since they share with prototypes the idea that categorization is similarity-based and probabilistic.

Alternative philosophical accounts of the phenomenon of vagueness exist, which do not require that concepts be prototypes. In the case of epistemological uncertainty, however, it may be possible for peaceful coexistence between an externalist account of concepts and a prototype-based account of our mental representations of those concepts (Prinz, 2002). When it comes to the use of concepts as elements of thoughts, to be combined compositionally through logical operations, then prototypes do not have the right properties. They have been shown to combine in nonlogical ways and do not respect the clean rules of set logic. To some, this is devastating news for prototypes as a component of the future of cognitive science. Our conceptual thought is logical, so our thought cannot be based on prototypes. To others, this fact about prototypes goes some way to explaining the vast literature on human reasoning—we just are very bad at thinking logically most of the time, whereas we are pretty good at shifting the meaning of our terms mid-argument if it will suit our purposes.

IV. Typicality

Variation in the typicality of category members is often cited as one of the core tenets of Prototype Theory. However, it is questionable whether the simple fact of typicality variation itself is particularly discriminating between Prototype Theory and other accounts of concepts. The problem is that when instructed to judge typicality or goodness-of-example it may be unclear just what aspect of the category members people may be attending to. Barsalou (1985) found that there were several different factors involved in determining mean typicality scores for common taxonomic categories like Bird or Fruit, including resemblance to other category members (as predicted by Prototype Theory) but also frequency of instantiation (how often the item is encountered) and fit to ideals (how well the item meets some goal or purpose—for example, for artifact concepts). Subsequently, Medin and Atran (2004) have reported that in nonstudent populations the notion of "goodness-of-example" as originally introduced by Rosch is much more likely to be determined by fitness to goals or ideals than by similarity to other category members. The point was driven home by Armstrong, Gleitman, and Gleitman (1983), who showed that participants were just as happy to rate the typicality of well-defined categories, such as "odd-number," as they were to judge typicality in allegedly prototype categories such as "fruit" [see Larochelle, Richard, and Soulières (2000) for evidence about how typicality effects in well-defined categories differ from those in other kinds of category].

The moral would seem to be that given a task in which category members have to be ranked or rated for goodness-of-example, people will quite reasonably attend to whatever dimension is available to provide sufficient information to rank the items. For natural kinds this may include similarity to prototype and frequency of instantiation, for artifacts it may include ability to meet the functional goals of the artifact, and for mathematical concepts it may reflect familiarity, simplicity, or yet other dimensions. In fact, there may be very few open-ended categories that do not have reliably measurable typicality differences within them. After all, John is a more typical name for a British male than is Tyrone, but this is presumably not because it is more similar to other names.

So, the demonstration of reliable typicality differences may be neither here nor there—prototype concepts would certainly be expected to show such differences but then so might other kinds of concepts given the ambiguity of the task. It is therefore important to go beyond the ratings themselves and examine what other behavioral effects can be associated with typicality differences. Here, the results suggest that variations in typicality proper (i.e., rather than frequency or familiarity) have strong and robust effects on a range of psychological tasks, consistent with similarity-based models (which would include Exemplar models). It is therefore encumbent on theories of concepts that have little or nothing to say about typicality to provide an alternative explanation of these effects. In the following section I review some of these results.

A. Some Typicality Effects

One of the first demonstrations of typicality effects was the finding that typical category members are more rapidly categorized than atypical (McCloskey & Glucksberg, 1979; Rips, Shoben & Smith, 1973). But is this effect due to degree of similarity to the prototype or due to associative strength between the member and its category?

Hampton (1997a) explored two dimensions of category gradedness and their effects on the speed of categorization of category members. Using the British category norms published by Hampton and Gardiner (1983), two sets of materials were constructed. One set provided a contrast between words that were of high typicality and others of low typicality, while holding constant their production frequency (PF) in the category norms. For example, for the category Birds, typical items *nightingale, swift*, and *dove* were compared with atypical items *ostrich, penguin*, and *emu*. Both kinds of word were equally likely to be generated as exemplars of the category and were rated as equally familiar, but one set was judged as typical and the other set as atypical. The second set of materials arranged the converse comparison—a contrast between words of high PF and words of low PF, with the rated typicality held constant. For example, high PF birds *eagle, hawk*, and *duck* were contrasted with low PF *cuckoo, peacock*, and *turkey*. These sets were matched for typicality and familiarity, but the high PF words were generated frequently when listing category members and the low PF words were not.

These two different contrasts were measured under two experimental manipulations. One factor (adapted from McCloskey & Glucksberg, 1979) varied the difficulty of the categorization task by manipulating whether the false items, to be rejected, were obviously false and unrelated to the category (bus–bird) or whether they included related items that would bear some similarity to the category (bat–bird). In one condition therefore false items could be easily rejected and the instructions emphasized speed of response, whereas in the other condition false items were confusable and the instructions emphasized accuracy of the response. The second factor that was manipulated was priming of the availability of half of the items by providing a prior task in which they were categorized at a more superordinate level (sparrow–animal).

The purpose of these two manipulations was to show that typicality and associative strength (PF) could be doubly dissociated in the context of speeded categorization of words. False relatedness was intended to make the atypical items harder to categorize and so enhance the typicality effect, whereas priming was expected to temporarily increase the accessibility of all items and so reduce the PF effect, which relies on the inaccessibility of low PF items.

The results showed that introducing related false items did increase the effect of typicality on response time but did not interact with PF. Alternatively, priming decisions with a superordinate category reduced the PF effect in the easy condition but did not interact with typicality. Error data confirmed the picture, with false relatedness and accuracy instructions increasing "no" responses to atypical items but reducing "no" responses to low PF items.

Data such as these provide strong support for the general notion that categorization of items in common semantic categories can involve a similarity-based comparison of the item with some generic representation of the category. Increasing the difficulty of discriminating the false items from the true items requires that a greater amount of information needs to be retrieved, with the result that a greater difference is seen in response time for typical versus atypical items, and atypical items are more likely to be rejected from the category. Associative links between items and the category name provide a separate and dissociable source of variance between items affecting categorization time. Hence, typicality is not just associative strength.

Typicality continues to prove itself an important variable. A study by Kiran and Thompson (2003) will serve to illustrate this. They set out to treat naming deficits in four patients with fluent aphasia. Over many weeks the patients were trained in category sorting and naming of pictures, identifying semantic attributes applicable to target pictures and answering yes/no questions about the features of the target. Patients were either trained with a set of 8 typical category items or with a set of 8 atypical items, and generalization was tested to 16 other category members. The results were striking. Training on atypical items generalized to the rest of the category whereas training on typical items did not. If one conceives of the category concept as being represented by a prototype in a feature space then clearly activation of widely spaced atypical examples will generalize to the whole region of the space, whereas activation of a cluster of typical examples near the center will generalize less widely. [Similar conclusions were drawn from a quite different paradigm—the release from Proactive Interference in short-term recall—by Keller and Kellas (1978).]

B. STABILITY OF TYPICALITY JUDGMENTS

As with categorization decisions, there is also considerable variability in people's typicality judgments. Barsalou (1987) conducted a series of studies of the instability of typicality ratings and rankings and concluded that the high levels of shift in an individual's ratings from one occasion to another argued for prototypes being constructed in working memory anew each time a typicality rating task was presented. In a study conducted with my student Lara Olufon, we set out further to investigate the within-participant stability of typicality ratings. In particular, we tested a prediction of Prototype Theory that had not been tested before. One plausible source of variability in typicality judgments would be variation in the relative weight given to different aspects of the prototype. Perhaps on one occasion a person feels that being sweet is the most important feature of a typical fruit, whereas on other occasions they feel that being round is more important. The effect of this variation will be that the relative similarity of items to the prototype will change. However, this change will *only* be observed for items that have one but not the other of the features. Items that have all of the features will still be the most typical, regardless of any shift in weight from one feature to another. In spatial terms, shifts in dimensional weight that stretch or shrink different dimensions will leave the center of the category unmoved, although distance of atypical items from the center will be affected. We therefore predicted that the items judged most typical would be least likely to shift their ranking on a retest a week later.

One should note that it is also true that items with few or none of the prototype features should show less variability. However, lacking enough features, these items would not fall in the category and so would not be included in a list of category members. We hypothesized that all items in the category would have at least half of the full set of weighted features. Hence, variability should increase monotonically across the typicality scale within the category.

A possible confound here is the extra stability of items at the two ends of a sequence. For example, the item judged most (or least) typical will still tend to be most typical if its typicality increases and will only risk a change in rank if its typicality decreases. So the chances of a change are half as great for an end item as they are for an item in the middle of the ranking order in which a change either up or down on the scale risks a change in the rank position. Items in the middle of a rank order are also more likely to be jumped over by items on each side, than items at the end that have items on one side only. To control this confound, we compared the stability of items at the top end of the ranking (most typical), with those at the bottom end (least typical). Confounds due to position in the list relative to the end and the middle should be equal for both ends, so the predicted extra stability of typical items should show up as greater stability for the top end of the list compared with the bottom end of the list.

Nine category members were selected in each of eight common taxonomic categories studied by Hampton and Gardiner (1983) such as birds, clothing, and weapons. Care was taken to space the items equally along the typicality scale. In addition, nine category features were selected for each category. Participants ranked the items for typicality and the features for their importance. They did the same task on two occasions a week apart, and correlations were calculated between the ranks given on each occasion. Median correlation between the first and second rankings was 0.77 for both feature importance and typicality rankings. Results also showed greater stability for the top four ranks in the list than the bottom four ranks. Mean probability of the top four most typically ranked items retaining the same typicality rank was 0.33, and for the bottom four atypically ranked items was only 0.27. The difference was significant on an ANOVA with end (top or bottom) and distance from the end (1–4) as within-subjects factors.

Consistent with the hypothesis that instability in people's concepts may reflect changes in the weights attributed to different prototype features, we therefore found that typical category members were more consistently ranked than were atypical category members.

As a final demonstration that typicality is an effect of similarity, rather than availability or some other variable, I conducted a short study with Wenchi Yeh in which participants gave typicality judgments for items that (unknown to them) were constructed in quadruples. Within a quadruple were two pairs of similar items, which when re-paired within the quadruple would constitute two pairs of dissimilar items. For example, the pairs "goose and turkey" and "pelican and toucan" were similar pairs, which were then re-paired as "goose and pelican" or "turkey and toucan" to create dissimilar pairs. The measure taken was very simple—the degree of correlation in the ratings or rankings given to each member of a pair, across the different participants in the experiment. Thus, for example, one group of students rated all the items for typicality, and then the correlation was calculated across individuals of the ratings given to each member of a similar pair, such as *goose:turkey,* and to each member of a matched dissimilar pair such as *goose:pelican.* The idea was that if individuals vary in the weight that they attach to different dimensions of a prototype, then there should be a stronger correlation for similar pairs than for dissimilar pairs. Having the same feature profile, similar pairs would move up or down together as feature weights changed across individual raters whereas dissimilar pairs would not. This was what was found. The stronger the similarity between a pair of items the larger the correlation between the ratings given to the items by different people.

C. Conclusions about Typicality

In sum, typicality effects can be identified that are not simply to do with the familiarity or availability of category members. Theories of concepts that do not base categorization on similarity tend to be dismissive of typicality effects. Armstrong et al.'s (1983) results are often cited as discrediting the use of typicality to argue for prototype representations. However, it is increasingly clear that a great many tasks are influenced by typicality effects, and these effects are rooted in differences of similarity or degree of match between an item and a conceptual representation. For prototype and exemplar theory, similarity-based typicality effects are a central plank of the models. The wide range of such effects is therefore a key piece of evidence for this type of theory.

V. Genericity

Genericity in linguistics and the philosophy of language refers to sentences that either (a) refer to a kind rather than a particular or (b) assert general properties *typically* true of a class or individual. The following sentences illustrate these two phenomena.

> The potato was first cultivated in South America.
> John smokes a cigar after dinner.
> (Examples and definition from Krifka et al., 1995, p. 2.)

In the first sentence "the potato" refers to the kind, not to an individual potato, whereas in the second the sentence implies that this is John's usual habit and not that John never has dinner without smoking a cigar afterward.

The two kinds of genericity coincide when people are asked to give general properties of a kind—which is the task that Rosch and Mervis (1975) used to develop Prototype Theory. For our purposes then, genericity refers to the finding that people generate descriptions that are typically true of the concept, where "typically true" implies that typical category members will have the property but atypical category members may not.

A commonly observed phenomenon in all natural languages is the fact that many sentences may be neither universally true, nor simply false but may instead be true under some notion of "generally true" or "typically true." When asked to describe birds and say what is distinctive about them compared with other related categories, people will commonly start with "has wings" and "flies" and then go on to describe other distinguishing features, such as two legs, feathers, hatched from eggs and migratory. There appears to be no intuitive difference to the respondent between the relevance of saying that birds fly and saying that they have feathers. This in spite of the fact that there are well-known examples of flightless birds, and many species of insect that fly, whereas all birds (at least before they are prepared for the oven) and only birds have feathers. Given that there is a single defining feature—feathers—that is both necessary and sufficient to discriminate birds from other types of creature, why do people not recognize this fact and define the word's meaning in this simple way?

In fact, birds turn out to be a rather special and potentially misleading case. Early theories of semantic memory, such as the classic paper by Smith, Shoben, and Rips (1974), took the fact that birds have a clear set of defining features and other features that merely characterize typical birds as a basis for proposing a distinction between Defining and Characteristic Features, in spite of difficulties in establishing such a distinction for a broader range of concepts (Hampton, 1979, 1981; McNamara & Sternberg, 1983).

People's knowledge of what distinguishes other types of creature, such as fish, insects, reptiles, or amphibians, is much less easily captured in terms of a small set of necessary features. It appears that we apply a general approach to representing most of the conceptual classes that we distinguish in the external world—that is to represent them in terms of a set of information about what they typically are like, where they can be expected to be found, how they typically behave, or what humans typically use them for. Russell may have been right that "things are what they are," but our way of grasping reality involves setting up classifications that groups things together into classes or types—which almost necessarily will involve fuzziness in the categorization and the involvement of information that is distinctive and very useful to know, even though it lacks logical rigor.

Genericity is important evidence for the most central tenet of Prototype Theory (and more generally of similarity-based theories, including Exemplar theory). This tenet is that:

Concepts are represented by their most common and distinctive attributes—if using a spatial metaphor, then they are represented as a region in semantic similarity space centered on a particular point corresponding to the most typical potential example of the category.

A corollary of this proposal is that the category boundary between one sort of thing and the next is not directly represented. We easily identify things when they are a good match to our stored representation, but we do not find it easy to draw fine distinctions at the category boundary. This proposal contrasts, for example, with rule-based categorization, in which it is the rule determining membership (and hence the boundary) that is represented and not the collection of typical or usual features normally found in the category.

Genericity has been little challenged within psychology, although a number of different approaches to the problem of how to characterize the meaning of generic sentences have been proposed within philosophical semantics (Carlson & Pelletier, 1995).

A. GENERICITY EFFECTS

Genericity applies to most (but not all) statements of conceptual knowledge. Penguins live in cold climates (except for those in the Los Angeles zoo), tigers have stripes (except those born as albinos), and trees have leaves (except for deciduous trees in winter). One exception to the rule would be very general properties. Thus, "penguins hatch from eggs," "tigers need food and water to live" are almost certainly universally true. (Or perhaps it just gets harder and harder to imagine the scenario that would falsify them). In an early study (Hampton, 1982) I showed that even category membership statements need not be universally quantified. It might appear that to say "X is of type Y" is to mean that all Xs are Ys. However, this constraint does not apply to all of our superordinate categories. People will say that a car headlight is a type of lamp and that a lamp is a type of furniture, but the headlight is clearly not furniture. It is possible that this intransitivity is only observed with certain types of superordination—for example, it does not occur readily with biological taxonomies. This point is made by Wierzbicka (1984), who argues that categories like furniture are really collections not types—in the way that tableware is stuff you put on your table, so furniture is just stuff that you use to furnish your house. However, it is still puzzling why collections should not obey transitivity in the way we expect true classes to.

Some research I conducted with Martin Jönsson of Lund University, Sweden, examined the degree to which people's acceptance of the truth of generic statements changes as the subject noun is modified (Hampton & Jönsson, 2005). Taking our inspiration from a study by Connolly, Fodor, Gleitman, & Gleitman (2003), we considered sentences of the following type.

Ravens are black.
Jungle ravens are black.
Young jungle ravens are black.

In keeping with Connolly et al.'s (2003) reported results, we found that as more modifiers are added to the subject noun, so the degree to which people think the sentence is likely to be true decreases. Connolly et al. (2003) interpreted this result as showing that people do not use the default prototype information for a general class (raven) when judging a subordinate (jungle raven) and as therefore undermining the notion that prototypes are involved in forming complex concepts such as jungle ravens. Our alternative account is that, following published models of how prototypes combine in intersective concept combination (Hampton, 1987, 1997b), one would expect there to be a reduction in the importance or weight of features that are true of one concept but not of the other. Thus, if jungle creatures are not generally black, the intersection of ravens and jungle creatures will have less weight attached to that feature.

We thought it would be interesting to see how people responded when the sentences were universally quantified. Suppose now that you are asked to judge the likelihood that the following statements are true.

All ravens are black.
All jungle ravens are black.
All young jungle ravens are black.

If people use their prototypes for constructing complex concepts in order to make these judgments, then they should continue to say that the sentences are less likely to be true as the number of modifiers increases. However, if the presence of a universal quantifier triggers Fodorian atomistic concepts and logical intersection, then it cannot be the case that the first statement is more true than the others. Clearly, in all worlds in which it is true that "all ravens are black," it is also true that "all jungle ravens are black" and similarly that "all young jungle ravens are black." If a property holds true of a whole class it must necessarily be true of any arbitrarily defined subset of that class.

Our results were overwhelmingly in favor of the Prototype Theory. Across both individuals and items the large majority had lower estimates of truth likelihood for the modified sentences than for the unmodified. We refer to this as the Inverse Conjunction Fallacy, since it takes the opposite form of Tversky and Kahneman's Conjunction Fallacy (Tversky & Kahneman, 1983) in which likelihood estimates are *greater* for a conjunction of facts than for a single component fact.

We followed this experiment with one in which we varied the *mutability* of the attributes in the predicate part of each sentence. Mutability has been established by Sloman, Love, and Ahn (1998) as an important variable within conceptual representations. As discussed in an earlier section, certain attributes in a conceptual representation are involved in many causal or other dependency relations with other attributes—for example, the motor of a car is involved in causal relations with the car's function, its need of fuel, its contribution to pollution, etc. Such attributes tend to be less mutable—it is harder to imagine an example of the concept that is like other examples in every respect except missing just this one feature. We gave people a task in which they had to choose the more likely of two generic sentences with modified subjects, one with a mutable predicate (e.g., "Brazilian doves are white") and one with a less mutable predicate (e.g., "Brazilian doves have wings"). We discovered a strong preference for the sentence expressing the less mutable feature. Thus not only is attribute information inherited by the complex concept (Brazilian dove) from the simple noun concept prototype (dove), but the degree of confidence with which it is inherited depends on the internal structure of the prototype, in keeping with Hampton's (1987) account of the formation of Composite Prototypes.

B.   CONCLUSIONS ABOUT GENERICITY

Genericity is crucially important in the argument for prototypes. If it is true that we represent a concept in terms of its typical features, then there is no requirement that those features will be true of all members of the category, and people may not even be aware, without conducting a memory search, of which features are universally true and which are not. Exemplar models would also not expect all features to be true of all category members, but here an important failing of exemplar models comes to the fore. Since they have been developed almost exclusively with respect to the categorization of individual particulars, there is very little that the models have to say about categorization of whole classes or kinds or the truth of generic statements about a class. While they do a good job of predicting the learning dynamics and generalization performance for certain kinds of category structure, they have not been set the task of deciding whether a class as a whole has a particular property or whether a class as a whole belongs in a super-ordinate class. In effect, the development of the models has been too restricted to tightly controlled artificial stimulus sets to offer much help with understanding many of the effects observed in natural language.

VI. Opacity: The Failure of Category Definitions

The fourth phenomenon considered to support a prototype view of concepts is the difficulty that has been encountered in generating good accurate definitions of the meanings of content words (particularly nouns and verbs) in any language. This problem was famously expounded in Wittgenstein's *Philosophical Investigations* (1953) in relation to the category of games. It appears that (in keeping with the earlier discussion of genericity), people know lots of things about games—they involve people, they take place over a period of time, they are done for their own sake, they involve rules, they involve winning and losing, and they are unpredictable—but no set of these different features can be found that discriminates games from nongames, except by using a prototype rule.

In work originally done for my PhD (Hampton, 1979), I interviewed people about their definitions of eight different semantic categories. The questions included asking what was true of all category members, what was true of typical members, what would make something a borderline case—what features it would have, and what it would lack, and even what the word might mean if applied metaphorically to a thing or a person. Features were then listed, regardless of where in the interviews they were generated, and a separate group of people judged whether each of a list of potential category members had those features. Finally, a third group categorized the list of items and made judgments about how good a member they were or how related a nonmember they were. The question was whether the set of category members could be distinguished in terms of a set of common features. The results were that half of the categories could be defined in this way but half could not. A similar proportion of definable categories was found by McNamara and Sternberg (1983) using a procedure in which each individual's definitions was compared to their own category judgments.

Of course, the procedure is perhaps unnecessarily restrictive in its insistence on relying only on empirical evidence generated by respondents.

Semanticists certainly take a much more unconstrained view of how the task should be done. Thus:

> ... semanticists are not obliged to take informants' judgments at face value.
>
> (Wierzbicka, 1990),

or

> ... why should the "real meaning" of a word correspond to what people think of as the meaning of that word? Folk theories should no more be a criterion in semantics that they are in syntax or any other aspect of linguistics."
>
> (Bouchard, 1995).

There is a serious issue here that arises frequently at the interface between psychology and other branches of cognitive science such as linguistics or philosophy. In a way reminiscent of the externalist theory of concepts propounded by philosophers, it is common for semanticists to see the analysis of word meaning as being the analysis of an abstract cultural artifact such that a word's "true meaning in English" need not correspond directly to its current usage. This is a knotty problem that will take some unraveling. On the one hand, psychological methods can be accused with some justification of being crude and open to unwanted demand characteristics. We know, for example, that when generating features of a word's meaning people are driven by pragmatic considerations of trying to be as relevant as possible. Thus, they may neglect to mention many features of birds (such as "has a heart") that they would nonetheless agree to be true, simply because they are less relevant to the perceived communicative goal of distinguishing birds from other creatures. Psychologists have also taken to asking people for metalinguistic reflections on concept meaning—for example, rather than asking for the definition of a term, asking whether the term *has* a definition (Armstrong et al., 1983) or asking whether membership in a class is all-or-none or graded (Estes, 2004; Kalish, 1995). This methodology, while instructive, is also subject to the same question—at what level should we take what people say about how their mind works as a constraint on our theory of the mind? We do not study perception or attention this way (although researchers may get some useful ideas via introspection), but somehow one feels that conceptual contents just *are* what people claim they are. One is reminded of the wag who claimed that Wagner's music is not nearly as bad as it sounds.

There are some writers who still hold that given proper attention to the task and a degree of training, definitions of word meanings can be provided. Sutcliffe (1993) suggested that in following Wittgenstein psychologists have been looking in the wrong place for monothetic definitions of classes—it is not the many ways in which games resemble each other or differ that will tell you what constitutes a game, it is at the more abstract level in which games are differentiated from other broad classes of human activity. Wierzbicka (1972, 1985, 1987) has been the most tireless proponent of getting on with the task of actually giving definitions. For example, her answer to Wittgenstein was the following (Wierzbicka, 1990, p. 469).

Games
1. Things that people do
2. When they do something for some time
3. For pleasure
4. Imagining that they are in a world
5. Where they want to cause some things to happen
6. Where they know what they can do and what they cannot do
7. And where no one knows all that will happen

This definition is proposed to apply to board games, card games, ball games, etc. and to exclude nongames, such as a child idly throwing a ball against a wall and catching it again, which according to Wierzbicka would not be called a game in English. It is, in my view, a great pity that such definitions are not put to the test against a panel of competent speakers of English, rather than being tested against the author's (albeit expert) intuitions. It is easy to suggest potential counterexamples—category members that the definition excludes such as games that are played for money rather than pleasure (poker, professional golf) or games that are entirely predictable (simple computer games like space invaders) and nonmembers that are included such as watching Reality-TV shows and voting for one's least or most favorite participant in the show or standing on the touchline and shouting your support for your sports team. You may be influencing the outcome, you know what you are and are not allowed to do, but watching the game is not playing it.

The general ease with which definitions can be discredited explains the tendency of less brave individuals (in which group I include myself) to discuss the problem in general terms, without actually doing the descriptive work of proposing definitions for any particular term. A dedicated prototype theorist should be willing to take on the task of generating prototype representations, complete with feature weights, dependencies between features, and parameters for individual and group variability that would completely fit a range of data of the kind described in this chapter for some set of concept terms. To date, only fragments of this project have been attempted and probably with good reason. In the mean time, the prototype theorist takes some (unearned) comfort in the general failure of definitional approaches to word meaning.

For other psychological theories of concepts (other than exemplar theory), opacity may possibly be an embarrassment. If concepts derive their meaning from their role in a naïve theory, then what is to stop individual respondents from explaining that theory and hence providing the appropriate account of the concept. Theory-based models seem to be even more remiss than prototype models in making general claims about concepts, without providing a description of the actual contents of a concept. Their case would be much stronger if they could find a way to elicit the naïve theory for one or more domains from their respondents and then show how the theory affects decisions about the concepts within it. The experience of those interviewing experts in the course of developing knowledge-based systems in artificial intelligence (AI) is that eliciting people's theories of a domain in an explicit format is a very difficult and time-consuming process.

In responding to the problem of opacity and not favoring the prototype approach, philosophers have turned to two alternative accounts of word meaning, which for completeness sake I will briefly outline.

A. DEFERENCE

For deference, a famous paper by Putnam (1975) puts the case in terms of a linguistic division of labor. Just as people accept that it is quite possible that they may be using a word in the wrong sense and would refer to a dictionary to check—they also accept that for many terms referring to natural kinds, such as Elephant or Gold, there may be expert biologists with DNA testing kits or expert chemists with chemical assay kits who know the crucial tests of category membership. It is reasonable in such cases for lay speakers to defer to the relevant experts. As a result, in Putnam's memorable phrase "Cut the pie any way you like, "meanings" just ain't in the head!"

Studies by Braisby (2005) suggest that people are willing to change their minds about a categorization if an expert opinion differs from their own. However, he found that there are quite restricted circumstances in which this will work, and in fact there is a considerable minority of individuals who strongly resist any attempt to influence their decisions by reference to experts. The notion of deference may therefore not offer a complete account of opacity. It also leaves us with two interesting questions: first how do the experts solve the problem of defining the concept and second what happens for all those concepts for which there is no recognized body of experts?

B. ATOMISM

Probably the best way to define an elephant is to say that it is the result of two elephants breeding. This definition captures all and only elephants. It is not a truism, since it captures the commonly held belief that natural kinds have a particular set of features because of some germ-like essence, which in the case of biological kinds gets passed from generation to generation. It even covers the concepts of more sophisticated individuals with a knowledge of evolutionary biology, for whom the concept of elephant would be vague at some point in the past as the species evolved from its predecessor.

The difficulty with this definition is twofold. First, how do you know that two creatures who are about to have an offspring are elephants? You seem to have doubled the problem you started with. And second, how do you know what kind of creature the parents of the creature now in front of you were? However, one should note that these are problems of how we could come to know for sure what something is, rather than problems of not having the right definition. Fodor's atomist view is [roughly, Fodor (2000)] that our minds contain an atomic symbol for the concept elephant. Through exposure to a world in which there are such things as elephants and, presumably, cultural representations of elephants together with a word "elephant" in one's native language, this symbol comes to refer indexically to those things, and the word "elephant" comes to be the name of that symbol, through which we can frame thoughts and statements about elephants. Any attempt therefore to define the meaning of the word will be doomed to failure, since the word just means ELEPHANT, and it derives the nontrivial part of its meaning through its reference relation to that (self-perpetuating) class of things in the real world.

This is not the place to explore the different accounts of how the appropriate indexical relation is established or how the atomic concept gets associated with the prototype (or stereotype as it is sometimes called) of a concept. The key advantage of atomism is that it makes a clean distinction between the concept and what we know about it. A descriptivist account of the contents of a concept will involve some set of features (i.e., broadly speaking a prototype). As a result, if you and I differ in whether we think one of the features applies, then in effect we have *different concepts.* Given the data on instability described earlier, it would then follow that like stepping in the proverbial river, we never access the same concept twice. An answer needs to be given to this challenge, but (happily) space and time do not permit such a venture at this point. Just to note that it is a challenge not just to Prototype Theory but to all of cognitive science in as much as the latter aims to individuate concepts by representing conceptual contents (Fodor, 1998).

VII.   Conclusions

I have covered a considerable amount of ground in this discussion of current issues concerning prototype representations. I hope to have convinced the reader that in spite of the unpopularity in certain quarters of Prototype Theory as a serious contender for representing concepts, the phenomena of prototypes are still with us and still in need of explanation. Four major types of phenomenon have been reviewed, all of which seem to fit best with the prototype theory.

a. Membership in conceptual categories is vague, not only because people do not know enough about the domain but also because word meanings are flexible and cannot be pinned down.

b. Degrees of typicality within a category influence a wide range of cognitive processes—from category-based induction, through memory interference and sentence processing, to the treatment of aphasics, and variation in typicality is not just about familiarity or availability of concepts in memory but about similarity to the rest of the class.

c. The problem of how to treat the semantics of generic sentences is of major importance, and Prototype Theory is the only account of concept representation that explains why so much of our semantic knowledge takes the form of statements that are "typically" true, rather than having a universally quantified truth. It is also the only approach that explains the nonlogical combination of concepts under different forms of linguistic connective.

d. Finally, the difficulty of defining word meanings remains a live issue. Prototype concepts cannot by their nature be simply defined. The problem can be stipulated away by taking an atomistic view, or it can be pushed back a level by taking a deference view, but neither of these will ever be a complete account of how the individual brain is able to use its internal representation of concepts for understanding, thinking, and talking about its world.

At various points, I have tried to bring into the discussion notions that are common currency in philosophy, such as the Externalist view of conceptual contents, and ideas of deference and conceptual atomism. The integration of philosophy, lexical semantics, and psychology into a true cognitive science of concepts is still a rather distant goal. Not only are the methods of enquiry of the three fields very different but also the value placed on different kinds of evidence varies widely as do the intuitive assumptions that drive the development of theory. However, the goal remains a crucially important one. It should be possible, for example, for philosophy to set interesting research agendas for psychology and for the data from psychology and linguistics to pose theoretical challenges for philosophy. The final unifying theory of concepts will need to explain how people's use of language is vague, variable, generic, and opaque, as well as explaining how concepts can be reduced to atomic symbols for the understanding of logical reasoning.

After all, Gödel and Frege, Wittgenstein and Russell developed their notions of the logical forms of natural reasoning with just the same biological apparatus as the rest of us. The mistake is to take our ability to appreciate the logical necessity of simple arguments, such as $A{\wedge}B \rightarrow A$, as the paradigm case of thought that requires explaining. Our minds have evolved to find it much less effortful to run down the vaguely drawn channels characterized by the range of phenomena reviewed here. The central notion of a prototype remains at the heart of our understanding of this way of thinking.

REFERENCES

Aarts, B., Denison, D., Keizer, E., & Popova, G. (2004). *Fuzzy grammar: A reader*. Oxford: Oxford University Press.

Armstrong, S. L., Gleitman, L. R., & Gleitman, H. (1983). What some concepts might not be. *Cognition, 13*, 263–308.

Ashby, F. G., Alfonso-Reese, L. A., Turken, A. U., & Waldron, E. M. (1998). A neuropsychological theory of multiple systems in category learning. *Psychological Review, 105*, 442–481.

Barsalou, L. W. (1985). Ideals, central tendency, and frequency of instantiation as determinants of graded structure in categories. *Journal of Experimental Psychology: Learning, Memory, and Cognition, 11*, 629–654.

Barsalou, L. W. (1987). The instability of graded structure: Implications for the nature of concepts. In U. Neisser (Ed.), *Concepts and conceptual development: Ecological and intellectual factors in categorization* (pp. 101–140). Cambridge: Cambridge University Press.

Berlin, B., & Kay, P. (1969). *Basic color terms: Their universality and evolution*. Berkeley: University of California Press.

Bouchard, D. (1995). Fuzziness and categorization, Section 1.5.1. of *The semantics of syntax: A minimalist approach to grammar*. Chicago: University of Chicago Press. Reprinted in Aarts et al. (2004) op. cit. pp. 479–485.

Braisby, N. R. (2005). *Flexibility and pragmatics in categorizing natural kinds*. Paper presented at the 9th European Congress of Psychology. Granada, Spain, July.

Braisby, N. R. (1993). Stable concepts and context-sensitive classification. *Irish Journal of Psychology, 14*, 426–441.

Carlson, G. N., & Pelletier, F. J. (1995). *The generic book*. Chicago: University of Chicago Press.

Cohen, B., & Murphy, G. L. (1984). Models of concepts. *Cognitive Science, 8*, 27–58.

Connolly, A. C., Fodor, J. A., Gleitman, L. R., & Gleitman, H. (2003). *Why stereotypes don't even make good defaults*. University of Pennsylvania: unpublished MS, October.

Estes, Z. (2004). Confidence and gradeness in semantic categorization: Definitely somewhat artifactual, maybe absolutely natural. *Psychonomic Bulletin & Review, 11*, 1041–1047.

Fodor, J. A. (1998). *Concepts: Where cognitive science went wrong*. Oxford: Oxford University Press.

Fodor, J. A. (2000). Multiple review of concepts: Where cognitive science went wrong, replies to critics. *Mind & Language, 15*, 350–374.

Fodor, J. A., & Lepore, E. (1994). The red herring and the pet fish: Why concepts still can't be prototypes. *Cognition, 58*, 253–270.

Frege, G. (1903–1970). Concepts. In P. Geach and M. Black (Eds.), *Translations from the philosophical writings of Gottlob Frege*. Oxford: Blackwell. Reprinted in Aarts et al. (2004) op. cit., p. 33.

Gärdenfors, P. (2000). *Conceptual spaces: The geometry of thought.* Cambridge, MA: MIT Press.

Hampton, J. A. (1979). Polymorphous concepts in semantic memory. *Journal of Verbal Learning and Verbal Behavior, 18,* 441–461.

Hampton, J. A. (1981). An investigation of the nature of abstract concepts. *Memory & Cognition, 9,* 149–156.

Hampton, J. A. (1982). A demonstration of intransitivity in natural categories. *Cognition, 12,* 151–164.

Hampton, J. A. (1987). Inheritance of attributes in natural concept conjunctions. *Memory & Cognition, 15,* 55–71.

Hampton, J. A. (1995). Testing prototype theory of concepts. *Journal of Memory and Language, 34,* 686–708.

Hampton, J. A. (1996). Conjunctions of visually based categories: Overextension and compensation. *Journal of Experimental Psychology: Learning, Memory, and Cognition, 22,* 378–396.

Hampton, J. A. (1997a). Associative and similarity-based processes in categorization decisions. *Memory & Cognition, 25,* 625–640.

Hampton, J. A. (1997b). Conceptual combination. In K. Lamberts and D. R. Shanks (Eds.), *Knowledge, concepts and categories* (pp. 135–162). Hove: Psychology Press.

Hampton, J. A. (1997c). Psychological representation of concepts. In M. A. Conway (Ed.), *Cognitive models of memory* (pp. 81–110). Hove: Psychology Press.

Hampton, J. A. (1998). Similarity-based categorization and fuzziness of natural categories. *Cognition, 65,* 137–165.

Hampton, J. A. (2004). *Reasons for vagueness.* Paper presented at the Annual Meeting of the Psychonomic Society, Kansas City, November.

Hampton, J. A. (2005). *Typicality, graded membership and vagueness.* London: City University, unpublished MS.

Hampton, J. A., Dubois, D., and Yeh, W. (2006). Effects of classification context on categorization in natural categories. *Memory & Cognition.*

Hampton, J. A., & Estes, Z. (2000). *Appearance versus reality: How essential are essences?* Paper presented at the Annual Meeting of the Psychonomic Society, New Orleans, November.

Hampton, J. A., & Gardiner, M. M. (1983). Measures of internal category structure: A correlational analysis of normative data. *British Journal of Psychology, 74,* 491–516.

Hampton, J. A., & Jönsson, M. (2005). Paper presented at 46th Annual Meeting of the Psychonomic Society. *Effects of noun modification on the plausibility of attribute information,* Toronto, November.

Henle, M., & Michael, M. (1956). The influence of attitudes on syllogistic reasoning. *The Journal of Social Psychology, 44,* 115–127.

Homa, D. (1984). On the nature of categories. In G. H. Bower (Ed.), *The psychology of learning and motivation* (Vol. 18, pp. 49–94). New York: Academic Press.

Homa, D., Sterling, S., & Trepel, L. (1981). Limitations of exemplar-based generalization and the abstraction of categorical information. *Journal of Experimental Psychology: Human Learning and Memory, 7,* 418–439.

Kalish, C. W. (1995). Essentialism and graded membership in animal and artifact categories. *Memory & Cognition, 23,* 335–353.

Kamp, H., & Partee, B. (1995). Prototype theory and compositionality. *Cognition, 57,* 129–191.

Keefe, R., & Smith, P. (1997). Theories of Vagueness. In R. Keefe and P. Smith (Eds.), *Vagueness: A reader* (pp. 1–57). Cambridge: MIT Press.

Keller, D., & Kellas, G. (1978). Typicality as a dimension of encoding. *Journal of Experimental Psychology: Human Learning and Memory, 4,* 78–85.

Kempton, W. (1978). Category grading and taxonomic relations: A mug is a sort of cup. *American Ethnologist, 5,* 44–65.

Kiran, S., & Thompson, C. K. (2003). The role of semantic complexity in treatment of naming deficits: Training semantic categories in fluent aphasia by controlling exemplar typicality. *Journal of Speech, Language, and Hearing Research, 46*, 608–622.

Krifka, M., Pelletier, F. J., Carlson, G. N., ter Meulen, A., Chierchia, G., & Link, G. (1995). Genericity: An introduction. In G. N. Carlson and F. J. Pelletier (Eds.), *The generic book* (pp. 1–124). Chicago: University of Chicago Press.

Lakoff, G. (1987). *Women, fire, and dangerous things*. Chicago: University of Chicago Press.

Larochelle, S., Richard, S., & Soulières, I. (2000). What some effects might not be: The time to verify membership in "well-defined" categories. *Quarterly Journal of Experimental Psychology, 53A*(4), 929–961.

McCloskey, M., & Glucksberg, S. (1978). Natural categories: Well-defined or fuzzy sets? *Memory & Cognition, 6*, 462–472.

McCloskey, M., & Glucksberg, S. (1979). Decision processes in verifying category membership statements: Implications for models of semantic memory. *Cognitive Psychology, 11*, 1–37.

McNamara, T. P., & Sternberg, R. J. (1983). Mental models of word meaning. *Journal of Verbal Learning and Verbal Behavior, 22*, 449–474.

Medin, D. L., & Atran, S. (2004). The native mind: Biological categorization and reasoning in development and across cultures. *Psychological Review, 111*, 960–983.

Medin, D. L., & Schaffer, M. M. (1978). Context theory of classification learning. *Psychological Review, 85*, 207–238.

Mellor, D. H., & Oliver, A. (1997). Introduction. In D. H. Mellor and A. Oliver (Eds.), *Properties* (pp. 1–33). Oxford: Oxford University Press.

Millikan, R. (1998). A common structure for concepts of individuals, stuffs and real kinds: More mama, more milk and more mouse. *Behavioral and Brain Sciences, 21*, 55–66.

Murphy, G. L., & Medin, D. L. (1985). The role of theories in conceptual coherence. *Psychological Review, 92*, 289–316.

Murphy, G. L. (2002). *The big book of concepts*. Cambridge, MA: MIT Press.

Nosofsky, R. M. (1988). Similarity, frequency, and category representations. *Journal of Experimental Psychology: Learning, Memory, and Cognition, 14*, 54–65.

Osherson, D. N., & Smith, E. E. (1981). On the adequacy of prototype theory as a theory of concepts. *Cognition, 9*, 35–58.

Osherson, D. N., & Smith, E. E. (1982). Gradedness and conceptual conjunction. *Cognition, 12*, 299–318.

Osherson, D. N., & Smith, E. E. (1997). On typicality and vagueness. *Cognition, 64*, 189–206.

Posner, M. I., & Keele, S. W. (1968). On the genesis of abstract ideas. *Journal of Experimental Psychology, 77*, 353–363.

Prinz, J. J. (2002). *Furnishing the mind: Concepts and their perceptual basis*. Cambridge MA: MIT Press.

Putnam, H. (1975). The meaning of "meaning". In H. Putnam (Ed.), *Mind, language, and reality: Philosophical papers* (Vol. 2, 215–271). Cambridge: Cambridge University Press.

Quine, W. V. (1948). *On what there is. Review of Metaphysics* (Vol. 2, pp. 21–38). Reprinted in W. V. Quine (1953). *From a logical point of view* (pp. 1–19). Cambridge, MA: Harvard University Press.

Randall, R. A. (1976). How tall is a taxonomic tree? Some evidence for dwarfism *American Ethnologist, 3*, 543–553.

Rey, G. (1983). Concepts and stereotypes. *Cognition, 15*, 237–262.

Rips, L. J. (1989). Similarity, typicality, and categorization. In S. Vosniadou and A. Ortony (Eds.), *Similarity and analogical reasoning* (pp. 21–59). Cambridge: Cambridge University Press.

Rips, L. J. (2001). Necessity and natural categories. *Psychological Bulletin, 127*, 827–852.

Rips, L. J., Shoben, E. J., & Smith, E. E. (1973). Semantic distance and the verification of semantic relations. *Journal of Verbal Learning and Verbal Behavior, 12,* 1–20.

Rosch, E. R., & Mervis, C. B. (1975). Family resemblance: Studies in the internal structure of categories. *Cognitive Psychology, 7,* 573–605.

Rosch, E. R., Simpson, C., & Miller, R. S. (1976). Structural bases of typicality effects. *Journal of Experimental Psychology: Human Perception and Performance, 2,* 491–502.

Rosch, E. R. (1978). Principles of categorization. In E. R. Rosch and B. B. Lloyd (Eds.), *Cognition and categorization* (pp. 27–48). Hillsdale, NJ: Erlbaum.

Ross, J. R. (1973). Nouniness. In O. Fujimura (Ed.), *Three dimensions of linguistic research.* Tokyo: TEC Company Ltd. Reprinted in Aarts et al. (2004). op. cit. pp. 351–422.

Roth, E. M., & Mervis, C. A. (1983). Fuzzy set theory and class inclusion relations in semantic categories. *Journal of Verbal Learning and Verbal Behavior, 22,* 509–525.

Russell, B. (1923). Vagueness. *Australasian Journal of Philosophy and Psychology, 1,* 84–92. Reprinted in Aarts et al. (2004) op. cit. pp. 35–40.

Sloman, S. A., Love, B. C., & Ahn, W. (1998). Feature centrality and conceptual coherence. *Cognitive Science, 22,* 189–228.

Smith, E. E., & Sloman, S. A. (1994). Similarity-versus rule-based categorization. *Memory & Cognition, 22,* 377–386.

Smith, E. E., Shoben, E. J., & Rips, L. J. (1974). Structure and process in semantic memory: A featural model for semantic decisions. *Psychological Review, 81,* 214–241.

Smith, J. D., & Minda, J. P. (2000). Thirty categorization results in search of a model. *Journal of Experimental Psychology: Learning, Memory, and Cognition, 26,* 3–27.

Sutcliffe, J. P. (1993). Concept, class, and category in the tradition of Aristotle. In I. van Mechelen, J. A. Hampton, R. S. Michalski, and P. Theuns (Eds.), *Categories and concepts: theoretical views and inductive data analysis* (35–65). London: Academic Press.

Tversky, A., & Kahneman, D. (1983). Extensional versus intuitive reasoning: The conjunction fallacy in probability judgment. *Psychological Review, 90,* 293–315.

Verbeemen, T., Storms, G., & Verguts, T. (2004). Similarity and taxonomy in categorization. In K. Forbus, D. Gentner, and T. Regier (Eds.), *Proceedings of the 26th Annual Conference of the Cognitive Science Society* (pp. 1393–1398). Mahwah, NJ: Erlbaum.

Wierzbicka, A. (1972). *Semantic primitives.* Frankfurt: Athenaum-Verlag.

Wierzbicka, A. (1984). Apples are not a kind of fruit: The semantics of human categorization. *American Ethnologist, 11,* 313–328.

Wierzbicka, A. (1985). *Lexicography and conceptual analysis.* Ann Arbor, Michigan: Karoma.

Wierzbicka, A. (1987). *English speech act verbs: A semantic dictionary.* New York: Academic Press.

Wierzbicka, A. (1990). "Prototypes save": On the uses and abuses of the notion of "prototype" in linguistics and related fields. In S. L. Tsohatzidis (Ed.), *Meanings and prototypes: Studies in linguistic categorization* (pp. 347–367). London: Routledge.

Williamson, T. (1994). *Vagueness.* London: Routledge.

Winman, A., Wneerholm, P., Juslin, P., & Shanks, D. R. (2005). Evidence for rule-based processes in the inverse base-rate effect. *Quarterly Journal of Experimental Psychology, 58A,* 789–815.

Wittgenstein, L. (1953). *Philosophical investigations.* New York: Macmillan.

Zadeh, L. (1965). Fuzzy sets. *Information and control, 8,* 338–353.

AN ANALYSIS OF PROSPECTIVE MEMORY

Richard L. Marsh, Gabriel I. Cook, and Jason L. Hicks

I. Introduction to Our Thesis

Creating dichotomies and classification schemes that segregate related phenomena from one another is a pervasive tendency in cognitive psychology (and many other disciplines as well). In the study of memory, for example, distinctions are drawn between recognition, free recall, and cued recall. Similarly, memories are often classified as episodic or semantic, or according to Brewer and Pani's (1983) classification scheme as personal, skill, or semantic memories. Although such subdivisions can often serve as useful heuristics for highlighting some differences, the general cost associated with classification is that scholars may not carefully consider fundamental similarities among the subclasses, and therefore, may overlook functional relationships that exist across the heuristic boundaries of a classification scheme. Failure to seek out and uncover these similarities can seriously impede the development of larger scale models and theoretical frameworks whose goal is to integrate, rather than segregate, research findings.

We believe that this exact state of affairs has occurred in the study of prospective memory, or memory for one's intentions; and one of the basic motivations in this chapter is to demonstrate that better integrating retrospective memory theories (and principles) with research on prospective memory can profitably advance our understanding of prospective memory. To date, virtually every article on prospective memory makes the point that prospective memories are encoded representations about activities that are

THE PSYCHOLOGY OF LEARNING
AND MOTIVATION VOL. 46
DOI: 10.1016/S0079-7421(06)46004-7 planned for the future, whereas retrospective memories are encoded representations of what has transpired in one's personal past. Although this distinction is valid, adhering to the dichotomy has probably prevented those who are interested in understanding prospective memory from building on established frameworks and theories that have been extensively tested in the retrospective memory literature (Crowder, 1996; Roediger, 1996). Consequently, in this chapter we attempt to elucidate some similarities and functional relationships between retrospective and prospective memory phenomena that have heretofore been overlooked in the research reports on prospective memory (or given only cursory attention). By making explicit the uniformities and analogous components of prospective and retrospective memory, we hope to provide an overarching approach for generating new ideas for empirical work on prospective memory, which in turn, should advance the development of more comprehensive theories of prospective memory. We also hope to attract interest in the topic of prospective memory from a larger body of researchers schooled primarily in retrospective memory phenomena so that they may propagate additional empirical and theoretical foundations concerning people's memory for their intentions.

At the outset of this endeavor, we must acknowledge that there have been important reasons to date for appealing to a strict dichotomy that somewhat segregated prospective from retrospective memory phenomena. First, the distinction justified studying prospective memory when there was virtually no published research investigating people's memory for intentions to complete tasks in the future. Characterizing prospective memory as an antithesis of retrospective memory helped justify publishing early empirical findings. Second, there was immense intuitive appeal to the idea that memories of forward-looking plans would behave differently from memories of backward-looking experiences. But, just as the intuitive appeal of sharp distinctions between short-term and long-term memory in the modal model (Atkinson & Shiffrin, 1968) ultimately proved untenable, we believe that intuition can be a somewhat shaky basis for indefinitely sustaining scientific distinctions. Third, prospective memory *tasks* were distinguished from retrospective memory *tasks* in the same way that recognition and free recall have been characterized as different *tasks*. Unfortunately, the danger of a dichotomy based on task analysis is that it denies that many underlying component cognitive processes can be shared across tasks. After all, Jacoby (1991, 1998) demonstrated that no memory task is process pure and may be subserved by the same cognitive processes albeit in different relative contributions from each. Fourth, and finally, early researchers debated whether retrospective and prospective memory performances were correlated (Cherry & LeCompte, 1999; Einstein & McDaniel, 1990; Kidder, Park, Hertzog, &

Morrell, 1997). Support was proffered for continuing the distinction between prospective and retrospective memory when correlations were absent between the two. Nevertheless, preserving a strong dichotomy has probably outlived its usefulness in the quest for truly understanding the intricacies of memory for intentions.

II. The Appeal to Principles of Retrospective Memory

The cost associated with any strict adherence to the dichotomy between prospective and retrospective memory is that decades of scientific inquiry on retrospective memory are declared "different from" prospective memory phenomena. We believe strongly that doing so may impede theory development in the area of prospective memory. Adopting the idea that retrospective and prospective memory may be more alike than different, as we will do here, is to embrace the notion that all memories must begin as some representation of a mental experience, be that experience reflecting on an event in the future or one that happened in the recent past. For example, observing the winning goal in a soccer match (a retrospective memory) and planning to take the trash out after dinner (a prospective memory) are both episodic representations that may be stored in memory in a similar fashion. We propose that what is different between these two memories are the characteristics associated with them, the degree to which they are elaborated, and the degree to which they are associated with other memories and the environment surrounding the rememberer at the time of memory formation. In this sense, the encoding operations may be the same cognitive processes operating on prospective and retrospective memories, but the outcome results in mental representations that differ in degree. That point is the core of our thesis, and to reiterate it, prospective and retrospective memory qua memory do not differ at all (Roediger, 1996). Rather, the average qualities and features of these memories may differ, and the cognitive processes that operate on them (in terms of frequency or kind of processing) may differ.

Several brief examples may serve to highlight this point. In the retrospective memory literature, a classic distinction has been made between flashbulb memories and other episodic, retrospective memories with the former being characterized as more vivid and durable than the latter (Brown & Kulik, 1982; Conway, 1995). However, the recent theorizing about flashbulb memories is that their mental representation is actually no different from other memories insofar as they are subject to forgetting and distortion just like all other episodic memories (Christianson & Safer, 1996). Flashbulb memories may be retrieved more frequently, revised more often, and thereby come to have a distribution of information associated with them that is dissimilar to the "average" episodic memory such as attending a friend's birthday dinner. In terms of prospective memories, they may also be retrieved more often, reformulated, or discarded as containing plans that are no longer relevant (Marsh, Hicks, & Landau, 1998). The retrieval and reflective processes that operate on both prospective and retrospective memories changes their character in much the same way that memories in the source-monitoring framework have different distributions of qualitative information (Johnson, Hashtroudi, & Lindsay, 1993). In that framework, memories of externally derived information contain more perceptual and spatio-temporal details than internally derived information from imagination or elaboration, which contains relatively more information about cognitive operations that were used in their initial generation. Therefore, just as memories from different sources may have different average distributions of information, we propose that prospective versus retrospective memories are essentially the same, but differ in the distribution of characteristics that comprise them.

In the remaining sections of this chapter, we consider how those cognitive processes that are well established in the retrospective memory literature might change the mental representation of prospective memories. Our basic assumption is that the outcome of any process on a prospective memory has an effect that is analogous to a process that has been well studied in the retrospective memory literature, and our goal is to elucidate these connections. As a basic framework, we adopt the notion that prospective memories are established by encoding operations, must be maintained over some retention interval, and finally must be retrieved (see Ellis, 1996). Like retrospective memories, prospective memories undergo cyclical periods of dormancy (retention interval) broken by retrieval or use. As in the flashbulb memory example given earlier, the cycles of retention interrupted by recollection may be far more important than any processing at initial encoding. Our goal is to speculate on the changes in the mental representation of prospective memories that occur at each stage of processing and identify the similarities between memories for intentions and "standard" retrospective memories. In the process of considering each of these stages, we will recapitulate very selectively the findings from the prospective memory literature. As such, this chapter is intended neither to be comprehensive nor exhaustive as a review, but it will give the reader a strong flavor of the level of analysis that we believe will advance theoretical inroads in the area of prospective memory. Before considering in some depth each of the standard stages of encoding, retention, and retrieval, we first briefly summarize the terminology and the laboratory paradigms that have become standard in the prospective memory literature.

III. Types of Prospective Memory Tasks

The goals and intentions that people form vary widely in the time frame established for completion, their specificity, and the conditions that are expected to initiate their retrieval and completion. For example, some intended activities are habitual (e.g., taking medication or feeding one's pet), others are novel (e.g., applying for a marriage license), and some occur with intermittent regularity (e.g., maintenance on the exterior of one's home). Some intentions need to be completed sooner (e.g., filling the gas tank in one's car) and others have the characteristics of longer-term goals (e.g., authoring a paper or a textbook). Whereas some must be completed at a specific time or in a specific context (e.g., arriving for a doctor's appointment) others can be completed within a broader time frame and have less contextual constraints (e.g., phoning a family member or friend). If one overlays on these dimensions a multitude of other characteristics, such as the social contract that may be associated with an intention and the personal importance of completing it, the difficulty in developing any comprehensive rubric of prospective memories becomes quickly apparent. Nevertheless, most laboratory tasks that have been used to date have been broadly classified (as an organizing structure) as event based, time based, or activity based (Einstein & McDaniel, 1990; Kvavilashvili & Ellis, 1996; Schaeffer, Kozak, & Sagness, 1998).[1]

Event-based prospective memory tasks are those in which the rememberer sets up a contingency to let an environmental cue serve as a reminder to complete an activity. For example, leaning a package or a book against the back door serves as a good cue to take it with you when leaving for work. Similarly, a person to whom a message is to be delivered should serve as a good cue to do so. Presumably, the cue or category of cues is decided upon at intention formation (and perhaps refined before completion). In the laboratory, verbal and pictorial cues have been associated with overt target actions that participants perform (e.g., pressing a key on a keyboard when the cue is encountered; Einstein, Holland, McDaniel, & Guynn, 1992; Ellis & Milne, 1996; Maylor, 1996, 1998).

By contrast, time-based tasks are ones in which the rememberer must monitor the passage of time in order to fulfill the intention (Cook, Marsh, & Hicks, 2005; Hicks, Marsh, & Cook, 2005). For example, keeping a lunch date requires self-initiated processing to disengage from one's

---

[1] Like the distinction between prospective and retrospective memory that we are attempting to deemphasize in this chapter, these distinctions among types of intentions are probably only useful heuristics. As more is learned about each of them, perhaps the time will come to discard this classification scheme too. Nevertheless, we appeal to it for expository purposes.

current activity to check the time and suspend the activity at an appropriate moment in order to be successful. In a similar way, completing an activity after some specified time period has elapsed (e.g., calling someone again after 15 min has elapsed) is also a time-based intention (and cooking tasks represent good examples of such everyday intentions). Time-based intentions usually occur as steps or pulses (Ellis, 1988). The former can be completed in a larger window of time (from hours to days or weeks) and the latter must be completed at a specific time (e.g., 11 AM). Activity-based intentions are ones that establish a contingency between completing one activity and commencing a different one (Kvavilashvili, 1987). For example, the intention to visit a colleague or run a quick errand can be linked to a transition point in one's current activity (e.g., finish writing the current paragraph) or to a transition point that will occur somewhere in the day (e.g., after a lunch or before attending a colloquium talk).

Although research has been conducted on other sorts of intentions, the vast majority of the current theorizing on prospective memory has focused on event-based and time-based intentions; and even then, the former has received the lion's share of researchers' efforts. Most theorists have preferred to study one or another of these types of intentions, and only rarely have they been directly compared (Einstein, McDaniel, Richardson, Guynn, & Cunfer, 1995; Kidder et al., 1997; Kliegel, Martin, McDaniel, & Einstein, 2001; Sellen, Louie, Harris, & Wilkins, 1997). But direct comparison would highlight similarities such as the fact that many of the intentions just described require an association between a cue (or event, or transition) and some expected context in which the cue or transition will occur. Even time-based intentions require an association between the action to be performed and time-checking behavior (either overt as in checking a clock or covert in terms of time estimation).

Hopefully, the foregoing description of the terminology used in the prospective memory literature will allow the reader to understand the commonalities (and differences) we propose exist across the retrospective memory representations of different types of intentions, and how the cognitive processes that operate on them can change those representations. We begin the remainder of this chapter by analyzing how various intentions are formed in memory (encoding), consider next how they are realized (retrieved), and finally scrutinize how representations of intentions can change over the interval between formation and realization. Each of these topics is considered in a separate section, and we conclude in a final section with some further generalizations that may prove useful for future work on prospective memory.

IV. Intention Formation

Recall that our basic thesis is that the memory representation of intentions need not be any different from retrospective memories. By this account, they have no different qualitative characteristics as defined in the source-monitoring framework (Johnson et al., 1993), but have different distributions of those characteristics on average than certain kinds of retrospective memories. We make occasional reference to the source-monitoring framework because the description of its elements should be more intuitive to the typical reader than more complicated mathematical models of similar elements, such as context information in the ICE model (Murnane, Phelps, & Malmberg, 1999), or the BCDMEM model (Dennis & Humphreys, 2001). In many ways, the source framework shares Bower's (1967) idea that all memories are composed of attribute vectors and that certain vectors are more important (i.e., weighted differently) on different occasions depending on the mental agenda for encoding and retrieval (see also Anisfield & Knapp, 1968, on attribute bundles and Underwood, 1969). In the case of intentions, the desire to perform some action in the future results in a memory representation that is generally internally derived. In other words, the self is usually the original source of the memory. Internally generated memories are imbued with cognitive operations from reflection, planning, and elaborating on the activity to be performed. Most kinds of retrospective memories record perceived events, such as listening to others engage in conversation or watching a television show; and therefore, they will mainly contain perceptual, spatial, and temporal characteristics. By this account, prospective and retrospective memories can differ on the relative quantity of internal versus external qualities.

A. Internal Generation

As it relates to all kinds of memories, the act of generation often results in better retention for the information than obtaining it from an external source. This outcome is the basis of the classic generation effect (Mulligan & Lozito, 2004; Slamecka & Graf, 1978). For example, participants who generate the ending words of sentences better recollect those endings than equivalent words provided to them. The same is true of generating antonyms, synonyms, or category exemplars. Ostensibly, the process of generation is akin to a problem solving task and increases attention toward the resulting "product" (Glisky & Rabinowitz, 1985). In the course of solving the generation task, the item selected has conferred on it both item specific information about why it is the best choice as well as relational information back to the task at hand (McDaniel, Waddill, & Einstein, 1988). From this perspective, intentions should, on average, be better remembered than otherwise equivalent information stored in memory that has no associated intentionality. Consistent with this idea, Maylor, Darby, and Della Salla (2000) found that healthy adults could recall greater numbers of intentions (planned activities) per unit of time than they could recall otherwise equivalent activities that they had performed over the preceding days. In addition, Einstein and McDaniel (1996) have reported that over 50% of the episodes of forgetting that people can remember are instances in which they forgot to complete an intention. Thus, even in the absence of fulfilling intentions, recollection of them appears to be superior to material without any intentionality.[2]

Just as intentions are usually self-generated, most intentions are self-referential. That is, they relate to a highly elaborated, detailed, and organized mental construct, namely, that of one's self. In memory studies, the self-reference effect is that material (especially positive material) associated with one's self is recollected better than the equivalent material processed without regard to one's self (Klein & Kilhstrom, 1986; Rogers, Kuiper, & Kirker, 1977). Integrating information with a preexisting network (or schema) provides more associations and retrieval cues, and therefore, improves recollection. In addition, Marsh and Hicks (2002) have shown that decisions associated with to-be-encoded information improve both item and context memory as compared with cases in which the decision component is absent. Intentions usually involve decisions about several different courses of action, such as when to perform an activity and in what context, or scheduling completion around external constraints such as time demands or other people's schedules. Therefore, the generation effect, the self-reference effect, and associated decision making are three influences at intention formation that all converge on the notion that intentions may be better remembered because of the cognitive processes used to establish them in the first place. If this is true, otherwise comparable information that lacks intentionality may be retained more poorly only because it lacks the equivalent elaborated cognitive processing at encoding.

Activities that receive equivalent processing (but are not intentions) should be just as well recollected as intentions, and those that receive more of this processing should be retained better than prospective memories. For example, certain significant autobiographical memories such as the birth of one's child, the loss of a relation, or learning that one has successfully secured a desired career advancement, are likely to be better remembered

---

[2] Of course, we are cognizant of the fact that it would be difficult in practice to demonstrate "equivalence" between a prospective and retrospective memory. However, just because we are not clever enough today to devise such experimental conditions does not mean they do not exist and that some clever scholar will not find such conditions.

than the average intention because of the associated cognitive elaboration that such events evoke (and because there are perceptual details to augment internally generated records of reflection). According to this line of reasoning, intentions that are formed in haste or that lack true commitment will have weaker memory representations than those that are formed with deliberation and commitment. If the declarative representation in memory of an intention is correlated with ultimately fulfilling it, intentions of the former types should be fulfilled less frequently than those of the latter type.

Empirical evidence is consistent with this assertion insofar as Gollwitzer and Schaal (1998) found that implementation intentions have a higher probability of being carried out (see also Chasteen, Park, & Schwarz, 2001; Gollwitzer, 1999). Implementation intentions are those that are elaborated at formation with a specific plan for carrying them out. For example, dieters who plan specific strategies for losing weight are more successful, people who plan specific route deviations to run an errand after work have a higher completion rate, etc. We are not saying that prospective memories have more elaborated representations as compared to retrospective memories. Rather, we are saying that both prospective and retrospective memories vary in how elaborately they are encoded, and that elaboration will determine their durability in memory, but with prospective memories that durability is likely to affect their completion rate.

The exact mechanisms that could mediate better prospective memory after more elaborate intention formation are unclear. Here we speculate on two as potential avenues for additional inquiry. First, more deeply encoded intentions may come to mind (i.e., be reactivated) more often during the retention interval and receive additional processing. The additional strengthening that could be associated with such rehearsals of the intention will be discussed in depth in a later section, but could be prompted either by self-initiated processing or increased sensitivity to relevant retrieval cues in the environment. To our knowledge, only Hicks, Marsh, and Russell (2000) have attempted to measure how often an event-based intention is spontaneously retrieved, and they did not compare intentions that varied on the dimension of how elaborately they were encoded initially. But, several attempts have been made to record time-checking behavior for time-based intentions (Hicks et al., 2005; Park, Hertzog, Kidder, Morrell, & Mayhorn, 1997; Sellen et al., 1993). Second, how well an intention is learned may affect a person's metacognitive belief about the ease with which they will recollect it and complete the task. Ironically, in the case of event-based intentions, more elaborated encoding may cause less attention to be devoted to monitoring for the occurrence of intention-relevant cues and actually decrease prospective memory performance (Cockman, 2003). Later we describe how possessing an intention may interfere with ongoing processing, and therefore, how an intention is learned could have consequences for cue detection or performance of the ongoing activity in which cues occur.

Of course, not all intentions are internally generated. Some intentions are derived from the wishes of others (e.g., a request from a spouse to perform a task), or set forth as requirements from superiors (e.g., work or school-related tasks). To date, very little is known about whether the completion rate differs for such intentions as compared with intentions that are self-generated. In these cases, the intention may be associated with the person making the request, the environmental context in which it is made (i.e., perceptual details), as well as any internal reactions to the request. Consequently, predicting whether such intentions have greater or lesser elaborated memory representations would be difficult, and perhaps the variability of encoding across internally versus externally derived intentions makes this a somewhat impractical question to answer. In addition, the social contract inherently involved with externally derived intentions that is absent with internally derived intentions complicates such a comparison as well. Nevertheless, a careful consideration of these (and other factors) could make such a comparison very informative and add valuable knowledge to the field.

B. IMAGINATION AND CUE–ACTION CONTINGENCIES

Regardless of whether an intention is wholly self-referential or is formed in response to the wishes or demands of others, people often imagine at intention formation the environmental and spatio-temporal contextual details in which it can be carried out. The mental complexity of doing so, it seems, would require visuospatial resources and goal-directed problem solving behavior at intention formation. This would be especially true for novel as compared with more routine intentions. For example, the intention to retrieve a picture at the local art framing shop is likely to represent a relatively novel intention as compared with replenishing milk, despite the fact that the two stores are geographically proximal. However, despite the intention of buying milk being more important, the novel intention may receive more planning, elaboration, and visuospatial imagination at intention formation. Consequently, the novel intention may have more episodic details associated with it than a relatively routine or habitual intention.

As it relates to imagination, Johnson, Kounios, and Reeder (1994) have shown that imagined items are more available at earlier processing deadlines during retrieval than comparable material experienced as pictures. That is, less time is needed to retrieve and render accurate judgments for imagined as compared to perceived material. If intentions have more imagined details and other records of cognitive operations than retrospective memories, then they may be relatively more accessible (or revive more quickly) than retrospective memories. Consistent with this hypothesis, intention related material is processed more quickly than the identical material that lacks any intentionality at all (Freeman & Ellis, 2003; Goschke & Kuhl, 1993, 1996; Marsh, Hicks, & Bink, 1998; Marsh, Hicks, & Bryan, 1999). This outcome has been dubbed the intention-superiority effect, and as mentioned earlier, appears to manifest itself with both laboratory-based and real-world intentions (Maylor et al., 2000). According to this analysis, novel intentions may be fulfilled more often than routine ones because their mental representations in memory are more elaborate. Although we know of no empirical data comparing novel to routine intentions, Marsh et al. (1998) did find that commitments (appointments) went uncompleted only 17% of the time whereas more mundane (routine) intentions went uncompleted approximately 38% of the time.

One aspect of forming an event-based intention is that part of the imagined conditions will be a specification of the cue (or category to which a cue belongs) that will signal intention retrieval and fulfilling the intention. For example, the intention to buy cereal may be linked with the thought that passing the grocery store will serve as a good cue to complete the intention. McDaniel, Guynn, Einstein, and Breneiser (2004) have demonstrated that cue–action pairings that are highly related tend to evoke fulfilling the intention more automatically as compared with those whose cue–action associations are less related (Marsh, Hicks, Cook, Hansen, & Pallos, 2003). In their laboratory experiments, *spaghetti* serves as an automatic cue to fulfill the intention to respond *sauce*, whereas the same cue requires more processing resources to remember to respond *steeple*. As applied to the cereal example, seeing the grocery store, which may be associated with many other intentions (past and present) and consequently, may serve as a poor cue relative to seeing the dry cleaners and remembering to retrieve one's laundry.

Aside from McDaniel, Guynn, Einstein, and Breneiser (2004) clear prediction that strength of association between cue and target activity is one predictor of event-based remembering, we are asserting that the relative fan of target activities that have been (or are currently) associated with a cue may also predict intention completion. According to either a cue overload account (Watkins & Watkins, 1975) or its extension to the fan effect in memory (Anderson, 1974; Anderson & Reder, 1999), cues may become less effective at retrieving prospective memories in much the same way that they become less effective at retrieving retrospective memories. We know of no empirical tests of this prediction, but one could imagine asking research participants to form intentions to novel cues over the course of an experiment and compare that performance with cues that have been used repeatedly in the past (for a potential paradigm that may be easily adapted to this end, see Einstein, McDaniel, Smith, & Shaw, 1998).

The strength of the cue to the associated action is only one of several potentially important variables involved with intention formation. The specificity of the cue also determines performance, with more specific cues eliciting higher fulfillment rates than less specific cues (Ellis & Milne, 1996; McDaniel & Einstein, 1993). For example, the intention to respond to specific category exemplars (e.g., *table, chair*) results in better prospective memory than intending to respond to exemplars from the category of *furniture*. According to one theory, activation spreads (as in the fan effect described in the preceding paragraph) to many category exemplars in the ill-defined (category) case, dividing activation among many exemplars, thereby making each cue relatively less efficient than having studied fewer, specific cues (Ellis & Milne, 1996). By contrast, we know of no investigations that have examined well- versus ill-specified *actions* to the same event-based cue. However, real-world intentions do vary along this dimension as well. For example, one may plan to purchase *chicken* at the grocery store for today's dinner or one may plan on purchasing *something* for the same meal. Whether driving past the grocery serves as a better or worse retrieval cue will depend on the nature of the representation left in memory after encoding these two slightly different types of intentions. A well-specified intention may be recorded more quickly, and hence, receive less elaboration than perhaps considering the possibilities of what to buy when forming the intention about dinner in the *something* case. Although alternative predictions could be constructed easily, the point is that virtually nothing is known about the mental representation of well- versus ill-defined intentions and this could be a productive area of inquiry to pursue.

When considering the quality of memorial representations, one important source of information for theoretical analysis is special populations. We will consider just one briefly, namely, performance of healthy older adults, but prospective memory has been studied in children (Ceci & Bronfenbrenner, 1985; Kvavilashvili, Messer, & Ebdon, 2001) and in neuropsychologically impaired populations as well (Maylor, Smith, Della Sala, & Logie, 2002; McDaniel, Glisky, Rubin, Guynn, & Routhieaux, 1999; West, Herndon, & Ross-Munroe, 2000). Some debate exists as to whether older adults have worse prospective memory as compared with younger adults (Maylor, 1996, 1998). Moreover, highly educated, high-functioning older adults may have no deficit at all (Cherry & LeCompte, 1999). However, their self-reports indicate that completing intentions is one of the most challenging changes in cognitive performance that older adults face in aging (Park & Kidder, 1996). Older adults have trouble in binding information into integrated representations, as for example with contextual details (Chalfonte & Johnson, 1996; Ferguson, Hashtroudi, & Johnson, 1992). Unless they are given a lot of environmental support at the time of recollection, they generally have poorer retrospective memory performance (e.g., Craik & Anderson, 1999; Park & Shaw, 1992). Because their information processing speed is compromised, cues that otherwise would be sufficient for younger adults do not cue retrospective memories as readily for older adults. As it relates to encoding intentions, older adults may fail to elaborate sufficiently at intention formation, or elaborate only as well as they have over the course of their lives, not realizing that they need more elaborate representations to compensate for slower and less efficient information uptake. According to this line of reasoning, a deficit in prospective memory in older adults can be partially attributed to declarative representations that are too sparse to easily evoke the intention from memory at the time the activity could be performed. Consistent with this line of reasoning, more elaborate encoding associated with implementation intentions raised older adults performance (Chasteen et al., 2001).

C.   SUMMARY OF ANALYSIS FOR ENCODING

Although prospective memories need not have more elaborate mental representations after initial encoding as compared to retrospective memories, the analysis we have done suggests that they might. The act of generation, the relation to ones' self, and cognitive processes associated with imagination, are some retrospective memory principles that converge on that conclusion. Although we have suggested some possible avenues of inquiry, many more retrospective memory paradigms are available that could be used to probe the nature of the mental representation left after initially forming an intention. Some of these include reaction time latencies, output order in free recall, interitem recall latencies, clustering measures, memory accrual rate measures such as response-signal paradigms, and so forth, that can be used to complement the standard dependent variable of whether an intention was successfully completed.

V.   Retrieving Intentions

Many principles of retrospective memory could inform how retrieving prospective memories at opportune times enhances their rate of completion. Because there has been very little effort to tie prospective and retrospective memory more tightly together, applying any of these could provide valuable directions for further analysis and inquiry. In this section, we consider just a few of these principles in order to provide what will hopefully serve as some guideposts for this much-needed analysis. These retrospective memory principles include transfer of appropriate processing, transient states of accessibility (sometimes due to cues and their association strength to intentions), the amount of attention or degree of monitoring as found in studies of divided attention or contributions of executive resources to retrieval, and the time spent retrieving (or the number of retrieval attempts) as in studies of classic hypermnesia.

A.   RETRIEVAL CUES

Once an intention is recorded into memory, it should behave much like other retrospective memories that possess similar distributions of qualitative details and contextual associations. According to our analysis, a retrospective and a prospective memory that are otherwise equivalent in their representations should be equally well recollected, say, when presented with the same cue. The power of that cue is going to depend on the degree to which it is noticed in the environment and the degree to which it uniquely specifies the memory that "needs" to be retrieved on that occasion. As discussed earlier, the strength of the association between the cue and target action in prospective memory tasks can be established at encoding, determined through the amount of practice retrieving it as would be the case of having a habitual or routinized intention, or may be changed over the retention interval (as will be discussed in a later section).

For the present purposes, differences in the effectiveness of cues to evoke either a prospective or a retrospective memory will be determined not only by the strength of the association between the two, but also by standard transfer appropriate effects. Regarding the latter, if a cue is processed at retrieval in the same way as it was processed during learning (as when an intention was formed), then retrieval will be better than a case in which the two processing episodes are different (Roediger, Weldon, & Challis, 1989). Consistent with this interpretation, McDaniel, Robinson-Riegler, and Einstein (1998) demonstrated that a homograph (e.g., bat or chest) that is encoded with one meaning serves as an exceptionally poor prospective memory cue if the meaning was changed during test. Similarly, a cue studied as a picture versus a word triggers remembering an intention more often if the cue occurs in the same format (picture versus word) as it did during intention formation. In the same research report, McDaniel et al. (1998), also demonstrated standard environmental context effects (albeit marginally significant). Intentions learned in one environment (a particular room) had a higher completion rate if the testing phase was carried out in the same room than in a different one. Consequently, at least with event-based prospective memory, the extra cues conferred by the environment appear to function in the same beneficial way as they do for retrospective memory (Smith & Vela, 2001; Wickens, 1987).

McDaniel et al. (2004) and McDaniel and Einstein (2000) argue that cues that are bound tightly with intended actions are retrieved reflexively and automatically, in much the same way that Moscovitch (1992) argues that strong associations between retrospective memories are bound in a reflexive, hippocampal neural circuit (see also Einstein, McDaniel, Thomas, Mayfield, Shank, Morrisette, & Brenesier, 2005). All of the cases just discussed of remembering either an intention or a retrospective memory are instances of what Ebbinghaus (1885) labeled *involuntary* retrieval insofar as no strategic search of memory needed to be conducted. However, cues can evoke more conscious search strategies for either retrospective or prospective memories. In the latter case, Einstein and McDaniel (1996) have argued for a conscious search component in their noticing plus search model. By their account, noticing occurs because of heightened familiarity or a discrepancy in familiarity between the cue and the background material in which it is encountered, and this familiarity difference elicits a conscious search for what the cue might signify (see McDaniel et al., 2004). For this reason, highly unusual cues, those that are distinctive from the background, and those of low frequency in their class of items, increase event-based prospective memory because they ensure that a cue is noticed and a search of memory for their meaning ensues (McDaniel & Einstein, 1993). Therefore, cues need not always invoke automatic or involuntary retrieval, but rather, can invoke conscious and voluntary retrieval strategies. This is true for both retrospective and prospective memories.

Most people realize that in everyday life odd retrieval cues (i.e., those that are distinctive from their background) substantially increase fulfilling intentions. In fact, such cues form the basis of standard mnemonic techniques for completing everyday tasks (see Harris, 1980; Park, Smith, & Cavanaugh, 1990). People will tie strings around their fingers, write on their hands, turn their watch so that the face is toward their wrist, and so forth as cues to completing intentions. Such strategies work because they invoke a conscious (voluntary) search for the intention. A strategic search through memory is the basis for improving retrospective memory as well. Numerous studies of autobiographical memory have investigated the efficacy of different kinds of retrieval cues for obtaining accurate reports of events that have occurred in one's past. These have included the Galton cuing method (1883), Linton's (1982), and Wagenaar's (1986) self-study of their memory abilities, and a host of applied and clinical measures for improving memory reports such as the cognitive interview technique (Memon & Higham, 1999).

B. ACCESSIBILITY VERSUS AVAILABILITY

Similar to retrospective memory, the failure of a cue to evoke spontaneously a memory of the intended action or to cause a conscious search for its significance does not mean the intention has been forgotten. In many studies of prospective memory, research participants are asked to recall what cue(s) should have served to remind them to complete intentions. Despite failing to respond to them earlier, when queried in this direct way people have near perfect memory for what they should have done. This outcome is exactly what would be expected from theories and data on retrospective memory. Free recall performance is worse than cued recall, and cued recall is generally worse than recognition in which a "copy cue" of the memory itself is presented. As Tulving and Pearlstone (1966) argued long ago, retrieval failure in the free or cued recall cases does not indicate forgetting, but instead highlights a distinction between memory *availability* and memory *accessibility*. A memory can be temporarily inaccessible because the person does not self-generate the correct retrieval cues, does not engage in the correct search strategy (or does so too quickly), or because the environmental cue is not processed correctly or deeply enough as might happen under cognitive distraction or divided attention. In these cases, the memory is available to be recollected, but is not drawn into working memory to be inspected, and therefore, labeled a failed recollection at that moment in time.

As it relates to inaccessibility of prospective memories, we are aware of only two studies that systematically examined the fate of unique cues, which once missed, are presented later for a second opportunity for completing the intention (Marsh, Hicks, Cook, & Mayhorn, in press; Marsh, Hicks, Hancock, & Munsayac, 2002). Although it was not our focus, such an experimental paradigm could be informative about the variables that make prospective memories temporarily inaccessible under some conditions but not others. The same underlying idea was expressed when Maylor (1996; see also West & Craik, 1999) developed metrics of remembering and forgetting functions for event-based prospective memory. In brief, these metrics assess successful prospective remembering following failures to respond to cues, and they assess forgetting following successes to respond to cues (i.e., remembering). Therefore, together the functions are consistent with the idea that, like retrospective memories, prospective memories shift between being inaccessible and accessible despite being available to memory under more ideal cuing conditions (e.g., a direct query).

Although it has been couched in other terms, the accessibility of intentions has been studied as a function of task demands and task characteristics, albeit mainly with event-based intentions. One of the ongoing debates in prospective memory is whether retrieval is ever attention-free and automatic. McDaniel et al. (2004) have argued that salient cues, strong cue–action associations, and ongoing tasks that focus attention on the relevant features of cues will cause automatic (involuntary) retrieval of the intention even under extreme cognitive load. Marsh and Hicks (1998) demonstrated that dividing attention with tasks tapping central executive resources drastically reduced event-based performance, whereas divided attention tasks that were more peripheral had no effect at all (see also Einstein, Smith, McDaniel, & Shaw, 1997). But, this result has not been consistently obtained.

In a similar vein, Marsh, Hancock, and Hicks (2002) argued that task switching within an ongoing activity makes the task more demanding in terms of the central executive resources that are required as compared with ongoing activities that do not switch. Consistent with this interpretation, they found worse cue detection in tasks that switched randomly between the judgments being made as compared with those that did not switch at all. Although there is no agreement on whether retrieving an intention in the face of a cue is more akin to recognition or recall, the results of dividing attention and demanding ongoing activities in prospective memory tasks do display a striking resemblance to dividing attention in standard retrospective memory tasks.

In those retrospective memory studies, cognitive load unequivocally decreases free recall and cued recall (Baddeley, Lewis, Eldridge, & Thompson, 1984; Craik, Govoni, Naveh-Benjamin, & Anderson, 1996). The debate has concerned recognition memory which was, at one time, believed to be a privileged process that was immune to disruption (Craik et al., 1996) but has since been shown that it can be reduced by divided attention (Hicks & Marsh, 2000; Lozito & Mulligan, in press). One noteworthy point here is that cognitive load appears to reduce both prospective and retrospective memory, and it may do so because of the cognitive components that are shared by both tasks. Another notable point is that cognitive load never eliminates recollection for prospective and retrospective information, it only reduces memory for it. Therefore, finding reductions in either retrospective or prospective memory due to divided attention does not mean that, say, executive resources are always recruited in every instance of prospective or retrospective memory retrieval. Rather, such reductions indicate that some optimal level of those executive resources benefit retrieval but is not necessarily required because some (reduced) level of prospective and retrospective recollection occurs anyway. From this perspective, Jacoby's (1991, 1998) arguments that no memory task is process pure insofar as it recruits both conscious/voluntary and unconscious/involuntary processes seems to apply to both prospective and retrospective memories.

C.   RESOURCE SHARING AND TASK CHARACTERISTICS

The debate about what resources are required for retrieving intentions often examines the speed with which an ongoing task can be performed when an intention is active versus when it is not. Some researchers have found that maintenance of an intention slows ongoing task latencies (Marsh et al., 2003;

Smith, 2003). Although the intention could be actively maintained in working memory through maintenance rehearsal, this interpretation would be inconsistent with prospective memory performance that is usually far below ceiling performance. Therefore, the slowing observed when an intention is active must have some other locus. Because the slowing is sometimes positively correlated with prospective memory performance, it must have some functional effect on cue detection and/or intention retrieval. One interpretation is that attentional resources are being shared by maintaining the intention and so fewer are available to complete the ongoing cognitive activity. Marsh et al. (2003), describe this trade-off as setting attentional allocation policies differently when an intention is active as compared to when it is not (Marsh, Hicks, & Cook, 2005). By this account, faster ongoing task latencies should straddle cues that are missed, and slower latencies should covary around the time cues are detected and the intention is retrieved (West & Craik, 1999).

According to this analysis, the momentary accessibility or inaccessibility of cues to evoke intentions within a given individual could be accounted for by variability in how well people can maintain their attentional allocation policies over time. To the extent that attention varies toward an activity in which cues are embedded, successful recollections will follow failed recollections, and thus, Maylor's (1996) remembering and forgetting metrics may actually be indexing how well people can maintain their attentional allocation policies. Clearly, further work needs to investigate how her measures relate to task interference caused by holding an intention, as well how they relate to more specific latencies that straddle successful versus failed retrievals. Any further discussion of the resource trade-off issues related to these effects is somewhat beyond the scope of this paper. However, the overarching connection to retrospective memory is that increased attention and time spent retrieving often improve retrospective memory. For example, in the SAM model of memory people sample memory until they reach some subjective stopping point (Gillund & Shiffrin, 1984; Raaijmakers & Shiffrin, 1981). People who sample more, retrieve more. In the hypermnesia literature, people who are given multiple retrieval trials recollect more unique material from the learning episode (Payne, 1987; Roediger & Payne, 1985). In response-signal procedures where a signal indicates that a memory judgment must be rendered, memory performance is worse with shorter lengths of time to inspect memory (Johnson et al., 1994; Reed, 1973). In sum, increased attention and time are beneficial to both prospective and retrospective memory.

Task characteristics also affect prospective and retrospective memory in similar ways. In the older work on transfer appropriate processing, the cognitive operations performed on material at test fostered retrospective recollection if they matched the cognitive operations used at encoding

(Morris, Bransford, & Franks, 1977). For example, semantic testing yielded better memory for material studied under semantic orienting tasks than phonetic (e.g., rhyming) ones. Likewise, phonetic tests (identifying rhyming words) yielded better performance when material was processed phonetically at study as compared with when it was processed semantically. A similar outcome occurs in prospective memory (Darby & Maylor, 1998; Marsh, Hicks, & Hancock, 2000). When intentions and their related cues are semantic in nature (e.g., finding exemplars of fruits) completion is better when the ongoing processing in which the cues are embedded is semantic in nature (e.g., rating material for pleasantness) than when the processing focuses people on orthographic characteristics of the material. The reverse is true insofar as when the intention is orthographic (finding palindromes, or finding words with double letters in them), then an orthographic processing task results in better prospective memory than a semantic one (Marsh et al., 2005). Therefore, in terms of ongoing processing characteristics, the retrieval of intentions appears to follow the same regularities as the retrieval of information that has no associated intentionality at all.

Much of the foregoing discussion has focused on event-based prospective memory and little has been explicitly said about retrieving time-based intentions. There are at least two good reasons for this omission. First, not much is known about time-based prospective memory because very little research has investigated it. Consequently, there are very few empirical findings that can be used to link it to the retrospective memory literature. Second, once a time-based intention is formed, there are (ostensibly) no cues in the environment to remind the person to monitor the passage of time (otherwise, the intention would be a hybrid event-based and time-based intention, and we have purposefully side-stepped considering such intentions herein). Rather, successful time-based memory has been characterized as requiring significantly more self-initiated processing during a retention interval (Craik, 1986; Einstein et al., 1995; but see Hicks et al. (2005), for a counter-claim). In fact, the only (now somewhat antiquated) model of time-based prospective memory is the test-wait-test-exit (TWTE) model (Harris & Wilkins, 1982). The notion here is that people periodically test to see if the required time has elapsed (or the exact time to engage in activity has arrived), and if not, they cycle through a period of waiting and testing until it has. The exact nature of what causes this self-initiated retrieval is relatively unknown. However, our hypothesis is that it is driven by a set of cognitive processes that are more characteristic of those that occur over a retention interval, rather than a set of processes specifically classified as intention retrieval (of the ilk that have been discussed in this section). Therefore, we hold in abeyance any further consideration of time-based intentions for the next section of this paper.

D. Summary of Analysis for Retrieval

Retrieval of intentions appears to be governed by many of the same basic principles as standard retrospective memories. As McDaniel et al. (2004) have recognized, intentions are drawn to mind by both involuntary (spontaneous) and voluntary (conscious search) retrieval; and specifying the conditions that foster each type of retrieval has only just begun (a more recent treatment can be found in Einstein et al., 2005). Improvements in fulfilling intentions have been observed when the retrieval operations reinstate the cognitive processing used during encoding, and decrements have been observed when attention is divided and in certain populations that often mirror laboratory-induced divided attention such as older adults, schizophrenics, and anxiety patients. In addition, task demands that focus attention on relevant features of potential cues increases recollection of intentions. Much remains to be learned about what causes temporary inaccessibility of memories for intentions, but we believe that many of the answers to these questions probably lie somewhere near the cross-roads of where memory and attention interface.

VI. Changes Over the Retention Interval

In this section, we consider issues related to the fate of prospective and retrospective memories over a retention interval. The processes that take place after memory formation represent an interesting amalgam of the cognitive processes that take place both at encoding and at retrieval. Consequently, we chose to discuss them subsequent to presenting arguments for both encoding and retrieval phenomena. Our rationale in this section is simple and derives itself from the basic principles of retrospective memory: Memories that are revisited become refreshed and strengthened in the process of reconsidering them; and, they also can be changed and distorted by these same episodes of recollection as well. Consider the case of retrospective memory for certain autobiographical events. Retelling the event has a certain probability of changing it. Details that were never present in the original memory are added, details that others resonate to during the retelling process take on new salience and prominence, parts are totally forgotten and become confabulated with inference on the part of the teller, the listener's inferences can become the teller's inferences, and so forth. The original event need not be particularly salient for these processes to occur, as for example, in discussing one's memory for attending a colloquium. On the other hand, highly salient events, such as those that rate as flashbulb memories, do not immunize the memory representation against these distortions of random strengthening and confabulation that occur to the component parts of an episode recorded in memory (Conway, 1995). We propose that any changes in the representation of a prospective memory are potentially subject to the same strengthening and distortion processes that apply to retrospective memories.[3]

A. EXPANDED RETRIEVAL PRACTICE

One standard finding in the retrospective memory literature is that spaced practice results in more durable memory representations than massed practice (Bahrick & Phelps, 1987; Ebbinghaus, 1885; Glenberg, 1976). This principle applies to all manner of materials including episodic as well as procedural information. As a simple example, material that is studied for 1 min in each of three successive hours (i.e., spaced learning) will be better retained on the following day than the same material studied for 3 min at either the first or third hours (i.e., massed learning). There are many theories for why this result occurs, but they all converge on the two ideas that spaced practice increases the variability of contextual cues associated with the memory (hence providing more retrieval cues at test), and that more attention is devoted to seemingly novel material in the spaced learning case as opposed to a learner habituating to the material in the massed learning case (for one discussion of novelty monitors in memory see Metcalfe, 1991; and for a slightly different approach see Malmberg & Shiffrin, 2005).

A related finding is that practice retrieving is more effective for retention than another study episode (Bjork, 1988). Retrieval practice occurs when a person attempts to recall information on a subsequent occasion rather than engaging in another study episode. For example, in vocabulary learning, practice at retrieving the definition for a word is more beneficial than another study episode with both the word and the definition together. The spaced practice and retrieval practice principles have been combined to argue for the benefits of expanded retrieval practice. In this case, retrospective memory is enhanced by progressively lengthening the time between attempted retrieval episodes (Landauer & Bjork, 1978). Although both the spaced learning and retrieval practice principles have been found to benefit retrospective memory representations, we propose that they will have similar influences on prospective memories as well.

---

[3] For the purposes of the present chapter, we will remain agnostic about the actual cognitive processes that "change" memories. We certainly do not mean to imply that new memories overwrite old ones, but rather, that additional information is added that was not part of the original memory and information is also lost over time. The specifics of how memory is changed (e.g., new traces are added and are retrieved in addition to or instead of the target memory) will vary according to one's preferred theory of memory.

In one study, people recorded that they naturally reviewed and rehearsed their intentions about 18 times per day (Marsh et al., 1998). Assuming that one or more of these rehearsals involves retrieval practice (say in the absence of a daily planner or a palm pilot-type device), and further, that all of these rehearsals involve spaced practice of revisiting the intentions after their formation, then intentions may be very strongly represented in memory. Moreover, the phenomena related to spaced practice and retrieval practice argue for better memory under these conditions, not that massed practice or another study episode does not also improve memory as compared with not revisiting the memory at all. Our point is that prospective memories may, on average, be recalled and rehearsed more often than standard retrospective memories. Each of these revisitations to a previously established intention has the potential to change its distribution of characteristics as discussed earlier, or more generally, to strengthen its memory representation even further.

The strengthening of prospective memories in this way is consistent with some researchers' beliefs that intentions reside in memory with an above-baseline level of activation or can be revived from baseline more quickly than equivalent material that has no associated intentionality (Freeman & Ellis, 2003; Goschke & Kuhl, 1993; Marsh et al., 1998; Maylor et al., 2000).[4] Based on the foregoing analysis, there may be no a priori reason to believe that prospective memories have this special above-baseline status at the time of their formation, but rather, any special status of heightened activation may accrue over time as a function of their strengthening due to revisiting and rehearsal processes. Because this is a brand new interpretation of the intention-superiority effect that has hitherto been overlooked, it warrants some careful empirical scrutiny before being considered a viable alternative theoretical explanation. Moreover, Freeman and Ellis (2003) have made the argument that the intention-superiority effect may represent deeper, motoric encoding (as in the subject-performed task literature), and this new interpretation needs to be weighed against our new interpretation as well.

Just as explicit memory for material improves with more rehearsal, we are arguing that the same occurs with prospective memories as well. Under the assumption that retrospective memories for events are rehearsed less

---

[4] The astute reader will notice that throughout we have from time to time appealed to a strength theory of memory. Of course, strength theories qua activation have been refuted in cognitive psychology because what constitutes strong versus weak is going to depend on a host of factors, including the factors that prevail on a particular retrieval occasion. Thus, our appeal to strength acknowledges that what makes one memory strong or weak depends on many factors; but for simplicity one can speak about strong versus weak in a generic sense.

frequently than prospective memories, lengthening retention intervals may hurt recollection of retrospective memories and improve retention of prospective memories. For example, if the average person reviews their plans 18 times a day (Marsh et al., 1998), then intentions (or subsets of them) will be rehearsed frequently. When factoring in that intentions are often spread across multiple days, they may receive extraordinary amounts of rehearsal. By contrast, retrospective memories are probably rehearsed much less frequently. Finding such an ironic effect depends on differential rehearsal of prospective and retrospective memories over a retention interval, but the assumption seems reasonable given that the average individual has more events to record as retrospective memories than they do intended activities. In fact, event-based prospective memory has been observed to *increase* over longer retention intervals as compared with retrospective memory (Hicks et al., 2000). In addition, prospective memory was also observed in the Hicks et al. (2000) report to increase with an increasing number of intervening task changes during a retention interval of a fixed duration. For example, a retention interval of 15 min with one intervening task resulted in worse prospective memory than a 15 min interval with 5 embedded 3-min tasks.

One explanation for this outcome is that there may be a cognitive tendency to rehearse one's near-term plans upon completion of one task and prior to commencing the next task. In other words, the act of planning one's next task may bring with it a consideration of the possible options in terms of one's unfulfilled intentions. For some people this may be a natural mental activity, and for the truly organized individual, it may involve consulting an external list. For now, we limit consideration to the former, mental activity. Consistent with our interpretation of mentally refreshing prospective memories is one research report that investigated workers in an office setting (Sellen et al., 1997). The workers were asked to press electronic badges whenever they were thinking about their intentions and the badges recorded (among many other things) people's physical locations. Many of these natural prospective memory rehearsals occurred in the corridors, stairwells, kitchen areas, and rest rooms as opposed to when people where behind their desks working. Together, studies of Marsh et al. (2000) and Sellen et al. (1997) provide fairly convincing evidence for quite frequent natural rehearsal and revisiting of prospective memories after their formation. We hypothesize that each of these rehearsals provides an opportunity to strengthen or change the representation of the intention.

B. CHANGES ASSOCIATED WITH RETRIEVAL

The cognitive processes that cause people to review and rehearse their intentions are unclear at this time. We believe that many of these episodes involve self-initiated searches of memory for near-term goals that need to be completed. As just mentioned, the completion of one task may automatically serve as a cue to consult memory for the next task that can be reasonably accomplished given one's constraints at the time. If this indeed occurs, virtually nothing is known about the factors that mediate such cognitive processes; and therefore, this is one issue that deserves serious empirical inquiry. In doing so, however, one issue that would have to be considered carefully is the fact that measuring self-initiated rehearsal processes requires people to make an overt record that they had done so. The record keeping is by itself a prospective memory task, and so one would be studying a process (prospective memory for intentions) using another layer of that process (prospective memory to record). Nevertheless, not all rehearsals of intentions involve self-initiated retrieval. As discussed earlier, people set up salient external reminders and odd retrieval cues to ensure that they complete intended activities. A note taped to a dash board or a medicine bottle in the middle of the stove will serve as an explicit retrieval cue. If the intention cannot be fulfilled immediately, the cue will nonetheless engage the cognitive processes that refresh and revise the memory representation of the intended activity.

For example, suppose the note on the dash board serves to remind one to retrieve clothes from the dry cleaner. If one cannot do it at the time of seeing the note, one is likely to reflect on when the next opportunity might present itself (e.g., on the way home from work, the following morning before work, etc.). People report that much of their cognitive processing about intentions involves reprioritizing and postponing their intentions to later time frames than initially planned (Marsh et al., 1998). Such episodes not only strengthen the representation of an intention but also elaborate it by increasing its complexity and associations to other material or other intentions (as would be the case if one decides to replenish a dwindling supply of pet food after retrieving the clothes from the cleaner). Such instances of elaboration may increase the retrieval sensitivity (to use Mäntylä's, 1993, term) such that the next encounter with the retrieval cue (note on dash board) serves as an even more effective reminder to complete the intention. Even aside from external reminders, normal reprioritization and postponement are activities that occur over a retention interval that may increase later completion of an intention by changing the representation of a prospective memory.

However, there are limits on the effectiveness of external reminders. If the intention goes unfulfilled in the face of repeated exposure to the retrieval cue, then people tend to habituate to the cue and it loses its effectiveness (Vortac, Edwards, & Manning, 1995). Therefore, an inverted-U shaped function may operate in which initial exposures to retrieval cues increase the probability of completing an intention through rehearsal and elaboration of the prospective memory, but there exists some point beyond which reminders decrease the probability of intention fulfillment (or at least no longer assist in completion). Very little is known about the temporal or frequency characteristics that affect the utility of reminders. But, we suspect that just as the efficacy of spaced practice depends on both temporal and frequency characteristics, so too will these factors mediate reminder effectiveness (for retrospective memory, see Glenberg, 1976).

Only several studies of reminders exist, and these reports appear somewhat inconsistent with each other. On the one hand, reminders that contain both the activity and the context in which it is to be performed were more effective than reminders about one or the other of just the activity or when it is to be performed (Guynn, McDaniel, & Einstein, 1998). On the other hand, a post-it note or a blue dot on a screen prevents forgetting an intention (Einstein & McDaniel, 1990; McDaniel, Einstein, Graham, & Rall, 2004). Obviously, the cognitive consequences of reminders that occur during a retention interval are not completely understood. Further research needs to examine how the strength of the memory representation is affected by both externally-cued and internally-cued (self-initiated) recollection of intentions over a retention interval.

In this regard, one fruitful course might be to adapt the reaction time paradigm used in assessing the intention-superiority effect. A straightforward prediction is that strengthening occurs (and reaction time declines) as a function of the number of reminders. In addition to assessing whether such a function exists, such experimentation would allow one to test an alternative theoretical stance that frequency of reminders is irrelevant to intention completion but their presence versus absence is the critical variable (Ellis, Kvavilashvili, & Milne, 1999). In this case, strengthening would be a function of one reminder and additional reminders have no net effect on the reaction time variable at all. Another course of experimentation should also investigate how partial-match cues serve as reminders and what consequences such retrievals have on the memorial representation of intentions (Taylor, Marsh, Hicks, & Hancock, 2003; West & Craik, 1999). For example, walking down a particular aisle of a grocery store may trigger the intention to purchase salad dressing, but if that store does not carry one's preferred brand, then the cue is only a partial match (i.e., a lure) because the context does not allow one to complete the intention of placing the bottle in one's shopping cart. Partial-match cues (or lures) also have the potential to invoke slowing in the ongoing cognitive activity (Marsh et al., 2003; Smith, 2003). For example, just as possessing an intention can slow ongoing tasks in some cases, seeing a coworker to whom a message must be delivered but who is engaged in conversation might invoke a strategy to monitor for when the conversation has ended. Therefore, the consequences of processing lures are not known in terms of changing: (a) the mental representation of an intention, (b) ongoing task processing, and (c) ultimate completion rate of intentions. Because Taylor et al. found better event-based prospective memory after encountering lures, we suspect that understanding partial-match cues could be a productive avenue for further research.

As a final thought on strengthening, very little is known about the differences between novel and habitual intentions. Habitual intentions may already be well represented in memory as compared to novel tasks. Consequently, processing habitual versus novel intentions could behave in an analogous fashion to processing high versus low-frequency words. For example, the increment to activation of low-frequency representations is much greater and dissipates much more slowly than the identical exposure to a high-frequency representation (Jacoby & Dallas, 1981; Mandler, 1980). If the analogy is accurate, then novel intentions may accrue more activation when reprocessed and that activation may dissipate more slowly as compared with retrieving the desire to complete a more habitual task. Obviously, this idea could be tested in a number of ways, but two of these ways include measuring revival rates of the two memories at varying time points subsequent to explicit reminders and/or measuring cue detection at such time points.

C.   Working Memory and Rapid Forgetting

Similarities also exist between retrospective and prospective memories in how easily they can be displaced from working memory once they are retrieved. For example, the sight of a favorite pen, or the pen holder it was retrieved from, can momentarily draw into consciousness a retrospective memory of the occasion on which it was received as a gift. Ongoing cognitive tasks and one's other thoughts can, however, relegate that memory back outside the focus of current attention (see Cowan, 1995). The identical phenomenon can happen with prospective memories as well. Upon seeing a cue to accomplish an intention (e.g., remove clothes from the dryer, take medication, etc.), or having a self-initiated thought to do so, one can initiate the activity. What was previously an intention that was out of awareness, now becomes an "intention in action" (Dalla Barba, 1993; Searle, 1983). In the course of fulfilling it, unfortunately, other thoughts and activities can derail its successful completion. One example to which every reader should be able to relate is standing in one's kitchen (or other room) and not remembering what caused you to go there in the first place because the intention has been momentarily forgotten. Therefore, forgetting an intention can occur over exceptionally short retention intervals and it occurs for the same reasons that other thoughts and memories are squeezed out of working memory, namely, limited capacity (Kahneman, 1973).

Einstein, McDaniel, Manzi, Cochran, and Baker (2000) have captured this phenomenon with a laboratory analog in which participants must wait a very short period of time (e.g., 10–30 s) before being able to execute the intended action (see also McDaniel et al., 2004). They have discovered that activity-filled delays reduce completion as compared to delays that allow constant rehearsal. They also found that interruptions that focus attention on an entirely different activity displace the intention thereby drastically reducing completion of the intended activity (Cook & Marsh, submitted for publication). In addition, healthy older adults appear more prone to such rapid forgetting of intentions than younger adults.

D. RETENTION INTERVALS IN TIME-BASED INTENTIONS

When considering just how rapidly forgetting can occur for intentions in action, it is somewhat amazing that people perform as well as they do at many time-based prospective memory tasks. As mentioned earlier, one older model of time-based intention completion involves a sequence of test–wait cycles until the time arrives to complete an activity (e.g., attend a meeting, remove food from the oven). The waiting periods between intermittent tests (as in checking a clock) are justifiably classified as retention intervals and test periods are justifiably called instances of refreshing and rehearsing the time-based intention. As mentioned in an earlier section, very little research has directly compared time-based and event-based prospective tasks (but see Kidder et al, 1997; Kliegel et al., 2001; Sellen et al., 1997) so it is unclear if the instances of recollection that occur in time checking might have the same effect on time-based prospective memories as we have speculated occurs for other intentions. However, our intuition is that time-checking is usually prompted by self-initiated processes (as opposed to external reminders like alarms), and consequently, it is a manifestation of a deeper underlying set of cognitive processes. In this sense, time checking provides a window on a complicated cognitive process, but it is not the process itself that scientists should be primarily interested in.

Time-based prospective memories are probably completed with the aid of internal clocks, which estimate the passage of time over the retention interval (Block & Zakay, 1997; Friedman, 1993). These clocks are constantly recalibrated to external time keeping devices (Ceci & Bronfenbrenner, 1985) and this is one aspect of time-checking behavior. In addition to the influences on internal time keeping accuracy, time-based prospective memories may be accomplished with reference to one's schema for a typical day. A dentist appointment or a veterinary appointment would require changing one's activities for a morning or an afternoon. Such consequential disruptions to one's day may also aid in completing time-based memories (Ellis, 1988).

However, none of these influences are informative about how self-initiated reminders occur for time-based intentions or whether they change the mental representation of the intention in similar ways. One simple account is that the self-reminding that occurs is no different from those remindings that occur for other sorts of intentions such as wanting to remember to place paid bills in the outgoing mail. In this case, the amount of elaboration or reflection that occurs will be function of the same factors that determine how much one reflects on other intentions.

A quick clock check could be associated with verifying that a critical time has not arrived in which case any prospective intention associated with it may not receive a great deal of rehearsal or elaboration. Or, a clock check may be associated with contemplating what can be accomplished before a critical time will arrive, in which case a decision to complete a different activity first will associate its completion with commencing the time-based intention. In this sense, time-based intentions may receive extended rehearsal just like other prospective and retrospective memories. All of this is to say that the fate of memories over a retention interval has not been studied very extensively, and the general lack of research on time-based prospective memory makes speculation even more difficult.

E.   Canceling Intentions

There is, of course, one fundamental activity that can occur for prospective memories that cannot occur for retrospective memories during a retention interval. That is, the intention associated with a prospective memory can be canceled (or become impossible to complete). Only two research reports have investigated canceling an intention and both of these were conducted to investigate the intention-superiority effect (Marsh et al., 1998, 1999). In these studies, canceling an intention eliminated the heightened activation level that the prospective memory previously enjoyed. In this sense, a canceled prospective memory came to resemble a retrospective memory. Because no one has measured the long-term recollection of completed, canceled, and unfulfilled intentions, doing so may provide some insight into the dynamics of the forgetting functions for intention-related material as compared with neutral material that never had any associated intentionality.

F.   Summary of Analysis of Retention Intervals

We have argued that intentions are periodically refreshed over retention intervals just as autobiographical memories are. And once retrieved, they can be elaborated on or very rapidly forgotten, depending on one's current mental activities. The retrieval of intentions may act like spaced retrieval of episodic material (like facts or skills) and serve to heighten the strength and durability of its representation. Perhaps repeated retrievals over a retention interval explain why people have very good memory for those occasions when they forget to complete their intentions. We even suggested that processes that occur over a retention interval could account for the intention-superiority effect. Although we do not know exactly what causes self-initiated retrievals, we suspect that there may be analogous cues and pauses in the day when one reflects back on what one has done and what else one wants to accomplish. But regardless of whether the retrieval of an intention is in response to self-initiated cognitive processing or external cues, reminders, or lures in the environment, using dependent measures other than completion rate that are used in the retrospective memory literature (such as retrieval speed or revival rates) could represent new, informative approaches. Before presenting our concluding comments, we offer the reader a brief précis of some of the major conclusions that we derived in the course of our analysis; and these are presented in Table I that may be useful to readers who come back to the chapter later seeking clarification of a specific set of points that we made.[5]

VII. Conclusions

Remembering to complete previously established intentions is an important, practical task that virtually everyone engages in daily. The label scientists have used (prospective memory) clearly identifies it as an ability that depends on the neural substrates comprising the human memory system. That same label has also served to segregate somewhat the research on prospective memory from over a century of work on retrospective memory. A recent *PsycINFO* search for "prospective memory" revealed that over 360 articles have been published on the topic, and the vast majority have appeared since 1990 when Einstein and McDaniel's seminal articles first started to appear in print. We tabulated the number of citations for 2-year periods and that data is shown in Fig. 1. As the reader will see, the field of prospective memory is burgeoning and the rate of articles being published has dramatically increased since McDaniel's (1995) treatise was published in this series exactly one decade ago. Although the relative number of articles is small by most standards, we believe that is sufficient to declare that research on prospective memory is well beyond its infancy. Unfortunately, theory development in this area has been slow. At one time we were convinced that this was a consequence of needing more empirical data around which such theories could be constructed. Although elements of this argument are still

---

[5] We thank Brian Ross for suggesting that we create this table.

TABLE I

A Brief Retrospective Summary of Some of the Conclusions Drawn in this Chapter

Section		Summary statement
IV	Intention formation	
	IV. A Internal generation	Prospective memories may be remembered better because of different distributions of rehearsal as compared with retrospective memory
	IV. B Imagination	Prospective memories may be more elaborately encoded and they are linked to both a present and future context
V	Retrieving intentions	
	V. A Retrieval cues	Standard transfer appropriate processing effects are obtained in prospective memory. Cues operate in much the same way as in retrospective memory
	V. B Accessibility	Temporary inaccessibility does not mean a prospective memory will not be available on another occasion
	V. C Resource sharing	Attentional allocation policies affect prospective memory in many of the same ways that they affect retrospective memory
VI	Changes over the retention interval	
	VI. A Retrieval practice	Retrieval of prospective memories may change their representation; and consequently, provide an alternative explanation of the intention-superiority effect
	VI. B Changes	Reminders have mixed success and the "strength" of a prospective memory can be increased by them unless habituation of the cue occurs
	VI. C Working memory	Once retrieved, intentions can be forgotten rapidly
	VI. D Time-based intentions	Retrieval of time-based intentions may not affect the representation of the intention in the same ways as event-based intentions
	VI. E Canceling intentions	Canceling an intention transforms it into a retrospective memory, but little work has been conducted in this area

true, we also became convinced that existing theories and principles governing retrospective memory could be used profitably to interpret the results of experiments on prospective memory. This chapter attempted to demonstrate that applying these principles to memory for intentions can explain the existing data in potentially interesting ways, and further, the analysis from the viewpoint of retrospective memory principles served to generate many avenues for future work (all of which are freely available for an interested reader to pursue).

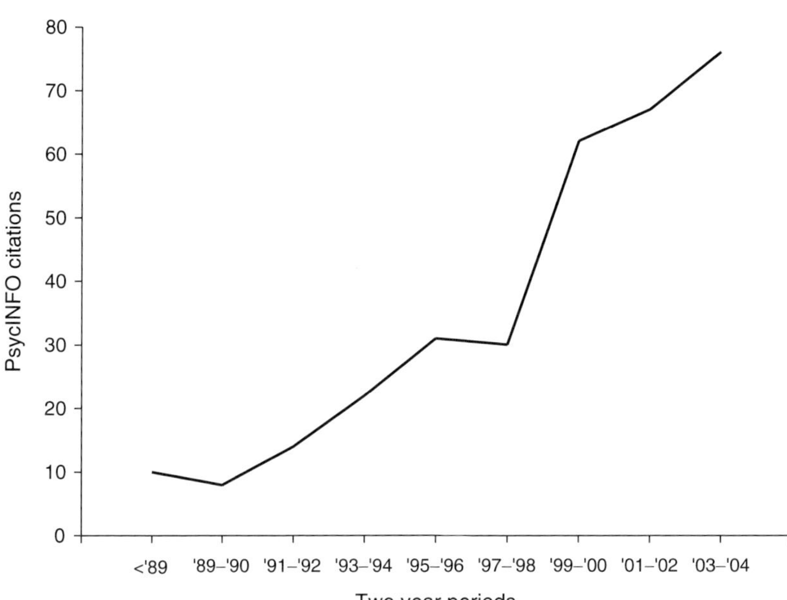

Fig. 1.   The total number of citations in PsycINFO summed over 2-year period except at the first data point.

We readily admit that we have provided no new theories of prospective memory in this chapter, but that was never the intention. Rather, a framework has been provided for integrating prospective memory with the principles of retrospective memory that may prove more valuable to the field over the next several years than, say, yet another theory of event-based prospective memory. We are not advocating replicating decades of findings from the retrospective memory literature and discovering whether they apply to memory for intentions, although some of this sort of work is inevitably necessary and likely to prove interesting. Instead, we are suggesting that empirical results from studies on prospective memory can sometimes be explained by existing theories and the history that surrounds these existing theories is bound to faithfully guide research on prospective memory. Recall that we reanalyzed the finding of better prospective memory over longer retention intervals (Hicks et al., 2000) by appealing to principles of distributed practice and recollection. So, even an outcome that appears prima facie to contradict long-established canons of retrospective memory can be explained by other principles of retrospective memory.

The reader may now be convinced that there are many more similarities between prospective and retrospective memory than has hitherto been explicitly acknowledged in the research reports on prospective memory. What differences do occur, however, may be explained by understanding how cognitive processes change the nature of the memorial representation of an intention in memory. Very few studies, if any, have systematically investigated how the characteristics of the memorial representation of an intention affect the completion rate of the intended activity. None have investigated how representations change over time due to completion or omission, or as a function of whether they represent preexisting memorial representations (as with novel versus habitual intentions). All of this is experimentally tractable and amenable to controlled laboratory study by using modifications of paradigms that are standards in the repertoire of techniques used in the retrospective memory literature.

There are distinct advantages to seriously considering the memorial representation of an intention in the same terms as retrospective memories have been considered. New terms like "cue sensitivity" or "retrieval sensitivity" are obviated if one considers the strength of the memory trace or the number and types of associations that are linked with a retrieval cue. Because all intentions must have memorial representations, the analysis of any differences in qualitative characteristics or associations between particular types of intentions (e.g., time-based versus activity-based) is made much easier by this approach. The association to a future context may be different when expecting a time will arrive as opposed to when a cue will arrive in one's environment. In this case, the association or its strength is different and perhaps could be analyzed with the principles already known about associations from the verbal learning tradition. More generally, the unifying principle across different types of intentions is the association to an imagined context, but differences among intentions can be characterized as differences in the dimension that unifies them (as opposed to believing that time-based and event-based prospective memory are governed by entirely different principles). For a more detailed treatment of the role that contextual associations play in prospective memory, the interested reader may wish to examine Marsh, Hicks, and Cook's (in press) book chapter.

The work that has been conducted on prospective memory to date has proven extremely valuable in more applied settings because it has already been used productively to ameliorate difficulties in certain subpopulations. The argument put forth here is that the theoretical and empirical work, which is the fodder for such applications, will be advanced more quickly by analyzing memory for intentions in a similar manner to all other retrospective memories. In doing so, we do not advocate returning to the old idea that the retrospective memory representation is "remembering what to do" and prospective memory is "remembering to do it." That characterization was relatively unproductive in advancing the field. In fact, our argument is just the reverse: there is only one memory representation for an intention, and students of memory (like ourselves) should be asking questions about how that representation is accessed under certain conditions, what its characteristics are, what associations it has, how fragile or durable it is, and how various cognitive processes change it. In summary, prospective memory should be defined as its own separate area of inquiry, but it should be reintegrated with (and informed by) the theories and principles of memory from whence it originally came.

ACKNOWLEDGMENT

Richard L. Marsh and Gabriel I. Cook, Department of Psychology, University of Georgia; Jason L. Hicks, Department of Psychology, Louisiana State University. Correspondence concerning this chapter should be addressed to Richard L. Marsh, Department of Psychology, University of Georgia, Athens, GA 30602–3013. Electronic inquiries and requests may be sent to rlmarsh@uga.edu, gabriel.cook@claremontmckenna.edu, or jhicks@lsu.edu.

REFERENCES

Anderson, J. R. (1974). Retrieval of propositional information from long-term memory. *Cognitive Psychology, 6*, 451–474.

Anderson, J. R., & Reder, L. M. (1999). The fan effect: New results and new theories. *Journal of Experimental Psychology: General, 128*, 186–197.

Anisfield, M., & Knapp, M. (1968). Association, synonymity, and directionality in false recognition. *Journal of Experimental Psychology, 77*, 171–179.

Atkinson, R. C., & Shiffrin, R. M. (1968). Human memory: A proposed system and its control processes. In K. W. Spence and J. T. Spence (Eds.), *The psychology of learning and motivation: Advances in research theory* (pp. 89–195). New York: Academic Press.

Baddeley, A., Lewis, V., Eldridge, M., & Thomson, N. (1984). Attention and retrieval from long-term memory. *Journal of Experimental Psychology: General, 113*, 518–540.

Bahrick, H. P., & Phelps, E. (1987). Retention of Spanish vocabulary over 8 years. *Journal of Experimental Psychology: Learning, Memory, and Cognition, 13*, 344–349.

Block, R. A., & Zakay, D. (1997). Prospective and retrospective duration judgments: A meta-analytic review. *Psychonomic Bulletin & Review, 4*, 184–197.

Bower, G. H. (1967). A multi-component theory of the memory trace. In K. W. Spence and J. T. Spence (Eds.), *The psychology of learning and motivation* (Vol. 1, pp. 229–325). New York: Academic Press.

Bjork, R. A. (1988). Retrieval practice and the maintenance of knowledge. In M. Gruneberg, P. Morris, and R. Sykes (Eds.), *Practical aspects of memory: Current research and issues* (Vol. 1, pp. 396–401). New York: Wiley.

Brewer, W. F., & Pani, J. R. (1983). The structure of human memory. In G. H. Bower (Ed.), *The psychology of learning and motivation: Advances in research and theory* (Vol. 17, pp. 1–38). New York: Academic Press.

Brown, R., & Kulik, J. (1982). Flashbulb memories. In U. Neisser (Ed.), *Memory observed: Remembering in natural contexts* (pp. 23–40). San Francisco: Freeman.

Ceci, S. J., & Bronfenbrenner, U. (1985). "Don't forget to take the cupcakes out of the Oven": Prospective memory, strategic time-monitoring, and context. *Child Development, 56*, 152–164.

Chalfonte, B. L., & Johnson, M. K. (1996). Feature memory and binding in young and older adults. *Memory & Cognition, 24*, 403–416.

Chasteen, A. L., Park, D. C., & Schwarz, N. (2001). Implementation intentions and facilitation of prospective memory. *Psychological Science, 12*, 457–461.

Cherry, K. E., & LeCompte, D. C. (1999). Age and individual differences influence prospective memory. *Psychology and Aging, 14*, 60–76.

Christianson, S. A., & Safer, M. A. (1996). Emotional events and emotions in autobiographical memories. In D. C. Rubin (Ed.), *Remembering our past* (pp. 218–243). New York: Cambridge University Press.

Cockman, D. (2003). *Monitoring in event-based prospective memory tasks.* Unpublished Master's thesis, Baton Rouge, Louisiana: Louisiana State University.

Conway, M. A. (1995). Flashbulb memories. Hillsdale, NJ: Erlbaum.

Cook, G. I., & Marsh, R. L. (submitted for publication). Investigating task interruptions in the delay-execute prospective memory task.

Cook, G. I., Marsh, R. L., & Hicks, J. L. (2005). Associating a time-based prospective memory task with an expected context can improve or impair intention completion. *Applied Cognitive Psychology, 19*, 345–360.

Cowan, N. (1995). *Attention and memory: An integrated framework.* New York: Oxford University Press.

Craik, F. I. M. (1986). A functional account of age differences in memory. In F. Klix and H. Hagendorf (Eds.), *Human memory and cognitive capabilities: Mechanisms and performance* (pp. 409–422). New York: Elsevier Science.

Craik, F. I. M., & Anderson, N. D. (1999). Applying cognitive research to problems of aging. In D. Gopher and A. Koriat (Eds.), *Attention and performance XVII: Cognitive regulation of performance: Interaction of theory and application* (pp. 583–615). Cambridge: MIT Press.

Craik, F. I. M., Govoni, R., Naveh-Benjamin, M., & Anderson, N. D. (1996). The effects of divided attention on encoding and retrieval processes in human memory. *Journal of Experimental Psychology: General, 125*, 159–180.

Crowder, R. G. (1996). Commentary: The trouble with prospective memory: A provocation. In M. Brandimonte, G. O. Einstein, and M. A. McDaniel (Eds.), *Prospective memory: Theory and applications* (pp. 143–148). Hillsdale, NJ: Erlbaum.

Dalla Barba, G. (1993). Prospective memory: A "new" memory system. In F. Boller and J. Grafman (Eds.), *Handbook of neuropsychology* (Vol. 8, pp. 239–251). Amsterdam: Elsevier.

Darby, R. J., & Maylor, E. A. (1998). Effects of the relationship between background and prospective task requirements on age differences in prospective memory. Presented at the Seventh Cognitive Aging Conference, Atlanta, GA.

Dennis, S., & Humphreys, M. S. (2001). A context noise model of episodic word recognition. *Psychological Review, 108*, 452–478.

Ebbinghaus, H. (1885). *On memory.* Leipzig, Germany: Duncker and Humboldt.

Einstein, G. O., Holland, L. J., McDaniel, M. A., & Guynn, M. J. (1992). Age-related deficits in prospective memory: The influence of task complexity. *Psychology and Aging, 7*, 471–478.

Einstein, G. O., & McDaniel, M. A. (1990). Normal aging and prospective memory. *Journal of Experimental Psychology: Learning, Memory, and Cognition, 16*, 717–726.

Einstein, G. O., & McDaniel, M. A. (1996). Retrieval processes in prospective memory: Theoretical approaches and some new empirical findings. In M. Brandimonte, G. O.

Einstein, and M. A. McDaniel (Eds.), *Prospective memory: Theory and applications* (pp. 115–142). Hillsdale, NJ: Erlbaum.

Einstein, G. O., McDaniel, M. A., Manzi, M., Cochran, B., & Baker, M. (2000). Prospective memory and aging: Forgetting intentions over short delays. *Psychology and Aging, 12,* 671–683.

Einstein, G. O., McDaniel, M. A., Richardson, S. L., Guynn, M. J., & Cunfer, A. R. (1995). Aging and prospective memory: Examining the influences of self-initiated retrieval processes. *Journal of Experimental Psychology: Learning, Memory, and Cognition, 21,* 996–1007.

Einstein, G. O., McDaniel, M. A., Smith, R. E., & Shaw, P. (1998). Habitual prospective memory and aging: Remembering intentions and forgetting actions. *Psychological Science, 9,* 284–289.

Einstein, G. O., Smith, R. E., McDaniel, M. A., & Shaw, P. (1997). Aging and prospective memory: The influence of increased task demands at encoding and retrieval. *Psychology and Aging, 12,* 479–488.

Einstein, G. O., McDaniel, M. A., Thomas, R., Mayfield, S., Shank, H., Morrisette, N., & Brenesier, J. (2005). Multiple processes in prospective memory retrieval: Factors determining monitoring versus spontaneous retrieval. *Journal of Experimental Psychology: General, 134,* 327–342.

Ellis, J. A. (1988). Memory for future intentions: Investigating pulses and steps. In M. M. Gruneberg, P. E. Morris, and R. N. Sykes (Eds.), *Practical aspects of memory: Current research and issues* (Vol. 1, pp. 371–376). Chichester, England: Wiley.

Ellis, J. A. (1996). Prospective memory or the realization of delayed intentions: A conceptual framework for research. In M. Brandimonte, G. O. Einstein, and M. A. McDaniel (Eds.), *Prospective memory: Theory and applications* (pp. 1–22). Hillsdale, NJ: Erlbaum.

Ellis, J., Kvavilashvili, L., & Milne, A. (1999). Experimental tests of prospective remembering: The influence of cue-event frequency on performance. *British Journal of Psychology, 90,* 9–23.

Ellis, J., & Milne, A. (1996). Retrieval cue specificity and the realization of delayed intentions. *Quarterly Journal of Experimental Psychology, 49,* 862–887.

Ferguson, S. A., Hashtroudi, S., & Johnson, M. K. (1992). Age differences in using source-relevant cues. *Psychology and Aging, 7,* 443–452.

Freeman, J. E., & Ellis, J. (2003). The representation of delayed intentions: A prospective subject-performed task? *Journal of Experimental Psychology: Learning, Memory, and Cognition, 29,* 976–992.

Friedman, W. J. (1993). Memory for the time of past events. *Psychological Bulletin, 113,* 44–66.

Galton, F. (1883). *Inquiries into human faculty and its development.* Everyman Edition, London: Dent.

Gillund, G., & Shiffrin, R. M. (1984). A retrieval model for both recognition and recall. *Psychological Review, 91,* 1–67.

Gollwitzer, P. M. (1999). Implementation intention: Strong effects of simple of plan. *American Psychologist, 54,* 493–503.

Gollwitzer, P. M., & Schaal, B. (1998). Metacognition in action: The importance of implementation intentions. *Personality and Social Psychology Review, 2,* 124–136.

Goschke, T., & Kuhl, J. (1993). The representation of intentions: Persisting activation in memory. *Journal of Experimental Psychology: Learning, Memory & Cognition, 19,* 1211–1226.

Goschke, T., & Kuhl, J. (1996). Remembering what to do: Explicit and implicit memory for intentions. In M. Brandimonte, G. O. Einstein, and M. A. McDaniel (Eds.), *Prospective memory: Theory and applications* (pp. 53–91). Hillsdale, NJ: Erlbaum.

Glenberg, A. M. (1976). Monotonic and nonmonotonic lag effects in paired-associate and recognition memory paradigms. *Journal of Verbal Learning & Verbal Behavior, 15*, 1–16.

Glisky, E. L., & Rabinowitz, J. C. (1985). Enhancing the generation effect through repetition of operations. *Journal of Experimental Psychology: Learning, Memory, and Cognition, 11*, 193–205.

Harris, J. E. (1980). Memory aids people use: Two interview studies. *Memory & Cognition, 8*, 31–38.

Harris, J. E., & Wilkins, A. J. (1982). Remembering to do things: A theoretical framework and an illustrative experiment. *Human Learning, 1*, 123–136.

Hicks, J. L., & Marsh, R. L. (2000). Toward specifying the attentional demands of recognition memory. *Journal of Experimental Psychology: Learning, Memory, and Cognition, 26*, 1483–1498.

Hicks, J. L., Marsh, R. L., & Cook, G. I. (2005). Task interference in time-based, event-based, and dual intention prospective memory conditions. *Journal of Memory and Language, 53*, 430–444.

Hicks, J. L., Marsh, R. L., & Russell, E. J. (2000). The properties of retention intervals and their affect on retaining prospective memories. *Journal of Experimental Psychology: Learning, Memory, and Cognition, 26*, 1160–1169.

Jacoby, L. L. (1991). A process dissociation framework: Separating automatic and intentional uses of memory. *Journal of Memory and Language, 30*, 513–541.

Jacoby, L. L. (1998). Invariance in automatic influences of memory: Toward a user's guide for the process-dissociation procedure. *Journal of Experimental Psychology: Learning, Memory, and Cognition, 24*, 3–26.

Jacoby, L. L., & Dallas, M. (1981). On the relationship between autobiographical memory and perceptual learning. *Journal of Experimental Psychology: General, 110*, 306–340.

Johnson, M. K., Hashtroudi, S., & Lindsay, D. S. (1993). Source monitoring. *Psychological Bulletin, 114*, 3–28.

Johnson, M. K., Kounios, J., & Reeder, J. A. (1994). Time-course studies of reality monitoring and recognition. *Journal of Experimental Psychology: Learning, Memory, and Cognition, 20*, 1409–1419.

Kahneman, D. (1973). *Attention and effort*. Englewood Cliffs, NJ: Prentice-Hall.

Kidder, D. P., Park, D. C., Hertzog, C., & Morrell, R. W. (1997). Prospective memory and aging: The effects of working memory and prospective memory task load. *Aging, Neuropsychology, and Cognition, 4*, 93–112.

Kliegel, M., Martin, M., McDaniel, M. A., & Einstein, G. O. (2001). Varying the importance of a prospective memory task: Differential effects across time- and event-based prospective memory. *Memory, 9*, 1–11.

Klein, S. B., & Kilhstrom, J. F. (1986). Elaboration, organization, and the self-reference effect in memory. *Journal of Experimental Psychology: General, 115*, 26–38.

Kvavilashvili, L. (1987). Remembering intention as a distinct form of memory. *British Journal of Psychology, 78*, 507–518.

Kvavilashvili, L., & Ellis, J. (1996). Varieties of intention: Some distinctions and classifications. In M. Brandimonte, G. O. Einstein, and M. A. McDaniel (Eds.), *Prospective memory: Theory and applications* (pp. 23–52). Hillsdale, NJ: Erlbaum.

Kvavilashvili, L., Messer, D. J., & Ebdon, P. (2001). Prospective memory in children: The effects of age and task interruption. *Developmental Psychology, 37*, 418–430.

Landauer, T. K., & Bjork, R. A. (1978). Optimum rehearsal patterns and name learning. In M. M. Gruneberg, P. E. Morris, and R. N. Sykes (Eds.), *Practical aspects of memory* (pp. 625–632). New York: Academic Press.

Linton, M. (1982). Transformations of memory in everyday life. In U. Neisser (Ed.), *Memory observed: Remembering in natural contexts* (pp. 77–91). San Francisco: Freeman.

Lozito, J. P. & Mulligan, N. W. (in press). Exploring the role of attention during memory retrieval: Effects of semantic encoding and divided attention. *Memory & Cognition.*

Malmberg, K. J., & Shiffrin, R. M. (2005). The "One-Shot" hypothesis for context storage. *Journal of Experimental Psychology: Learning, Memory, and Cognition, 31,* 322–336.

Mandler, G. (1980). Recognizing: The judgment of previous occurrence. *Psychological Review, 87,* 252–271.

Mäntylä, T. (1993). Priming effects in prospective memory. *Memory, 1,* 203–218.

Marsh, R. L., Hicks, J. L., & Cook, G. I. (in press). On beginning to understand the role of context in prospective memory. In M. Kliegel, M. McDaniel, and G. Einstein (Eds.), *Prospective memory: Cognitive, neuroscience, developmental, and applied perspectives.* Hillsdale, NJ: LEA.

Marsh, R. L., Hancock, T. W., & Hicks, J. L. (2002). The demands of an ongoing activity influence the success of event-based prospective memory. *Psychonomic Bulletin & Review, 9,* 604–610.

Marsh, R. L., & Hicks, J. L. (1998). Event-based prospective memory and executive control of working memory. *Journal of Experimental Psychology: Learning, Memory, and Cognition, 24,* 336–349.

Marsh, R. L., & Hicks, J. L. (2002). Comparisons of target output monitoring to source input monitoring. *Applied Cognitive Psychology, 16,* 845–862.

Marsh, R. L., Hicks, J. L., & Bink, M. L. (1998). The activation of completed, incomplete and partially completed intentions. *Journal of Experimental Psychology: Learning, Memory and Cognition, 24,* 350–361.

Marsh, R. L., Hicks, J. L., & Bryan, E. S. (1999). The activation of unrelated and cancelled intentions. *Memory & Cognition, 27,* 320–327.

Marsh, R. L., Hicks, J. L., & Cook, G. I. (2005). On the relationship between effort toward an ongoing task and cue detection in event-based prospective memory. *Journal of Experimental Psychology: Learning, Memory, and Cognition, 31,* 68–75.

Marsh, R. L., Hicks, J. L., Cook, G. I., Hansen, J. S., & Pallos, A. L. (2003). Interference to ongoing activities covaries with the characteristics of an event-based intention. *Journal of Experimental Psychology: Learning, Memory, and Cognition, 29,* 861–870.

Marsh, R. L., Hicks, J. L., Cook, G. I., & Mayhorn, C. B. (in press). Comparing older and younger adults in an event-based prospective memory paradigm containing an output monitoring component. *Aging, Neuropsychology, & Cognition.*

Marsh, R. L., Hicks, J. L., & Hancock, T. W. (2000). On the interaction of ongoing cognitive activity and the nature of an event-based intention. *Applied Cognitive Psychology, 14,* S29–S42.

Marsh, R. L., Hicks, J. L., Hancock, T. W., & Munsayac, K. (2002). Investigating the output monitoring component of event-based prospective memory performance. *Memory & Cognition, 30,* 302–311.

Marsh, R. L., Hicks, J. L., & Landau, J. D. (1998). An investigation of everyday prospective memory. *Memory & Cognition, 26,* 633–643.

Maylor, E. A. (1996). Age-related impairment in an event-based prospective memory task. *Psychology and Aging, 11,* 74–79.

Maylor, E. A. (1998). Changes in event-based prospective memory across the adulthood. *Aging, Neuropsychology, and Cognition, 5,* 107–128.

Maylor, E. A., Darby, R. J., & Della Salla, S. (2000). Retrieval of performed versus to-be-performed tasks: A naturalistic study of the intention superiority effect in normal aging and dementia. *Applied Cognitive Psychology, 14,* S83–S98.

Maylor, E. A., Smith, G., Della Sala, S., & Logie, R. H. (2002). Prospective and retrospective memory in normal aging and dementia: An experimental study. *Memory & Cognition, 30*, 871–884.

McDaniel, M. A. (1995). Prospective memory: Progress and processes. In D. L. Medin (Ed.), *Psychology of learning and motivation: Advances in research and theory* (Vol. 33, pp. 191–221). San Diego, CA: Academic Press.

McDaniel, M. A., & Einstein, G. O. (1993). The importance of cue familiarity and cue distinctiveness in prospective memory. *Memory, 1*, 23–41.

McDaniel, M. A., & Einstein, G. O. (2000). Strategic and automatic processes in prospective memory retrieval: A multiprocess framework. *Applied Cognitive Psychology, 14*, S127–S144.

McDaniel, M. A., Einstein, G. O., Graham, T., & Rall, E. (2004). Delaying execution of intentions: Overcoming the costs of interruptions. *Applied Cognitive Psychology, 18*, 553–561.

McDaniel, M. A., Glisky, E. L., Rubin, S. R., Guynn, M. J., & Routhieaux, B. C. (1999). Prospective memory: A neuropsychological study. *Neuropsychology, 13*, 103–110.

McDaniel, M. A., Guynn, M. J., Einstein, G. O., & Breneiser, J. (2004). Cue-focused and automatic-associative processes in prospective memory retrieval. *Journal of Experimental Psychology: Learning, Memory, and Cognition, 30*, 605–614.

McDaniel, M. A., Waddill, P. J., & Einstein, G. O. (1988). A contextual account of the generation effect: A three-factor theory. *Journal of Memory & Language, 27*, 521–536.

McDaniel, M. A., Robinson-Riegler, B., & Einstein, G. O. (1998). Prospective remembering: Perceptually driven or conceptually driven processes? *Memory & Cognition, 26*, 121–134.

Memon, A., & Higham, P. A. (1999). A review of the cognitive interview. *Psychology, Crime & Law, 5*, 177–196.

Metcalfe, J. (1991). Recognition failure and the composite memory trace in CHARM. *Psychological Review, 98*, 529–553.

Morris, C. D., Bransford, J. D., & Franks, J. J. (1977). Levels of processing versus transfer appropriate processing. *Journal of Verbal Learning and Verbal Behavior, 16*, 519–533.

Moscovitch, M. (1992). A neuropsychological model of memory and consciousness. In R. L. Squire and N. Butters (Eds.), *The neuropsychology of memory*. New York: Guilford Press.

Mulligan, N. W., & Lozito, J. P. (2004). Self-generation and memory. In B. H. Ross (Ed.), *Psychology of learning and motivation* (pp. 175–214). San Diego: Elsevier Academic Press.

Murnane, K., Phelps, M. P., & Malmberg, K. (1999). Context-dependent recognition memory: The ICE theory. *Journal of Experimental Psychology: General, 128*, 1–13.

Park, D. C., Hertzog, C., Kidder, D. P., Morrell, R. W., & Mayhorn, C. B. (1997). Effect of age on event-based and time-based prospective memory. *Psychology and Aging, 12*, 314–327.

Park, D. C., & Kidder, D. P. (1996). Prospective memory and medication adherence. In M. Brandimonte, G. O. Einstein, and M. A. McDaniel (Eds.), *Prospective memory: Theory and applications* (pp. 369–390). Hillsdale, NJ: Erlbaum.

Park, D. C., & Shaw, R. J. (1992). Effect of environmental support on implicit and explicit memory in younger and older adults. *Psychology & Aging, 7*, 632–642.

Park, D. C., Smith, A. D., & Cavanaugh, J. C. (1990). Metamemories of memory researchers. *Memory & Cognition, 18*, 321–327.

Payne, D. G. (1987). Hypermnesia and reminiscence in recall: A historical and empirical review. *Psychological Bulletin, 101*, 5–27.

Raaijmakers, J. G. W., & Shiffrin, R. M. (1981). Search of associative memory. *Psychological Review, 88*, 93–134.

Reed, A. V. (1973). Speed-accuracy trade-off in recognition memory. *Science, 181*, 574–576.

Roediger, H. L., III. (1996). Commentary: Prospective memory and episodic memory. In M. Brandimonte, G. O. Einstein, and M. A. McDaniel (Eds.), *Prospective memory: Theory and applications* (pp. 149–156). Hillsdale, NJ: Erlbaum.

Roediger, H. L., III, & Payne, D. G. (1985). Response criteria do not affect recall level or hypermnesia: A puzzle for generate/recognize theories. *Memory & Cognition, 13*, 1–7.

Roediger, H. L., III, Weldon, M. S., & Challice, B. H. (1989). Explaining dissociations between implicit and explicit measures of retention: A processing account. In H. L. Roediger, III and F. I. M. Craik (Eds.), *Varieties of memory and consciousness: Essays in honour of Endel Tulving* (pp. 3–41). Hillsdale, NJ: Erlbaum.

Rogers, T. B., Kuiper, N. A., & Kirker, W. S. (1977). Self-reference and the encoding of personal information. *Journal of Personality and Social Psychology, 35*, 677–688.

Schaeffer, E. G., Kozak, M. V., & Sagness, K. (1998). The role of enactment in prospective remembering. *Memory & Cognition, 26*, 644–650.

Sellen, A. J., Louie, G., Harris, J. E., & Wilkins, A. J. (1997). What brings intentions to mind? An *in situ* study of prospective memory *Memory, 5*, 483–507.

Searle, J. R. (1983). *Intentionality: An essay in the philosophy of mind.* Cambridge: Cambridge University Press.

Slamecka, N. J., & Graf, P. (1978). The generation effect: Delineation of a phenomenon. *Journal of Experimental Psychology: Human Learning and Memory, 4*, 592–604.

Smith, R. E. (2003). The cost of remembering to remember in event-based prospective memory: Investigating the capacity demands of delayed intention performance. *Journal of Experimental Psychology: Learning, Memory, and Cognition, 29*, 347–361.

Smith, S. M., & Vela, E. (2001). Environmental context-dependent memory: A review and meta-analysis. *Psychonomic Bulletin & Review, 8*, 203–220.

Taylor, R. S., Marsh, R. L., Hicks, J. L., & Hancock, T. W. (2003). The influence of partial-match cues on event-based prospective memory. *Memory, 12*, 203–213.

Tulving, E., & Pearlstone, Z. (1966). Availability versus accessibility of information in memory for words. *Journal of Verbal Learning and Verbal Behavior, 5*, 381–391.

Underwood, B. J. (1969). Attributes of memory. *Psychological Review, 76*, 559–573.

Vortac, O. U., Edwards, M. B., & Manning, C. A. (1995). Functions of external cues in prospective memory. *Memory, 3*, 201–219.

Wagenaar, W. A. (1986). My memory: A study of autobiographical memory over 6 years. *Cognitive Psychology, 18*, 225–252.

Watkins, O. C., & Watkins, M. J. (1975). Buildup of proactive inhibition as a cue-overload effect. *Journal of Experimental Psychology: Human Learning and Memory, 1*, 442–452.

West, R., & Craik, F. I. M. (1999). Age-related decline in prospective memory: The roles of cue accessibility and cue sensitivity. *Psychology and Aging, 14*, 264–272.

West, R. L., Herndon, R. W., & Ross-Munroe, K. (2000). Event-related neural activity associated with prospective remembering. *Applied Cognitive Psychology, 14*, S115–S126.

Wickens, D. D. (1987). The dual meanings of context: Implications for research, theory, and applications. In D. S. Gorfein and R. R. Hoffman (Eds.), *Memory and learning: The Ebbinghaus Centennial Conference.* Hillsdale, NJ: Erlbaum.

ACCESSING RECENT EVENTS

Brian McElree

I. Introduction

It has long been recognized that our ability to actively attend to and concurrently process information is limited (Broadbent, 1958). Nonetheless, component operations in many cognitive skills often rely on the products of prior perceptual and cognitive analyses. For example, subgoals in problem solving and reasoning can rely on the products of earlier subgoals (Anderson, 1983). Similarly, in language understanding, comprehenders frequently need to resolve dependencies between elements separated by several phrases or clauses (McElree, 2000; McElree, Foraker, & Dyer, 2003). As ongoing operations will often displace past analyses from the current focus of attention, successful execution of many operations may depend on our ability to rapidly shunt information between memory and focal attention.

Many researchers have suggested that a working memory (WM) system partially compensates for our limited capacity to concurrently process information. Working memory is thought to provide a "workspace," where a few by-products of recent perceptual and cognitive processing can be maintained in a more accessible state than information in long-term memory (LTM). Working memory representations may be more accessible than LTM representations either because they are held in specialized stores (Baddeley, 1986; Baddeley & Hitch, 1974; Schneider & Detweiler, 1988; Shallice & Vallar, 1990) or simply because they have residual activation from recent processing

THE PSYCHOLOGY OF LEARNING
AND MOTIVATION VOL. 46
DOI: 10.1016/S0079-7421(06)46005-9

155

(Anderson, 1983; Conway & Engle, 1994; Cowan, 1995, 2001; Engle, 1996; Ericsson & Pennington, 1993).

If one posits a distinct WM system, as illustrated in Fig. 1A, information can be represented in three possible states, either in LTM, WM, or in the current focus of attention. Different forms of evidence have been used to motivate this type of tripartite architecture (Cowan, 1995, 2001). However, the evidence is indirect and can be challenged on several grounds (Crowder, 1993; Nairne, 1996; Wickelgren, 1973).

This chapter examines whether there is direct evidence for either qualitative or quantitative differences in retrieval for items that the framework in Fig. 1A posits to be in distinct representational states. Different states could be motivated by findings that a qualitatively different type of retrieval operation is used to access information in each state. Alternatively or additionally, the architecture in Fig. 1A could be motivated by discontinuities in retrieval speed. This prediction is illustrated in Fig. 1B. The ultimate success of retrieval will be limited by forgetting due to the passage of time or intervening items between study and test, which should lead to systematic declines in accuracy with diminished recency. However, a straightforward prediction of a tripartite architecture is that each state should be associated with a distinct retrieval speed. Information in the current focus of attention should exhibit a privileged form of access. Less recent representations—those that are outside the capacity of focal attention but still within the span of WM—should be accessed slower than items within focal attention but faster than LTM representations. Finally, information that resides in LTM should be associated with the slowest retrieval speed.

This chapter reviews studies on the speed and accuracy of accessing representations of recently processed information. It documents the types of retrieval operations used to access both item and order information. Evidence is presented indicating that item information is retrieved with a direct-access (content-addressable) process (Section II. B), whereas order information is retrieved by a slower serial search process (Section II. C). Crucially, however, in neither case do we find evidence for a qualitative or quantitative "break-point" between what a tripartite architecture posits as the divide between WM and LTM. Collectively, the temporal dynamics of retrieval are indicative of two rather than three representational states. These measures provide clear evidence for a distinction between information within the current focus of attention and information passively stored in memory but not a further distinction corresponding to WM and LTM. Rather, the evidence suggests the type of dichotomy illustrated in Fig. 2A in which there is only an architectural difference between representations in focal attention and representations in memory. The corresponding speed and accuracy profiles are illustrated in Fig. 2B. Like Fig. 1B, the probability

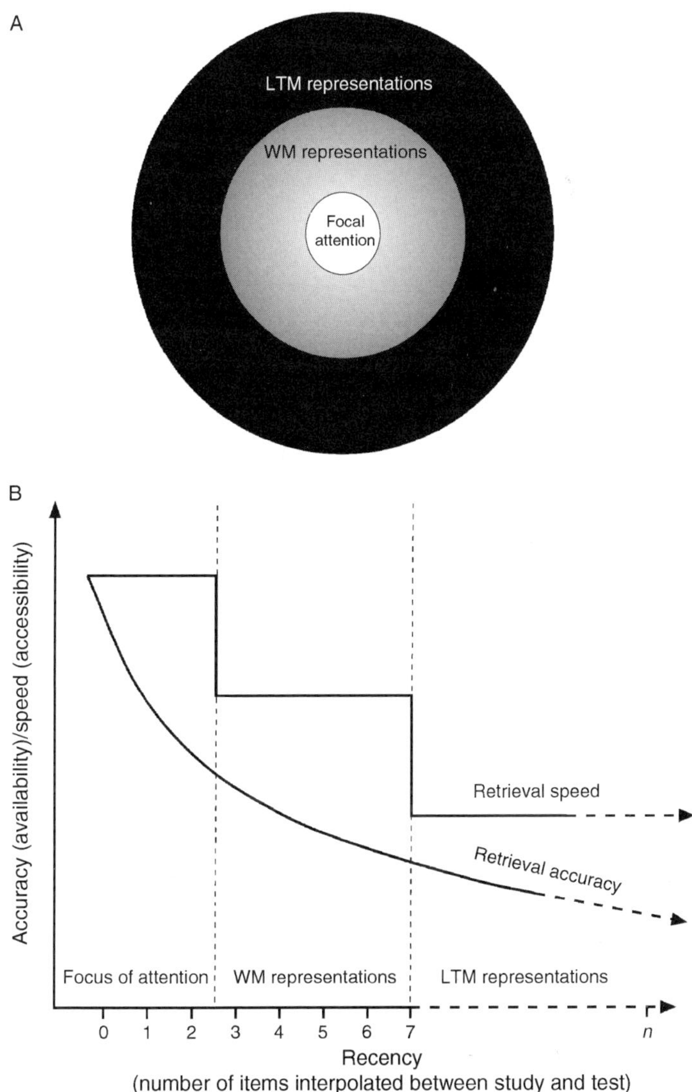

Fig. 1.   (A) Tripartite architecture assumed in many current approaches (Cowan, 1995). (B) Schematic illustration of how the speed and accuracy of retrieval are predicted to vary with recency. As more time and items are interpolated between study and test, the availability of a memory representation decreases continuously. In contrast, retrieval speed is predicted to show three distinct phases corresponding to the three states posited in (A).

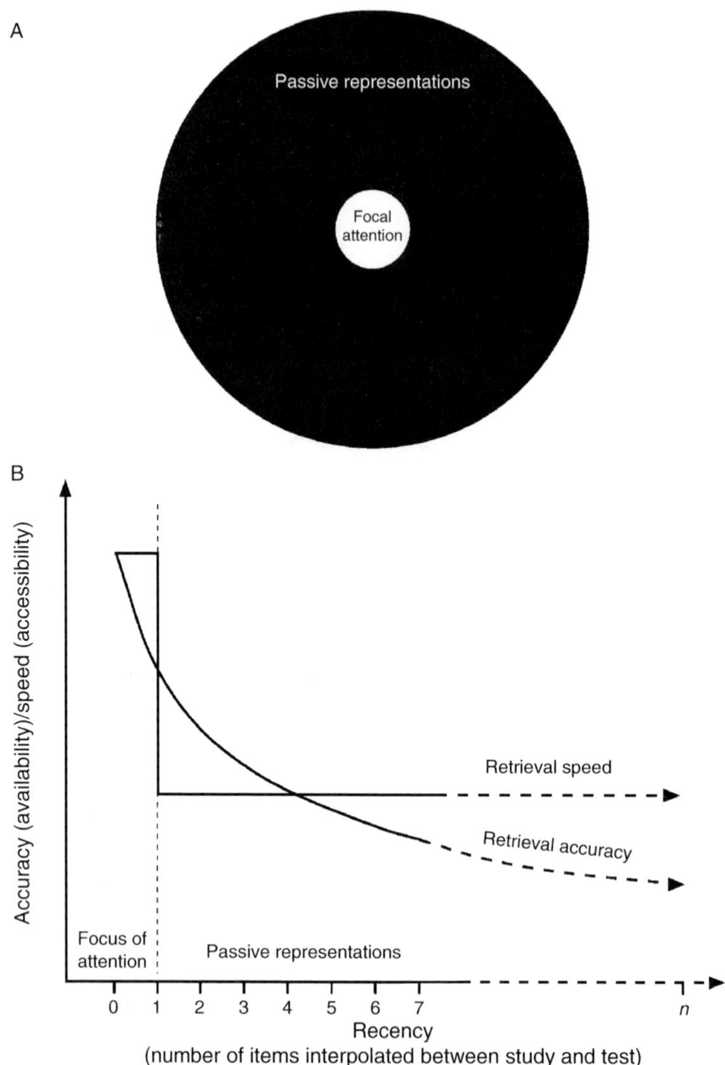

Fig. 2. (A) Bipartite architecture proposed on the basis of measures of the time-course of retrieval (McElree, 2001; McElree & Dosher, 1989; Wickelgren et al., 1980). (B) Schematic illustration of how the speed and accuracy of retrieval vary with recency. As more time and items are interpolated between study and test, the availability of a memory representation decreases continuously. Retrieval speed shows a dichotomous pattern—retrieval speed is constant across all serial positions except the last unit processed (recency = 1), which can be accessed faster than all other representations.

of retrieving an item from memory decreases continuously as more information is interpolated between study and test. Here, however, accessibility shows a sharply dichotomous pattern. Items within focal attention are accessed quickly, but all other items outside attention are accessed more slowly and with the same retrieval speed. The architecture in Fig. 2A hearkens back to the simple dichotomy James (1890) drew between primary memory, which he regarded as synonymous with conscious awareness, and secondary memory, the repository of all passive memory representations.

The second emphasis of the chapter is on the capacity of focal attention. Information in focal attention can be discriminated from information in a more passive state by its relatively fast retrieval dynamics (Section III. A). This view is reinforced by two new experiments that measure changes in retrieval dynamics that result from explicit attempts to shunt information from memory to focal attention (Sections III. B and III. C). Estimates of focal attention based on retrieval speed measures indicate that it has a much smaller capacity than has typically been assumed in some current approaches (Cowan, 2001). This view is reinforced further by studies that challenge subjects to attempt to retain items in focal attention while concurrently processing other information (Section III. D). The chapter ends with a brief discussion of neuroimaging findings.

II. Retrieval Processes

A. Measuring Retrieval

Reaction time (RT) paradigms are often used to investigate potential differences in the speed of memory retrieval. However, RT is not a pure measure of retrieval speed. Barring speed–accuracy trade-offs, there is little doubt that a difference in retrieval speed will be reflected in RTs derived from standard memory paradigms such as the probe recognition task (Sternberg, 1966, 1975). Crucially, however, the converse does not necessarily follow—we cannot infer a difference in retrieval speed from a difference in RT. Reaction time differences cannot be unequivocally attributed to a difference in retrieval speed unless we can be certain that there are no differences in the underlying strength (or quality) of the memory representations (Dosher, 1976, 1981; McElree & Dosher, 1989; Murdock, 1971; Ratcliff, 1978; Wickelgren, 1977; Wickelgren, Corbett, & Dosher, 1980).

That memory strength (or analogous properties) alone will engender differences in RT is a key property of explicit models of RT, and it is unlikely that any viable model of RT could be formulated without incorporating such a principle. To illustrate how strength affects RT consider an RT model like Ratcliff's diffusion model (Ratcliff, 1978; Ratcliff, Van Zandt, & McKoon,

1999). In any recognition task, memory strength will affect the degree of match between a test probe and its memory representation; specifically, it determines the resonance between the probe and its memory representation. A response is executed when the resonance exceeds a criterion value. In an RT task, a test probe with a high-resonance value will exceed a response criterion before a test probe with a lower resonance value, thereby engendering faster RTs, simply because the degree of match is better in the former than the latter. Crucially, RTs will differ even if both items are associated with the same underlying rate of information accrual.

Hence, we cannot use RT differences alone to infer a difference in retrieval speed unless we have independent evidence that the conditions of interest do not differ in strength. It is often assumed that there are no strength differences when performance in an RT task is nearly errorless. This reasoning is faulty, however. Perfect performance may simply reflect a limit on the performance scale and, hence, does not provide sufficient grounds for assuming equal strength.

It may be quite unusual to find cases in which conditions do not differ in underlying strength. Nevertheless, we can be certain that investigating differences between representations that are hypothesized to be in focal attention, WM or LTM is *not* one of these cases. Empirically derived forgetting functions show that the loss of memory strength is particularly dramatic across retention phases that correspond to standard assumptions concerning the break between focal attention, WM, and LTM (Dosher & Ma, 1998; McBride & Dosher, 1997, 1999; Rubin, Hinton, & Wenzel, 1999; Rubin & Wenzel, 1996; Wickelgren, 1972). This makes RT measures wholly unsuitable for differentiating possible representational states associated with focal attention, WM, and LTM.

A solution to this problem is to derive a full time-course function that describes how accuracy varies with retrieval time (Dosher, 1979; Reed, 1973, 1976; Wickelgren, 1977), which enables retrieval speed to be measured independently of potentially covarying differences in memory strength. The response-signal speed–accuracy trade-off (SAT) procedure derives such functions by tracking changes in the accuracy of a response as a function of processing time. In a probe recognition task, for example, participants are cued to respond to a response signal (typically a tone) presented at various times after the onset of the recognition probe. The response signal is varied across a range of times that span the full time course of retrieval (e.g., 100–3000 ms after the onset of the test probe), and accuracy is measured at the respective time periods by requiring participants to respond within a 100–300 ms of the signal. Figure 3 illustrates that SAT functions derived in this manner typically display three distinct phases, namely a

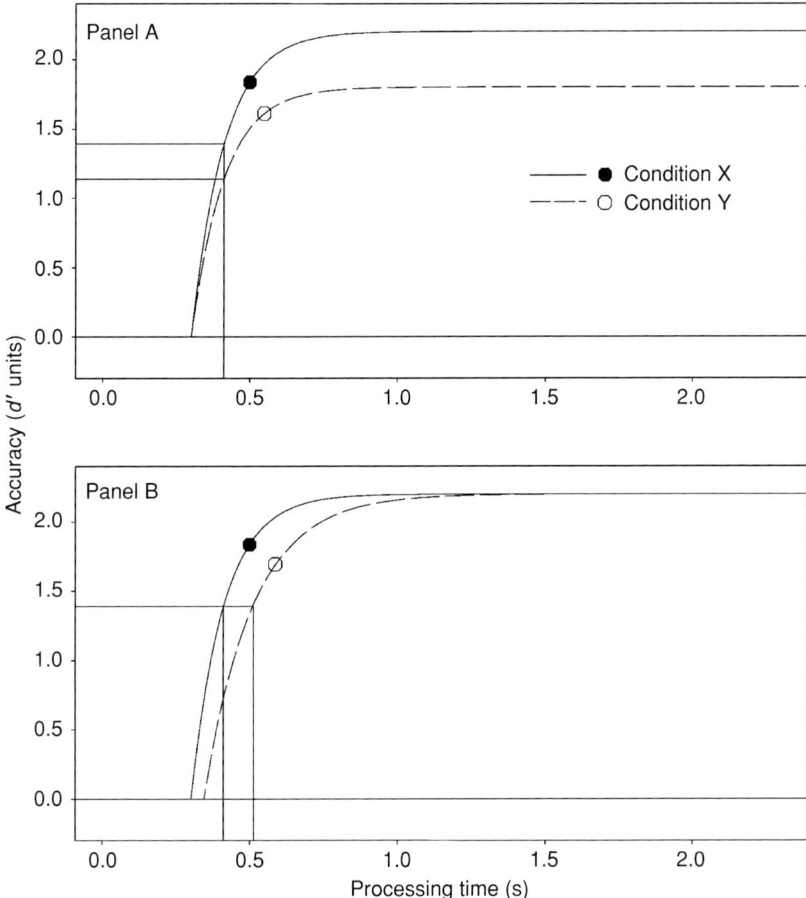

Fig. 3.   Illustrative SAT functions, plotted in d' units versus processing time (time of the response cue plus participant's average latency to respond). Panel (A) shows the pattern expected if an experimental factor increases memory strength alone. The functions differ in asymptotic accuracy but are associated with the same intercept (point when accuracy departs from chance) and proportional rate of information accrual. Panel (B) shows the pattern expected if the experimental factor affects retrieval speed (intercept and rate) alone. The functions display disproportional dynamics, reaching a given proportion of their asymptotes at different times. The solid symbols in both panels show hypothetical results from an reaction time (RT) variant of the task plotted in SAT coordinates (abscissa = mean RT; ordinate = accuracy), illustrating that RT differences can reflect differences in memory strength (panel A) or retrieval speed (panel B). The position of the RT points on the corresponding SAT functions are determined by the decision criteria that a participant uses to balance speed and accuracy.

period of chance performance, followed by a period of increasing accuracy, followed by an asymptotic period.[1]

The SAT asymptote is a measure of the overall probability of retrieval, and it provides an estimate of underlying memory strength. Panel A of Fig. 3 depicts two conditions that differ in asymptotic accuracy alone. The curves display proportional dynamics, indicating comparable underlying retrieval speeds. This is illustrated by the lines that intersect the ordinate and abscissa in Panel A, which show the time when each function reaches its $1 - 1/e$ (63%) point. When the retrieval speed is identical, as here, the functions reach this point at the same time, as indicated by the vertical line.

Retrieval speed is jointly measured by when information first becomes available, the SAT intercept, and the rate at which accuracy grows from chance to asymptote, the SAT rate. Panel B of Fig. 3 depicts a situation in which the functions are associated with different intercepts and rates of rise to asymptote (for expository purposes, the functions are shown rising to a common asymptote). A difference in either rate or intercept will engender disproportional SAT dynamics, in that the functions will reach a given proportion of their respective asymptotes (e.g., the $1 - 1/e$ point) at different times. Disproportional dynamics, whether due to differences in intercept or rate, indicate underlying differences in either the rate of continuous information accrual if processing is continuous or the distribution of finishing times if processing is discrete (Dosher, 1976, 1979, 1981, 1982, 1984; Meyer, Irwin, Osman, & Kounios, 1988; Ratcliff, 1988). Crucially, information that is in a more accessible state should be associated with an earlier intercept or faster rate, irrespective of differences in asymptote (Dosher, 1976, 1981, 1984; Hintzman & Caulton, 1997; Hintzman & Curran, 1994; Hintzman, Caulton, & Levitin, 1998; McElree, 1996, 1998, 2001; McElree & Dosher, 1989, 1993; McElree & Griffith, 1995; Ratcliff, 1978; Reed, 1973, 1976; Wickelgren, 1977).

The inability of RT data to uniquely isolate retrieval differences is illustrated by the filled symbols in Fig. 3, which show (hypothetical) data from an RT task plotted in speed–accuracy coordinates. The position of the RT points on the corresponding SAT functions is determined by the decision criteria that an observer uses to balance speed and accuracy.[2] Panel A illustrates that a difference in mean RT (distance on the abscissa) and RT accuracy (distance on the ordinate) can arise if the corresponding SAT

---

[1] Nonmonotonic functions have also been observed (Dosher, McElree, Rosedale & Hood, 1989; Reed, 1973), which motivate multiprocess models, as discussed in a later section.

[2] Direct comparisons of RTs and SAT functions have shown that participants typically respond at subasymptotic times in an RT procedure (Dosher, 1982; McElree & Dosher, 1993; Reed, 1973), often close to the two-thirds point as shown in Fig. 2.

time-course functions differ in asymptotic accuracy alone. Panel B illustrates that a nearly identical difference in mean RT and RT accuracy could arise from underlying differences in the dynamics of processing. Empirically, differences in RT have been found to reflect differences in asymptotic accuracy alone (Dosher, 1984; McElree, 1993; McElree & Dosher, 1989), differences in dynamics alone (Dosher, 1981; Dosher & Rosedale, 1989; McElree & Griffith, 1998), or mixtures of asymptotic and dynamics differences (McElree, 1996, 1998, 2001; McElree & Dosher, 1993; McElree & Griffith, 1998).

B. ACCESSING REPRESENTATIONS

1. *Qualitative Differences in Retrieval*

Is information thought to be stored in WM retrieved through a qualitatively different means than information stored in LTM? In a classic series of papers, Sternberg (1966, 1969, 1975) argued that it was. Sternberg proposed that items were retrieved from WM with a serial exhaustive search of the WM set, based on the finding that mean RT was a linear function of set size (the number of items studied) and that positive and negative responses engendered approximately equal slopes. Other researchers have proposed other specialized retrieval mechanisms to account for this pattern, including a serial self-terminating search model (Theios, 1973), a multiple serial scan model (Treisman & Doctor, 1987), and rate-varying parallel models (Murdock, 1971; Townsend & Ashby, 1983).

Despite salient differences among these approaches, all assert that WM retrieval is qualitatively different from LTM retrieval in involving some form of search through a limited set of items stored in WM. In contrast, episodic memory models (Clark & Gronlund, 1996; Gillund & Shiffrin, 1984; Hintzman, 1988; Murdock, 1982) and semantic memory models (Hinton, 1989; Kawamoto, 1988; Plaut, 1997) typically posit that LTM representations are retrieved with a direct-access or content-addressable operation.[3] Content-addressability can be implemented in models with diverse storage architectures, including those with localized representations and those with highly distributed representations (Clark & Gronlund, 1996). The defining property of a content-addressable retrieval process is that information (cues) in the retrieval context enables direct access to relevant memory representations, without the need to search through extraneous memory representations.

---

[3] Recall, which involves production of an item that is not presented at retrieval, may involve a series of operations to resample memory, possibly using modified sets of cues (Raaijmakers and Shiffrin, 1981).

Although it is not possible to discriminate between different retrieval models on the basis of mean RT alone, McElree and Dosher (1989) demonstrated that these models make distinctive predictions about the shape of the SAT curve as a function of two variables, either the size of the memory set or the serial position or recency of the (positive) test probe. In contrast to direct-access mechanisms, Sternberg's serial exhaustive scan model, as well as related models like Treisman and Doctor's (1987) multiple fast scan model, predict that retrieval dynamics will slow (longer SAT intercepts and/or slower growth rates) as the size of the memory set is increased. This follows directly from the assumption that the memory set must be exhaustively scanned (see McElree & Dosher, 1989 for specific simulations and McElree & Carrasco, 1999 for a related simulation in visual search). Serial self-terminating and rate-varying parallel models predict that retrieval dynamics will vary with the serial position or recency of the test probe rather than with set size. This follows from the fact that recency is assumed to affect the order of the serial comparisons in a serial self-terminating model (Theios, 1973) or the rate of information accrual in rate-varying parallel models (Murdock, 1971; Townsend & Ashby, 1983).

McElree and Dosher (1989) collected full time-course functions for serial positions within lists of three to six sequentially presented words. Figure 4 shows the full time-course profiles for each of the serial positions in set sizes of three (Panel A), four (Panel B), five (Panel C), and six (Panel D) words. The functions were fit (solid lines) with the exponential approach to a limit equation in Eq. (1), where λ estimates the asymptote of the function, δ estimates the intercept or discrete point in time when accuracy departs from chance, and β estimates the rate at which accuracy grows to asymptote:[4]

$$d'(t) = \lambda\left(1 - e^{-\beta(t-\delta)}\right), \quad \text{for } t > \delta, \text{else } 0 \tag{1}$$

Competitive model fits demonstrated that the size of the memory set affected asymptotic accuracy (λ) only, with larger set sizes yielding lower overall asymptotic levels. Within each set size, asymptotic performance decreased as the test probe was drawn from less recent serial positions, offset by a small primacy effect for the first position. Analyses of the retrieval functions for individual serial positions indicated that the impact of set size on asymptotic performance was largely a consequence of the inclusion of less recent serial positions in the (averaged across serial position) set size functions, with less recent test probes resulting in lower asymptotic performance. This suggests that observed asymptotic patterns are due to forgetting with

---

[4] The functions were also fit with the related three-parameter equation from Ratcliff's (1978) diffusion model (McElree & Dosher, 1989).

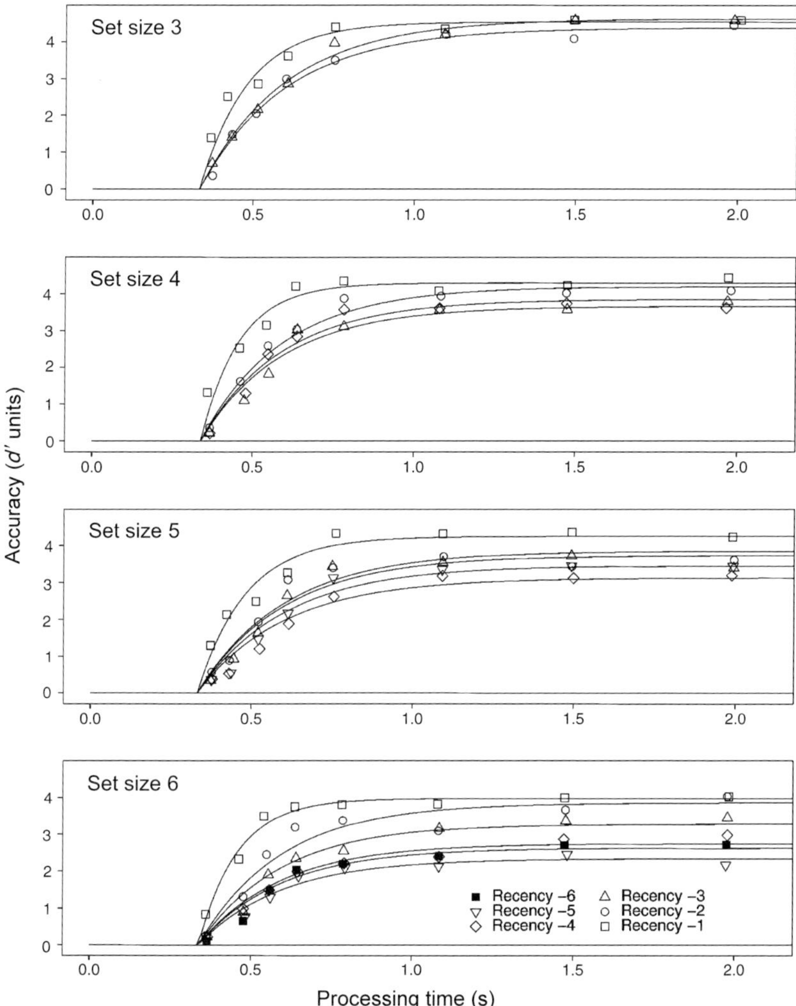

Fig. 4.   Average d' values as a function of total processing time for serial positions with set sizes of three (top panel), four (second panel), five (third panel), and six (bottom panel) words. Smooth functions show best fitting exponential models (Eq. 1). (Serial position is labeled in terms of recency, counting backward from the test item, position 0, to the study position of the probe, -1 for the most recent serial position, -2 for the next, and so on.) These functions are consistent with direct-access (content-addressable) retrieval process. (Based on data reported in McElree & Dosher, 1989.)

the passage of time and/or intervening study events. McElree and Dosher (1989) found that a simple forgetting model—Wickelgren and Norman's (1966) acquisition-primacy model—fully accounted for the asymptotic differences, which in turn could be used to model standard RT effects.

Crucially, there was no evidence that the size of the memory set *or* the recency of the test probe affected retrieval speed, with the exception of the last item on the study list (a case of immediate repetition between study and test; see later section). The dynamics of retrieval for different serial positions within and across various set sizes were indistinguishable. That is, save the last serial position, all the serial positions within and across the four set sizes were best fit by a single SAT intercept (δ) and a single SAT rate (β). When rates or intercepts were varied, neither did it improve the quality of the fits nor did it yield a set of consistently ordered parameter estimates across the fits of the individual subjects' data.

The observed retrieval dynamics are inconsistent with serial or parallel search models. The absence of a measurable effect of set size on retrieval speed is inconsistent with an exhaustive search of the memory set, whether the search process is viewed as serial (Sternberg, 1966, 1975; Treisman & Doctor, 1987) or parallel (Ratcliff, 1978).[5] The absence of an effect of serial position on retrieval speed is inconsistent with serial self-terminating models in which recency determines either the order of the serial comparisons (Theios, 1973) or the rate of information accrual of parallel comparisons (Murdock, 1971; Townsend & Ashby, 1983).

Identical retrieval speeds for different serial positions and for different set sizes indicate retrieval is mediated by a direct-access mechanism, such as a simple strength-accumulator (Reed, 1973), or parallel retrieval mechanisms (without an exhaustive decision rule) such as a simple diffusion process (McElree & Dosher, 1989; Ratcliff, 1978). Crucially, these types of mechanisms are consistent with a large class of LTM models that treat item recognition as an assessment of the global familiarity or strength of an item (Gillund & Shiffrin, 1984; Hintzman, 1984, 1988; Murdock, 1982, 1993). In short, full time-course measures indicate that retrieval from what is traditionally thought to be WM is mediated by the same mechanism that is typically argued to underlie retrieval from LTM.

---

[5] Ratcliff's (1978) treatment of Sternberg's effects assumed a self-terminating decision rule on positives but an exhaustive decision rule for negatives, which predicts substantial dynamics effects for different set sizes (McElree and Dosher, 1989).

2. Quantitative Differences in Retrieval

Time-course data do not support the idea that WM and LTM are retrieved with qualitatively different operations. Nonetheless, the distinction between WM and LTM inherent in the tripartite architecture, illustrated in Fig. 1A, could be motivated by findings that items within the span of WM are accessed faster than items outside the span of WM. This follows directly from the assumption that the functional role of WM is to maintain items in a highly accessible state; indeed, if there is any empirical content to that claim it is that WM representations should be accessed faster than LTM representations.

Wickelgren, Corbett, and Dosher (1980) tested this idea by examining the time-course profiles for various serial positions within lists of 16 sequentially presented consonants. Using a probe recognition task, they derived SAT retrieval functions for serial positions 16 (the last item on the list), 15, 14, and the averages of serial positions 13–11, 10–6, and 5–3. This provided three time-course profiles for what most researchers would consider subspan items (positions 16, 15, and 14) and three time-course profiles for supraspan items (13–11, 10–6, and 5–3).

The data showed a pattern analogous to Fig. 4. Asymptotic accuracy decreased monotonically with the decreasing recency of the tested item, indicating that memory strength systematically declines as time or activity is interpolated between study and test. Importantly, retrieval speed (SAT intercept and rate) was constant across sub- and superspan serial positions, with one exception. Serial position 16, the most recently studied position, was retrieved with a speed 50% faster than all other positions. Wickelgren et al. (1980) argued that this item remains active in focal attention because no activity intervened between study and test. Consequently, the recognition probe can be compared to the contents of focal attention directly, without deploying a retrieval process to restore the item to active processing. As with the McElree and Dosher (1989) study, retrieval is markedly distinct for the last unit processed only. Crucially, the lack of speed differences beyond the last serial position is inconsistent with approaches that posit an intermediate state between focal attention and LTM.

Figure 2B schematically summarizes the affect of recency on the time-course of retrieval. The probability of retrieving an item from memory, which is measured by the SAT asymptote, decreases continuously as more information is interpolated between study and test. In contrast, accessibility—the speed of retrieval measured by SAT intercept and rate—shows a sharply dichotomous pattern. The last item processed is accessed quickly, but all other items are accessed more slowly with the same retrieval speed. This pattern motivates a distinction between attended and nonattended states, as illustrated in Fig. 2A, but not a further distinction corresponding to what a tripartite architecture posits as the break between WM and LTM. In short, the temporal dynamics of retrieval are indicative of two rather than three representational states.

3. *Extensions*

The time-course patterns in these list-learning experiments appear to generalize to other naturalistic circumstances, language comprehension in particular. Natural language often contains dependencies between nonadjacent elements. For example, when processing the verb *embrace* in the sentence *This is the novel that the editor hoped the public would embrace*, comprehenders must incorporate the initial noun phrase *the novel* into a representation of the verb phrase as the direct object of the final verb *embrace*. As an indefinite amount of material can intervene between these types of nonadjacent dependencies, it is often the case that the earlier element will have been displaced from attention and must be retrieved from memory.

We have measured the dynamics of retrieval in such circumstances by systematically varying the distance between dependent constituents (e.g., *the novel* and *embrace* in the example given in paragraph above) and using SAT procedures to measure the dynamics of comprehension (McElree, 2000; McElree et al., 2003). Across several different types of sentence structures, the recency of the earlier constituent (e.g., *the novel* in the example above) was found to have the same effect on comprehension as recency had upon the probe recognition task. The SAT asymptotes indicated that amount of intervening material negatively impacts on the probability of computing an acceptable interpretation of the target sentence, consistent with the notion that recency affects the probability of maintaining in memory a representation of the earlier processed constituent. However, comprehension speed, measured by SAT intercept and rate, was unaffected by the amount or type of material intervening between the dependant constituents. This suggests that recency does not affect the speed of accessing a preserved representation, which in turn is consistent with the hypothesis that sentence comprehension is mediated by the same types of content-addressable memory structures that are found in tasks such as probe recognition.

Reinforcing this view further, we found that comprehension speed showed the same dichotomous pattern illustrated in Fig. 2B. Comprehension speed is generally unaffected by the number of phrases interpolated between the dependent elements. For example, *laughed* is interpreted at the same speed in The *editor that the book amused laughed,* The *editor that the book that won the award amused laughed,* and *The editor that the book that the journalist wrote amused laughed.* However, it is interpreted at a measurably faster rate when the dependant element, the subject and the verb, are adjacent to one another, for example, *The editor laughed.* This directly mirrors the patterns seen in probe recognition in which recognition speed is found to be exceptionally fast when no item intervenes between study and test. The findings in both domains suggest that processing is fast when information is active in focal attention, and, by hypothesis, retrieval can be circumvented.

C. ACCESSING RELATIONS

The time-course evidence indicates that access to a representation in memory is mediated by a direct-access or content-addressable mechanism. However, not all types of information may be recoverable with such a mechanism. The retrieval of relational information, both temporal and spatial order information, appears to be one such case. This section briefly outlines evidence indicating that relational information is retrieved with a different type of retrieval process than item information and then considers whether the retrieval of relational information provides any grounds for motivating a tripartite architecture.

1. Temporal and Spatial Order Information

The speed of retrieving order information can be effectively measured with a relative judgment of recency (JOR) task (Hacker, 1980; Hockley, 1984; Muter, 1979). Like the probe recognition task, a list of items is sequentially presented and followed immediately by a recognition probe. In the JOR task, however, the test probe consists of two items from the list, and subjects are asked to perform two-alternative forced-choice (2AFC) recency discriminations, choosing which of two items occurred more recently in a list.

The effects of recency on RTs and RT-accuracy in this task suggest that recency discriminations may be mediated by a serial search process (Hacker, 1980; Hockley, 1984; McElree & Dosher, 1993; Muter, 1979). Mean correct RT is inversely related to the study position of the more recent or *later* probe in the test pair. Reaction time increases as the later probe is drawn from more remote positions and is unaffected by the study position of the less recent or *earlier* probe. Accuracy decreases as the later probe is drawn from earlier study positions and, to a lesser extent, as the separation in recency between the two probe items decreases. This pattern is inconsistent with the order of the JOR probes being derived from a direct comparison of time tags explicitly coded in a memory trace (Hasher & Zacks, 1984; Yntema & Trask, 1963) or a direct comparison of mnemsic properties like trace strength (Hinrichs, 1970; Morton, 1968), trace fragility (Wickelgren, 1974), or attribute counts (Bower, 1972; Flexser & Bower, 1974). If any of these accounts were correct, RT should vary with the difference in recency between the two test items (Muter, 1979). That RT systematically decreases as the later item is drawn from less recent study positions suggest that the list is searched in a backward serial fashion, terminating on finding the first match to an item in the memory set (Hacker, 1980).

McElree and Dosher (1993) used an SAT version of a JOR task to directly test this claim. Participants studied 6-item lists and then were tested on combinations of all pairwise serial positions (1–2, 1–3, 1–4, 1–5, 1–6, 2–3, 2–4, etc). Figure 5A presents a subset of the 15 time-course functions (1–2, 1–3, 1–4, 1–5, and 1–6), which span the full range of the observed differences. Asymptotic accuracy varied with the recency of the later item in the test probe, with higher accuracies for more recent items. This pattern indicates that the availability of the more recent item in the test probe is the major determinant of asymptotic accuracy in this task. In contrast to item recognition, however, retrieval dynamics also depended on the recency of the most recent item in the test pair, with retrieval speed slowing as the most recent item in the test probe was drawn from less recent positions.

Model fits (using Eq. 1) indicated that both the SAT intercepts (δ) and SAT rates (β) varied with recency, with the most dramatic effects seen on the intercept. The intercepts varied as much as 500 ms across a list of six consonants. Although some parallel models can be consistent with differences in SAT rate (McElree & Carrasco, 1999), they are incompatible with large shifts in intercepts.[6] The form of dynamics differences implicates a serial search process in which the search began from the most recent position and extended backward in time. The SAT dynamics are consistent with a class of serial backward-search models, including serial-chaining operations that capitalize on pairwise associative information (Lewandowsky & Murdock, 1989). McElree and Dosher (1993) demonstrated that a variant of the backward-search model proposed by Hacker (1980) could adequately account for the full time-course patterns.

Sternberg (1973, 1975) pointed out that analysis of the shape of the RT distribution can provide additional evidence for a serial mechanism. A crucial prediction of a serial self-terminating model is that the minima of the (correct) RT distributions will vary with the experimental factor that determines the number of serial operations (Sternberg, 1973; Townsend & Ashby, 1983). Increasing the number of serial matching or comparison processes should shift the entire distribution—including the leading edge

---

[6] The rate of information accrual may vary for the component processes in parallel architecture, which can lead to differences in SAT rate. However, a defining property of a parallel model is that all processes are initiated at the same time, and this property is incompatible with substantial differences in SAT intercept.

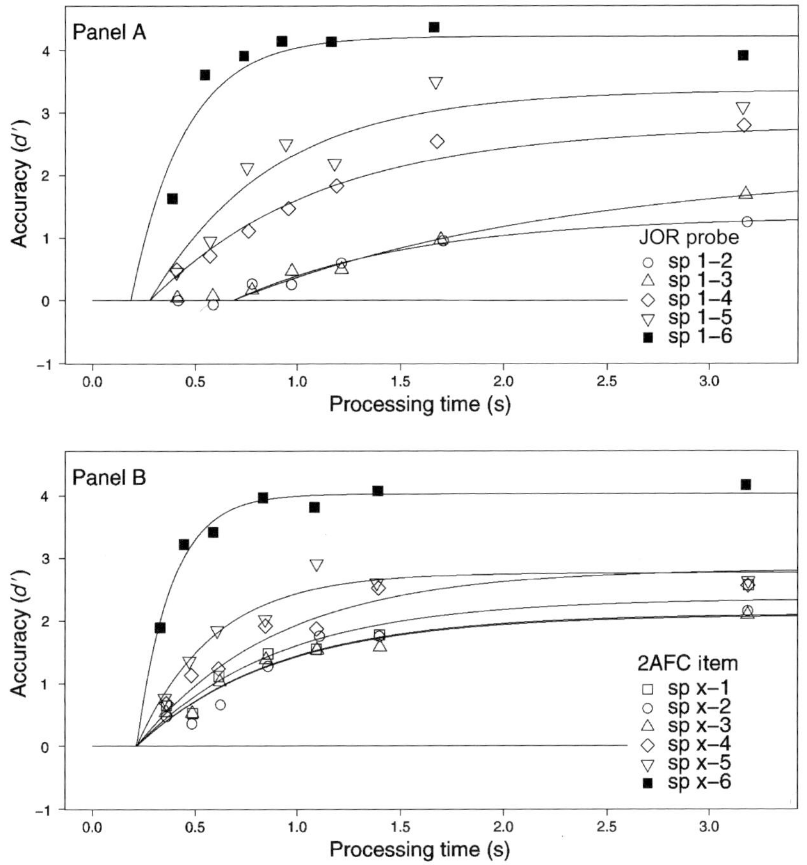

Fig. 5. Average d' values as a function of total processing time for judgments of recency (JOR) (top panel) and two-alternative force-choice (2AFC) item recognition (bottom panel). Smooth functions show best fitting exponential models (Eq. 1). (Based on data reported in McElree & Dosher, 1993.)

and mode of the distribution—toward longer times (Hockley, 1984; Ratcliff & Murdock, 1976). McElree and Dosher (1993) constructed RT distributions for individual subjects and for group data for each of the 15 JOR test probes. The distributions were fit with an Ex-Gaussian function (the convolution of a Gaussian and an exponential distribution; Ratcliff & Murdock, 1976) to summarize changes in the overall shape of the distributions. Fully consistent with a serial self-terminating search, the serial position of the later probe shifted the leading edge and mode of the RT distributions toward longer times. These shifts in the leading edge paralleled the large changes in

SAT intercept seen in Fig. 5A. Comparable RT distributions for item recognition, in which recency does not affect SAT dynamics, have shown that recency does not affect the leading edge or mode, only the rightward tail of the distribution (McElree, 1998; Ratcliff, 1978).

The effect of recency on retrieval dynamics in the JOR task but not in item recognition tasks suggests that item and order information are retrieved by qualitatively different mechanisms, one direct or parallel and the other serial. However, one concern with the studies reported so far is that the JOR task involves 2AFC judgments, whereas the reported SAT studies of item recognition have used yes–no judgments. To ensure that the divergent patterns were not due to different response demands, McElree and Dosher (1993) conducted an SAT study using a 2AFC item recognition task. A list of sequentially presented items was followed by a test probe consisting of two test items, one new and the other drawn from one of the six study positions in the list. In other relevant respects, the experimental parameters were matched to the 2AFC JOR task.

Figure 5B shows the average SAT functions for the six serial positions, along with the best fitting exponential functions (Eq. 1). The same pattern is evident in this figure as in other yes–no recognition tasks (Fig. 4). Asymptotic accuracy graded directly with recency of study, coupled with a small primacy advantage for the first item on the list. There was a large dynamics (rate) advantage for the last serial position, the case of immediate repetition across study and test, but retrieval speed was constant beyond this position. This can be easily seen in Fig. 5B. The function for serial position 6, the last serial position, reaches its asymptote at around 800 ms; in contrast, the functions for all other serial positions are still rising at 800 ms, and all appear to reach their respective asymptotes around 1000–1200 ms. These data show the same direct-access signature pattern seen in other item recognition studies. Hence, there is little reason to suppose that the seriality evident in the recovery of order information is a consequence of performing 2AFC judgments.

Gronlund, Edwards, and Ohrt (1997) compared the retrieval of item and spatial order information in three SAT experiments. Participants studied either pairs or triples of words and were tested on a single word in a particular spatial position. For example, if ABC was studied, the test might consist of A _ _, where the dashes indicated the spatial position of the test item. When a positive response required verifying the correct position of the item in the triple, SAT dynamics were substantially delayed relative to item judgments irrespective of position. Gronlund et al. did not systematically investigate recency, so it is not possible to determine whether the same mechanism is used for the retrieval of spatial information as for temporal information. However, the slower time-course for spatial order judgments indicates that participants used a qualitatively different retrieval mechanism to recover spatial information.

2. Does the Seriality of Order Judgments Motivate a WM System?

Does evidence for seriality in the recovery of order information contradict the architecture illustrated in Fig. 2A? One might argue that a serial search process is an inefficient and therefore implausible mechanism for the recovery of long-term information, and so the apparent use of this process in tasks, such as JOR, suggests that participants must be serially searching representations maintained in a specialized short-term store. There are, however, several questionable features of this argument.

First, it is not clear that a serial search process is in fact implausible as a mechanism for recovering the order of remote events. There appears to be multiple bases on which to determine the order of past events, be they recent or distant. Many events, particularly salient events, might be directly associated with specific times or dates (Bower, 1972; Estes, 1985; Yntema & Trask, 1963). In other cases, item strength (familiarity, distinctiveness, trace fragility, and related constructs) might serve as a proxy for recency (Bower, 1972; Flexser & Bower, 1974; Hinrichs, 1970; Morton, 1968; Peterson, 1967; Wickelgren, 1972, 1974).[7] Discriminating between the recency of two time-tagged events or two events differing in strength may require little beyond a direct comparison of properties retrieved from each. However, without time-tags or salient differences in strength, we may need to *reconstruct* the order of remote events by chaining through a sequence of associated events with processes similar to what is observed in the JOR task. For example, we might determine which of two locations we visited last on a vacation by reconstructing our travel sequence. That process may differ from JOR in its use of richer forms of information (e.g., causal relations) to establish links between events, but it may nevertheless exhibit the same type of seriality found in the JOR task.

What would motivate a distinct WM system is clear evidence that serial operations are only applicable to events stored in WM and that the retrieval process changes to a different type when events stored in LTM are accessed. Recency effects on order retrieval have not been as systematically investigated as item retrieval, but current evidence does not suggest an obvious break point corresponding to WM and LTM. No one has examined JORs in lists as long as those used by Wickelgren et al. (1980) in their probe

---

[7] Even in short-term tasks, such as the JOR, subjects may forgo a slower serial search for a rapid assessment of familiarity in some circumstances. McElree and Dosher (1993) found clear evidence in the JOR time-course profiles that participants relied on a fast assessment of strength to judge recency when there was not sufficient time to complete the slower search.

recognition task. However, Muter (1979) used lists of 10 items and reported RT patterns reflecting a serial process extending back to all 10 items. This would exceed what most would consider the span of WM.

What limits the applicability of a serial process appears to be the availability of the items in memory. Availability, however, declines continuously with recency, with no discontinuities that could be plausibly mapped on to a break between WM and LTM. Figure 6 plots availability estimates for each of the six serial positions in the McElree and Dosher (1993) SAT task and in the Hacker (1980) RT tasks with three presentation rates (170-ms/study item, 110-ms/study item, and 50-ms/study item).[8] These estimates are derived from Hacker serial scan model (see figure 6 legend). Estimated availability is higher in the SAT task than the RT tasks, and the rate of decline with recency is slower. This is consistent with the fact that subjects in the RT task operate on a point on the SAT curve that is substantially less than the maximal asymptotic level of performance (Fig. 3). Hence, RT task is likely to underestimate the true availability of the items in memory. Nonetheless, in all cases, availability systematically declines with recency, consistent with standard forgetting as time or activity is interpolated between study and test. The smooth functions show a simple fit of an exponential forgetting function to each of the estimates.

Hence, although relational information appears to be retrieved with a different process than item information, this fact alone does not appear to provide any grounds on which to motivate a distinct WM system. Importantly, there is no evidence to suggest that order judgments over short and long retention periods engender different operations or that the use of a serial retrieval process is crucially linked to specialized WM representations. In summary, measures of retrieval dynamics for both item and relational information provide clear evidence for a distinction between information within the current focus of attention and information passively stored in memory, but neither provides evidence for a qualitative or quantitative break point between what a tripartite architecture posits as the divide between WM and LTM.

III. Focal Attention

Measures of speed of accessing representations in memory show a sharply dichotomous pattern (Fig. 2B). In tasks, such as probe recognition, retrieval is exceptionally fast when no item or activity intervenes between study and

---

[8] Unfortunately, Muter (1979) only reported the proportion of highly confident responses, so it is not possible to calculate availability estimates for his data.

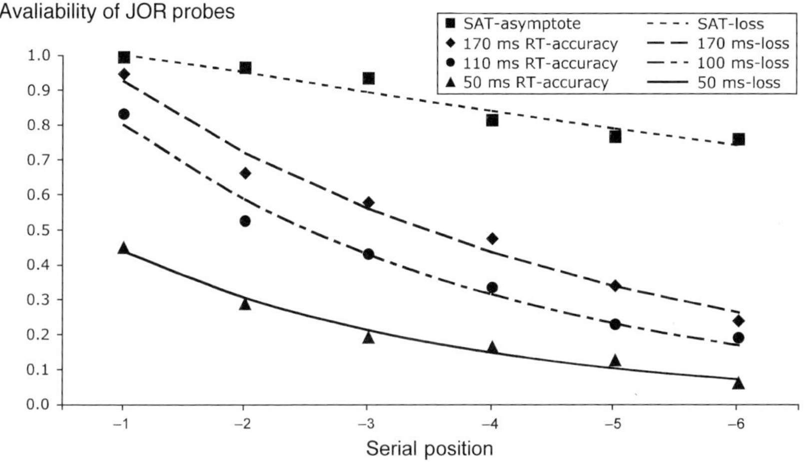

Fig. 6. The estimated availability of different serial position in four different JOR tasks. The most recent serial position is labeled -1, the next most recent position -2, and so on. Square symbols show estimates from the SAT study of McElree and Dosher (1993). The diamonds, circles, and triangles show estimates from Hacker (1980) RT with different rates of presentation (170, 110, and 50 ms/item, respectively). The availability estimates are derived from Hacker's (1980) serial self-terminating model. Test probes are compared to elements in memory in a serial fashion, starting with the most recent and moving backward through the memory representation. The scan is self-terminating in that the first test probe that matches an item in the memory representation is chosen as the more recent. If the later probe is unavailable (with probability $\mathrm{pr} = 1 - a_i$), the earlier probe is incorrectly chosen as the more recent. If both probes are unavailable, the subject is assumed to be guessing. At test, the probability that any particular item is still available in memory is represented in the model by an availability parameter ($0 \leq a_i \leq 1$). Availability for item i in the test probe, a_i, can be estimated from the probability correct, viz., $P_{ij} = a_i + 0.5(1 - a_i)(1 - a_j)$.

test, approximately 40%–50% faster than other items (McElree & Dosher, 1989; Wickelgren et al., 1980). Dosher (1981) reported a similar advantage for the last pair of items in a word–word paired associate recognition task. McElree et al. (2003) found the same essential pattern in an online sentence comprehension task. Retrieval speed continuously declines with recency in the retrieval of order information, but here too there is evidence, albeit indirect evidence, for a discontinuity in retrieval. McElree and Dosher (1993) found that fits of serial search models to the JOR time-course data had to be augmented with a fast matching process to accommodate the exceptionally fast dynamics for JOR probes with the item from the last serial position (SP 1–6 in Fig. 5A). McElree (2001) also found that fits of a serial model to time-course data from an n-back task had to be augmented in exactly the same way (Section III. C).

Evidence is presented below that the most consistent interpretation of these findings is that the last study event typically remains within focal attention, circumventing the retrieval operations that are otherwise needed to restore passive representations outside focal attention to active processing. In many tasks, the event maintained in focal attention will typically be the last item in the study list prior to test. However, as outlined later, the contents of focal attention may consist of more than one item if the task encourages participants to encode items into a chunk (McElree, 1998). Additionally, an item other than the last item may exhibit privileged access if the task induces participants to maintain a nonrecent item in focal attention (Sections III. B and III. C).

A. FURTHER EVIDENCE FOR FOCAL ATTENTION

Does the retrieval advantage for the most recent event truly reflect a special state associated with focal attention, as depicted in Fig. 2A? A concern might be that this advantage is mediated by a low-level physical or visual match (Posner, Boies, Eichelman, & Taylor, 1969). However, several facts suggest that the advantage is mediated by a more abstract or conceptual representation. For example, imposing a pattern mask between study and test does not attenuate the advantage (McElree, 1996, 1998; McElree & Dosher, 1989, 1993) nor does varying letter case between study and test (McElree, 1996, 1998; McElree & Dosher, 1989).

Perhaps the most compelling evidence that the advantage is mediated by an abstract representation comes from an SAT comparison of recognition based on phonological and semantic cues. McElree (1996) presented five-word lists followed by a recognition probe that was either a word from the list (item judgments), rhymed with a list item (rhyme judgments), was synonymous with a list item (synonym judgments), or an unstudied (non-rhyming and nonsynonymous) word. After study, a high, medium, or low-tone cued subjects to make item, rhyme, or synonym judgments about the test probe. The SAT retrieval functions exhibited the same pattern as illustrated in Figs. 4 and 5B. For each type of judgment, recency affected asymptotic accuracy in a continuous fashion. However, retrieval speed (SAT intercept and rate) was equivalent for all serial positions within each judgment, except for the most recently studied position, which showed a large retrieval advantage. Synonym and rhyme judgments were associated with slower SAT dynamics than item judgments, consistent with the idea that subjects used the phonological or semantic information in the test probe as a cue to redingrate the appropriate studied item. The exception to this pattern was the last serial position in which the dynamics were approximately equal across the three judgments. These data indicate that the representation that is responsible for the fast processing dynamics must be abstract enough to enable phonological and semantic properties of the test probe to be directly matched to it.

Other findings more directly implicate the role of focal attention. If the retrieval advantage truly reflects representations in focal attention, then the advantage should extend beyond the most recent item in circumstances in which more than one item is processed concurrently. Dosher (1981) reported an advantage for the last pair of items in a word–word paired associate recognition task. McElree (1998) showed that the advantage extends to the last group of items when task demands induce concurrent encoding of more than one item. Nine-item lists, consisting of three instances from three categories, were presented for study. The words were presented sequentially but were blocked by category membership to encourage subjects to encode members of a category as a chunk. Like prior studies, asymptotic accuracy decreased with the recency of the test probe, but there were also bowed serial position effects within the categories. The latter provides independent evidence that subjects were using the category structure to encode the list. As with other probe recognition studies, two retrieval speeds were found. However, in this case, all three items from the last category were associated with a fast retrieval speed and all items from the first two categories were associated with a second, slower rate. This study provides strong support for the notion that the retrieval advantage stems from representations in focal attention. New evidence for this claim is presented in the next two sections.

B. Shunting Information into Focal Attention: Explicit Retrieval

In all of the studies outlined in earlier section, the advantage in processing speed was limited to the last unit encountered, either to the last studied item or to the last group of studied items. The last event is likely to remain active in focal attention when no activity intervenes between study and test, but in general there need not be a direct coupling of focal attention and the most recent event. One function of an attentional mechanism should be to maintain whatever information is relevant to ongoing processing, even if it is not the most recently processed information. The studies reported in the next three sections show through different means that the retrieval advantage need not be linked to the last event if the task is structured in ways that encourage subjects to attempt to restore previously processed information to focal attention (this section and Section C) or to actively maintain earlier information (Section D).

These studies motivate the general point that task demands often require shunting information between memory and focal attention. They also provide additional evidence for the claim that the observed advantage in processing speed truly reflects the contribution of focal attention. One could imagine an alternative account of the retrieval advantage formulated in terms of the distinctiveness of contextual cues (Nairne, 1996). For example, when no activity intervenes between study and test, the retrieval context at test is nearly identical to the context used to encode the last event. As a consequence, retrieval speed may be exceptionally fast because of the high degree of overlap between study and test.

The studies reported in this section test this notion. Subjects studied sequentially presented six-item lists, consisting of three instances from two categories blocked by category membership (e.g., CAT, MOOSE, WOLF, DOCTOR, COP, LAWYER). On half the trials, subjects received a category cue or prime, consisting of the category label (e.g., ANIMAL or PROFES-SIONS) before receiving a recognition probe. In one experiment, the category cue and the associated retention interval was short, 1 s. Subjects were told to attend to the cue, as it might help them in judging the list status of the probe item. In the other experiment, the category cue and the associated retention interval was 3 s, providing time for subjects to use the cue to attempt to actively retrieve the studied items from that category. In this case, subjects were explicitly instructed to use the retention interval to recover the relevant items presented on the list.

The rationale for these studies was that the retrieval advantage should extend to items from the first category if the subjects are able to use the category cue to retrieve items from memory and restore them to focal attention. But, this should only be possible with sufficient time to retrieve the relevant items. Speed–accuracy trade-off dynamics in these tasks suggest that it takes at least 1 s to recover one item (McElree, 1998), so it should only be possible to retrieve the category members with the long retention interval. Alternatively, if the retrieval advantage is driven by cues in the retrieval context, we might expect the presentation of a category cue, even with a short retention interval, to alter the pattern seen in McElree (1998) in which an advantage is found for the last category only. The advantage should extend to items on the first category in all cases in which the category cue is given before the test item.

1. Experimental Details

Five subjects participated in the first experiment (1-s retention interval) and seven subjects in the second experiment (3-s retention interval). The first-experiment consisted of fifteen 1-h sessions, plus an initial 1-h practice ses-sion that served as training for the SAT procedure. The second experiment consisted of ten 1-h sessions, plus an initial 1-h practice session.

In both experiments, a trial consisted of the sequential presentation of a six-word study list (400 ms/word). Each list contained three words from two common categories drawn from the Battig and Montague (1969) category norms, and the presentation was blocked by category membership. Equal numbers of positive and negative test probes were used. Positive probes were drawn from each of the six serial positions equally often. One-third of the negative trials used an unstudied member from one of the categories in the study list. Another third used lures drawn from a category not presented in the study list. The remaining third used a lure drawn from one of the three words presented on the last category of the prior trial.

After presentation of the study list, a pattern mask (a collection of non-letter symbols) appeared for 500 ms. In the first experiment, the mask was followed by either a 1-s blank retention interval or a 1-s presentation of a category label (e.g., ANIMAL or PROFESSIONS). In the second experiment, the mask was followed by either a 3-s blank retention interval or a 3-s presentation of a category label. The type of retention interval (cue or no cue) was fully crossed with all other experimental factors. Following the retention interval, the test probe was presented. It remained on the screen until the presentation of a 50-ms (2000 Hz) tone, which cued subjects to respond by pressing one of two (yes–no) response keys. In the first experiment, the tone was randomly presented at 43, 200, 300, 500, 800, 1500, or 3000 ms after the test probe appeared. In the second experiment, the tone was presented at 100, 300, 500, 800, 1500, or 3000 ms after the test probe appeared. Following a response, visual feedback on the subject's latency to respond to the interruption tone was presented. Subjects were instructed to respond within 270 ms of the tone. They were told that responses longer than 270 ms were too long and that responses faster than 120 ms were anticipations.

In the short retention interval experiment, half of the cues were valid when the probe was positive (viz., matched the category of the test probe) and half were invalid (viz., matched the other category on the list). In the long retention interval experiment, the cue was always valid when the probe was positive. This was done to encourage subjects to continue to attempt to retrieve studied items from the category throughout the experiment.

2. Findings and Implications

A d' measure was constructed for each subject's data by scaling the hit rate for the serial positions against the false alarm rate for lures from the respective category. The full time-course d' functions were fit with the exponential function in Eq. 1. A competitive model-testing scheme was used to determine the best fitting exponential model.

Figure 7 shows the d' data and best fitting functions for the average (over subjects) data in the no-cue condition (top panel) and 1-s cued condition (bottom panel). Both conditions show standard recency effects on SAT asymptotes—accuracy systematically declined as the probe was drawn from more remote serial positions, coupled with a small primacy advantage for the first item on the list. The estimated d' asymptote was comparable across the noncued and cued conditions—listing from serial position 1–6: 2.4, 1.9, 2.6, 3.4, 3.4, and 3.7 versus 2.3, 2.0, 2.6, 3.4, 3.5, and 3.8, respectively.

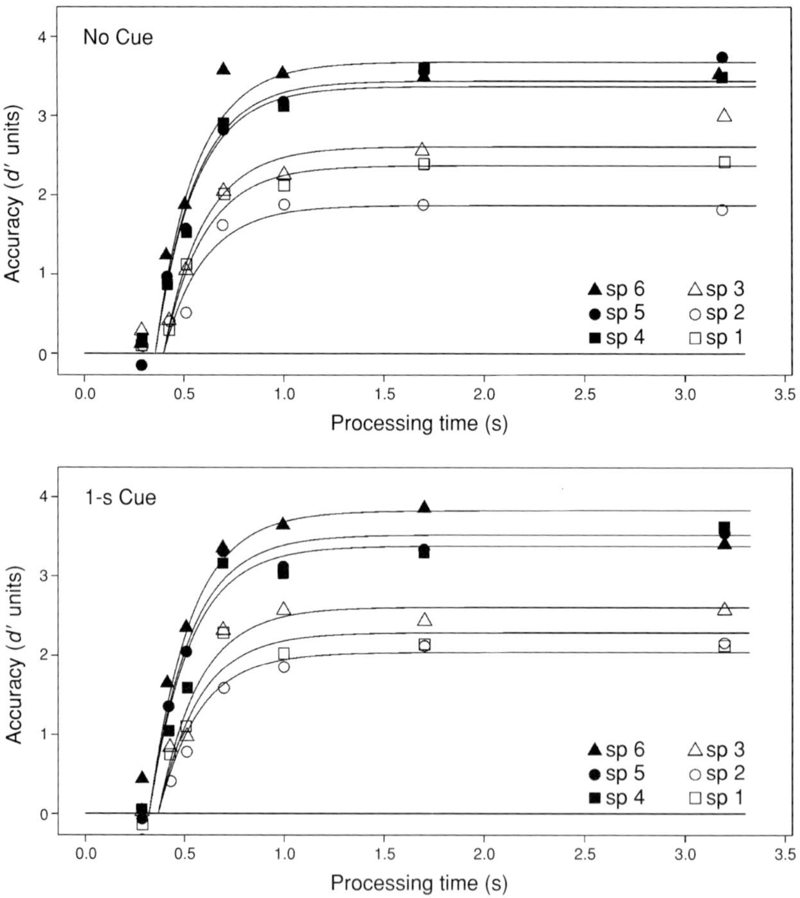

Fig. 7. Average d' values as a function of total processing time for serial positions with set sizes of six word with no retrieval cue (top panel) or 1-s category cue (bottom panel). Smooth functions show best fitting exponential models (Eq. 1) (sp = serial position of the test probe).

Measures of retrieval speed replicated the pattern found in McElree (1998). In the no-cue condition, there was a clear retrieval advantage for items from the last category (serial positions four to six), which was best expressed as a 45 ms advantage in intercept in fits of the average data. The same pattern was evident in fits of all individual subjects' data, with intercept differences that ranged from 84 to 29 ms. Importantly, however, the same pattern was evident in the cued condition. Here, there was a 43 ms advantage in intercept for items from the last category. Again, all subjects showed this intercept advantage, with differences ranging from 98 to 23 ms. Cueing appeared to speed retrieval slightly, as presentation of the category cue reduced the intercepts by 29 ms overall. However, the effect was quite similar for items from the first and second category—the intercept difference between the no-cue and cued condition was 29 ms for items from the first category and 31 ms for items from the last category. Overall, then, there was no evidence indicating that contextual cues affected the retrieval advantage.

Figure 8 shows the corresponding d' data and best fitting functions for the average data from the experiment with the 3-s retention interval in the no-cue condition (top panel) and cued condition (bottom panel). The SAT asymptotic profiles are quite similar to the first experiment—again, accuracy systematically declined as the probe was drawn from more remote serial positions, coupled with a small primacy advantage for the first item on the list. Here, the estimated d' asymptotes were slightly lower for the no-cue than the cued conditions, viz., 2.5, 2.3, 2.6, 3.2, 3.2, and 3.3 versus 2.7, 2.6, 2.9, 3.4, 3.5, and 3.5, listing from serial position 1–6.

Crucially, however, the dynamics showed a different pattern. In the no-cue condition, there was a clear retrieval advantage for items from the last category (serial positions 4–6), which was best expressed as a 35 ms advantage in intercept in fits of the average data. This difference was evident in 6 of the 7 subjects and ranged from 102 to 26 ms. In the cued condition, however, there was no evidence for a dynamics difference between the first and second category. When the average data were fit with separate intercepts or rates, the estimated values were nearly indistinguishable (intercepts: 314 ms versus 311 ms; rates ($1/\beta$): 156 ms versus 162 ms). Additionally, no consistent trend was observed in the fits of the individual subjects' data. Again, cueing appeared to speed retrieval, but the effect was on items from the first category only—the intercept difference between the no-cue and cued condition was 41 ms for items from the first category.

The pattern of results favors an account that attributes the retrieval advantage to focal attention. The category cue alone does not eliminate the advantage. To eliminate the advantage, subjects required sufficient time to implicitly generate list members consistent with the category cue. When the last category on the list was cued, presumably subjects attempted to

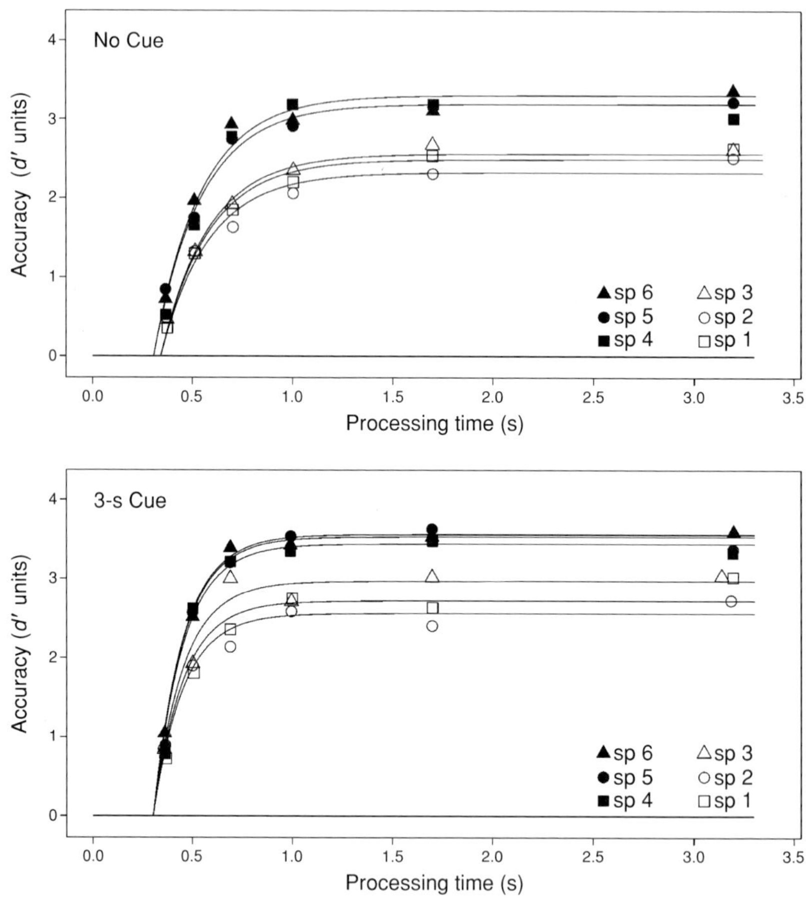

Fig. 8. Average d' values as a function of total processing time for serial positions with set sizes of six word with no retrieval cue (top panel) or 3-s category cue (bottom panel). Smooth functions show best fitting exponential models (Eq. 1) (sp = serial position of the test probe).

maintain items from the last category in focal attention. When the first category was cued, presumably they used the 3-s retention interval to generate the items from the first category. One would expect that success in the latter case would depend on the availability of items in memory, and the SAT asymptotes are largely consistent with this claim. Although the category cue sped the retrieval of items from the first category to a point where they matched the retrieval of items from the last category, the category cues had only a small effect on asymptotic accuracy, and the overall levels for the first category remained well below the levels for the last category.

The absence of a difference in retrieval speed in the cued condition with a 3-s retention interval is consistent with subjects actively shifting attention to list items consistent with the cue. Measuring the dynamics for unattended items would provide an alternative and particularly strong test of this notion. For example, when the first category is cued, retrieval dynamics for the items from the last category on the list should shift to longer times, effectively reversing the pattern seen in the no-cue condition. Testing this prediction requires including trials with invalid cues (e.g., cuing the first category but testing items from the last category). However, the inclusion of these trials is very likely to induce subjects to stop attempting to retrieve items that match the category cue during the retention interval. For this reason, all of the cues in the second experiment were designed to be valid.

C. SHUNTING INFORMATION INTO FOCAL ATTENTION: COVERT REHEARSAL

Arguments for a unique WM store have often been based on the role of phonological coding and covert rehearsal in the maintenance of information over the short term. For example, Baddeley et al. (Baddeley, 1986, 1993; Baddeley, Lewis, & Vallar, 1984; Vallar & Baddeley, 1982) proposed that verbal information is maintained in a limited capacity phonological store, capable of holding 1.5–2 s of auditory information. To maintain information for an extended period, a central executive must selectively apply rehearsal processes to fast decaying items within the store. The argument for 1.5–2 s store is based on the relationship between articulation (or reading) time and memory span—when articulation time for a list of words is used to derive a measure of temporal span, Baddeley (1986) reports that span corresponds to the number of items that can be articulated in 1.5–2 s.

However, Dosher and Ma (1998; Cowan et al., 1992; Schweickert & Boruff, 1986) have argued that this logic crucially ignores the fact that forgetting occurs during recall (output) of the list, which is often 4–6 s in duration. Consequently, 1.5–2 s is not a viable estimate of either trace duration or the capacity of the store; rather, as argued by Dosher and Ma (1998), it represents the correlation of output time and articulation time. Dosher and Ma (1998) demonstrated that span performance follows from a simple forgetting model without assuming a separate store that serves as a buffer for rehearsal.

The approach to subvocal rehearsal pursued here is that a subvocalized item is the current focus of attention and that the subvocalizing process involves sequentially shunting items between focal attention and memory. The latter is similar to traditional arguments that rehearsal provides a means of refreshing fast decaying items, but, unlike approaches such as those of Baddeley et al., no specialized store is assumed.

If the retrieval advantage found in past research reflects the current content of focal attention, then the advantage should track directly with covert rehearsal. A control rehearsal procedure (Seamon & Wright, 1976) was coupled with an SAT probe recognition task to test this notion. Prior to receiving a recognition probe, subjects subvocally rehearsed the items from a five-item study list for either a 2- or 4-s retention period. The numbers 1 and 2 (2-s retention interval) or 1–4 (4-s retention interval) were presented for 1 s each during the retention interval to serve as an external timing cue for rehearsal. The prediction was that a retrieval advantage should be observed around serial position 2 in the 2-s retention interval and around serial position 4 in the 2-s retention interval, rather than on the final items, as has been observed in other list studies.

1. Experimental Details

Five subjects participated in the experiment. It consisted of fifteen 1-h sessions, plus an initial 1-h practice session that served as training for the SAT procedure.

A trial consisted of the sequential presentation of a five-consonant study list (400 ms/consonant). Equal numbers of positive and negative test probes were used, with positive probes being drawn from each of the six serial positions equally often. After presentation of the study list, a pattern mask (a collection of nonletter symbols) was presented for 500 ms. On half the trials, the mask was followed by a sequential visual presentation of the numbers 1 and 2 for 1 s each. On the other half of the trials, the mask was followed by the numbers 1–4, presented for 1 s each. Subjects were instructed to use the number to time their rehearsal, using the numbers to rehearse the corresponding consonant on the list. Following the final number (2 or 4), the test probe was presented, enclosed in asterisks to clearly mark it as a recognition probe. The probe remained on the screen for either 43, 257, 400, 600, 800, or 3000 ms, at which time the probe disappeared and a 50 ms (2000 Hz) tone sounded to cue the subject to respond. Following a response, visual feedback on the subject's latency to respond to the interruption tone was presented. Subjects were instructed to respond within 270 ms of the tone. They were told that responses longer than 270 ms were too long and that responses faster than 120 ms were anticipations.

2. Findings and Implications

A d' measure was constructed for each subject's data by scaling the hit rate for various serial positions against the false alarm rate for each condition. The full time-course d' functions were fit with the exponential function in Eq. 1.

Figure 9 shows the d' data and best fitting functions for the average (over subjects) data in the 2-s rehearsal condition (top panel) and the 4-s rehearsal condition (bottom panel). A notable aspect of these data is the attenuation of the robust recency effects found in other probe recognition studies (McElree, 1996, 1998; McElree & Dosher, 1989; Wickelgren et al., 1980). In the 2-s rehearsal conditions, the estimated asymptotes (λ) were 3.47, 3.80, 3.89, 3.93, and 3.50 d' units for serial position 1–5. In the 4-s rehearsal conditions, the corresponding values were 3.78, 3.63, 3.79, 3.84, and 3.70. The absence of recency effects on the SAT asymptotes is consistent with

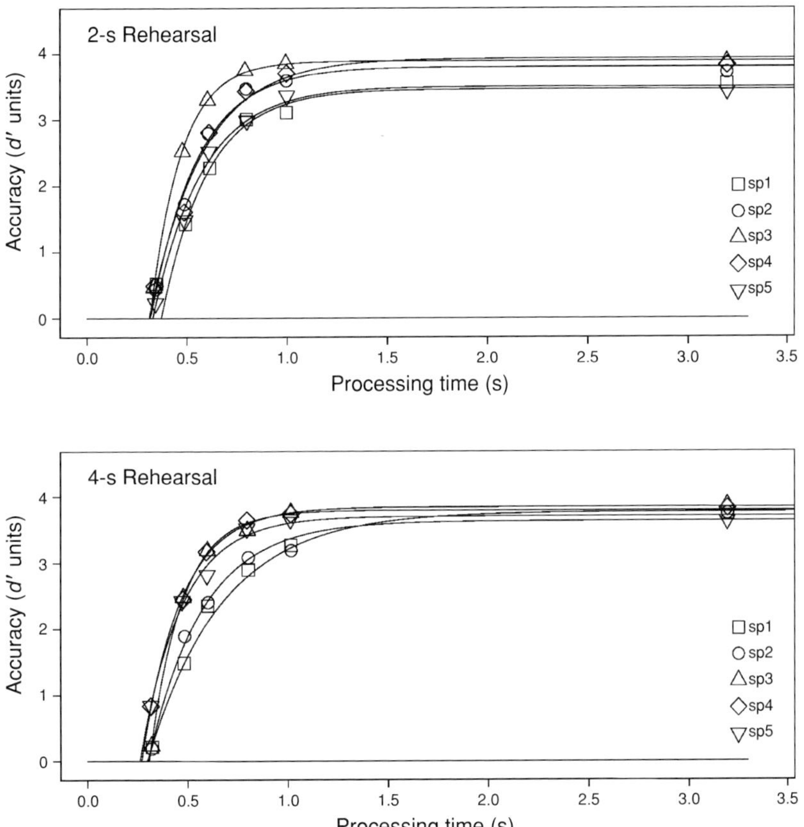

Fig. 9. Average d' values as a function of total processing time for serial positions with set sizes of five word with 2 s of cued rehearsal (top panel) or 4 s of cued rehearsal (bottom panel). Smooth functions show best fitting exponential models (Eq. 1) (sp = serial position of the test probe).

Sternberg's (1966, 1969, 1975) original reports that the serial position of the positive test probes did not affect response latency or accuracy. McElree and Dosher (1989) speculated that the few researchers who obtained no serial position effects in this type of task used longer retention intervals (>1 s), which allowed partial rehearsal to alter subjective recency. They noted that this view is generally consistent with data from controlled-rehearsal studies (Seamon & Wright, 1976). The absence of recency effects on the asymptotes here provides additional support for this contention.

Competitive model fits found clear evidence for dynamics differences, but they were unlike the standard patterns that have been found in similar studies (McElree, 1995, 1998; McElree & Dosher, 1989; Wickelgren et al., 1980). Notably absent from both conditions is the general advantage for the last item on the list. This is consistent with rehearsal displacing the last item from focal attention. The dynamics differences are best illustrated by allowing both rate and intercept to vary with serial position. However, because rate and intercept can sometimes trade with one another in model fits, it is best to compare conditions with a composite measure, $\delta + 1/\beta$, which provide an estimate of the average retrieval speed. In the 2-s rehearsal conditions, the estimated retrieval speeds were 598, 551, 467, 572, and 573 ms. There is a clear advantage for position 3 and to a lesser extent position 2. If subjects were rehearsing the list in approximate time to the rehearsal cue, then these are exactly the positions that would be predicted to be in focal attention at test time. In the 4-s rehearsal conditions, the estimated retrieval speeds were 667, 574, 470, 463, and 468 ms. Here, there is a clear advantage for the positions 3–5, with the minimum at position 4. Again, these are the positions that are predicted to be in focal attention at test. The broader dispersion of the advantage is likely to have resulted from general variability in timing and from the greater likelihood of encountering retrieval difficulties in the 4 s as compared to 2-s conditions. For example, if a subject failed to retrieve one of the items in positions 1–4, then they would be predicted have the item from position 5 in focal attention at test time. Conversely, if there was momentary difficulty in retrieving items at position 1–4, then it is reasonable to expect that subjects may lag behind the cue by one or two items. Additionally, order exchanges (Estes, 1985) could also contribute to the broader distribution of the advantage in the 4-s condition.

Collectively, the time-course profiles in Fig. 9 provide strong evidence that items in focal attention are associated with faster dynamics than items in a more passive memory state outside of attention. Covert rehearsal can be regarded as a process that gates items between focal attention and memory by retrieving items from memory and restoring them to active processing.

D. THE CAPACITY OF FOCAL ATTENTION

Cowan (2001) argued that data from several paradigms indicate that focal attention has a capacity of three to five chunks. The strongest support for this claim has come from studies examining processing limits in multielement displays, in which all elements are simultaneously displayed and the task encourages concurrent processing of the elements. These include multi-object tracking, enumeration tasks, and visual search tasks. Cowan also proposed that the same capacity limit holds when information is distributed across time, viz., when information is *sequentially* rather than *simultaneously* presented and processed. However, McElree and Dosher (2001) point out that the evidence for a three to five-item limit is very indirect in tasks in which information is distributed across time. For example, as evidence for the capacity of focal attention, Cowan forwards findings that the absolute or estimated number of items recalled in short-term tasks is often three or four. However, recall levels are determined by factors other than the capacity of focal attention. For example, recall of representations outside focal attention will partly contribute to overall recall scores, with the amount contributed being determined by forgetting over the learning phase and during the recall process (Dosher & Ma, 1998). There is simply no reason to assume that the number of items recalled exclusively denotes items recalled from focal attention and hence that the number of items recalled provides a veridical estimate of the capacity of focal attention.

Notably, Cowan's estimate of the capacity of focal attention is inconsistent with other data, including RT patterns in a switching task, which suggest that only one object can be maintained in focal attention (Garavan, 1998). Crucially, this estimate is inconsistent with the observed discontinuities in retrieval speed, which provide perhaps the most direct evidence of what is in focal attention. As outlined earlier, this evidence indicates that focal attention is able to maintain only one temporally extended event across a dynamically changing environment. This is usually the last item processed (McElree, 1996; McElree & Dosher, 1989; McElree et al., 2003; Wickelgren et al., 1980), but it may include more than one nominal item if those items can be simultaneously coded into a chunk that forms a single processing epoch (McElree, 1998; Section II. B). McElree and Dosher (2001) suggested that the capacity of attention may differ across space and time—we may be able to attend to more than one simultaneously presented element, but we do not appear able to attend to more than one temporally extended epoch.

1. Sustaining and Refocusing Attention

Collectively, direct measures of retrieval speed indicate that focal attention is more limited than what is suggested by the indirect measures proposed by

Cowan (2001). Further evidence for this claim comes from an investigation of the temporal dynamics in the *n*-back task (McElree, 2001). This task requires determining whether an item matches the *n*th-item back in a sequentially presented list of items, for example, 1-back, 2-back, 3-back, and so on. The task directly challenges subjects to maintain the *n*-back item in focal attention while concurrently processing new items. Additionally, the task places substantial demands on control (executive) processes, as the response set must be continually updated when new items are encountered. For example, when a new item is presented, the former *n*-back item changes from a target to a distractor, the item that was formerly $n - 1$ back becomes the target item, and all items less than *n*-back must be marked as future targets. As such, the task provides a good experimental analog to real world situations in which we must focus on an item or event while continuing to process other information that may be useful in the future.

Just as in the controlled-rehearsal study reported in Section II. C, we would expect that if the *n*th-item back is successfully maintained in focal attention, then it should be immediately available for matching to the test probe. Conversely, if subsequent processing usurps the *n*-back item from focal attention, then the *n*-back target must be retrieved from a more passive memory state. The *n*-back task requires the retrieval of temporal order information, as a positive response must be given only to an item in a particular position in the sequence. Consequently, when the item is outside of focal attention, retrieval is likely to require the same type of slow, search-like process used to recover order information in tasks such as JOR (McElree & Dosher, 1993).

McElree (2001, Experiment 1) examined 1-back, 2-back, and 3-back conditions with the SAT procedure to further investigate the capacity of focal attention. If Cowan's capacity estimate of three to four items is correct, then we would expect that subjects can maintain the *n*-back target in focal attention across one or two intervening items. This predicts that access speed should be fast and should not vary across the 1–3-back conditions. Conversely, if subjects cannot accurately maintain three items in focal attention, then retrieval speed should systematically slow as *n* is increased, for two reasons. First, there are two ways to make a correct judgment (ignoring guessing), either by maintaining the *n*-back item in focal attention or by successfully retrieving it from memory. If the latter is slower than the former and the probability of maintaining an item in focal attention decreases as more items are interpolated between study and test, then retrieval speed will slow as *n* increases. Second, the speed of retrieving order information decreases with recency (McElree & Dosher, 1993), so recovering a 3-back item will take more time than a 2-back item, and 2-back item will take more time than a 1-back item.

The standard version of the *n*-back task uses a continuous recognition paradigm, in which judgments are made after each item is presented. However, this procedure is not optimal for collecting time-course data. McElree (2001) implemented the task demands in a standard *n*-back paradigm by using randomly varying lists of 6–15 letters, followed by a recognition probe. In different blocks of trials, subjects judged whether the probe matched the item occurring 1, 2, or 3 positions back. The unpredictable list length challenged subjects in exactly the same way as a continuous recognition task—because subjects did not know when the test item would appear, the response set had to be modified as new items were presented. The SAT procedure was used to collect time-course data by cueing subjects to respond at 43, 200, 300, 500, 800, 1500, or 3000 ms after the onset of the probe.

Figure 10 shows the average full time-course functions for the three *n*-back conditions. Asymptotic accuracy decreased as *n* increased—the average d' score at the longest interruption time (3 s) was 3.9 for 1-back, 3.5 for 2-back, and 2.6 for 3-back. These differences indicate that the probability of identifying the *n*-back target decreased as more items intervened between study and test. Prima facie, the significant differences in asymptotic levels demonstrate that participants were not completely successful in maintaining the *n*-back target in focal attention and that they were less likely to retrieve the *n*-back target from memory when more items intervened between study and test.

Additionally, competitive model fits of the exponential function (Eq. 1) revealed that retrieval significantly slowed as *n* increased. This is also inconsistent with an attentional capacity of three or more items. The speed

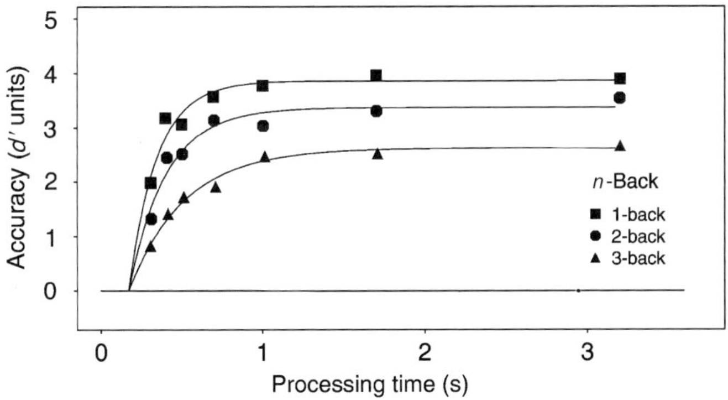

Fig. 10.   Average d' accuracy (symbols) as a function of processing time (lag of the response cue plus latency to respond to the cue) for the 1-back, 2-back, and 3-back conditions. Smooth curves show the best fits of Eq. 1. (Based on data reported in McElree, 2001.)

difference was best expressed as a rate (β) difference—the average rate estimates were 231 in ($1/\beta$) ms units for 1-back, 344 ms for 2-back, and 581 ms for 3-back, and this order was evident in all 6 subjects. The systematic slowing of the SAT rate indicates that the target item was not perfectly maintained in focal attention across 1–3-back conditions and that a retrieval operation was required to restore the target item to active processing on some portion of trials. McElree (2001) showed that the time-course profiles are adequately modeled by probabilistic mixtures of two processes. When the n-back item was maintained in focal attention, judgments were mediated by a fast matching process; when the target had been displaced from focal attention, judgments were mediated by a slower backward or recency-based search process of the type used to model the recovery of order information in the JOR task.[9]

In a second experiment, McElree (2001) modified the task to further induce subjects to attempt to maintain all three items in focal attention. The experiment used two variants of a 3-back condition. In one, a standard 3-back condition, subjects were required to respond positively to a test item only if it matched the item three positions back. This condition was referred to as 3-back exclusion, because subjects were required to exclude all positions other than 3-back. In the second condition, referred to as 3-back inclusion, subjects were required to respond positively to all items up to and including 3-back (viz., 1-back, 2-back, and 3-back). This condition was expected to challenge subjects to maintain three items rather than just one item within the focus of attention.

Figure 11 shows the average full time-course functions for the 3-back exclusion (open squares) and the three n-back inclusion conditions (filled symbols). Consider the latter first. As with the first experiment, asymptotic accuracy significantly decreased as n increased—here, the average d' score at the longest interruption time (3 s) was 3.3 for 1-back, 3.1 for 2-back, and 2.7 for 3-back. Again, these differences provide prima facie evidence that three n-back targets could not be perfectly maintained in focal attention and that the probability of recovering the relevant target from a memory representation decreased as more items intervened between study and test. Again, retrieval significantly slowed as n increased, best expressed as a rate (β) difference—the average rate estimates were 238 in ($1/\beta$) ms units for 1-back, 386 ms for 2-back, and 629 ms for 3-back, and this ordering was evident in

---

[9] In JORs, recency engendered large shifts in SAT intercept, which were not found in the n-back data. However, as the SAT intercept is determined by the first process to complete, shifts in intercept are not expected when a serial process is mixed with a fast matching process. The mixture model demonstrated that the impact of a serial process in such cases is to engender progressively slower rates as more serial comparisons are required (McElree, 2001).

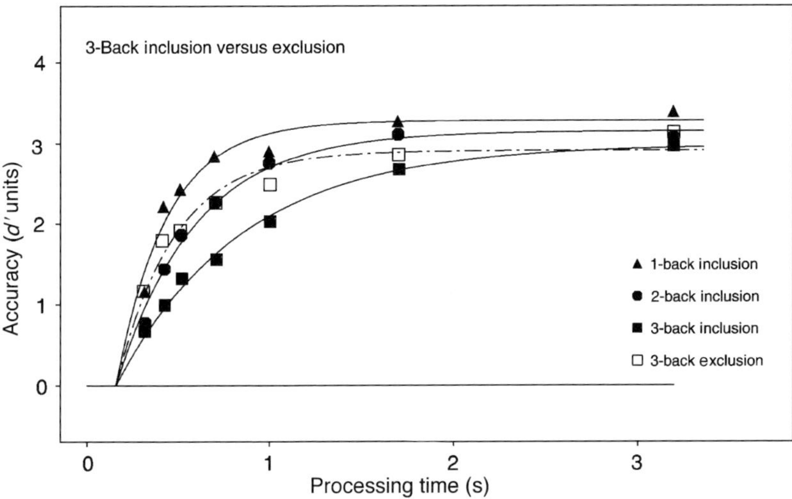

Fig. 11.   Average d' accuracy (symbols) as a function of processing time (lag of the response cue plus latency to respond to the cue) for the 1-back, 2-back, and 3-back inclusion conditions and the 3-back exclusion condition. Smooth curves show the best fits of of Eq. 1. (Based on data reported in McElree, 2001.)

all 7 subjects. These differences again indicate that subjects could not maintain all three items in focal attention.

The inability to maintain all three items in focal attention is also demonstrated by a comparison of the 3-back inclusion and exclusion conditions. The 3-back exclusion was associated with significantly faster dynamics than 3-back inclusion. In direct model fits, the rate estimates were 317 ms for 3-back exclusion versus 689 ms for 3-back inclusion, with all subjects showing this difference. One should note that asymptotic performance is comparable in both conditions. Hence, subjects were equally likely to ultimately access the 3-back item, but they were slower to do so in the 3-back inclusion condition. The speed difference suggests that there is a higher probability of maintaining the 3-back item in attention with one rather than three potential targets. With more targets, there is a greater probability that the 3-back item will be displaced from focal attention and will then require a more costly search process. Consistent with this interpretation, when the mixture model was fit to these data, the probability of maintaining an item in focal attention was estimated to be lower in the 3-back inclusion condition than in the 3-back exclusion condition.

Results from the *n*-back inclusion task indicate that the upper bound on the number of units that can be actively maintained in focal attention is less than three items. For example, the mixture model reported in McElree (2001) estimated that subjects had to search for either the 2-back or 3-back target on 86% of the trials.[10] The data unequivocally indicate that three items could not be maintained in focal attention, and overall the time-course differences between 3-back exclusion and inclusion are fully consistent with prior results suggesting that the limit on focal attention is one unit. Arguably, the *n*-back task provides stronger evidence for the limited nature of focal attention than other time-course studies. Tasks, such as item recognition, can be easily accomplished with an efficient direct-access process, so there may be little incentive for subjects to deploy more cognitively engaging operations to maintain more than the last item in focal attention. In the *n*-back task, in contrast, a strategy of maintaining more than one item in focal attention would ostensibly circumvent the more difficult process of recovering order information (McElree & Dosher, 1993). It is reasonable to assume, therefore, that subjects would have attempted to maintain three items if they were capable of doing so.

In summary, measures of retrieval speed provide a relatively direct means of estimating the capacity of focal attention, as information in focal attention can be distinguished from information passively held in memory by its exceptionally fast response dynamics. Crucially, whether information is maintained in focal attention because no significant mental activity has intervened between study and test (McElree, 1996, 1998; McElree & Dosher, 1989, 1993; Wickelgren et al., 1980) or because task demands induce participants to attempt to maintain nonrecent items in focal attention (Sections III. B , III. C, and III. D), estimates of the capacity of focal attention based on measures of retrieval speed suggest a much smaller upper-limit than the three to five items that Cowan (2001) has proposed on the basis of various indirect measures. Measures of retrieval dynamics suggest that we may be able to maintain only one temporally extended event across a dynamically changing environment.

---

[10] In fact, this is a very conservative estimate. The mixture model assumes that subjects always maintained the 1-back item in focal attention. However, if subjects were attempting but unable to maintain all three items in focal attention, an effective strategy would have been to cycle through the last three items. If the last item was not in focal attention every time it was tested, then the baseline estimate of the time to match an item to the contents of focal attention is inflated by those trials when additional time was needed to search for the 1-back target. The net effect of overestimating the time to match a test item to focal attention would be to underestimate the proportion of searches necessary to respond to a 2-back or 3-back target.

IV. Neuroanatomical Substrates

The behavioral evidence used to motivate a unique WM system assumed in tripartite architectures has been questioned on several grounds (Crowder, 1993; Nairne, 1996; Wickelgren, 1973). Measures of retrieval speed outlined in this chapter provide grounds for drawing a distinction between focal attention and passive memory representations, but they are inconsistent with an intermediate WM state assumed in tripartite architectures. However, recent neuroimaging work might provide another source of evidence for a WM store. The tripartite architecture has been used as a framework for interpreting several neuroimaging studies. This section briefly considers whether proposed mappings between components of this architecture and different neuroanatomical substrates provide new evidence for a WM store.

For example, imaging studies of the n-back task have found significant activations that scale with n in the dorsolateral prefrontal cortex (DLPFC), Broca's area, and areas of the left inferior parietal cortex (Awh et al., 1996; Cohen et al., 1994, 1997; Ravizza, Delgado, Chein, Becker, & Fiez, 2004; Smith & Jonides, 1997, 1999). Smith and Jonides (1997, 1999) argued that activation in the DLPFC and Broca's area are reflections of executive or control processes, with the latter specifically linked to rehearsal processes (Henson, Burgess, & Frith, 2000). Activation in left inferior parietal areas is said to reflect WM storage rather than control processes, particularly the locus of the phonological buffer postulated in Baddeley's (1986) WM model. In this construal, increased activation in left inferior parietal areas reflects the neural activity directly associated with increased storage demands. This proposal is generally consistent with this area also being active in probe recognition tasks (Henson et al., 2000; Jonides et al., 1997; Ravizza et al., 2004).

However, given that the time-course data shows that n-back judgments are in part mediated by a search process and that the complexity of the search depends on n, activation in the posterior parietal region could equally well reflect correlates of the search or reconstructive process (McElree, 2001). Because imaging studies of the probe recognition task have been conducted in a manner that allowed for rehearsal, which involves the reconstruction of serial order, it is also possible to interpret results from these tasks in this manner.

Fiez et al. (Chein, Ravizza, & Fiez, 2003; Fiez, 2001; Ravizza et al., 2004) argued that several facts are inconsistent with the left inferior parietal region acting as a phonological store. Their analysis suggests that two regions in the inferior parietal region have functionally dissociable roles, neither of which is fully consistent with the notion of a phonological store. A dorsal region appears to be recruited in high-load condition, when attentional demands are high. They suggest that it might be more proper to view this region as part of a frontal–parietal executive system and that it may serve to focus attention on items rather than as a storage site (Chein et al., 2003). They note that this is generally consistent with this region being important for retaining temporal order information (Marshuetz, Smith, Jonides, DeGutis, & Chenevert, 2000), for reactivating sources of information (Corbetta, Kincade, & Shulman, 2002), and for attention switching (LaBar, Gitelman, Parrish, & Mesulam, 1999). A more ventral region is sensitive to information type, showing activation when the task involves verbal coding. Crucially, however, this region does not appear to be sensitive to memory load and is active in conditions with very few memory demands. Thus, it does not appear to function as a short-term store, which would be expected to show an effect of high-verbal load when rehearsal processes are deployed to refresh and update the store (Ravizza et al., 2004). The suggestion is that this region is involved with basic speech processing.

Although brain imaging data hold great potential for addressing issues of functional architecture, the evidence to date does not appear to provide additional grounds on which to motivate a unique storage structure associated with WM.

V. Conclusions

The direction taken in recent neuroimaging work appears to parallel directions in research on individual differences and age-related changes in cognition. Traditionally, the capacity of WM was thought to be an important constraint on cognitive processing and to provide a basis on which to characterize differences among individuals and special populations. However, recent work has appealed more to differences in control and automatic processes than to differences in storage capacity (Engle, 1996; Engle & Kane, 2004; Kane & Engle, 2003; Stoltzfus, Hasher, & Zacks, 1996), processes that appear to be associated with frontal–parietal systems. Measures of retrieval speed appear to dovetail with both of these recent directions in emphasizing that the successful execution of complex cognitive operations may depend more on our ability to shunt information between focal attention and memory than on the existence of a temporary store.

ACKNOWLEDGMENTS

Preparation of this chapter was supported by a grant from the National Science Foundation (BCS-0236732). The author would like to thank Julie Van Dyke and Ilke Öztekin for helpful comments. Address correspondence to Brian McElree, Department of Psychology, New York University, 6 Washington Place, New York 10003, USA.

REFERENCES

Anderson, J. R. (1983). *The architecture of cognition.* Cambridge, MA: Harvard University Press.

Awh, E., Jonides, J., Smith, E. E., Schumacher, E. H., Koeppe, R. A., & Katz, S. (1996). Dissociation of storage and rehearsal in verbal working memory: Evidence from positron emission tomography. *Psychological Science, 7,* 25–31.

Baddeley, A. D. (1986). *Working memory.* Oxford: Oxford University Press.

Baddeley, A. D. (1993). Working memory or working attention? In A. Baddeley and L. Weiskrantz (Eds.), *Attention, selection, awareness, and control: A tribute to Donald Broadbent* (pp. 152–170). Oxford: Oxford University Press.

Baddeley, A. D., & Hitch, G. (1974). Working memory. In G. H. Bower (Ed.), *The psychology of learning and motivation: Advances in research and theory* (Vol. 8, pp. 47–89). New York: Academic Press.

Baddeley, A. D., Lewis, V. J., & Vallar, G. (1984). Exploring the articulatory loop. *Quarterly Journal of Experimental Psychology: Human Experimental Psychology, 36*(A), 233–252.

Battig, W. F., & Montague, W. E. (1969). Category norms for verbal items in 56 categories: A replication and extension of the Connecticut category norms. *Journal of Experimental Psychology Monograph, 80,* 1–46.

Bower, G. H. (1972). Stimulus sampling theory of encoding variability. In A. W. Melton and E. Martin (Eds.), *Coding processes in human memory.* New York: V. H. Winston.

Broadbent, D. E. (1958). *Perception and commucation.* London: Pergamon Press.

Chein, J. M., Ravizza, S. M., & Fiez, J. A. (2003). Using neuroimaging to evaluate models of working memory and their implications for language processing. *Journal of Neurolinguistics, 16,* 315–339.

Clark, S. E., & Gronlund, S. D. (1996). Global matching models of recognition memory: How the models match the data. *Psychonomic Bulletin & Review, 3,* 37–60.

Cohen, J. D., Forman, S. D., Braver, T. S., Casey, B. J., Servan-Schreiber, D., & Noll, D. (1994). Activation of the prefrontal cortex in a nonspatial working memory task with functional MRI. *Human Brain Mapping, 1,* 293–304.

Cohen, J. D., Perlstein, W. M., Braver, T. S., Nystrom, L. E., Noll, D., Jonides, J., & Smith, E. E. (1997). Temporal dynamics of brain activation during a working memory task. *Nature, 386,* 604–608.

Conway, A. R. A., & Engle, R. W. (1994). Working-memory capacity as long-term memory activation: An individual-differences approach. *Journal of Experimental Psychology: General, 123,* 354–373.

Cowan, N. (1995). *Attention and memory: An integrated framework.* Oxford: Oxford University Press.

Cowan, N. (2001). The magical number 4 in short-term memory: A reconsideration of mental storage capacity. *Behavioral and Brain Sciences, 24,* 87–185.

Cowan, N., Day, L., Saults, S., Keller, T. A., Johnson, T., & Flores, L. (1992). The role of verbal output time in the effects of word length on immediate memory. *Journal of Memory and Language, 31,* 1–17.

Corbetta, M., Kincade, J. M., & Shulman, G. L. (2002). Neural systems for visual orienting and their relationships to spatial working memory. *Journal of Cognition Neuroscience, 14,* 508–523.

Crowder, R. G. (1993). Short-term memory: Where do we stand. *Memory and Cognition, 21,* 142–145.

Dosher, B. A. (1976). The retrieval of sentences from memory: A speed-accuracy study. *Cognitive Psychology, 8,* 291–310.

Dosher, B. A. (1979). Empirical approaches to information processing: Speed-accuracy tradeoff or reaction time. *Acta Psychologica, 43*, 347–359.

Dosher, B. A. (1981). The effect of delay and interference: A speed-accuracy study. *Cognitive Psychology, 13*, 551–582.

Dosher, B. A. (1982). Effect of sentence size and network distance on retrieval speed. *Journal of Experimental Psychology: Learning, Memory and Cognition, 8*, 173–207.

Dosher, B. A. (1984). Degree of learning and retrieval speed: Study time and multiple exposures. *Journal of Experimental Psycholog: Learning, Memory and Cognition, 10*, 541–574.

Dosher, B. A., & Ma, J. J. (1998). Output loss or rehearsal loop? Output-time versus pronunciation-time limits in immediate recall for forgetting-matched materials. *Journal of Experimental Psychology: Learning, Memory, and Cognition, 24*, 316–335.

Dosher, B. A., McElree, B., Hood, R. M., & Rosedale, G. R. (1989). Retrieval dynamics of priming in recognition memory: Bias and discrimination analysis. *Journal of Experimental Psychology: Learning, Memory & Cognition, 15*, 868–886.

Dosher, B. A., & Rosedale, G. (1989). Integrated retrieval cues as a mechanism for priming in retrieval from memory. *Journal of Experimental Psychology: General, 118*, 191–218.

Engle, R. W. (1996). Working memory and retrieval: An inhibition resource approach. In J. Richardson, R. Engle, L. Hasher, R. Logie, E. Stoltzfus, and R. Zacks (Eds.), *Working memory and human cognition* (pp. 89–119). Oxford: Oxford University Press.

Engle, R. W., & Kane, M. J. (2004). Executive attention, working memory capacity, and a two-factor theory of cognitive control. In B. Ross (Ed.), *The psychology of learning and motivation* (Vol. 44, pp. 145–199). New York: Elsevier.

Ericsson, K. A., & Pennington, N. (1993). The structure of memory performance in experts: Implications for memory in everyday life. In G. M. Davis and R. H. Logie (Eds.), *Memory in everyday life* (pp. 241–272). Amsterdam: North Holland.

Estes, W. K. (1985). Memory for temporal information. In J. A. Michon and J. L. Jackson (Eds.), *Time, mind, and behavior* (pp. 149–168). Berlin: Springer-Verlag.

Fiez, J. A. (2001). Bridging the gap between neuroimaging and neuropsychology: Using working memory as a case-study. *Journal of Clinical and Experimental Neuropsychology, 23*, 19–31.

Flexser, A. J., & Bower, G. H. (1974). How frequency affects recency judgments: A model of recency discriminations. *Journal of Experimental Psychology, 103*, 706–716.

Garavan, H. (1998). Serial attention within working memory. *Memory & Cognition, 26*, 263–276.

Gillund, G., & Shiffrin, R. M. (1984). A retrieval model for both recognition and recall. *Psychological Review, 91*, 1–67.

Gronlund, S. D., Edwards, M. B., & Ohrt, D. D. (1997). Comparison of the retrieval of item versus spatial position information. *Journal of Experimental Psychology: Learning, Memory, and Cognition, 23*, 1261–1274.

Hacker, M. J. (1980). Speed and accuracy of recency judgments for events in short-term memory. *Journal of Experimental Psychology: Learning, Memory and Cognition, 6*, 651–675.

Hasher, L., & Zacks, R. T. (1984). Automatic processing of fundamental information: The case of frequency of occurrence. *American Psychologist, 39*, 1372–1388.

Henson, R. N., Burgess, N., & Frith, C. D. (2000). Receding, storage, rehearsal and grouping in verbal short-term memory: An fMRI study. *Neuropsychologia, 38*, 426–440.

Hinrichs, J. V. (1970). A two process memory-strength theory for judgments of recency. *Psychological Review, 77*, 223–233.

Hinton, G. E. (1989). Implementing semantic networks in parallel hardware. In G. E. Hinton and J. A. Anderson (Eds.), *Parallel models of associative memory* (pp. 191–217). Hillsdale, NJ: Erlbaum.

Hintzman, D. L. (1984). MINERVA 2: A simulation model of human memory. *Behavior Research Methods, Instruments, & Computers, 16*, 96–101.

Hintzman, D. L. (1988). Judgments of frequency and recognition memory in a multiple-trace memory model. *Psychological Review, 95*, 528–551.

Hintzman, D. L., & Caulton, D. A. (1997). Recognition memory and modality judgments: A comparison of retrieval dynamics. *Journal of Memory and Language, 37*, 1–23.

Hintzman, D. L., Caulton, D. A., & Levitin, D. J. (1998). Retrieval dynamics in recognition and list discrimination: Further evidence for separate processes of familiarity and recall. *Memory & Cognition, 26*, 448–462.

Hintzman, D. L., & Curran, T. (1994). Retrieval dynamics of recognition and frequency judgments: Evidence for separate processes of familiarity and recall. *Journal of Memory and Language, 33*, 1–18.

Hockley, W. E. (1984). Analysis of response time distribution in the study of cognitive processes. *Journal of Experimental Psychology: Learning, Memory, and Cognition, 10*, 598–615.

James, W. (1890). *The Principles of Psychology* (pp. 646–647). New York: Henry Holt.

Jonides, J., Schumacher, E. H., Smith, E. E., Lauber, E., Awh, E., Minoshima, S., & Koeppe, R. A. (1997). The task-load of verbal working memory affects regional brain activation as measured by PET. *Journal of Cognitive Neuroscience, 9*, 462–475.

Kane, M. J., & Engle, R. W. (2003). Working memory capacity and the control of attention: The contributions of goal neglect, response competition, and task set to Stroop interference. *Journal of Experimental Psychology: General, 132*, 47–70.

Kawamoto, A. (1988). Distributed representations of ambiguous words and their resolution in a connectionist network. In S. L. Small, G. W. Cottrell, and M. K. Tanenhaus (Eds.), *Lexical ambiguity resolution: Perspectives from psycholinguistics, neuropsychology, and artificial intelligence* (pp. 195–228). San Mateo, CA: Morgan Kaufmann.

LaBar, K. S., Gitelman, D. R., Parrish, T. B., & Mesulam, M. (1999). Neuroanatomic overlap of working memory and spatial attention networks: A functional MRI comparison within subjects. *Neuroimage, 10*, 695–704.

Lewandowsky, S., & Murdock, B. B., Jr. (1989). Memory for serial order. *Psychological Review, 96*, 25–53.

Marshuetz, C., Smith, E. E., Jonides, J., DeGutis, J., & Chenevert, T. L. (2000). Order information in working memory: fMRI evidence for parietal and prefrontal mechanisms. *Journal of Cognitive Neuroscience, 12*, 130–144.

McBride, D. A., & Dosher, B. A. (1997). A comparison of forgetting in an implicit and explicit memory task. *Journal of Experimental Psychology: General, 126*, 371–392.

McBride, D. A., & Dosher, B. A. (1999). Forgetting rates are comparable in conscious and automatic memory: A process-dissociation study. *Journal of Experimental Psychology: Learning, Memory, and Cognition, 25*, 583–607.

McElree, B. (1993). The locus of lexical preference effects in sentence comprehension: A time-course analysis. *Journal of Memory and Language, 32*, 536–571.

McElree, B. (1996). Accessing short-term memory with semantic and phonological information: A time-course analysis. *Memory & Cognition, 24*, 173–187.

McElree, B. (1998). Attended and non-attended states in working memory: Accessing categorized structures. *Journal of Memory & Language, 38*, 225–252.

McElree, B. (2000). Sentence comprehension is mediated by content-addressable memory structures. *Journal of Psycholinguistic Research, 29*, 111–123.

McElree, B. (2001). Working memory and focal attention. *Journal of Experimental Psychology: Learning, Memory, and Cognition, 27*, 817–835.

McElree, B., & Carrasco, M. (1999). The temporal dynamics of visual search: Speed-accuracy tradeoff analysis of feature and conjunctive searches. *Journal of Experimental Psychology: Human Perception and Performance, 25*, 1517–1539.

McElree, B., & Dosher, B. A. (1989). Serial position and set size in short-term memory: Time course of recognition. *Journal of Experimental Psychology: General, 118*, 346–373.

McElree, B., & Dosher, B. A. (1993). Serial retrieval processes in the recovery of order information. *Journal of Experimental Psychology: General, 122*, 291–315.

McElree, B., & Dosher, B. A. (2001). The focus of attention across space and across time. *Behavioral and Brain Sciences, 24*, 129–130.

McElree, B., Foraker, S., & Dyer, L. (2003). Memroy structures that subserve sentence comprehension. *Journal of Memory and Language, 48*, 67–91.

McElree, B., & Griffith, T. (1995). Syntactic and thematic processing in sentence comprehension: Evidence for a temporal dissociation. *Journal of Experimental Psychology: Learning, Memory, and Cognition, 21*, 134–157.

McElree, B., & Griffith, T. (1998). Structural and lexical constraints on filling gaps during sentence processing: A time-course analysis. *Journal of Experimental Psychology: Learning, Memory, and Cognition, 24*, 432–460.

Morton, J. (1968). Repeated items and decay in memory. *Psychonomic Sciences, 10*, 219–220.

Murdock, B. B., Jr. (1971). A parallel-processing model for scanning. *Perception and Psychophysics, 10*, 289–291.

Murdock, B. B., Jr. (1982). A theory for the storage and retrieval of item and associative information. *Psychological Review, 89*, 609–626.

Murdock, B. B., Jr. (1993). TODAM2: A model for the storage and retrieval of item, associative, and serial-order information. *Psychological Review, 100*, 183–203.

Muter, P. A. (1979). Response latencies in discriminations of recency. *Journal of Experimental Psychology: Learning, Memory and Cognition, 5*, 160–169.

Meyer, D. E., Irwin, D. E., Osman, A. M., & Kounios, J. (1988). The dynamics of cognition and action: Mental processes inferred from speed-accuracy decomposition. *Psychological Review, 95*, 183–237.

Nairne, J. S. (1996). Short-term/working memory. In E. L. Bjork and R. A. Bjork (Eds.), *Memory* (pp. 160–169). San Diego: Academic Press.

Peterson, L. R. (1967). Search and judgment in memory. In B. Kleinnmuntz (Ed.), *Concepts and the structure of memory* (pp. 1–16). New York: Wiley.

Posner, M. I., Boies, S. J., Eichelman, W. H., & Taylor, R. L. (1969). Retention of visual and name codes of single letters. *Journal of Experimental Psychology Monographs, 79* (1, Pt. 2).

Plaut, D. C. (1997). Structure and function in the lexical system: Insights from distributed models of word reading and lexical decision. *Language and Cognitive Processes, 12*, 765–805.

Ravizza, S. M., Delgado, M. R., Chein, J. M., Becker, J. T., & Fiez, J. A. (2004). Contribution of the inferior parietal cortex to verbal working memory. *NeuroImage, 22*, 562–573.

Raaijmakers, J. G., & Shiffrin, R. M. (1981). Search of associative memory. *Psychological Review, 88*, 93–134.

Ratcliff, R. (1978). A theory of memory retrieval. *Psychological Review, 85*, 59–108.

Ratcliff, R., Van Zandt, & McKoon, G. (1999). Connectionist and diffusion models of reaction time. *Psychological Review, 106*, 261–300.

Ratcliff, R. (1988). Continuous versus discrete information processing: Modeling the accumulation of partial information. *Psychological Review, 95*, 238–255.

Ratcliff, R., & Murdock, B. B. (1976). Retrieval processes in recognition memory. *Psychological Review, 83*, 190–214.

Reed, A. V. (1973). Speed-accuracy trade-off in recognition memory. *Science, 181*, 574–576.

Reed, A. V. (1976). The time course of recognition in human memory. *Memory and Cognition, 4*, 16–30.

Rubin, D. C., Hinton, S., & Wenzel, A. (1999). The precise time course of retention. *Journal of Experimental Psychology: Learning, Memory and Cognition, 25*, 1161–1176.

Rubin, D. C., & Wenzel, A. E. (1996). One hundred years of forgetting: A quantitative description of retention. *Psychological Review, 103*, 734–760.

Schneider, W., & Detweiler, M. (1988). The role of practice in dual-task performance: Toward workload modeling in a connectionist/control architecture. *Human Factors, 30*, 539–566.

Schweickert, R., & Boruff, B. (1986). Short-term memory capacity: Magic number or magic spell? *Journal of Experimental Psychology: Learning, Memory, and Cognition, 12*, 419–425.

Seamon, J. G., & Wright, C. E. (1976). Generative processes in character classification: Evidence for a probe encoding set. *Memory & Cognition, 4*, 96–102.

Shallice, T., & Vallar, G. (1990). The impairment of auditory-verbal short-term storage. In G. Vallar and T. Shallice (Eds.), *Neuropsychological impairments of short-term memory* (pp. 11–53). New York, NY: Cambridge University Press.

Smith, E. E., & Jonides, J. (1997). Working memory: A view from neuroimaging. *Cognitive Psychology, 33*, 5–42.

Smith, E. E., & Jonides, J. (1999). Storage and executive processes in the frontal lobes. *Science, 283*, 1657–1661.

Sternberg, S. (1966). High speed scanning in human memory. *Science, 153*, 652–654.

Sternberg, S. (1969). The discovery of processing stages: Extensions of Donders' method. In W. G. Koster (Ed.), *Attention and performance II* (pp. 276–315). Amsterdam: North Holland.

Sternberg, S. (1973). *Evidence against self-terminating memory search from properties of the RT distribution.* Paper presented at the Meeting of Psychonomic Society. St. Louis, November.

Sternberg, S. (1975). Memory-scanning: New findings and current controversies. *Quarterly Journal of Experimental Psychology, 27*, 1–32.

Stoltzfus, E. R., Hasher, L., & Zacks, R. T. (1996). Working memory and aging: The current status of the inhibitory view. In J. Richardson, R. Engle, L. Hasher, R. Logie, E. Stoltzfus, and R. Zacks (Eds.), *Working memory and human cognition* (pp. 66–88). Oxford: Oxford University Press.

Theios, J. (1973). Reaction time measurement in the study of memory processes: Theory and data. In G. H. Bower (Ed.), *The psychology of learning and motivation* (Vol. 7, pp. 44–85). New York: Academic Press.

Townsend, J. T., & Ashby, F. G. (1983). *The stochastic modeling of elementary psychological processes.* New York: Cambridge University Press.

Treisman, M., & Doctor, E. (1987). Memory scanning: A comparison of the dynamic stack and exhaustive serial scan models with an extension of the latter. *Acta Psychologica, 64*, 39–92.

Vallar, G., & Baddeley, A. D. (1982). Short-term forgetting and the articulatory loop. *Quarterly Journal of Experimental Psychology: Human Experimental Psychology, 34*(A), 53–60.

Wickelgren, W. (1972). Trace resistance and the decay of long-term memory. *Journal of Mathematical Psychology, 9*, 418–455.

Wickelgren, W. (1973). The long and the short of memory. *Psychological Bulletin, 80*, 425–438.

Wickelgren, W. (1974). Single-trace fragility theory of memory dynamics. *Memory & Cognition, 4*, 775–780.

Wickelgren, W. (1977). Speed-accuracy tradeoff and information processing dynamics. *Acta Psychologica, 41*, 67–85.

Wickelgren, W. A., Corbett, A. T., & Dosher, B. A. (1980). Priming and retrieval from short-term memory: A speed-accuracy tradeoff analysis. *Journal of Verbal Learning and Verbal Behavior, 19*, 387–404.

Wickelgren, W. A., & Norman, D. A. (1966). Strength models and serial position in short-term recognition memory. *Journal of Mathematical Psychology, 3*, 316–347.

Yntema, D. B., & Trask, F. P. (1963). Recall as a search process. *Journal of Verbal Learning and Verbal Behavior, 2*, 65–74.

SIMPLE: FURTHER APPLICATIONS OF A LOCAL DISTINCTIVENESS MODEL OF MEMORY

Ian Neath and Gordon D. A. Brown

I. Introduction

It has long been common practice to divide memory into one system that operates from 0 to 500 ms (sensory memory), a second system that operates for up to a few seconds (short-term or working memory), and a third system that operates on all temporal durations from minutes to years (long-term memory). A scale invariant view of memory, in contrast, suggests that the fundamental principles of memory apply regardless of the time scale, whether remembering occurs immediately after an event or several years later. Brown, Neath, and Chater (2002) proposed a model, Scale Invariant Memory and Perceptual Learning (SIMPLE), which explicitly states that key principles of memory retrieval hold regardless of the time scale and thus regardless of the presumed underlying memory system. Brown et al. (2002) applied the model to a range of data from serial and free recall, and here we extend the range of application of the model.

Our aim is to illustrate the basic properties of SIMPLE by examining its ability to account for data and paradigms not studied by Brown et al. (2002). We first provide an overview of the model and then apply it to new data on serial position effects in absolute identification tasks, arguing for a link between discrimination in absolute identification and discrimination of memories in traditional serial recall paradigms. Next we fit key

THE PSYCHOLOGY OF LEARNING
AND MOTIVATION VOL. 46
DOI: 10.1016/S0079-7421(06)46006-0

data that support the idea that people represent items based on temporal rather than ordinal position in many paradigms and then offer a unified account of serial position effects that traditionally would have been described as being due to iconic memory, long-term memory, and semantic memory. We briefly show how SIMPLE is beginning to be applied to data used to support the idea of working memory and then return to the important issue of whether items are best thought of as being encoded using ordinal or temporal position cues. We end by addressing some arguments against the idea that unitary memory principles may apply over different time scales.

II. The Model

Perhaps the easiest way to describe SIMPLE is in terms of its application to a typical absolute identification experiment, in which subjects are exposed to a set of stimuli that vary systematically along only one dimension (e.g., nine tones of different frequencies, seven lines of different lengths, eight boxes of different weights). A label is associated with each stimulus; these labels are usually digits that correspond to each item's ordinal position on the continuum. After exposure to the stimuli, the test begins. On each of many trials, one stimulus from the continuum is shown and the subject is asked to identify the item with the correct label. Feedback regarding the correct response is normally given after each trial.

Following Murdock (1960), Helson (1964), Bower (1971), and many others, SIMPLE assumes log-transformed representations.[1] On each trial, the physical value of the stimulus undergoes a logarithmic transform and is then compared to the log-transformed representations in memory, which are associated with possible responses. The response that is produced is determined by the similarity between the transformed stimulus value and the relevant memory representations. In line with many other models, it is assumed that similarity falls off as a decreasing function of the separation between any two representations on the internal scale (Shepard, 1987).

The similarity, $\eta_{i,j}$, between two log-transformed memory representations, M_i and M_j, is given by Eq. (1), where c is the main free parameter in SIMPLE:

---

[1] The assumption of a log transform rather than some other function (e.g., power) is relatively unimportant for the model. Log transforms have the advantages of: (1) requiring no additional parameters and (2) allowing simple ratio-based formulations of similarity when exponential similarity-distance functions are used (Brown et al., 2002).

$$\eta_{i,j} = e^{-c|M_i - M_j|} \tag{1}$$

The probability of producing the response associated with item i, R_i, when given the cue for stimulus j, C_j, is given by Eq. (2) (i.e., the Luce choice rule), where n is the number of items in the response set:

$$P_r(R_i|C_j) = \frac{\eta_{i,j}}{\displaystyle\sum_{k=1}^{n}\eta_{j,k}} \tag{2}$$

SIMPLE can be seen as a direct descendant of global distinctiveness models such as the one proposed by Murdock (1960).[2] In a global distinctiveness model, the distinctiveness of an item is given by the degree to which it differs from *all* the other items. As Bower (1971) pointed out, such a view is problematic because there are many situations in which performance is affected more by near items than by far items (Neath, Brown, McCormack, Chater, & Freeman, 2006).

In contrast to global distinctiveness models, SIMPLE is a local distinctiveness model because it allows for near and far items to affect the distinctiveness of a given item differentially. It does this through the one free parameter, c, in Eq. (1). As Fig. 1 shows, as c increases, the similarity between a given item and other items further away decreases.

There are really two versions of SIMPLE. The basic version, described earlier, has only one free parameter, and the goal is to account qualitatively for the general pattern of data observed. The second version of SIMPLE adds additional parameters and assumptions so that data can be fit quantitatively. According to both versions, memory retrieval, regardless of the paradigm, is fundamentally discrimination in terms of location along a dimension, whether that dimension is frequency, temporal position, or ordinal position.[3] Here, we focus primarily on the basic version—the aim is to emphasize explanatory transparency by illustrating how the basic ideas underlying SIMPLE account for serial position effects in a variety of different paradigms.

[2] See Neath and Brown (in press) for a discussion of the relation between various distinctiveness models of memory and absolute identification.

[3] Obviously, this does not preclude the use of two or more dimensions.

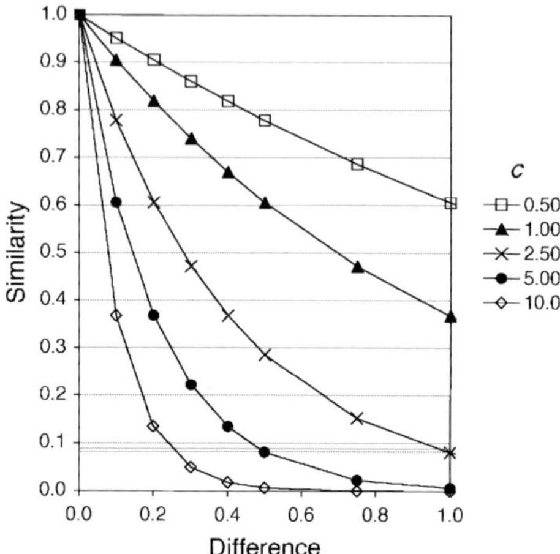

Fig. 1.   Similarity, η, for various differences between two memory representations, $|M_i - M_j|$, as a function of different values of c.

III.   Serial Position Effects in Absolute Identification

When accounting for serial position effects in memory paradigms, such as free recall, we will often invoke time as a principal dimension along which items are located, and we will be concerned with the effect that recalling one item might have on recalling later items. As our goal is to explicate the basic principles of operation of the model as transparently as possible, we consider first the simple one-parameter version in a paradigm in which only one response is made per trial and in which the choice of the underlying dimension on which the items are represented is less controversial. Our aim here, following Murdock (1960), is to make an explicit link between serial position effects in absolute identification and serial position effects in memory retrieval and to illustrate the claim that common mechanisms of distinctiveness and discrimination are involved in the two cases. It should be remembered, however, that the basic version of SIMPLE is not intended as a complete explanation of these data, and we note that more sophisticated models are necessary to account for additional phenomena in this paradigm such as sequential effects (Stewart, Brown, & Chater, 2006).

A.   SCALE INVARIANCE

Performance in absolute identification experiments is largely unaffected by the spacing of items along the perceptual scale; that is, increasing the spacing by a constant factor typically has almost no effect, provided the items are not sufficiently similar to be confused when presented pairwise (Alluisi & Sidorsky, 1958; Eriksen & Hake, 1955; Garner, 1962; Miller, 1956; Pollack, 1952; Shiffrin & Nosofsky, 1994). Neath and Brown (2005, Experiment 1) ran an experiment to replicate this scale invariance in absolute identification and to illustrate the role of the main free parameter, c, in contributing to scale-invariant effects within SIMPLE.

There were three conditions, narrow, medium, and wide, each of which had nine pure tones as the stimuli to be identified. In the "narrow" group, each tone was approximately 3.73% higher in frequency than the previous tone; in the "medium" group, each tone was 5% higher than the previous; and in the "wide" group, each tone was 7.59% higher then the previous. Table I lists the exact frequencies used. These frequencies were chosen so that all three sets would have three frequencies in common (420.00, 486.20, and 562.84 Hz).

In each condition, the tone with the lowest frequency was labeled "1" and the tone with the highest frequency was labeled "9." During the stimulus familiarization phase, as each tone was played, its number was shown on the screen. An identification trial consisted of the presentation of a single tone. Immediately after, the computer presented nine different buttons on the screen, each labeled with a digit 1–9. The subject was asked to use a mouse to click on the appropriate button that identified the tone that had just been played. Immediate feedback was then given to the subjects, informing them that they had made the correct response or informing them what the correct response should have been. Figure 2 shows the proportion of times each

TABLE I

THE FREQUENCY (Hz) OF EACH OF THE NINE TONES IN THE THREE CONDITIONS IN EXPERIMENT 1 AND PROPORTION CORRECT

Narrow		Medium		Wide	
Frequency (Hz)	Proportion correct	Frequency (Hz)	Proportion correct	Frequency (Hz)	Proportion correct
420.0	0.653	400.0	0.647	362.8	0.660
435.7	0.473	420.0	0.453	390.4	0.450
451.9	0.353	441.0	0.367	420.0	0.397
468.7	0.327	463.1	0.313	451.9	0.383
486.2	0.327	486.2	0.300	486.2	0.367
504.3	0.340	510.5	0.383	523.1	0.413
523.1	0.400	536.0	0.380	562.8	0.437
542.6	0.447	562.8	0.420	605.6	0.480
562.8	0.647	591.0	0.623	651.6	0.670

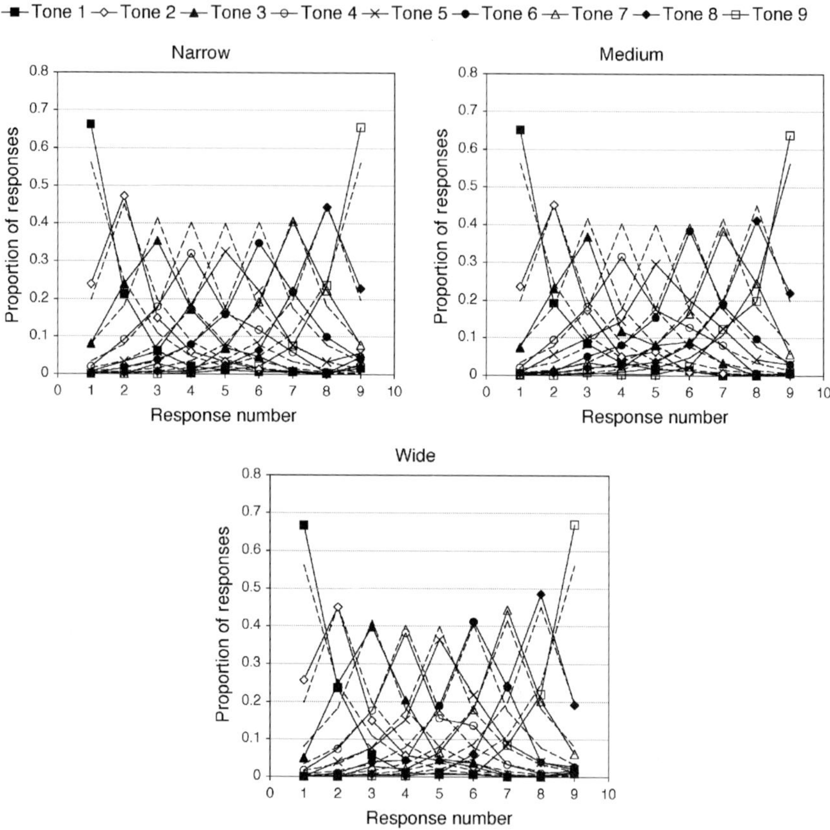

Fig. 2. Proportion of times each response (1–9) was given for each stimulus for the narrow (left), medium (right), and wide (bottom) conditions in Experiment 1 (symbols and solid lines) and predictions of SIMPLE (dashed lines).

response (1–9) was given for each tone for each condition (symbols and solid lines).

There are three things to note in the data. (1) The proportion correct (i.e., the "peaks") is roughly comparable in all three conditions, indicative of scale invariance—increasing the absolute difference between the tones did not result in improved identification. Statistically, performance on the first tones (420.00, 400.00, and 362.80 Hz) was equivalent—0.653, 0.647, and 0.660 in the narrow, medium, and wide groups, respectively. Similarly, performance on the last tones (562.80, 591.00, and 651.60 Hz) was statistically equivalent—0.647, 0.623, and 0.670 in the narrow, medium, and wide groups, respectively. (2) The error gradients are roughly comparable in all three conditions, again suggestive of scale invariance. Statistically, there are no differences between the conditions. (3) The error gradients are reminiscent of error gradients seen with serial and free recall data.

One way of conceptualizing the scale invariance of perceptual identification is in terms of the "stretchedess" of the internal scale used to represent the items in question. It is as if subjects have a fixed quantity of dimensional capacity, which can be stretched or contracted to accommodate the task demands most efficiently. In the case of the tones in the narrow condition, for example, the memory representations will cover a range of 0.292 units on the internal scale. This range is determined by taking the log of 562.84 (6.33) and subtracting the log of 420 (6.04): $6.33 - 6.04 = 0.29$. The range covers 0.390 and 0.585 units in the medium and wide conditions, respectively. The resolution of the scale in absolute frequency space will depend on the task demands. This flexibility has the advantage that sensitivity can be task dependent and that adaptation can occur (Helson, 1964). The concomitant disadvantage is that participants have no direct access to information about absolute magnitudes.

We incorporated this assumption into the model by assuming that the parameter c is inversely proportional to the logarithmic range covered by the experimental stimuli. In the experiment, the ratios of frequency ranges spanned are 1.0:1.3:2.0 (narrow:medium:wide). The values of c that we used in fitting the results were 22, 16.5, and 11. The inverse of these values stand in the same ratio to one another as the frequency ratios. The effect of this is to produce the same similarity value, $\eta_{i,j}$, for the largest difference. Thus, the largest difference in the narrow condition is 0.293 and with c set to 22.5, η is 0.001596. This is the same value as when the difference is 0.390 and c is 16.5 and when the difference is 0.585 and c is 11.

The results of the simulation are shown as dashed lines in Fig. 2. These results were produced using the values of c described earlier and the frequencies listed in Table I. One should note that the model is capturing the important qualitative aspects of the data, including not only proportion correct but also the error gradients. The model is not perfect—it systematically under predicts performance on the end items and slightly over predicts performance on middle items. It should be remembered, however, that this fit is produced with the basic one-parameter version of SIMPLE and is accounting for 81 data points per panel. Better quantitative fits can be obtained using a more complex version of the model such as that described by Neath et al. (2006). For current purposes, however, it is the qualitative fit and the perspective on scale invariance that is important—if one adjusts c in a way independently determined by the range of the internal scale used, the approach predicts equivalent performance.

B.   Primacy and Recency Effects

Two fundamental characteristics of the ubiquitous serial position curve are the primacy effect, better memory for early items in the sequence, and the recency effect, better memory for final items in the sequence.[4] Our claim is that in both memory retrieval and absolute identification, such effects arise due to differential discriminability of items along a particular dimension (Murdock, 1960). Neath & Brown (2005, Experiment 2) ran an experiment to illustrate this idea within the context of an absolute identification paradigm.

There were two conditions, primacy and recency, each of which had nine pure tones as the stimuli to be identified. In the primacy condition, the tones in the first part of the continuum were constructed so that they were relatively more distinct and thus should be identified more accurately. Specifically, the tones increased in frequency by decreasing ratios—tone 2 was 10% higher than tone 1, tone 3 was 9% higher than tone 2, and so on. The recency condition was simply the "reverse" of the primacy condition, so items in the latter part of the continuum should be identified more accurately. Thus, tone 2 was 3% higher than tone 1, tone 3 was 4% higher than tone 2, and so on. The exact frequencies used are listed in Table II; one should note that both the first and last tones were identical in the two groups.

Figure 3 shows the proportion of times each response (1–9) was given for each tone for each condition (symbols and solid lines). Clearly, the observed serial position curves are analogous to those seen in memory, with the "primacy" line reminiscent of serial recall data, with a larger primacy and smaller recency effect, and the "recency" line more akin to free recall data, with a smaller primacy and larger recency effect.

According to SIMPLE, the ability to identify an item depends on the extent to which it "stands out" from its near neighbors. End items have an automatic advantage, as there are no neighbors on one side and so (on average) there are fewer confusable near items. This end-item advantage is called an edge effect. In the primacy condition, the distance between the items systematically decreases, and so performance drops until there is a recency effect due to edge effects at the end of the sequence. In the recency condition, the pattern of data is a mirror image of the primacy condition because the distances are the reverse. An important point is that the absolute

---

[4] There are a variety of ways of measuring the magnitude of a primacy or recency effect. Unless otherwise specified, in this chapter, a larger primacy (or recency) effect is one in which absolute performance of the first (or last) item is greater, and a smaller primacy (or recency) effect is one in which absolute performance of the first (or last) item is lower, relative to some other condition.

TABLE II

THE FREQUENCY (HZ) OF EACH OF THE NINE TONES IN BOTH CONDITIONS IN
EXPERIMENT 2 AND PROPORTION CORRECT

Primacy		Recency	
Frequency (Hz)	Proportion correct	Frequency (Hz)	Proportion correct
360.0	0.723	360.0	0.483
396.0	0.453	370.8	0.403
431.6	0.377	385.6	0.327
466.2	0.357	404.9	0.297
498.8	0.323	429.2	0.340
528.7	0.383	459.3	0.400
555.2	0.413	496.0	0.437
577.4	0.400	540.6	0.480
594.7	0.503	594.7	0.717

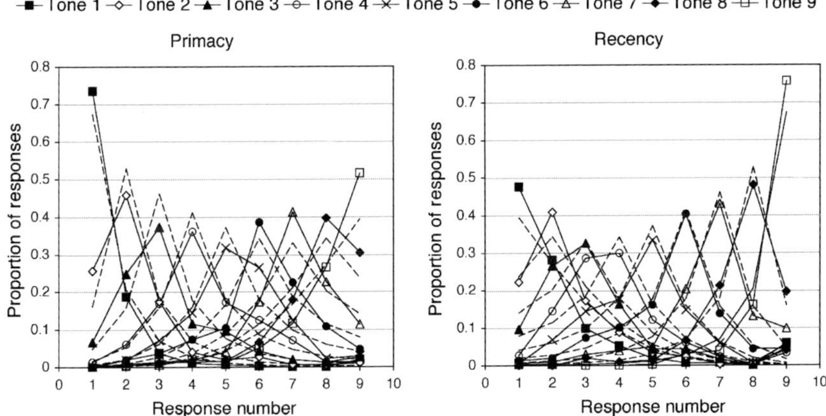

Fig. 3. Proportion of times each response (1–9) was given for each stimulus for the primacy (left) and recency (right) conditions in Experiment 2 (symbols and solid lines) and predictions of SIMPLE (dashed lines).

frequency is irrelevant—what matters is the relative distance between a given frequency and its neighbors.

The value of the free parameter, c, was set based on information from the first experiment.[5] The range on the log scale covered by both conditions

---

[5] This is appropriate here, as the two experiments were run at the same time with subjects drawn from the same pool.

in Experiment 2 was 0.502. The ratio of this value to the range in the narrow condition in Experiment 1 was 1.0:1.72. Because the value of c in the narrow condition in Experiment 1 was 22, we set $c = 12.8$; the ratio of the inverse of these values is 1.0:1.72.

Figure 3 (dashed lines) shows the results of a simulation with c set to 12.8 (for both conditions) and using the frequency values specified in Table II. The simulation captures the important qualitative aspects of the results—the primacy and recency conditions are mirror images, and the error gradients are appropriate. The model does slightly under predict the amount of recency in the primacy condition (and the amount of primacy in the recency condition), and undoubtedly better fits could be obtained with a more complex version of SIMPLE (Neath et al., 2006). Nonetheless, the simulation can be taken as an existence proof—a local distinctiveness model, which posits that memory performance, is fundamentally discrimination in terms of location along a dimension produces results just like those observed in an absolute identification experiment.

IV.   Relative Temporal Distinctiveness

The results from the two absolute identification experiments emphasize the importance of relative distinctiveness. In this section, we consider results from two memory paradigms that are analogous to the absolute identification data discussed earlier and use these results to argue that in many memory paradigms, the principal underlying dimension is relative temporal position.

A.   SHIFT FROM RECENCY TO PRIMACY (AND VICE VERSA)

It is important to distinguish between absolute time and relative time. According to SIMPLE, memory in many situations depends on how locally distinct an item is on a dimension based on relative time. The first experiment reported earlier demonstrated that the total absolute range of stimuli in an absolute identification task did not affect performance; in an analogous way, SIMPLE predicts that total absolute time will not affect performance in a memory task (all other factors being equal). Rather, it is relative time that is important.

Brown et al. (2002) highlight this difference between absolute and relative time by showing how SIMPLE accounts for the ratio rule observed in free recall (Bjork & Whitten, 1974; Crowder, 1976; Glenberg, Bradley, Kraus, & Renzaglia, 1983). If one defines recency as the slope of the best fitting line for the final three items in the list, then one may state the ratio rule as saying recency will be proportional to the ratio of the time separating items in the list (the interitem presentation interval or IPI) and the time following the final item until recall (the retention interval or RI). Because this is a ratio, the units do not matter—the same recency effect is expected whether the units are seconds or weeks (Glenberg et al., 1983).

Here, we focus on a different pattern of results that also offers support for the role of relative rather than absolute time. In general, immediate recall results in substantial recency and little primacy, but as the duration of the RI increases, recency decreases and primacy increases. Specifically, if the duration of the IPI is held constant, recall of the final item decreases and recall of the first item increases as the duration of the RI increases (Bjork, 2001; Neath, 1993). This pattern has been observed with single-item probe recognition of nonverbal stimuli (Neath, 1993), verbal stimuli (Neath & Knoedler, 1994), auditory stimuli (Knoedler, Hellwig, & Neath, 1999; Surprenant, 2001), and even sentences (Knoedler et al., 1999). What is surprising is that recall of a particular item *increases* as the test is delayed. As with the ratio rule data, memory can be better after a longer interval than after a shorter interval, a pattern of results problematic for views of memory that posit a role for absolute time but one predicted by views of memory that focus on relative time.

The key idea to fit SIMPLE to this general pattern of results is similar to that used to account for scale invariance in absolute identification—the value of parameter c is made inversely proportional to the range on the log-transformed scale occupied by the to-be-remembered items. The simulation examines memory for a list of four items. Each item occurs 1 s after the prior item, and the RI is either 1, 3, or 10 s. The 1-s RI condition occupies 1.386 units on the log-transformed temporal dimension, the 3-s RI condition occupies 0.693 units, and the 10-s RI condition occupies 0.262 units. The ratio is thus 1.0:2.0:2.64 so the values of c were 3, 6, and 15.85. The results are shown in the left panel of Fig. 4.

The simulation shows that SIMPLE produces the appropriate pattern of results—recall of the final item decreases and recall of the first item increases as the duration of the RI increases. The reason that SIMPLE produces this pattern is because the same range is "stretched" to accommodate all three conditions. In the absolute identification data, stretching the range resulted in equal performance because the items' representations changed by a constant. Here, the change is *not* constant—rather, the relative distinctiveness of the first item in the longer RI condition is greater than the corresponding distinctiveness in the shorter RI condition.

Neath and Knoedler (1994) examined what happens when the RI is held constant but the IPI increases. Under this arrangement, recency increases with increased RI and primacy decreases. SIMPLE was applied to this type

                                    Neath and Brown

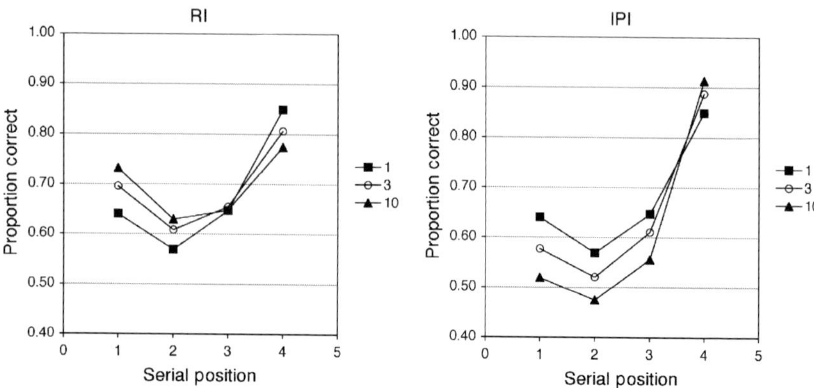

Fig. 4. Simulation from SIMPLE showing the decrease in recency and the increase in primacy as the duration of the RI increases (left panel) and the increase in recency and the decrease in primacy as the duration of the interitem presentation interval increases (right panel).

of experiment, using the same parameters as before. The results are shown in the right panel of Fig. 4. This time, recall of the final item increases and recall of the first item decreases as the duration of the IPI increases, the same pattern observed by Neath and Knoedler (1994). The IPI manipulation does not affect the temporal value of the final item (or more specifically, its log-transformed value), but the temporal values of other items become much larger, with the largest effect for the first item. Because the log transform condenses large values more than small values, the first item (with the largest temporal value) is particularly affected and becomes relatively closer to its neighbors. The relative distinctiveness of the final item is slightly enhanced because of the changes to the other log-transformed values.

B. SCHEDULES OF PRESENTATION

Experiment 2 of Neath and Brown (2005), described above, was designed, in part, to exclude the possibility that tones that differed in frequency were identified in terms of their position along an ordinal dimension (e.g., as represented by the numbers 1–9) rather than in terms of their position along the frequency dimension. If subjects were using this ordinal representation, there should have been no difference in performance between the two groups. However, the experiment found that the closeness of neighbors in frequency, rather than the closeness of neighbors along the positional dimension, determined performance. A similar question can be asked in the memory case.

In most experiments, items' positions on a relative temporal dimension and on an ordinal position dimension are perfectly correlated, as will always be the case when presentation rate is constant. However, the dimensions can be separated experimentally in order to compare positional and temporal effects. Neath and Crowder (1990) conducted an experiment in which items' places on the positional and temporal dimensions varied due to either increasing or decreasing the presentation rate throughout the course of list presentation. We illustrate with data from two presentation schedules in their Experiment 3. In both conditions, five word pairs (object names) were presented for 2.5 s and subjects were asked to indicate which of the two objects was the larger. After the final item, there was 8 s of distractor activity (solving math problems). The two schedules differed in the amount of distractor activity that occurred between the presentation of the word pairs.

In the increasing condition, there was 0 s of distractor activity between the first and second pair, 8 s between the second and third, 16 s between the third and fourth, and 32 s between the fourth and fifth. Thus, the duration of the distractor intervals systematically increased throughout the list. In the decreasing condition, the same gaps were used but in the reverse order (i.e., 32 s between the first and second item, 16 s between the second and third item, and so on). Although both lists lasted exactly the same amount of time, the relative time of occurrence of an item in a given position in one condition differed from that in the other condition.

If subjects represented the items on a position dimension, there should be no difference between the conditions. As Fig. 5 shows (solid lines, filled

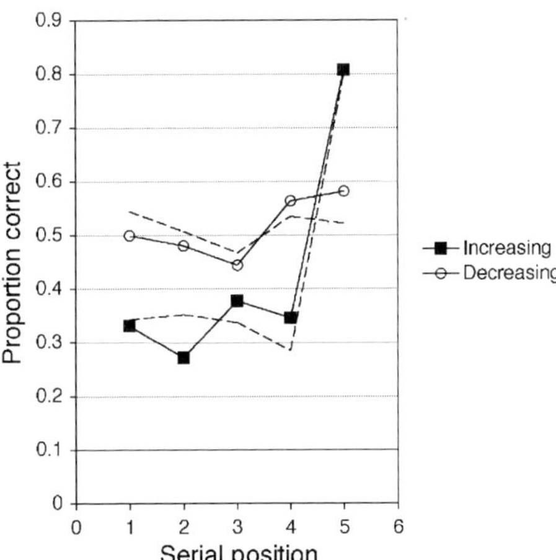

Fig. 5. Data (symbols and solid lines) from Neath and Crowder (1990) and simulation results (dashed line) from SIMPLE. Data from Neath, I., & Crowder, R. G. (1990). Schedules of presentation and distinctiveness in human memory. *Journal of Experimental Psychology; Learning, Memory, and Cognition, 16*, 316–327. Copyright © 1990 American Psychological Association.

symbols), the two conditions were quite different—the increasing condition exhibited very little primacy and extensive recency. In contrast, the decreasing condition was closer to a horizontal line, with substantially less recency and more primacy relative to the increasing condition.

In order to provide a version of SIMPLE to model free recall, some additional considerations are necessary. In absolute identification, a cue elicits either the correct response or an incorrect response. In serial recall, a cue elicits either the item that occurred in that position or an incorrect item. In free recall, however, an item will be scored correct regardless of the cue that elicited its retrieval. For example, if the list to be recalled is A B C D E, a temporal–positional recall cue for the second item might retrieve B with probability 0.6, A with probability 0.1, C with probability 0.1, and so on. Whichever item is recalled, in free recall it is a correct response. In modeling free recall, we took the recall probability for a given item to be the sum of its recall probabilities over all retrieval cues (subject to a maximum of 1).

A second, related, issue concerns omission errors. The basic version of SIMPLE does not omit responses; the sum of the individual item recall probabilities at each recall attempt adds up to 1.0. There are a variety of ways in which omissions could be implemented. One straightforward way is to assume that low-retrieval probabilities (as estimated by the model) should be most likely to lead to omissions. Omissions can be created by establishing a threshold—any items whose retrieval probabilities fall below the threshold will be omitted. We use a sigmoid function to increase recall probabilities that are already high and reduce recall probabilities for items whose recall probabilities are already low.

Equation 3 shows the implementation, which calculates output probability, P_o, based on the estimated recall probability, P, from the one-parameter model used hitherto:

$$P_o = \frac{1}{1 + e^{-s(P-t)}} \tag{3}$$

The parameter t is the threshold, and parameter s is the slope of the transforming function (which can be interpreted as the noisiness of the threshold). For example, if t is set to 0.8 and s is very large, the transformation will approximate a system that recalls (with 100% probability) all items with relative strengths greater than 0.8 and omits (with 100% probability) all items with strengths less than 0.8. As s becomes smaller, the transition from low to high recall probabilities becomes more gradual. The effect of various values of s on output probability for a fixed value of t is shown in the left panel of Fig. 6. The effect of various values of t on output probability for a

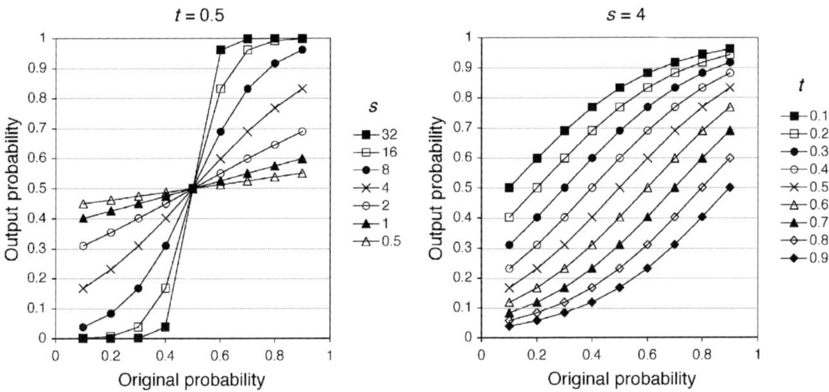

Fig. 6. Output probability when t is set to 0.5 and s varies (left panel) and when s is set to 4 and t varies (right panel).

fixed value of s is shown in the right panel. In applying SIMPLE to free recall, then, there are three free parameters—c (distinctiveness of memory representations), t (threshold), and s (threshold noise).

The free recall version of SIMPLE provides a reasonable qualitative account of the effects of nonconstant presentation schedule on free recall probability (the dashed lines in Fig. 5). With $c = 0.383$, $t = 0.307$, and $s = 29.91$, SIMPLE predicts relatively poor performance for the early-list items in the increasing schedule, because those items are in more crowded temporal neighborhoods, and substantial recency, because those items are in a relatively more sparse neighborhood. In the decreasing schedule, in contrast, with c set to the same value but $t = 0.319$ and $s = 22.40$, performance is reduced for late-list items but improved for early list items (compared with the increasing schedule). Put another way, the experimental data are consistent with the predictions of SIMPLE that relative temporal position, rather than relative ordinal position, will determine how free recall varies as a function of serial position.[6]

In free recall, there is clear evidence that a model based on relative temporal position, rather than ordinal position, as the principal dimension provides a satisfactory account. In serial recall, however, the case maybe different. Although results similar to those shown in Fig. 5 are found when increasing and decreasing schedules are used in a serial recall task (Neath &

[6] Although SIMPLE can produce an appropriate pattern of results with $c = 0.432$, $s = 25.75$, and $t = 0.319$ for both conditions, the qualitative fit is better if s and t are different in the two conditions. Part of the reason might be that Neath and Crowder (1990) used word pairs, whereas we simulate lists of single items for simplicity.

Crowder, 1996), effects of temporal isolation are not observed when presentation schedule is temporally random (Nimmo & Lewandowsky, in press). One way of interpreting this is that subjects can and do use relative temporal position in serial recall when it is a useful cue, as in the case of the predictable temporal sequences in Neath and Crowder's experiment. However, they rely on a different cue when temporal position becomes less useful, as in Nimmo and Lewandowsky's experiment. In this latter case, ordinal position is predictable on every trial and so is likely to be a more efficient cue. SIMPLE can readily be augmented with a positional dimension to accommodate the absence of temporal distinctiveness effects under such circumstances (Lewandowsky & Brown, 2005; Lewandowsky, Brown, Wright, & Nimmo, 2006).

V. Serial Position Effects and Time Scale

SIMPLE stands for Scale Invariant Memory and Perceptual Learning, and scale invariance in this context refers to the idea that there exists a unified explanation of serial position effects that holds over a wide variety of time scales and paradigms. Brown et al. (2002) have shown how SIMPLE accounts for serial position effects and position error gradients for intermediate RIs (e.g., 30 s, 4 h, and 1 day). SIMPLE predicts, however, that similar-looking functions should be observable in both shorter and longer timescales. In this section, we examine recall after approximately 1.3 s (very short-term memory) and 2.5 weeks (long-term memory).

A. VERY SHORT-TERM MEMORY

The standard modal model of the 1960s posited the existence of sensory memory systems, with iconic memory being the system responsible for visually presented information (Neath & Surprenant, 2003, Chapter 2). Information first passed through this system prior to being registered in short-term memory. In this section, we consider an experiment (Neath, 2005) that examined serial position effects using a time scale commonly found only in studies of iconic memory. According to SIMPLE, standard-looking serial position curves and error gradients should obtain.

The subjects saw a five-item list of consonants presented at a rate of approximately one item every 50 ms and approximately 1000 ms elapsed between the offset of the final item and the appearance of the test. The test was a standard serial reconstruction of order task. Five buttons appeared on the screen displaying the letters that had appeared on that trial in a new random order. The subject's task was to click on the five buttons in the original presentation order.

The data are shown as filled squares in the top row of Fig. 7. Each panel shows the proportion of times the indicated item was recalled in each of the five possible positions. Primacy and recency effects are evident, and the position error gradients are entirely typical—when an item is recalled in the wrong position, it is mostly likely to be recalled in an adjacent position. This procedure produces serial position curves and position error gradients that look almost identical to those observed in standard immediate serial recall (Nairne, 1992); the time scale in the current experiment, however, is less than 1.3 s.

The basic one-parameter version of SIMPLE can be applied to these data, with just one modification. Recall of the first item is the same as described previously. For simplicity, the final (fifth) item is presented 1 s prior to the retrieval. Each succeeding item is an additional 0.05 s earlier. Thus, the first item is presented 1.2 s prior to its attempted retrieval. Recall of all five items takes time. On the plausible assumption that each retrieval takes 1 s, the second item is retrieved 2.15 s after presentation, although it occurred 1.15 s prior to the recall attempt of the first item. With this assumption and with c set to 51.86, SIMPLE produces an appropriate pattern of results, as shown as open circles in the top panel of Fig. 7.[7] SIMPLE produces serial position curves and appropriate error gradients in iconic-like paradigms for the same reason it produces them at longer intervals.

B. LONG-TERM MEMORY

Huttenlocher, Hedges, and Prohaska (1992) asked subjects to recall the day on which they had participated in a telephone survey. The telephone survey had taken place between 1 and 10 weeks prior to the dating question and could have occurred on any day of the week. Subjects were asked to name the day on which the survey occurred. The data to be fit come from weeks 1–5 (the top panel of Table V of Huttenlocher et al., 1992) and are shown as filled squares in the bottom row of Fig. 7.[8]

The serial position curves and position error gradients are remarkably similar to those observed in the very short-term memory experiment described earlier, despite the fact that the average RI here is increased from approximately 1.3 s in the very short-term case to the order of 1.3 *million*

---

[7] We note that an explanation in terms of positional (rather than temporal) representation, together with output interference, may be possible (Lewandowsky, Duncan, & Brown, 2004).

[8] We ignore Saturday and Sunday for simplicity. One key empirical finding in the dating literature is that people use whatever useful knowledge or fixed points they can to figure out the time of occurrence; one very common distinction is weekend versus weekday (Friedman, 1993). It is quite rare for subjects to say that a weekday event occurred on a weekend or vice versa (Huttenlocher, Hedges, & Bradburn, 1990; Huttenlocher et al., 1992). The data from Saturday and Sunday could be accommodated by adding a second dimension reflecting weekend versus weekday.

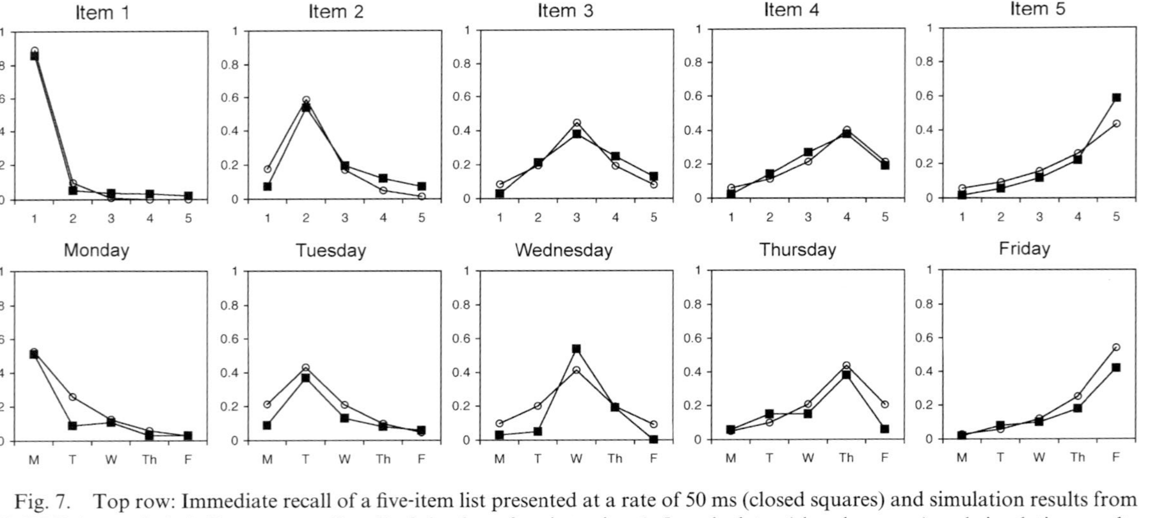

Fig. 7.   Top row: Immediate recall of a five-item list presented at a rate of 50 ms (closed squares) and simulation results from SIMPLE (open circles). Bottom row: Recall of the day of an interview 1–5 weeks later (closed squares) and simulation results from SIMPLE (open circles). Note: Data from Huttenlocher et al. (1992).

seconds. One characteristic of scale invariance in this context is that if the scale was not labeled on the figures, it would be impossible to determine the time scale just by looking at the results—either pattern could have come from any time frame.

SIMPLE simulates these data. Unlike in the very short-term case, only one response was made here—subjects were asked when the interview had taken place. Because the RI varied between 1 and 5 weeks, we used a value of 2.5 weeks (17.5 days). Monday was thus given a value of 21.5 days, Tuesday a value of 20.5 days, and so on. With c set to 14.22, SIMPLE produces the pattern of results shown with open circles in the bottom row of Fig. 7.

According to SIMPLE, the same principles underlie primacy and recency effects regardless of the time scale or the hypothetical underlying memory system. An item is well recalled to the extent that it stands out from its near neighbors, although the first and last item have an advantage due to edge effects.

C. SEMANTIC MEMORY

If SIMPLE's account is correct, then one should be able to observe serial position effects and position error gradients in memory systems other than the episodic system. Here, we examine serial position effects in semantic memory.[9] Maylor (2002) examined recall of the order of verses of popular hymns. By most multisystem accounts of memory, such information should be in the semantic memory system rather than in the episodic memory system. Maylor's subjects belonged to a denomination in which the same versions of the hymns have been used since 1933 and one which routinely sings all verses of a hymn. The subjects were given six verses from a hymn and were asked to reconstruct the original order. Each subject received 18 hymns, and the results are shown in the left panel of Fig. 8.

The results have all the hallmarks of data from an episodic memory task—there are clear primacy and recency effects, and the error gradients show that when a verse was placed in the wrong order, it was most often placed in an adjacent position.

To simulate these results, we first assumed an underlying dimension of 1–6. With $c = 2.28$, SIMPLE produced the results shown in the middle panel of Fig. 8. Although similar to the data, the results from SIMPLE differ in two ways—recall of the first and last items is lower and recall of the middle items is higher than in the data. Maylor (2002, p. 819) pointed out that it is

---

[9] The most well-known example of serial position effects in semantic memory is Roediger and Crowder's (1976) recall of US presidents. We do not fit those data as it is unclear what the underlying dimension should be.

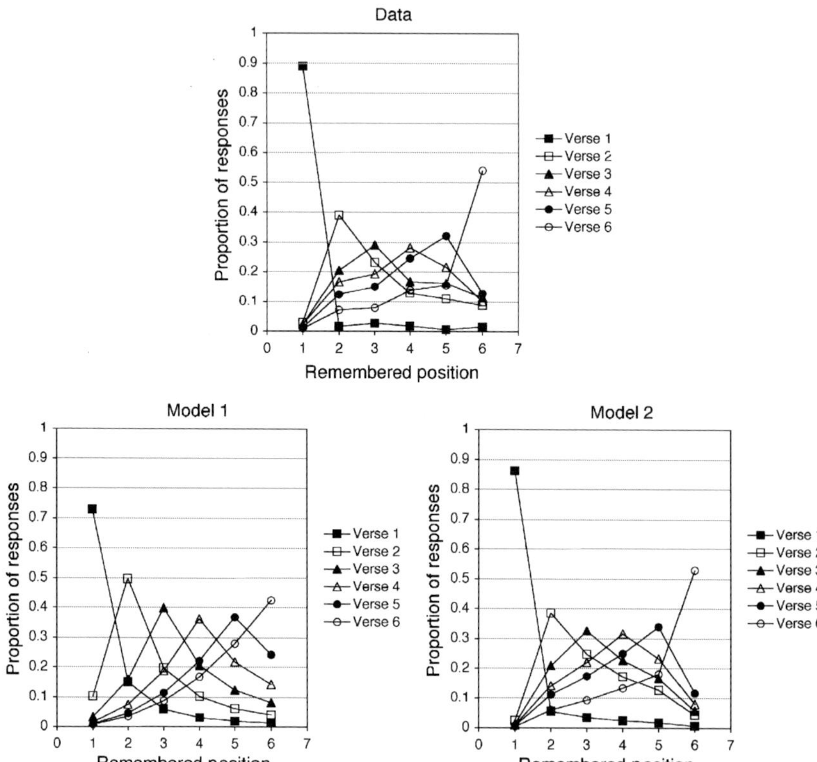

Fig. 8.   Data from Maylor (2002) showing recall by church goers of the order of six-verse hymns (top) and simulations from two versions of SIMPLE. Model 1 (left) uses an equally-spaced dimension, whereas Model 2 (right) has the first and last verse more distinct. Data from Maylor, E. A. (2002). Serial position effects in semantic memory: Reconstructing the order of verses of hymns. *Psychonomic Bulletin & Review, 9*, 816–820. Copyright © 2002 Psychonomic Society. Used with permission of the author.

likely that the first verse is slightly more familiar to her subjects because of its being included in the announcement of the hymns. If we adjust the values on the underlying dimension such that the values are 1, 4, 5, 6, 7, and 12 (rather than 1, 2, 3, 4, 5, and 6) and set c to 1.99, SIMPLE produces results much closer to the data, as shown in the right panel of Fig. 8.[10]

SIMPLE, then, offers the same explanation for the similar-looking serial position curves and error gradients observed in very short-term memory,

---

[10] Although the adjustment of dimensional values may appear somewhat post-hoc in this example, a more comprehensive approach could make use of an independently derived scaling solution to derive items' locations in psychological space.

immediate memory, long-term memory, and semantic memory. According to many alternate accounts of memory, there should not be these similarities. For example, according to the typical multiple memory systems view (Tulving, 2002), there are at least three different systems being assessed—two are varieties of episodic memory (short-term or working memory and long-term memory), so those similarities may be excusable, but the other, semantic memory, is supposed to be fundamentally different.

VI.   SIMPLE and Working Memory

In this section, we sketch a preliminary account of how SIMPLE might be applied to some benchmark data typically used to support the idea that there exists a separate working memory system (Baddeley, 1986). For processing verbal information, the important component of working memory is the phonological loop, which is divided into a storage system (the phonological store) and an active mechanism (the articulatory control process). The phonological store retains speech-based information for a short period of time. Unless rehearsed, the traces within the store are assumed to fade and decay within about 2 s, after which they are no longer usable. The articulatory control process is responsible for two different functions—it translates visual information into a speech-based code and deposits it in the phonological store; and it refreshes traces in the phonological store, offsetting the decay process.

The phonological loop was designed to account for four basic findings (Baddeley, 1986, 1994). The word-length effect is the finding that short words (in terms of pronunciation time) are recalled better than otherwise comparable long words in immediate serial recall tasks (Baddeley, Thomson, & Buchanan, 1975). According to working memory, this is because temporally longer words take longer to rehearse, and so fewer of them can be kept from decaying in the phonological store. The second result is the acoustic confusion effect,[11] the finding that dissimilar-sounding items are recalled better than similar-sounding items in immediate serial recall tasks (Conrad, 1964). According to working memory, this effect occurs because items in the phonological store are represented in a phonological code—items that sound similar will be confused with each other in some unspecified way and will thus be more difficult to retrieve.

The third finding that working memory was designed to account for is the irrelevant speech effect, the finding that immediate serial recall is impaired by

---

[11] This effect is often referred to as the "phonological similarity" effect, but it is not clear that all types of phonological similarity will cause a decrement.

the presence of irrelevant speech (Colle & Welsh, 1976). The original explanation was that phonemes from the irrelevant spoken material enter the
phonological store and interfere with phonemes from the to-be-remembered
items. The fourth finding, the concurrent articulation effect,[12] is the impairment of immediate serial recall when subjects are asked to speak during
list presentation (Murray, 1968). According to working memory, concurrent
articulation prevents rehearsal (the articulatory control process is required
to articulate). One should note that the phonological loop offers an explanation of not only the main effects but also the interactions among these
manipulations; for a description, see Chapter 4 of Neath and Surprenant
(2003). Here, we apply SIMPLE only to the first two main effects. Further
theoretical development is necessary before SIMPLE can be applied to the
latter two effects and their interactions.[13]

A.   WORD-LENGTH EFFECT

The standard account of the word-length effect relies on a trade-off between
decay (in the phonological store) and rehearsal (via the articulatory control
process). Because shorter items take less time to rehearse, more decaying
traces of short items can be refreshed than decaying traces of long items, and
therefore, more short items can be recalled. Here, we focus on just one set of
recent data that poses a challenge for the phonological loop hypothesis
(although there are other results problematic for the phonological loop
model, e.g., Neath, Bireta, & Surprenant, 2003).

Hulme, Surprenant, Bireta, Stuart, and Neath (2004) report a word-length
manipulation that used two types of lists. Pure lists contained either short
words (one syllable) or long words (three to five syllables). Pure short lists
were recalled better than the pure long lists, the standard word-length effect.
The second type of list was mixed, in that it contained equal numbers of
short and long items. An explanation of the word-length effect based on
rehearsal time must predict that these lists will be recalled intermediate
between the two pure lists; Burgess and Hitch (1999, Figure 16) show a
simulation of their version of the phonological loop model that predicts
exactly this. The reason is that a list of short words can be said fastest; a list
half composed of short and half composed of long items takes more time to
rehearse; and a list composed entirely of long words takes the greatest

---

[12] This effect is usually referred to as the "articulatory suppression" effect, but that name
implies just one specific effect of the manipulation. In contrast, "concurrent articulation" is
neutral with regards to the effects of the manipulation.

[13] It is possible that SIMPLE could explain the effects of concurrent articulation and irrelevant speech through the assumption that both reduce the distinctiveness of the representations,
in a way similar to the account offered by the feature model (Neath, 2000).

amount of time to rehearse. The longer the rehearsal time the fewer the number of decaying traces that can be refreshed. Hulme et al. (2004) disconfirmed this prediction—they found that items from mixed lists were recalled equally as well as the items from the pure short lists. From a working memory point of view, pronunciation time no longer accurately predicts subsequent recall performance.

Hulme et al. (2004; Hulme, Shostak, Stuart, Surprenant, Neath, & Brown, in press) describe how SIMPLE explains the results; our account here focuses on the revised explanation, which requires fewer assumptions than the original account. According to the revised SIMPLE account, items are represented on two dimensions, one corresponding to the usual temporal dimension and the other an item dimension. The second dimension captures the major difference between short and long words—short words are assumed to be more distinctive (i.e., easier to apprehend) due to the less complex phonological information. This is implemented by representing the items in different parts of the dimension and by having the difference between individual items in each of the two sets of items vary. For example, short items might have values beginning at 1.0 (on the arbitrary item scale) and each short item differs from other short items by 0.5. In contrast, long items might have values beginning at 0.1 (on the same scale) and each long item differs from each other by 0.1. Thus, the short and long items differ in their placement on the item scale.

Equation 1 is altered to include both dimensions. The similarity, $\eta_{i,j}$, between two memory representations, i and j, is given by

$$\eta_{i,j} = e^{-c(W_T|T_i-T_j|+W_I|I_i-I_j|)} \tag{4}$$

where T_i is the log of item i's value on the temporal dimension and I_i is item i's value on the item dimension. The weighting parameters, W_T (for the temporal dimension) and W_I (for the item dimension), are constrained such that $W_T + W_I = 1.0$. The main parameter c was set to 9, the starting value for short items was 1.0, the increment for short items was 0.5, the starting value for long items was 0.1, and the increment for long items was 0.1. There were 1000 trials per simulation; on each trial, values on the item dimension were randomly allotted to the list items. The weight on the temporal dimension, W_T, was 0.9, and the weight on the item dimension, W_I, was 0.1. Figure 9 shows that the model is clearly capturing the important aspects of the Hulme et al., data—there is a robust word-length effect for the pure lists (the overall proportion correct for the pure short list was 0.824 versus 0.697 for the pure long list) but recall of both short items (0.835) and long (0.831) items in the mixed list is indistinguishable from recall of short items in the pure list.

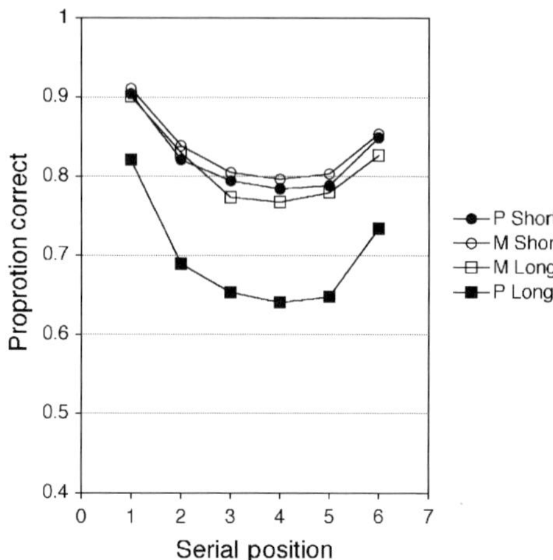

Fig. 9.   Simulation of recall of short and long items from pure and mixed lists.

According to SIMPLE, the reason that long items in the mixed list are recalled as well as short items from the pure list is that they benefit from emergent distinctiveness. Intuitively, this can be appreciated by considering the difference between two lists, a pure list of long words (e.g., PHYSIOLOGY, TUBERCULOSIS, PERIODICAL, REFRIGERATOR, ALUMINIUM, HIPPOPOTAMUS) and a list of both short and long items (e.g., MATHS, TUBERCULOSIS, SCROLL, REFRIGERATOR, ZINC, HIPPOPOTA-MUS). The long items in the second list stand out more than the comparable items in the pure list.

B.   ACOUSTIC CONFUSION EFFECT

The standard account of the acoustic confusion effect says that lists of similar-sounding items (e.g., B D P T V C) are more difficult to recall than otherwise comparable lists of dissimilar-sounding items (e.g., K M F Q Z L) because of unspecified interference in the phonological store (Baddeley, 1986). Brown et al. (2002) demonstrated how SIMPLE accounts for this effect through a local neighborhood-based discriminability mechanism. Here we extend SIMPLE to show that it can account for the reversal of the acoustic confusion effect observed when the RI increases; this interaction of confusability with RI is not readily accommodated by standard models.

Nairne and Kelley (1999) had subjects recall lists of five rhyming or nonrhyming nouns. Different items were used on each trial. One group recalled the order in which they had seen the items after 2 s, whereas another group recalled the order of the items after 24 s. During the RI, subjects were asked to read out loud a series of random digits to prevent rehearsal. At the short RI, a standard acoustic confusion effect was observed (top left panel of Fig. 10). At the long RI, however, a reverse effect was seen such that performance was better for the rhyming items (top right panel of Fig. 10).

Nairne and Kelley (1999) attribute the results to the need to locate items within a multidimensional space. At short RIs, the factor limiting performance is the nearness of each list item to other list items. If the items are close to one another phonologically as well as positionally, the task will be more difficult. At longer RIs, according to the Nairne–Kelley account, the factor limiting performance changes and becomes the problem

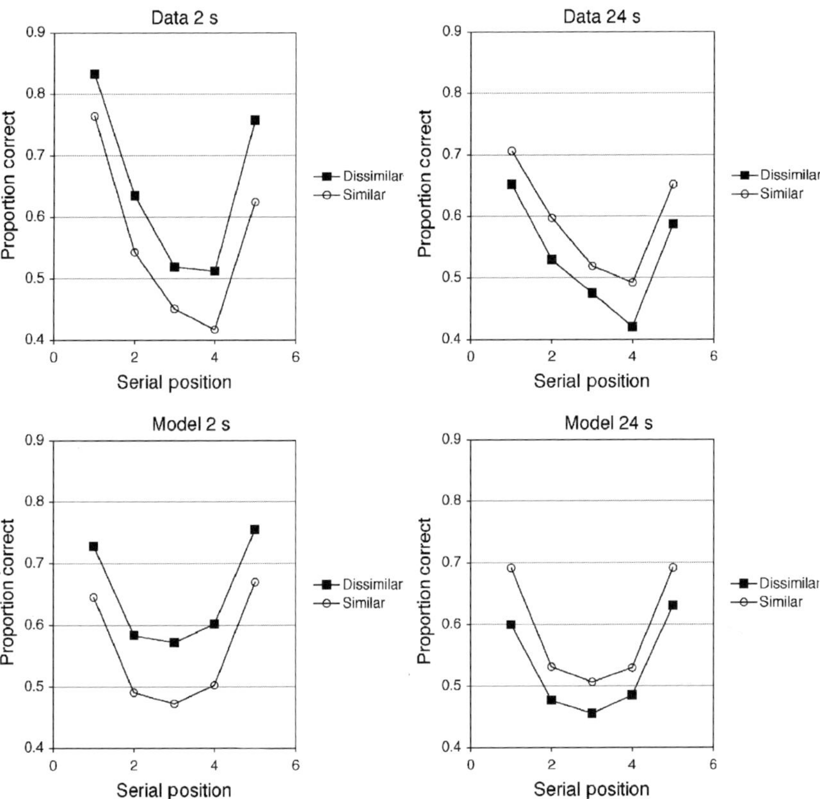

Fig. 10.   Data (top row) and simulation results (bottom row) for recall of lists of dissimilar- and similar-sounding items after a 2 s delay (left column) or after a 24 s delay (right column). Note: Data from Nairne, J. S., & Kelley, M. R. (1999). Reversing the phonological similarity effect. *Memory & Cognition, 27*, 45–53. Copyright © 1999 Psychonomic Society. Used with permission of the author.

of distinguishing one list from another. Within-list similarity may therefore help performance, because items within a list are similar to each other but all differ from items in neighboring lists, and so similarity can be used as a cue to aid list discrimination.

Nairne and Kelley (1999) do not provide a quantitative formulation of their account, but it is straightforward to implement such an account in SIMPLE. This simply requires a combination of features already introduced in other sections of this chapter. What is required is a multidimensional space, where the dimensions represent: (a) within-list position, (b) within-trial position, (c) position along a similarity dimension, and (d) elapsed time. At short RIs, there is little proactive interference from previous lists, and the performance-limiting factor is mainly the nearness of other list items (which, unlike items from previous lists, occupy similar positions along the temporal dimension). Performance will be worse on similar items for the same reasons illustrated in the previous demonstration. As the RI increases, items from different lists become closer to one another due to logarithmic compression. As these different-list items become closer to target-list items along the position-within-trial dimension, it becomes advantageous to use an additional cue (position along the similarity dimension) to distinguish the items.

We simulated recall after the longest and shortest RIs used by Nairne and Kelley (1999) as follows. Traces were represented along the logarithmically-transformed temporal dimension in the normal way, with a 2 s RI in the immediate recall condition and a 24 s RI in the delayed recall condition (as in the experiment). We assumed five lists of five items, to allow for the possibility of proactive interference. As in previous simulations (Brown et al., 2002), items in a "similar" list were assigned identical numbers on the "phonological confusability" dimension (one of the values 1 through 5 was given to every item within a list) and each item in a "dissimilar" list was assigned one of the values 1–5. Within-list position formed the third dimension, again as in previous simulations, and the final dimension (introduced here for the first time) was "list within trial." For phonologically confusable lists, each item was associated with a value between 1 and 5 representing the position of that item's list within the five-list series. Thus, this list-position giving value was perfectly correlated with phonological confusability value for the confusable lists. Useful values were assumed not to be available for nonconfusable lists; a value of 1 on this dimension was assigned to all dimensions. An attentional weight was allocated to each dimension, and these were constrained to sum to one. (One should note that the absolute magnitudes of values given to items' positions along dimensions is not important, because of the model's ability to allocate differential attentional weights to particular dimensions.) The mean additional effective RI was assumed to be 5 s. The behavior of the resulting model is illustrated in the bottom panels of Fig. 10, with c set to 6.5.

SIMPLE was able to reproduce the key qualitative pattern of behavior—a detrimental influence of phonological similarity on immediate recall, accompanied by a beneficial influence on delayed recall. Intuition suggests that the model achieves this by paying attention to the dimensions that are most useful for the particular RI it is faced with. Examination of the best-fit attentional weights reveals a psychological meaningful pattern. W_T, the attentional weight for the purely temporal distance dimension, reduced from 0.38 (RI = 2) to 0.29 (RI = 24). The weight assigned to the list-within-trial position dimension increased (0.48–0.52) as did the weight on the item-within-list position dimension (0.11–0.16). This supports the interpretation that less attention is paid to the temporal distance dimension as RI increases, and values on the temporal dimension become increasingly compressed. A greater weight is given to the list-within-trial position dimension as RI increases, and this leads to an advantage for phonologically confusable items at the longer RI only. At short RIs, confusable items suffer for the reasons discussed in previous simulations.

SIMPLE can account for some of the key data in working memory paradigms with the same set of retrieval principles used to account for other results over different timescales, hypothetical underlying memory system, and experimental paradigms. It remains to be seen whether SIMPLE can be extended to account for other working memory phenomena.

VII. Temporal Versus Positional Encoding: Evidence from Grouping

SIMPLE assumes that in many situations, people represent information on a log-transformed scale corresponding to the relative time between study and test. Using only this one dimension, SIMPLE can fit data showing temporal influences in both free recall (Neath & Crowder, 1990) and serial recall (Neath & Crowder, 1996). Moreover, the model can simulate the effects of varying the duration of the RI and the duration of the interitem presentation interval on relative primacy and recency and in data from very short-term memory and long-term memory. However, there exist several models of immediate serial recall in which memory relies on a purely positional code (Anderson & Matessa, 1997; Henson, 1998), and there is also evidence that purely positional information is relevant in serial recall (Henson, 1999; Lewandowsky & Brown, 2005; Lewandowksy et al., 2006; Ng & Maybery, 2002, 2005; Nimmo & Lewandowsky, in press).

The key question here concerns the nature of the underlying dimension(s) along which items are represented in memory. Our general position is that people use whatever cues are useful in a particular setting and that in many settings, temporal information is one cue used. We acknowledge that experiments can be designed in which position cues are made more useful than temporal cues. However, our interest here is the extent to which the version of SIMPLE that uses relative time as the primary dimension can model data from a variety of different paradigms. In this section, we turn to grouping experiments to examine further the issue of temporal versus positional (or ordinal) cues.

Consider serial recall of an eight-item list in which a temporal gap induces two groups of four items. Transposition errors typically preserve within-group position when group sizes are equal (Ryan, 1969a,b), a finding that could be accommodated by either a temporal coding account or an ordinal/positional coding account. Consider a second case, in which an odd number of items is used, resulting in two groups of different size. For example, a list of seven items, presented as a group of three followed by a group of four items: 1 2 3–4 5 6 7 where within-group presentation rate is constant. Movement errors might reflect either the absolute time or number of positions from the start of the groups (most confusable positions 1 and 4, 2 and 5, and 3 and 6); absolute time or number of positions from the end of the groups (most confusable positions 3 and 7, 2 and 6, and 1 and 5); or the relative distance along either the temporal or positional range spanned by the group (most confusable positions 1 and 4, and 3 and 7). Henson (1999; Experiment 1) found that transposition errors between positions 3 and 7 outnumbered errors between positions 3 and 6, and also that group-initial positions (1 and 4) were confusable. Similar effects are evident when errors across lists of different lengths are examined, for example, when a seven-item list follows a five-item list, the fifth item recalled from the first list is likely to intrude into the seventh rather than the fifth recall position for the second list (Henson, 1999, Experiment 2), suggesting end-relative instead of (or as well as) start-relative coding. Such results appear to provide a challenge to SIMPLE.

Figure 11 uses a two-dimensional representation to illustrate possible representations of the Henson (1999; Experiment 1) conditions. In SIMPLE, the retrievability of a given item will depend on its distance from its near neighbors in this two-dimensional space, in the same way as local neighborhood in a one-dimensional space (position along a simple temporal dimension) has governed performance in the simulations presented earlier. We assume that the distance of an item from any other item is simply the sum of its distances from that item along each of the two dimensions (i.e., we used a city block rather than Euclidean metric).

In all cases, the horizontal dimension in Fig. 11 represents (log transformed) temporal distance of items from the end of the list. The vertical

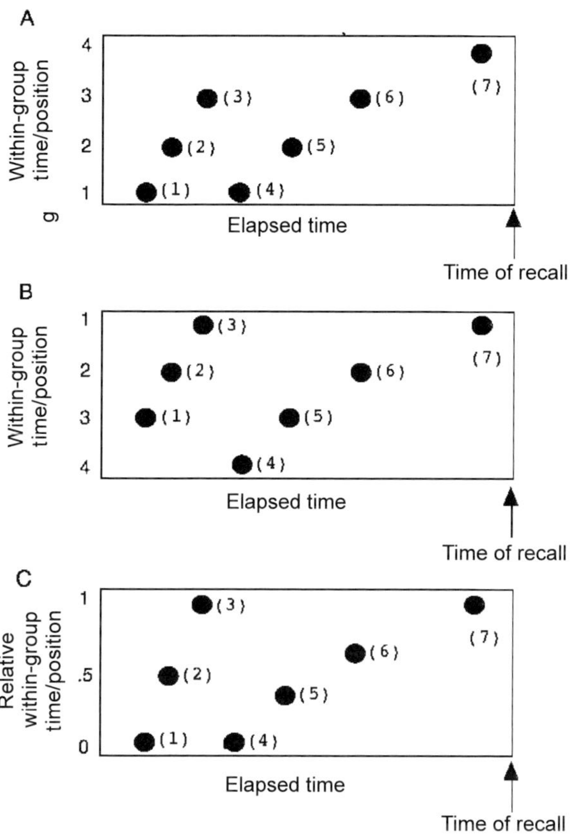

Fig. 11.   Possible psychological representations of within-group and within-list position.

dimension represents the location of items if encoded in terms of their position (or time) from the start of each group (panel A); their position (or time) from the end of each group (panel B), or their relative position (or relative time) through each group (panel C). The numerals beside each filled circle represent the positions in the presented list of each item. A three-dimensional possibility, according to which position (and/or time) from both ends of the group is relevant, is not pictured. We also ignore for now the possibility that both within-group time and within-group position are represented.

Ng and Maybery (2002) report a series of experiments designed to distinguish between: (a) position coding of within-group location and (b) encoding of within-group location in terms of the temporal distance of items from the beginning of the group. Ng and Maybery varied within-group SOA, such that for example a list of nine items might consist of an initial group of three fast-presented items (SOA = 0.5 s), followed by a group of three items presented more slowly (SOA = 1.0 s), followed by a final group of fast-presented items. Between-group SOA was held constant (at 4.0 s). When between-group order errors occur, a purely positional model of within-group encoding (according to which the timing of items within a group is not encoded on the within-group dimension) predicts under such conditions a preponderance of errors that preserve within-group position (e.g., item 5 being recalled in positions 2 or 8). A model of within-group encoding according to which items' location within a group is represented in terms of the absolute amount of time since group onset would, in contrast, predict movement errors that preserve time since group onset (e.g., item 5 being recalled in positions 3 or 9). In a variety of experiments and conditions, Ng and Maybery found the former pattern—movement errors reflected within-group position rather than time since group onset.

Intuitively, the Ng and Maybery (2002) results, which suggest movement errors preserve within-group position rather than time since group onset, are consistent with the positional interpretations of (A)–(C) in Fig. 11 or with the temporal interpretation of (C). Again in intuitive terms, the Henson (1999) demonstration that exchanges preserve location relative to the end of groups appear consistent with the temporal interpretation of (B), the positional interpretation of (B), and possibly the temporal or positional interpretation of (C). If movement errors simultaneously respect position from the start of the group (an issue on which the data are not yet clear when groups contain unequal numbers of items), both interpretations of (B) would additionally be excluded and the data would support either (C) or a model with additional dimensions.

We confirmed these intuitions by simulation of the Henson (1999) data. Henson (1999; Experiment 1) examined serial recall of seven-item lists presented as a group of three followed by a group of four items, as described earlier; as a group of four followed by a group of three, or ungrouped. A response was required in each output position. The resulting serial position curves (low-confidence responses included) are reproduced in Fig. 12. The analyses of particular interest focused on the proportion of order errors on critical positions (group-final and group-penultimate) that preserved position relative to the group's start (start-relative errors) in comparison to the number of order errors that preserved position relative to the group's end (end-relative errors). The main finding was that end-relative errors predominated.

We examined memory for a seven-item list in the model in both a grouped and an ungrouped condition. Because omissions were not permitted in the

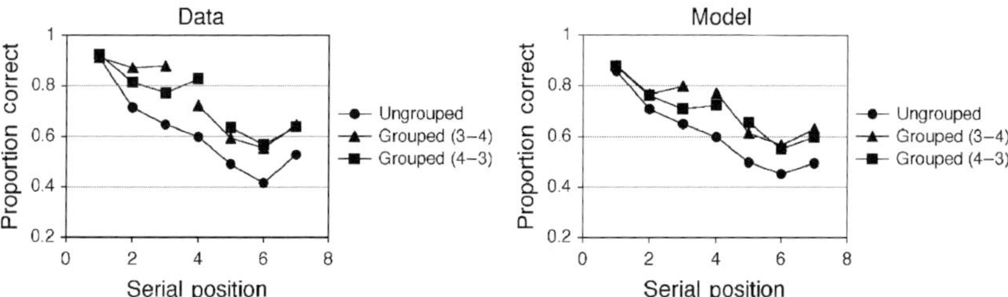

Fig. 12. Proportion correct recall on grouped and ungrouped lists and performance of SIMPLE. Data from Henson, R. N. A. (1999). Positional information in short-term memory: Relative or absolute? *Memory & Cognition, 27*, 915–927. Copyright © 1999 Psychonomic Society. Used with permission of the author.

Henson (1999) procedure, the threshold and threshold-noise parameters were not necessary. Within the model we varied the method of encoding within-group location, using each of the three schemes of representation illustrated in Fig. 11. The temporal schedule of item presentation for the model was identical to that used experimentally, but because the time course of output is not known, we made a similar assumption as in previous simulations (Brown et al., 2002) that output time increased as a power function (exponent $= 1.5$) of the output position.[14] For each method of encoding within-group location, we obtained best-fitting values of the three free parameters (the main parameter c; weight on the grouping dimension for the ungrouped list; and weight on the grouping dimension for the grouped list). With all three methods of encoding within-group location, it was possible to produce a reasonable qualitative fit to the serial position curves. For example, Fig. 12 shows serial positions obtained when position from the end of each group was encoded (panel b of Fig. 11). Parameter values were 9.3 (c); 0.04 (attentional weight on the grouping dimension for ungrouped lists) and 0.08 (attentional weight on the grouping dimension for grouped lists). Better fits can be obtained if parameters are allowed to vary between the two grouping conditions (3–4 and 4–3).

However, the key data concern the proportion of end-relative and start-relative errors on the critical positions (the third and fourth positions within a group). Henson (1999) found that end-relative errors predominated—the experimentally observed proportion of errors on critical positions that were start-relative (at 0.13) was lower than the proportion that was end-relative (0.17). In other words, movement errors tended to be between the ends of groups rather than between the third positions of groups. Consistent with

---

[14] We note the alternative possibility of output interference as an account of the extended primacy observed (Lewandowsky et al., 2004).

intuition, we were unable to obtain this pattern when the model encoded within-group location in terms of position from group start (panel A of Fig. 11)—start-relative errors predominated. However, end-relative errors (0.18) predominated over start-relative errors (0.06) when within-group location was encoded in terms of distance from the end of the group (panel B of Fig. 11) or when relative position within the group was encoded (panel C; 0.18 versus 0.08). Thus, the right qualitative pattern is observed, as expected, although the proportion of start-relative errors was smaller in the model than in the data (perhaps because of simplifications such as the ignoring of protrusions from previous lists). We also note that we did not analyze repetition errors in the simulation.

In summary, the data taken as a whole appear to suggest that coding of within-group position cannot be represented solely in terms of absolute temporal distance or number of positions from the start of the group or in terms of absolute temporal distance from the end of a group. A reasonable fit to the presently available data can be given if it is assumed that within-group position is encoded in terms of the positional distance from the end of the group or in terms of the relative time or position within a group.

VIII.   Challenges to SIMPLE's Account

SIMPLE proposes a single explanation for all serial position effects, including recency effects. In contrast, theoretical accounts descended from the modal model of the 1960s posit at least two different types of recency effect. According to these models, the recency effect observed in standard immediate free recall results from the immediate dumping of those items from a short-term store. This explanation cannot account for the so-called long-term recency effect observed in the continual distractor paradigm.[15] In a typical continual distractor experiment, each list item, including the final item, is followed by sufficient distractor activity (e.g., 30 s of solving math problems) that short-term memory should be flushed clean. Therefore, the two recency effects must be different.

Neath and Surprenant (2003, Chapter 4) review much of the evidence against the dual-store account of recency, and Brown et al. (2002) show how SIMPLE accounts for much of the data problematic for dual-store accounts, including the ratio rule. Davelaar, Goshen-Gottstein, Ashkenazi, Haarmann, and Usher (2005) argued that there exist five dissociations that

---

[15] This paradigm is frequently referred to as the "continuous" distractor paradigm despite the fact that distraction is not continuous.

support the idea that recency effects observed with immediate free recall are qualitatively different than those observed with the continual distraction paradigm and that unitary accounts cannot explain the dissociations. Here, we focus primarily on three of the dissociations, which naturally fall out of SIMPLE's architecture. In the final part of this section, we briefly consider the other two dissociations.

A. DIRECTED OUTPUT ORDER

Davelaar et al.'s (2005) first dissociation concerns the effects of directed output order. With immediate free recall, recency is present when subjects are asked to begin recall with the last item first, but recency is absent when subjects are asked to recall the first item first (Dalezman, 1976). In contrast, there are "no significant differences" in recall as a function of directed output order in the continual distractor paradigm (Whitten, 1978a, p. 689). SIMPLE is a unitary account of serial position functions and recency effects, and this pattern of results is exactly what SIMPLE predicts. In keeping with the goal of explanatory transparency, we present a simulation in which we strictly control output order. This simulation therefore differs somewhat from the procedure used by Whitten (1978a), who asked subjects to initiate recall with items from the first third of the list and then recall the remaining items in any order, or to initiate recall with items from the final third of the list and then recall the remaining items in any order.[16] The reason is that a simplified simulation affords a more transparent demonstration.

For the immediate free recall condition, 12-item lists were presented with a 1 s IPI, and recall was assumed to take 1 s per item. For the continual distractor condition, 12-item lists were again used, but there was 30 s between the presentation of each item and 30 s after the final item before recall began. Again, recall of each item was assumed to take 1 s per item. The simulation was either forwards or backwards recall. The results of the simulation, with $c = 5$, are shown in Fig. 13 and clearly demonstrate a huge effect of directed output order for immediate free recall but no such effect in the continual distractor paradigm.

SIMPLE produces this result because the logarithmic transform differentially affects small values and large values. A change from 30 to 41 s has almost no effect on the log-transformed values (e.g., 3.40 becomes 3.71) whereas a change from 1 to 12 s has a much larger effect (e.g., 0 becomes 2.48). The reason, according to SIMPLE, that there are no significant

---

[16] He also had a condition in which recall began with items from the middle third of the list; this did not affect recall either.

differences as a function of output order is that items in the continual distractor paradigm are represented in regions of psychological space in which the differences due to output order are too small to have a noticeable effect in typical paradigms.

One might be concerned that the simulation differs so much from the data cited by Davelaar et al. (2005). The reason for not showing a simulation closer to the paradigm used by Whitten (1978a) is solely that it requires additional steps and assumptions and quickly becomes very complex. The simulation reported, in contrast, emphasizes the fundamental role of the logarithmic transformation in selectively affecting immediate recall, and this effect holds regardless of other details of the simulation. The results shown in Fig. 13 serve as an existence proof that at least one unitary account of serial position effects accounts for the dissociation between directed output order and recall paradigm.

B. Dissociations with Amnesia

Davelaar et al.'s (2005) second dissociation concerns classic amnesic syndrome. With immediate free recall, the recency portion of the curve (i.e., the last three positions) does not differ between amnesic patients and healthy control subjects (Baddeley & Warrington, 1970). However, all other parts of the list in immediate free recall and *all* positions in the continual distractor recall are lower for patients than subjects.

Again, SIMPLE has no difficulty simulating these results (Brown & Lamberts, 2003; Brown, Della Sala, Foster, & Vousden, 2005). The critical

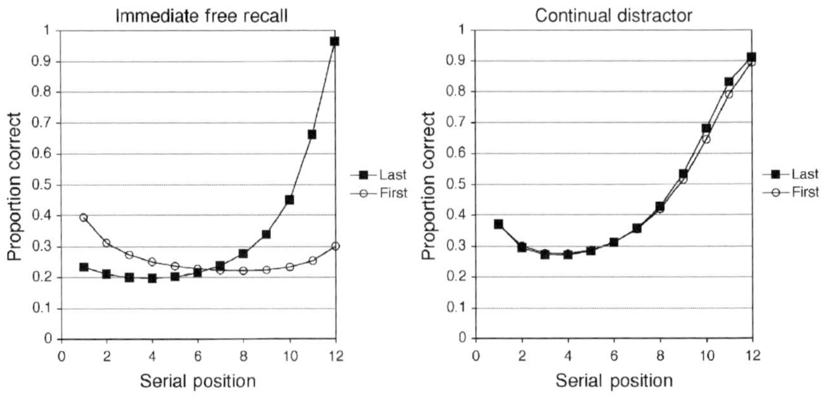

Fig. 13.   Simulations of recall of 12-item lists using either immediate free recall (left panel) or the continual distractor paradigm (right panel) as a function of whether recall begin with the last item in the list or with the first item in the list. Output order affects recency in immediate free recall but not in the continual distractor paradigm.

assumption has to do with when and how the items are rehearsed. For example, Brown et al. (2005) had an amnesic patient perform these tasks using the overt rehearsal procedure (Rundus, 1971; Tan & Ward, 2000). Brown et al. found that an amnesic patient engaged in fixed rehearsal rather than the cumulative rehearsal that is characteristic of unimpaired free recall. When the probability of recalling each item was plotted as a function of the temporal distance of last rehearsal for that item (Tan & Ward, 2000), both controls and amnesic showed extended recency and minimal primacy, and the resulting serial position curves were well fitted by SIMPLE.

C. PROACTIVE INTERFERENCE

Davelaar et al. (2005) report an experiment in which a prior list interfered with recall of the current list at all serial positions in a continual distractor task but interfered only with prerecency items in an immediate free recall task. SIMPLE can readily produce the appropriate pattern of data using an explanation similar to that used to explain the build-up (and release) of PI in the Brown–Peterson paradigm (Brown et al., 2002).[17] Because of the complexity of the experimental details, we again simplify the situation in order to emphasize the cause (within SIMPLE) of this effect.

Assume List 1 has been presented and recalled, and List 2 has been presented, the RI is over, but recall has not yet begun. Further assume a 60 s recall period (as was the case in the experiment). SIMPLE assumes a representation of 24 items (12 from each of the two lists). The final item of List 2 in the continual distractor condition has a temporal value of 15 s (the RI), the penultimate item has a value of 30 s (the RI plus a 15 s IPI) and so on through the list until the first item has a temporal value of 180 s. The last item of List 1 has a value of 180 s (the value of Item 1 of List 2) plus 60 s (the retrieval period) plus 15 s (the RI) for a total of 255 s. The penultimate item of List 1 has a value of 270 s (255 s plus 15 s IPI) and so on.

In the immediate free recall condition, in contrast, the final item of List 2 has a temporal value of 1 s (the RI), the penultimate item has a value of 2 s (the RI plus a 1 s IPI), and so on through the list until the first item has a temporal value of 12 s. The last item of List 1 has a value of 12 s (the value of Item 1 of List 2) plus 1 s (the retrieval period) plus 1 s (the RI) for a total of 73 s. The penultimate item of List 1 has a value of 74 s (73 s plus 1 s IPI), and so on. The rest of the model was similar to that used to produce the results in Fig. 6. The results of the simulation, with $c = 1.0$, $s = 20$, and $t = 0.25$, can

---

[17] A different way of explaining the data is to assume two dimensions, one corresponding to list and one to position within list, as with simulations of the Brown–Peterson paradigm (Brown et al., 2002).

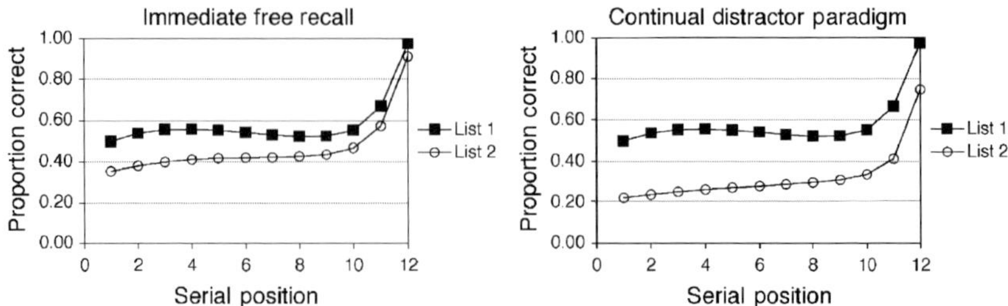

Fig. 14.   Sample simulations showing recall of two lists in either an immediate free recall task or a continual distractor paradigm task. The recency items in the former task are immune from proactive interference whereas those in the latter task are not.

be seen in the Fig. 14. Thus, the duration of the retrieval period (60 s) is large enough (relatively) to shield the recency items of List 2 from PI effects from List 1. However, the early part of List 1 is protected.

D.   OTHER DISSOCIATIONS

In addition to the three dissociations mentioned earlier, Davelaar et al. (2005) cite two more as being problematic for a unitary account of serial position effects, and thus these form the basis of postulating two separate types of recency effect.

One dissociation concerns the negative recency effect. On each trial in an experiment, subjects receive a list of items and perform immediate free recall. After the last trial, the subjects receive a surprise test that asks them to recall all of the items from all of the lists. On this surprise test, items from the recency portions of the individual lists are typically recalled worse than all other list items (Craik, 1970). In contrast, a surprise recall test of items that were presented in continual distractor lists shows no such disadvantage (Bjork & Whitten, 1974). A complete review of negative recency is beyond the scope of the current paper. However, a large number of studies suggest that negative recency occurs because subjects tend to process recency items in immediate free recall paradigms differently than prerecency items and also differently from recency items in continual distractor lists (Bartlett & Tulving, 1974; Marmurek, 1983; Maskarinec & Brown, 1974; Mazuryk, 1974; Watkins & Watkins, 1974; Whitten, 1978b). For example, negative recency can quite easily be turned into "positive recency" through either instructions or through experiencing different types of tests. It is possible that a version of SIMPLE in which a change in processing or experience altered the relative distinctiveness of the items, in a manner analogous to that used to explain the Nairne and Kelley (1999) data, could readily account for negative and positive recency. Within the SIMPLE framework, there is no need to restrict one type of processing to a particular memory system.

The final dissociation cited by Davelaar et al. (2005) as evidence against unitary accounts, such as SIMPLE, concerns the lag recency effect. The lag recency effect is the finding that the probability of recalling item j after recalling item i is larger the closer together items i and j were in the list (Kahana, 1996). The effect is asymmetric in that the probability is higher for items in the same input order than for items in reverse input order. That is, assuming the fourth item has just been recalled, the fifth item is more likely to be recalled than the third item. The dissociation concerns the finding that the asymmetry is greater for the first few recall transitions in immediate free recall, whereas in the continual distractor paradigm there is no such interaction between the asymmetry and output position. Currently, SIMPLE makes no predictions about lag recency; in order to determine whether SIMPLE could produce the appropriate pattern of results, a process version of the model would need to be developed.

Of the five problematic dissociations for unitary accounts of serial position curves described by Davelaar et al. (2005), three are not problems for SIMPLE, as the simulations reported here and elsewhere (Brown et al., 2005) demonstrate. Of the two remaining dissociations, we suggest negative recency is due to processes that could, in principle, be incorporated into the existing version of SIMPLE, but the final dissociation must await a process version before we can determine if it is a problem.

IX. Conclusions

We have focused on qualitative fits to emphasize the basic properties of SIMPLE. According to the model, memory performance depends on the extent to which an item is relatively distinct from its near neighbors on the dimension (or dimensions) underlying its representation. The combination of logarithmic transform, because it condenses large values more than small values, and edge effects give rise to the ubiquitous serial position curve. Systematic error gradients also arise from this cause. In most of the cases considered here, a model based on a temporal dimension provides an acceptable account, although we have noted that in some aspects of the serial recall literature, people might use other cues in combination with or as a replacement to temporal information. Our goal has not been to argue that the temporal dimension is fundamental in all memory situations, but rather, to see just how far a temporally-based local distinctiveness model can go. In this final section, we take the opportunity to speculate on possible reasons for the apparent success of models, such as SIMPLE, and briefly consider possible directions for future research.

The model explains key phenomena from a variety of memory tasks through its assumption that memories are organized in terms of their location along a temporal distance dimension. There are several reasons for believing that it may be adaptive to encode memory in temporal terms. For example, Anderson and Milson (1989; Anderson & Schooler, 1991) demonstrate that the probability with which some information will need to be recalled is related to the amount of time that has passed since the information was last required to be retrieved and, hence, suggest that an adaptively organized memory system will be structured in such a way as to make use of this temporal information. Gallistel (1990) points to the possible role of temporal coordinates in binding together elements of episodic memories (Brown & McCormack, in press). Brown and Chater (2001) and Brown and Vousden (1998) review a number of other reasons why memory may be chronologically organized. It is possible, therefore, that the success of the time-based SIMPLE model may partly reflect the adaptive role of temporal coding.

However, it is clear that not all tasks demand representation of memories along a temporal dimension, and indeed some tasks (such as memory for the serial order of short lists) seem likely to encourage ordinal encoding (this is the first item; this is the second, etc.). Consistent with this, evidence for time-based encoding is often stronger in free recall than in serial recall tasks (Brown, Morin, & Lewandowsky, 2005). A strength of SIMPLE is that, like exemplar models of categorization (Nosofsky, 1992) it assumes representation of items in multidimensional space (Brown et al., 2002). Thus, SIMPLE allows the addition of a temporal dimension into extant models of categorization and identification, and we speculate that the similarities in memory for different materials (such as the similar serial position curves and error gradients seen whether spatial location, positional location, or temporal location, etc. must be encoded) reflect a common retrieval mechanism. Of course, too much representational flexibility may lead to lack of falsifiablity, and it is therefore important to constrain the locations of items within multidimensional space as far as possible (e.g., by using MDS techniques).

SIMPLE is not a process model, and the lack of a process-level instantiation has both strengths and weaknesses. On the positive side, the adoption of a relatively economical high-level specification, and in particular the focus on computations based on ratios of temporal distances, gives clear prominence to the scale-invariant properties of the model. We suggest that these properties are just those needed to capture the scale-invariant properties of the structure of the world, as Chater and Brown (1999) have argued that psychological models must do in general. On the negative side, explanation of some phenomena will clearly require a model with a detailed process-level specification. For example, we noted earlier that we do not know whether a process version of SIMPLE could handle the asymmetric lag recency effect. As is often the case in psychological explanation, it is unclear which phenomena will need to make reference to a process-level explanation and which will not. Recent oscillator-based and temporal context models of memory (Brown, Preece, & Hulme, 2000; Burgess & Hitch, 1999; Glenberg & Swanson, 1986; Howard & Kahana, 2002) appear to implement many of the mechanisms needed to instantiate the more abstract specification in SIMPLE, and we anticipate that future work will focus on relating these different levels to each other as well as, of course, to relevant information from neuroscience.

According to SIMPLE, memory retrieval, regardless of the paradigm or the hypothetical underlying system, is fundamentally discrimination in terms of location along one or more dimensions. Thus, it explicitly renounces the multiple memory systems view, both when the distinction is based on time (e.g., short-term versus long-term memory) and when the distinction is based on other aspects of the to-be-remembered information (e.g., episodic awareness of the learning context as in the case of episodic versus semantic memory). As such, it emphasizes the search for common principles of memory that apply to memory as a whole (Neath & Surprenant, 2005). Further work will continue to examine the extent to which the basic local distinctiveness framework can accommodate data from supposedly different memory systems.

Finally, we note that SIMPLE, along with a number of other recent computational and mathematical models of human memory, is strongly antiassociationist in flavor. This antiassociationist emphasis, in combination with the focus on the representation of memories along a temporal relation, resonates strongly with recent approaches to learning and memory in non-human animals (Gallistel, 1990; Gallistel & Gibbon, 2000). Future work will, we suggest, need to build on the provocative similarities between temporal distinctiveness models of memory on the one hand and recent approaches to animal learning on the other.

ACKNOWLEDGMENT

Portions of this manuscript were written while the first author was a Visiting Fellow at the Department of Psychology, City University, London. This research was supported, in part, by ESRC Grant RES 000 231038 to the second author.

References

Alluisi, E. A., & Sidorsky, R. C. (1958). The empirical validity of equal discriminability scaling. *Journal of Experimental Psychology, 55*, 86–95.

Anderson, J. R., & Matessa, M. P. (1997). A production system theory of serial memory. *Psychological Review, 104*, 728–748.

Anderson, J. R., & Milson, R. (1989). Human memory: An adaptive perspective. *Psychological Review, 96*, 703–719.

Anderson, J. R., & Schooler, L. J. (1991). Reflections of the environment in memory. *Psychological Science, 2*, 396–408.

Baddeley, A. D. (1986). *Working memory.* New York: Oxford University Press.

Baddeley, A. D. (1994). Working memory: The interface between memory and cognition. In D. L. Schacter and E. Tulving (Eds.), *Memory systems 1994* (pp. 351–368). Cambridge, MA: MIT Press.

Baddeley, A. D., & Warrington, E. K. (1970). Amnesia and the distinction between long- and short-term memory. *Journal of Verbal Learning and Verbal Behavior, 9*, 176–189.

Baddeley, A. D., Thomson, N., & Buchanan, M. (1975). Word length and the structure of short-term memory. *Journal of Verbal Learning and Verbal Behavior, 14*, 575–589.

Bartlett, J. C., & Tulving, E. (1974). Effects of temporal and semantic encoding in immediate recall upon subsequent retrieval. *Journal of Verbal Learning and Verbal Behavior, 13*, 297–309.

Bjork, R. A. (2001). Recency and recovery in human memory. In H. L. Roediger, III, J. S. Nairne, I. Neath, and A. M. Surprenant (Eds.), *The nature of remembering: Essays in honor of Robert G. Crowder* (pp. 211–232). New York: APA.

Bjork, R. A., & Whitten, W. B. (1974). Recency-sensitive retrieval processes in long-term free recall. *Cognitive Psychology, 6*, 173–189.

Bower, G. H. (1971). Adaptation-level coding of stimuli and serial position effects. In M. H. Appley (Ed.), *Adaptation-level theory* (pp. 175–201). New York: Academic Press.

Brown, G. D. A., & Chater, N. (2001). The chronological organisation of memory: Common psychological foundations for remembering and timing. In C. Hoerl and T. McCormack (Eds.), *Time and memory: Issues in philosophy and psychology* (pp. 77–110). Oxford, England: Oxford University Press.

Brown, G. D. A., & Lamberts, K. (2003). Double dissociations, models, and serial position curves. *Cortex, 39*, 148–152.

Brown, G. D. A., & McCormack, T. (in press). The role of time in human memory and binding: A review of the evidence. In H. D. Zimmer, A. Mecklinger, and U. Lindenberger (Eds.), *Binding in human memory: A neurocognitive approach.* Oxford, England: Oxford University Press.

Brown, G. D. A., Preece, T., & Hulme, C. (2000). Oscillator-based memory for serial order. *Psychological Review, 107*, 127–181.

Brown, G. D. A., & Vousden, J. (1998). Adaptive sequential behaviour: Oscillators as rational mechanisms. In M. Oaksford and N. Chater (Eds.), *Rational models of cognition* (pp. 165–193). Oxford, England: Oxford University Press.

Brown, G. D. A., Della Sala, S., Foster, J. K., & Vousden, J. I. (2005). *Classical amnesia within a unitary model of memory* (submitted for publication).

Brown, G. D. A., Morin, C., & Lewandowsky, S. (in press). Evidence for time-based models of free recall *Psychonomic Bulletin & Review.*

Brown, G. D. A., Neath, I., & Chater, N. (2002). *A ratio model of scale-invariant memory and identification* (unpublished manuscript).

Burgess, N., & Hitch, G. (1999). Memory for serial order: A network model of the phonological loop and its timing. *Psychological Review, 106*, 551–581.

Burgess, N., & Hitch, G. J. (1999). Memory for serial order: A network model of the phonological loop and its timing. *Psychological Review, 106*, 551–581.

Chater, N., & Brown, G. D. A. (1999). Scale invariance as a unifying psychological principle. *Cognition, 69*, B17–B24.

Colle, H. A., & Welsh, A. (1976). Acoustic masking in primary memory. *Journal of Verbal Learning and Verbal Behavior, 15*, 17–32.

Conrad, R. (1964). Acoustic confusions in immediate memory. *British Journal of Psychology, 55*, 75–84.

Craik, F. I. M. (1970). The fate of primary memory items in free recall. *Journal of Verbal Learning and Verbal Behavior, 9*, 143–148.

Crowder, R. G. (1976). *Principles of learning and memory.* Hillsdale, NJ: Erlbaum.

Dalezman, J. J. (1976). Effects of output order on immediate, delayed, and final recall performance. *Journal of Experimental Psychology: Human Learning and Memory, 2*, 597–608.

Davelaar, E. J., Goshen-Gottstein, Y., Ashkenazi, A., Haarmann, H. J., & Usher, M. (2005). The demise of short-term memory revisited: Empirical and computational investigations of recency effects. *Psychological Review, 112*, 3–42.

Eriksen, C. W., & Hake, H. W. (1955). Absolute judgments as a function of stimulus range and number of stimulus and response categories. *Journal of Experimental Psychology, 49*, 323–332.

Friedman, W. J. (1993). Memory for the time of past events. *Psychological Bulletin, 113*, 44–66.

Gallistel, C. (1990). *The organization of learning.* Cambridge, MA: MIT Press.

Gallistel, C. R., & Gibbon, J. (2000). Time, rate, and conditioning. *Psychological Review, 107*, 289–344.

Garner, W. G. (1962). *Uncertainty and structure as psychological concepts.* New York: Wiley.

Glenberg, A. M., & Swanson, N. (1986). A temporal distinctiveness theory of recency and modality effects. *Journal of Experimental Psychology: Learning, Memory, and Cognition, 12*, 3–24.

Glenberg, A. M., Bradley, M. M., Kraus, T. A., & Renzaglia, G. J. (1983). Studies of the long-term recency effect: Support for a contextually guided retrieval hypothesis. *Journal of Experimental Psychology: Learning, Memory, and Cognition, 9*, 231–255.

Helson, H. (1964). *Adaptation-level theory: An experimental and systematic approach to behavior.* New York: Harper.

Henson, R. N. A. (1998). Short-term memory for serial order: The Start-End Model. *Cognitive Psychology, 36*, 73–137.

Henson, R. N. A. (1999). Positional information in short-term memory: Relative or absolute? *Memory & Cognition, 27*, 915–927.

Howard, M. W., & Kahana, M. J. (2002). A distributed representation of temporal context. *Journal of Mathematical Psychology, 46*, 269–299.

Hulme, C., Shostak, L., Stuart, G., Surprenant, A. M., Neath, I., & Brown, G. D. A. (in press). The distinctiveness of the word length effect. *Journal of Experimental Psychology: Learning, Memory, and Cognition.*

Hulme, C., Surprenant, A. M., Bireta, T. J., Stuart, G., & Neath, I. (in press). Abolishing the word length effect. *Journal of Experimental Psychology: Learning, Memory, and Cognition, 30*, 98–106.

Huttenlocher, J., Hedges, L. V., & Bradburn, N. M. (1990). Reports of elapsed time: Bounding and rounding processes in estimation. *Journal of Experimental Psychology: Learning, Memory, and Cognition, 16*, 196–213.

Huttenlocher, J., Hedges, L. V., & Prohaska, V. (1992). Memory for day of the week: A 5 + 2 day cycle. *Journal of Experimental Psychology: General, 121*, 313–326.

Kahana, M. J. (1996). Associative retrieval processes in free recall. *Memory & Cognition, 24*, 103–109.

Knoedler, A. J., Hellwig, K. A., & Neath, I. (1999). The shift from recency to primacy with increasing delay. *Journal of Experimental Psychology: Learning, Memory and Cognition, 25*, 474–487.

Lewandowsky, S., & Brown, G. D. A. (2005). Serial recall and presentation schedule: A micro-analysis of local distinctiveness. *Memory, 13*, 283–292.

Lewandowsky, S., Brown, G. D. A., Wright, T., & Nimmo, L. M. (2006). Timeless memory: Evidence against temporal distinctiveness models of short term memory for serial order. *Journal of Memory and Language, 54*, 20–38.

Lewandowsky, S., Duncan, M., & Brown, G. D. A. (2004). Time does not cause forgetting in short-term serial recall. *Psychonomic Bulletin & Review, 11*, 771–790.

Marmurek, H. H. (1983). Negative recency in final free recall: Encoding or retrieval. *American Journal of Psychology, 96*, 17–35.

Maskarinec, A. S., & Brown, S. C. (1974). Positive and negative recency effects in free recall learning. *Journal of Verbal Learning and Verbal Behavior, 13*, 328–334.

Maylor, E. A. (2002). Serial position effects in semantic memory: Reconstructing the order of verses of hymns. *Psychonomic Bulletin & Review, 9*, 816–820.

Mazuryk, G. F. (1974). Positive recency in final free recall. *Journal of Experimental Psychology, 103*, 812–814.

Miller, G. A. (1956). The magical number seven, plus or minus two: Some limits on our capacity for processing information. *Psychological Review, 63*, 81–97.

Murdock, B. B., Jr. (1960). The distinctiveness of stimuli. *Psychological Review, 67*, 16–31.

Murray, D. J. (1968). Articulation and acoustic confusability in short-term memory. *Journal of Experimental Psychology, 78*, 679–684.

Nairne, J. S. (1992). The loss of positional certainty in long-term memory. *Psychological Science, 3*, 199–202.

Nairne, J. S., & Kelley, M. R. (1999). Reversing the phonological similarity effect. *Memory & Cognition, 27*, 45–53.

Neath, I. (1993). Distinctiveness and serial position effects in recognition. *Memory & Cognition, 21*, 689–698.

Neath, I. (2000). Modeling the effects of irrelevant speech on memory. *Psychonomic Bulletin & Review, 7*, 403–423.

Neath, I. (2005). Serial position effects and position error gradients in "iconic" memory. Memory Lab Technical Report 2005–02, Purdue University.

Neath, I., & Brown, G. D. A. (2005). Scale invariance and primacy and recency effects in an absolute identification task. Memory Lab Technical Report 2005–01, Purdue University.

Neath, I., & Brown, G. D. A. (in press). Making distinctiveness models of memory distinct. In J. S. Nairne (Ed.), *The foundations of remembering: Essays in honor of Henry L. Roediger III.* New York: Psychology Press.

Neath, I., & Crowder, R. G. (1990). Schedules of presentation and distinctiveness in human memory. *Journal of Experimental Psychology: Learning, Memory, and Cognition, 16*, 316–327.

Neath, I., & Crowder, R. G. (1996). Distinctiveness and very short-term serial position effects. *Memory, 4*, 225–242.

Neath, I., & Knoedler, A. J. (1994). Distinctiveness and serial position effects in recognition and sentence processing. *Journal of Memory and Language, 33*, 776–795.

Neath, I., & Surprenant, A. M. (2003). *Human memory: An introduction to research, data, and theory* (2nd Edn.). Belmont, CA: Wadsworth.

Neath, I., & Surprenant, A. M. (2005). Mechanisms of memory. In K. Lamberts and R. L. Goldstone (Eds.), *Handbook of cognition* (pp. 221–238). London: Sage.

Neath, I., Bireta, T. J., & Surprenant, A. M. (2003). The time-based word length effect and stimulus set specificity. *Psychonomic Bulletin & Review, 10*, 430–434.

Neath, I., Brown, G. D. A., McCormack, T., Chater, N., & Freeman, R. (2006). Distinctiveness models of memory and absolute identification: Evidence for local, not global, effects. *Quarterly Journal of Experimental Psychology, 59*, 121–135.

Ng, M. L. H., & Maybery, M. T. (2002). Grouping in short-term verbal memory: Is position coded temporally? *Quarterly Journal of Experimental Psychology, 55*, 391–424.

Nimmo, L. M., & Lewandowsky, S. (in press). From brief gaps to very long pauses: Temporal isolation does not benefit serial recall. *Psychonomic Bulletin & Review.*

Nosofsky, R. M. (1992). Similarity scaling and cognitive process models. *Annual Review of Psychology, 43*, 25–53.

Pollack, I. (1952). The information of elementary auditory displays. I. *Journal of the Acoustical Society of America, 24*, 745–749.

Roediger, H. L., III, & Crowder, R. G. (1976). A serial position effect in recall of United States presidents. *Bulletin of the Psychonomic Society, 8*, 275–278.

Rundus, D. (1971). An analysis of rehearsal processes in free recall. *Journal of Experimental Psychology, 89*, 63–77.

Ryan, J. (1969a). Grouping and short-term memory: Different means and patterns of grouping. *Quarterly Journal of Experimental Psychology, 21*, 137–147.

Ryan, J. (1969b). Temporal grouping, rehearsal, and short-term memory. *Quarterly Journal of Experimental Psychology, 21*, 148–155.

Shepard, R. N. (1987). Toward a universal law of generalization for psychological science. *Science, 237*, 1317–1323.

Shiffrin, R. M., & Nosofksy, R. M. (1994). 7 plus or minus 2: A commentary on capacity limitations. *Psychological Review, 101*, 357–361.

Stewart, N., Brown, G. D. A., & Chater, N. (2005). Absolute identification by relative judgment. *Psychological Review, 112*, 881–911.

Surprenant, A. M. (2001). Distinctiveness and serial position effects in tonal sequences. *Perception & Psychophysics, 63*, 737–745.

Tan, L., & Ward, G. (2000). A recency-based account of primacy effects in free recall. *Journal of Experimental Psychology: Learning, Memory, and Cognition, 26*, 1589–1625.

Tulving, E. (2002). Episodic memory: From mind to brain. *Annual Review of Psychology, 53*, 1–25.

Watkins, M. J., & Watkins, O. C. (1974). Processing of recency items for free recall. *Journal of Experimental Psychology, 102*, 488–493.

Whitten, W. B. (1978a). Output interference and long-term serial position effects. *Journal of Experimental Psychology: Human Learning and Memory, 4*, 685–692.

Whitten, W. B. (1978b). Initial-retrieval "depth" and the negative recency effect. *Memory & Cognition, 6*, 590–598.

WHAT IS MUSICAL PROSODY?

Caroline Palmer and Sean Hutchins

Prosody is the music of everyday speech.
(Wennerstrom, 2001).

I. Introduction

Music performance is prevalent everywhere. Concert attendance, recording sales, and critics' reviews suggest that people are sensitive to and have definite preferences for particular performances. Performers add variation to music; they manipulate the sound properties, including frequency (pitch), time, amplitude, and timbre (harmonic spectrum) above and beyond the pitch and duration categories that are determined by composers. These manipulations are called "musical expression," and cognitive psychologists have speculated on why performances contain expression. One hypothesis is that musical expression communicates emotions (Juslin & Sloboda, 2001). Another is that it clarifies structure (Kendall & Carterette, 1990). That structure may be indicated by a composer in a musical score (Lerdahl & Jackendoff, 1983), as well as by a performer in an interpretation—the performer's shaping of the music according to his or her own intentions (Apel, 1972). Each of these hypotheses relies on the fact that music expresses something, and the object of study is often what is expressed in music. But to understand *what* is expressed requires that we understand *how* it is expressed; the *how* often delineates or identifies the *what*. Examples might include

THE PSYCHOLOGY OF LEARNING
AND MOTIVATION VOL. 46
DOI: 10.1016/S0079-7421(06)46007-2

245

remembering a familiar tune by its tempo or recognizing the end of a phase by marked decrease in tempo and loudness.

The ways in which musicians manipulate acoustic signals to create expression bear considerable resemblance to the ways in which talkers manipulate speech. In speech, the acoustic changes in frequency, amplitude, and duration that form grouping, prominence, and intonation are called "prosody"; these features are systematic within each language and are thought to be rule governed and distinct from other structural levels of linguistic analysis (Beckman, 1996; Pierrehumbert, 1999). We refer here to musical expression as "musical prosody" because, as in speech, performers manipulate music for certain expressive and coordinating functions. Acoustic properties of speech and music can be manipulated to a certain extent without changing the categorical information (the words as they might be written or the musical pitches as they might be notated). Because linguistic and musical items are constrained by different acoustic properties (e.g., timing defines duration categories in music but not in speech), some acoustic dimensions may play a larger role in one domain than in another. Thus, prosody reflects acoustic variations on dimensions within each domain, while maintaining important categorical distinctions. We focus here on the forms and functions of musical prosody and whether it is rule-governed and distinct from other forms of musical structure.

Not much attention has been paid to the role of musical prosody. One reason for this is an assumption that most aspects of memory for musical pitch or duration are relative (not absolute) and that subcategorical expressive features (such as frequency differences smaller than musical pitch categories) cannot be retained in memory once the items are perceived (Raffman, 1993). This position is similar to normalization views of speech perception in which extralinguistic speaker variation was treated as noise to be filtered out (Pisoni, 1997). Counterevidence to this position toward performer variation in music, however, is gaining to suggest that listeners do retain absolute details about pitch height (Levitin, 1994; Schellenberg & Trehub, 2003) and tempo of familiar music (Levitin & Cook, 1996), as well as subcategorical note-to-note variations in musical expression (Palmer, Jungers, & Jusczyk, 2001). Infants can remember the absolute details of tone intensities and durations as well (Palmer et al., 2001; Trainor, Wu, & Tsang, 2004). Thus, music is a good example of an intricate acoustic nonverbal system in which expression is remembered.

The role that prosodic features of music play in acquisition is particularly of interest; prosody may provide information to help novices (infants as well as late acquisition learners) parse a continuous acoustic stream into meaningful units and bootstrap learning of complex hierarchical relationships among those units. Listeners' knowledge of complex tonal and rhythmic structure in music is acquired through implicit knowledge gained from long-term exposure to music of a particular culture (Bharucha, 1987; Krumhansl, 1990; Trehub, 2000); it is unknown how much of that acquisition is influenced by prosodic features. Later in this chapter, we consider how prosodic features of music influence segmentation and implicit learning of musical structure.

A.   MUSICAL PROSODY IS OBLIGATORY

Musicians perform in a variety of ways in Western cultures. In many performances, musicians express their interpretation of previously composed music; the composition is learned either by reading a notated musical score or by hearing it performed. In improvisatory performance, musicians create the composition as they perform or create a variation on something they have heard or read. A musical composition denotes categorical pitches and durations. However, the physical instantiation of intensity, tempo (rate), articulation (relations of tone offsets to successive tone onsets, such as in staccato/legato), and timbre are usually underdetermined by the composition; in most cases, they must be determined by the performer. Because some instantiation of these factors is necessary, we consider prosody to be obligatory (not that there is an obligatory way in which prosody must be instantiated). Although frequency and timbre are fixed on piano and other keyboard instruments, most musical instruments permit variation in frequency and timbre, as well as variation in intensity and tempo. Some forms of expression are notated in a musical score; for example, intensity, tempo, and even emotional connotations can be indicated by composers or by editors, although these markings tend to be in a small number of large categories. However, the majority of acoustic features that the musician must choose are obligatory, in the same way that they are obligatory in speech (Pierrehumbert, 1999).

There are several ramifications of an obligatory prosody—first, every musical performance represents some choice of the physical variables that give rise to perception of stress, accent, rhythm, and intensity contour (including crescendos and decrescendos). Even computer-generated music, in which all tones have fixed and equivalent durations, intensities, and tempo, requires some choice of tempo and absolute intensity level by the composer/programmer. Those choices have important perceptual outcomes; computer-generated performances are perceived as flat or dull (Kendall & Carterette, 1990; Palmer, 1996b), similar to how computer-generated speech can be perceived as mechanical. Second, a musician tends to reproduce performances of the same music with the same prosodic choices. An example of a pianist's rendition of a Mozart piano sonata (Palmer, 1996a) is shown in Fig. 1; the prosodic choices of timing and intensity for each tone were highly similar across the repeated section of the performance (measures 1–16). Finally, musicians' prosodic choices change systematically with the musical context in which the tones appear. Excerpts from musical compositions are produced with different expressive nuances when performed in or out of a particular melodic context; for example, phrase-final lengthening (the choice of making final tones in a sequence longer than others) will be greater for the last tones in a musical excerpt when it is performed on its own than when it is embedded in a longer sequence. Also, musical excerpts are produced with different nuances when they are placed in one melodic context than in another (Palmer et al., 2001). One ramification is that experiments that use musical events produced in isolation, such as chords or tones, will reflect different prosodic structure

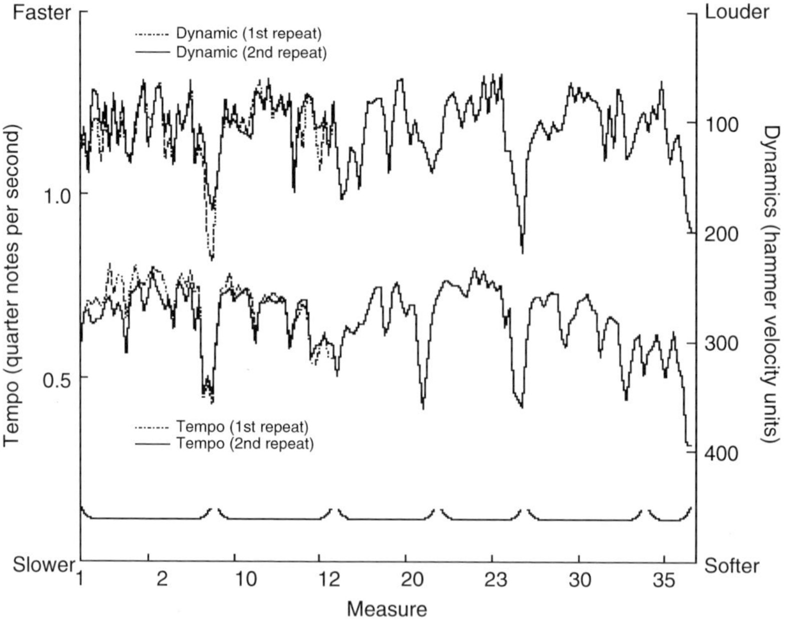

Fig. 1. Reprinted with permission from C. Palmer (1996a). Anatomy of a performance: Sources of musical expression. *Music Perception, 13*, 433–454, © by the Regents of the University of California. Performance of 54-measure section of a Mozart piano sonata; dynamics and tempo measures for the 16-measure section that the pianist performed twice. Both dynamics and tempo are consistent across repetitions.

from what is produced for the same musical events in context. Similar points have been made for speech (Pierrehumbert, 1999).

B. Musical Prosody Alters with Intent: Interpretations

One of the earliest empirical findings in music cognition was that musicians never perform events evenly (with equal duration, intensity, and articulation—note offset to successive note onset) (Seashore, 1938a). Performers often reproduce a musical performance with the same expression (Seashore, 1937), which indicates that the variations in how events are produced are not random. Furthermore, attempts to play mechanically (without expression) reduce the expressive nuances, and attempts to play exaggeratedly enhance the expressive nuances (Gabrielsson, 1987; Palmer, 1989a; Seashore, 1938b). An example of a pianist's intent to perform with a particular phrasing interpretation is shown in Fig. 2 (Palmer, 1989b). The difference between the expressive performance (solid line) and the intent to perform without expression (the dashed line) indicates the degree to which prosodic features of slowing down at phrase

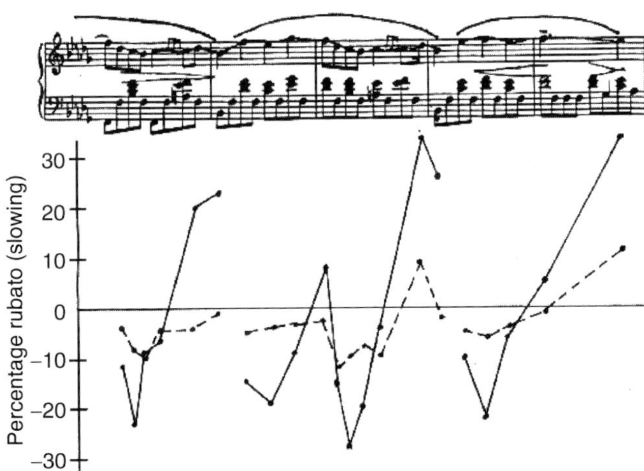

Fig. 2. Reprinted with permission from C. Palmer (1989b). Structural representations of music performance. In *Proceedings of the 11th Annual Conference of the Cognitive Science Society* (pp. 349–356). © Erlbaum. Tempo changes that alter with performer's interpretation from five measures of performance of a Prelude by Chopin. Solid lines above music notation indicate performer's intended phrasing. Tempo changes in expressive performance (solid line) show phrase-final lengthening near intended phrase boundaries. Inexpressive performance (dashed line) shows reduced phrase-final lengthening.

endings alter with intent. Thus, expressive nuances are systematic and at least some nuances correspond to musical intentions.

Most music contains some structural ambiguity with regard to where the phrase boundaries or metrical units will be, how important one musical voice is relative to another, etc. Musical interpretations allow the performer a certain degree of flexibility in how they apply prosodic features. Interpretations reflect a conductor's or performer's modeling of a piece according to their own musical thoughts or ideas (Apel, 1972). Music teachers often discuss the contents of interpretations with students, based on musicological and historical elements, aesthetic elements, and elements of expressive performance that are not necessarily conveyed by a printed score. Although interpretations permit a certain degree of freedom across musicians and performances, many theorists believe that some interpretations are more preferred or appropriate than others (Cyr, 1992; Neumann, 1982). For example, polyphonic music of J. S. Bach's era does not permit the same freedom of tempo change as romantic music of Chopin's era; measurements of rubato are greatest in performances of romantic music across a range of performers and compositions (Palmer & van de Sande, 1995; Repp, 1992a; Todd, 1985). Some expressive nuances, such as phrase-final lengthening or progressive slowing of tempo toward the end of major phrasal units, correspond to musical grouping structure as determined by the composition (Todd, 1985, 1992). Other expressive nuances seem tied to performers' individualistic decisions about the prominence given to some musical events over others, such as which tones form major phrase boundaries (Palmer, 1989a; Shaffer, 1992) or which tones in chords (simultaneities), are most important (i.e., the melody) (Palmer, 1989a, 1996b).

Given that most music contains structural ambiguity, one can ask whether musical prosody is the result of individualistic interpretations. Do performers have the freedom to express the musical features in acoustic signals in a primarily individualistic manner, or is this mapping constrained by cognitive principles shared across performers and listeners? If the former is true, then we should not expect to see perceptual or cognitive generalities across musical styles or cultures; other factors, such as historical period, geographical region, and instrument-specific degrees of freedom, may shape musical expression. Although there are many studies of musical expression within Western tonal cultures, there is a paucity of evidence to address cultural differences in musical expression. If the latter is true, we should see general principles of musical prosody both in the forms that it takes and the functions that it serves. This chapter focuses on whether the term "musical prosody" captures general principles of musical expression above and beyond individualistic features of musical interpretation.

II. Definitions of Prosody

To define musical prosody, we first consider definitions of linguistic prosody. Classical study of linguistic prosody, interestingly, returns us to music. In traditional study of classical grammar, which focused on poetry prosody was defined as the study of accent, or phonetic properties of syllables and words relevant to the measure of rhythm and meter, especially in verse (La Driere, 1993). Meter, which derives from the Greek *metron*, refers in both verse and in music to metrical units defined by accents, measured in syllables or feet in poetry and in beats in music (*American Heritage Dictionary of the English Language*, 2004). Grammatical and rhetorical elements were often combined with musical elements in the late Middle Ages, when poetry was again closely associated with music (La Driere, 1993). Thus, it is not surprising that aspects of metrical phonology have developed similarly in linguistic and music analyses.

Today, prosody is considered a distinct component of phonological theory, which posits a separate prosodic tier for metrical structure (Levelt, 1989; Liberman & Prince, 1977; Selkirk, 1984). Prosody can refer both to an abstract level of phonological structure and to its acoustic realization in speech (Cutler, Dahan, & Donselaar, 1997; Shattuck-Hufnagel & Turk, 1996). Prosodic cues in speech include acoustic variations in fundamental frequency, spectral information, amplitude, and relative durations of speech. One approach from phonological theory characterizes prosody in terms of the cognitive structures that are implicit in the minds of speakers in order to explain their use of these variations in speech production and speech perception (Pierrehumbert, 1999). Prosodic structure within the word is important in lexical access, influencing how segmentation works in each language and the set of active competitors for any given word at any given time (Cutler, 1995). Prosodic structure above the word level (phrasing and phrasal prominence) often reflects other dimensions of linguistic analysis, including syntax, semantics, and discourse structure (Ferreira, 2002).

Most definitions of speech prosody distinguish between pitch and time dimensions. For example, prosodic structure of rhythm, grouping, and prominence is often separated from intonational (melodic) structure (Cutler, 1999; Ferreira, 2002; Pierrehumbert, 1999). Intonational structure refers to pitch at the phonological phrase level, often described as the "melody" of the speech. Intonation is carried in the fundamental frequency of the voice, perceived as pitch. The primary functions attributed to intonation in non-tone languages (stress-timed or syllable-timed languages) are to mark the pragmatic information or the emotional information in an utterance (Pell, 2001). In lexical tone languages, such as Mandarin or Thai, lexical features interact with intonational features to determine pitch contours assigned to phrases. Intonation and rhythmic prominence (including meter) place simultaneous constraints on each other in prosody (Beckman, 1996).

In contrast to speech, musical pitch is relatively fixed by categorical constraints that are specified in a composition. Although most musical instruments allow some manipulation of fundamental frequency, performance conventions constrain the amount of pitch variability that can be introduced (vibrato, or a small fluctuation in pitch on a single tone, is an exception). While soloists may slightly alter their intonation at times, this is generally not feasible for ensemble musicians who must perform simultaneously with others, and is not possible for performance on instruments, such as keyboards, which only allow discrete pitch changes. Thus, most of our discussion of musical prosody focuses on rhythm, grouping, and prominence, and not intonation.

The temporal aspects of music and speech prosody bear important similarities, in particular, between musical meter and linguistic stress (Cooper & Meyer, 1960; Lerdahl & Jackendoff, 1983; Selkirk, 1984). The rhythm of speech involves patterning of strong beats that coincide with some syllables. Syllable-timed languages like Spanish are described as having a regular beat pattern in which each syllable coincides approximately with a beat, whereas stress-timed languages like English tend to have beats on stressed syllables and equal time intervals between stressed syllables (Pike, 1945). Vowels in stressed syllables are longer than in unstressed syllables in many (but not all) languages (Lehiste, 1972). Similar to how words differ in the amount of stress that is assigned to their constituent syllables, musical tones differ in the amount of prominence or accent assigned to them. Musical accent, like stress, is hierarchical—usually there are two to four levels of accent in a musical phrase (Cooper & Meyer, 1960; Lerdahl & Jackendoff, 1983). Metrical grids are a common formalism for representing both the different levels of stress that syllables receive and the levels of accent that musical tones receive (Lerdahl & Jackendoff, 1983; Liberman & Prince, 1977). Syllables that are stressed tend to be longer or bear a pitch accent (Ferreira, 2002), and musical tones that bear metrical accent tend to be longer or produced with greater intensity (Drake & Palmer, 1993; Sloboda, 1983).

A major difference in the temporal aspects of music and speech prosody is the degree of isochrony, or temporal regularity. Music of many cultures displays a strong beat regularity as evidenced in written notation and in aural traditions; furthermore, musically untrained listeners can clap along systematically to unfamiliar music that is performed with expressive tempo variations (Drake, Penel, & Bigand, 2000). Languages of the world do not display the same degree of regularity in production or perception. Interstress intervals tend to vary as a function of the material within the interval, although evidence of a tendency toward isochrony is seen in some studies when principle determinants of duration (sentential context, lexical content, etc.) are controlled for (Cooper & Eady, 1986; Kelly & Bock, 1988). Differences between speech and music in their degree of temporal regularity raise the possibility that prosodic variation may be constrained differently. Prosodic variation in music, whose temporal regularity is high, may permit more deviation and still yield perceptual constancy, whereas prosodic variation in speech, whose temporal regularity is lower, may be pressured to align with other structural (syntactic, semantic) dimensions.

In sum, although music and language differ on many important structural dimensions, both domains have realizations of prosody. Music may be more constrained in terms of pitch and duration categories, but both domains utilize the flexibility available within the domain. Temporal and pitch manipulations are used prosodically in music, although not to the extent permitted in speech. Linguistic stress and musical accent are both realized in duration and intensity, and are manipulated in similar ways for prosodic purposes. Linguistic meter and musical meter are modeled with similar hierarchical rules, and producers appear to manipulate those dimensions in similar ways to serve prosodic functions. The precise functions are discussed in later section.

III. Functions of Musical Prosody

What functions would musical prosody serve? Linguistic prosody serves several functions, some of which do not have direct equivalents in music performance. One such function is to signal the illocutionary intent of the speaker (such as making a statement or a request in "She has left the room (?)"). Another is to disambiguate the meaning of words with similar segmental structure (phonemic stress), such as "greenhouse" versus "green house." But other prosodic functions that relate less to semantic content may be similar to the functions of music prosody, such as segmenting a continuous acoustic stream into its component units, highlighting items of relative importance (focus and prominence), coordination among producers (including turn-taking), and attributing emotional states to producers. We consider here these functions that musical prosody may play.

A. SEGMENTATION

A major focus of auditory communication is how people segment a continuous signal into important events, their sources, and the relations among them (Bregman, 1990). Music and speech are organized in units of varying temporal extent. A short segment can serve as a unit at one level and then join with other segments to form longer units at higher levels of organization, in a hierarchical structure (Deutsch & Feroe, 1981; Lerdahl & Jackendoff, 1983). Musical tones combine to form melodic and rhythmic figures, phrases, and larger sections. Listeners, with and without musical training, are adept at segmenting the musical stream into these units. How do prosodic cues influence this segmentation?

One musical unit that is often marked for segmentation by prosodic cues is the phrase. A musical phrase varies in length and is described as a unit of meaning, often defined by elements at its boundaries (Cogan & Escot, 1976). Performers often mark phrase boundaries with changes in intensity, tone duration, and articulation (Henderson, 1936). Performers on a wide variety of musical instruments tend to use phrase-final lengthening at boundaries by increasingly lengthening successive tones as they approach a structural boundary, even when those tones are notated as equivalent duration in the musical composition (Gabrielsson, 1987; Kendall & Carterette, 1990; Palmer, 1989a,b; Todd, 1985). The patterns of tempo modulations often indicate a hierarchy of phrases, with the amount of slowing at a boundary corresponding to the depth of the phrase embedding (Shaffer & Todd, 1987; Todd, 1985, 1989). Todd (1985, 1989) proposed a computational model of phrase-final lengthening in music performance; the more important the musical segment in a given phrase, based on a hierarchical analysis of meter and grouping principles (Lerdahl & Jackendoff, 1983), the greater the phrase-final lengthening. The correspondence between phrase-final lengthening and intensity changes in music performance is also strong; unit boundaries are marked by both slowing in tempo and decreased amplitude (Drake & Palmer, 1993; Palmer, 1996b).

Are musical phrases always marked prosodically? Usually, yes. All published research on performance of Western tonal music shows phrase-final lengthening at boundaries. Compositional structure marks phrase boundaries as well with longer duration categories, and listeners attribute phrase structure in the absence of prosodic cues (Palmer & Krumhansl, 1987). Listeners are sensitive to phrase markings as early as infancy. When pauses were placed at appropriate phrase boundaries, infants displayed longer orientation times in a head-turn preference procedure task than to music with phrase boundaries placed at inappropriate phrase boundaries (based on the structural information in the compositional score) (Krumhansl & Jusczyk, 1990). Jusczyk and Krumhansl (1993) further demonstrated that the decreasing pitch height and increasing tone duration that typically marked phrase boundaries were critical for infants' sensitivity to music that is segmented at phrase boundaries. These two variables are the same ones suggested to underlie infants' segmentation of speech (Jusczyk et al.,

1992)—change in fundamental frequency at the ends of clauses and phrases, and lengthening of syllables before important syntactic boundaries. These similarities raise the possibility that listeners respond to general acoustic properties of acoustic signals, which serve to mark important events in auditory perception, rather than duplicating domain-specific segmentation mechanisms.

Other prosodic features of music help to distinguish simultaneities, such as musical voices from each other, presumably to aid listeners in focusing limited attentional resources. Performers often manipulate the relationship between the timing of individual parts that are notated as simultaneous, with intensity differences or onset timing differences; onset asynchronies are a primary aid to stream segregation (Bregman, 1990). Musical ensembles display inter-instrument onset asynchronies among tones notated as simultaneous (chords) that can help listeners distinguish between voices in multi-voiced music (Rasch, 1978). Ensemble players who produced the melody (voice of primary importance) tended to precede other voices in string and wind trios by 30–50 ms (Rasch, 1979, 1988). Palmer (1989a, 1996b; see also Thompson and Cuddy, 1997) showed further evidence of melodic leading in solo piano performance, giving evidence that timing asynchronies are the result of structural emphasis rather than solely a result of coordination between performers. Goebl (2001) showed that the amount of the melody leads correlated with hammer velocity differences (how fast the keys were struck to create louder sounds) on acoustic piano.

Do prosodic features influence music segmentation? Palmer et al. (2001) reported performances of the same musical excerpt (a musical measure, or metrical unit) placed in different melodic contexts. Figure 3 shows the original prosodic cues produced by a pianist for the excerpt (marked by the box) and the melody in which the excerpt was presented in music notation. Prosodic features of intensity and articulation were used to mark the metrical beats as implied by the meter in which the excerpt was presented. The prosodically marked excerpts were then spliced and placed in computer-generated melodic contexts whose musical structure either matched or mismatched the implicit structure of the prosodic cues. Musically trained and untrained listeners were then familiarized with a performance of the excerpts out of context, and later had to recognize which excerpts they had heard when the excerpts were placed in the computer-generated melodic contexts. All listeners were less able to recognize the excerpt when its prosodic cues matched the context; when the excerpt was heard in the incorrect context, it became more salient, suggesting that the prosodic cues influenced listeners' segmentation processes. In sum, prosodic cues may not always be necessary for segmentation in music, but when present, prosodic features have a significant influence on how segmentation occurs.

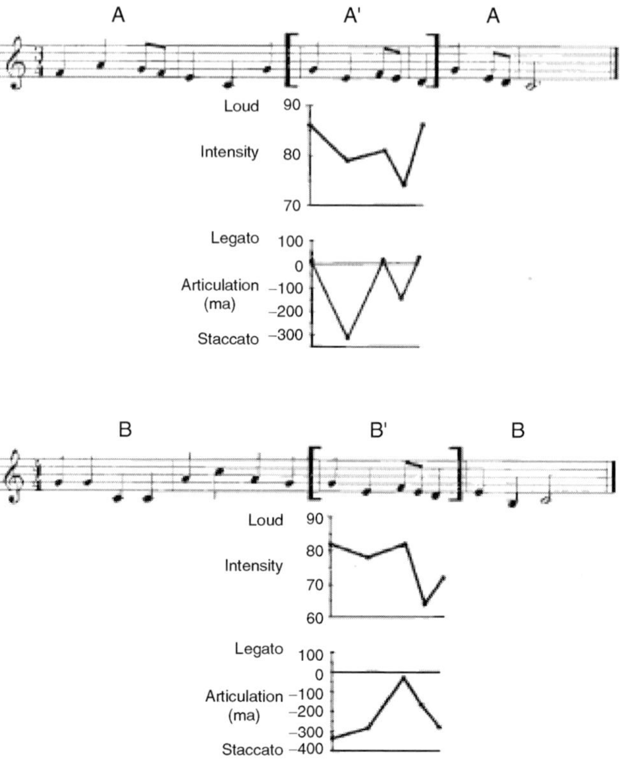

Fig. 3. Reprinted with permission from Palmer et al. (2001). Episodic memory for musical prosody. *Journal of Memory and Language, 45*, 526–545, © Elsevier. Musical expression changes with context and aids segmentation. Pianist's performance of musical excerpt placed in different metrical contexts (top: ternary meter, bottom: binary meter). Intensity and articulation patterns (legato/staccato) increase on metrical accents.

Does musical prosody carry information in the absence of tonal or rhythmic content? For example, listeners can still analyze major prosodic phrasing when segmental content is removed in low-pass-filtered speech or in hummed speech (Kreiman, 1982, with low-pass-filtered speech; Collier & Hart, 1975, with hummed sentences). Only a few studies have compared listeners' responses to musical prosody in the absence of pitch (monotonic tone) or rhythmic content (isochronous rhythm). When pitch variation was removed and only durational performance variation remained, listeners were able to identify the phrase structure on the basis of duration-lengthening (Palmer & Krumhansl, 1987). Likewise, when durational variation was removed and pitch variation remained, they were able to indicate phrase structure on basis of pitch variation. Thus, these results suggest that musical prosody is sufficient to signal phrase structure, similar to the speech findings.

B. PROMINENCE

Linguistic prominence, or acoustic highlighting with stress, accent, and other prosodic forms, is used to signal the focus, or the more significant elements of a sentence (Dogil, 2003). Musical prosody may also function to signal the relative prominence of events. Prominence is especially important in ambiguous forms of music for which the meter, phrasing, or the melody (most important voice) might be underdetermined by the composition. Performers use prosodic cues to emphasize the metrical and phrase structure of the music (above and beyond the segmental marking of boundaries), especially when the structure is ambiguous. Performers lengthen tones, perform them louder, or change the articulation (more legato or more staccato) to mark metrically important events (Sloboda, 1983, 1985). Gabrielsson (1974) documented in a wide variety of rhythms that musicians performed metrically important beats louder, longer, and more legato relative to other beats. Many studies document a decreased intensity and/or slowing tempo that performers introduce at phrase boundaries (Palmer, 1989b; Repp, 1992a; Shaffer, 1981; Todd, 1985), similar to phrase-final lengthening in speech. Vibrato, or small, rapid variations in pitch, is another method for increasing prominence. Although less research has addressed the use of vibrato, some studies indicate that singers and string players use vibrato to emphasize musical events (Seashore, 1938; Small, 1937).

Prominence can be used to exaggerate some aspects of musical structure at the expense of others, similar to the goals of contrastive focus in speech. For example, duration patterns that are intended to have certain ratios, such as 3:1, are often performed with higher ratios (>3:1), perhaps to distinguish them from similar (2:1) ratios commonly found in music (Gabrielsson, 1987). Shackford (1961, 1962) presented similar evidence from the production of simultaneous musical intervals; when two violinists performed a single tone a tritone apart from each other (a pitch interval of six semitones between the two tones), the interval they produced was exaggerated as a larger pitch interval when it was notated as an augmented fourth (an interval created by expanding a perfect fourth—an interval of five semitones) than when it was notated as a diminished fifth (an interval created by reducing a perfect fifth—an interval of seven semitones), even though the augmented fourth and the diminished fifth denote equivalent pitch intervals of six semitones. These exaggerations give prominence to a desired interpretation over an alternative interpretation, similar to how accented vowels tend to be articulated in a more exaggerated fashion and made more distinct from each other than unaccented vowels (Beckman, 1996; de Jong, 1995).

Performers and listeners develop expectations for the relationship between musical structure and prosodic prominence. Pianists are better at imitating the note-to-note prosodic variations in performances whose expressive timing deviations match the implicit phrase structure (Clarke, 1993; Clarke & Baker-Short, 1987); they are not as accurate at imitating expressive timing that does not match the structural expectations they form (Repp, 2000). Listeners develop structural expectations that influence their perception of prosodic cues as well; for example, a tone with increased duration is harder for listeners to detect when it occurs at a position in which lengthening is expected (toward the end of a phrase) relative to an unexpected position (in the middle of a phrase) (Repp, 1992c). Listeners' ability to detect lengthened tones placed in a computer-generated performance (one in which all tone durations, intensities, and tempo are constant) was inversely correlated with the points in time at which performers typically lengthen tones. Thus, structural expectations by performers and listeners can influence production and perception of prosody in systematic ways.

Interpretive (performer-specific) prosody also signals the relative prominence of musical events. Kendall and Carterette (1990) and Palmer (1989a) present evidence that different performers playing the same musical composition apply different prosodic cues to emphasize particular structural intentions. Palmer (1989a) documented correspondences between performers' notated interpretations of phrase boundaries and melody (primary voice) with melodic asynchrony, rubato, and articulation (staccato/legato) in pianists' performances of the same piece. Other studies document aspects of performance that are common between different performances of the same music (Gabrielsson, 1999; Repp, 1992b). In sum, musical prosody marks prominent musical events that are determined both by the composition and the performer.

C. Coordination

An important function of prosody in speech is to regulate turn-taking and interspeaker coordination in discourse, signaled primarily through intonation patterns and pauses (Cutler et al., 1997; Swerts & Geluykens, 1994). Most forms of music performance are collaborative; while they are not strictly turn-based, they require coordination between performers to achieve simultaneities. Sometimes, this is externally regulated by a conductor; however, in many small ensembles, performers must maintain coordination among themselves. Most research on synchronization among performers has focused on segmentation and prominence issues (described in an earlier section) and less on coordination. Performers must keep their onsets within

30–50 ms (Rasch, 1979) of each other for simultaneities to maintain cohesion. A conductor usually accomplishes this purpose in large ensembles by visual cues to the beat; more research is needed to investigate how performers maintain cohesion in ensembles without a conductor. It may be that one member is designated the "conductor" (perhaps the member who tends to lead in asynchronous performance), and other members follow their visual or auditory cues (Rasch, 1979). Synchronization may also be accomplished from memory or from schematic knowledge of stylistic norms.

Some researches address turn-taking among musicians. Perhaps the most important factor for regulating the coordination required for turn-taking is rate or tempo; a performance is considered a failure if performers do not maintain the same tempo. Jungers, Palmer, and Speer (2002) demonstrated that performers show strong tempo persistence from music they heard previously. Musicians and speakers heard sequences produced at different rates, and then produced sequences presented in written form. Musicians mimicked the rate of what they had just heard in their subsequent performances. This finding of rate priming can ensure successfully coordinated performances. Speakers' rates were also primed by the speech rates they had just heard, although to a lesser degree; their speech rate was better predicted by their preferred rate. Speech may show less rate priming because of the less strict demand for tempo coordination in spoken discourse than in music performance, which often requires that musicians perform simultaneously. However, other factors may ensure turn-taking in speech than in music; Jungers et al. (2002) found that speakers' intonational structure mimicked that of the speech they just heard; this parallel was not possible in the music because the primes were produced with equivalent loudness contours, and the notated music constrained the pitch values that were to be produced.

In some musical styles, such as improvisatory jazz, performers alternate creating solos in a stylistic turn-taking that is more like spoken discourse. Like conversation in which speakers elaborate upon their discourse partners' linguistic phrases (Fais, 1994), improvisatory jazz soloists elaborate upon previously heard performers' musical ideas (Johnson-Laird, 1991; Pressing, 1988). Although there is not much research on musical discourse, musical improvisation (in which the content is not predetermined) is an area, which would be an appropriate focus of questions such as: "Which prosodic cues distinguish the end of a musical solo from its middle?" and how much of turn-taking is prearranged or relies on learned musical patterns?

D. EMOTIONAL RESPONSE

Music has been characterized as the language of emotions (Peretz, Gagnon, & Bouchard, 1998), and cognitive approaches to music understanding have focused on the emotions that can be conveyed through music (Meyer, 1956). Until recently, little research focused on music's emotional content, both because of difficulties in defining musical emotion and possible lack of consensus in listeners' emotional response to music (Sloboda, 1992). There are distinctions between musical communication of emotional states and speech communication of emotional states. Whereas listeners often attribute emotional states to speakers based on their prosody (at least in everyday speech), listeners do not normally attribute the emotional state to the performer or assume that the sad music itself is suffering (Davies, 2001). Developments suggest there are some generalities in listeners' response to music that extends to infants and across cultures (Balkwill & Thompson, 1999), although the field of cross-cultural musical response is young. We do not know yet whether universals exist in emotional response to musical styles across cultures.

Study of emotional functions in music has paralleled speech research in separating emotional prosody from linguistic (structural) prosody. The term emotional prosody in speech refers to melodic and rhythmic components that listeners use to gain insight into a speaker's emotive disposition (Scherer, Ladd, & Silverman, 1984). The emotive significance of speech prosody tends to be considered as independent from linguistic-propositional content of prosody (Gandour, Wong, & Hutchins, 1998), in part due to empirical findings that speakers' emotional states were signaled in the fundamental frequency independent of the verbal content (Protopapas & Lieberman, 1997; Scherer et al., 1984). Neurological findings also suggest some dissociation between emotional and linguistic prosody (Heilman, Bowers, Speedie, & Coslett, 1984; Ross, Thompson, & Yenkosky, 1997). However, comparisons indicate that either right- or left-hemisphere damage can produce emotional prosody deficits of similar magnitude (Pell & Baum, 1997). A few studies suggest neurological dissociation between emotional response and structural response to music. Peretz, Belleville, & Fontaine (1997) tested a patient with brain damage whose musical abilities were impaired while her speech and intellectual functions were spared, a case of amusia without aphasia. The patient could classify happy and sad tunes correctly (emotional content), but she could not recognize familiar tunes or discriminate gross changes in pitch contour (Peretz, 2001; Peretz & Gagnon, 1999; Peretz et al., 1998).

Emotional expression in music performance is typically measured in experiments in which performers are instructed to express different emotions for the same piece of music in different performances. The performances are evaluated in listening experiments to see whether listeners recognize the intended expression (usually in a forced choice procedure), and the prosodic parameters of the performances are analyzed with regard to the intended emotion. The assumption is that because the structural contents of the music remain the same, any changes in performances or listeners' reactions must be due to the intended emotional expression. The focus of this research has been on five primary emotions (Ekman, 1973)—happy, sad, angry, fearful, and surprised.

The most successful emotions communicated in the prosodic features of music performance are happy and sad (Gabrielsson & Juslin, 1996; Krumhansl, 1997). Juslin (2001) conducted a meta-analysis of which expressive cues performers used to communicate the five basic emotions across studies. The primary means of expression included tempo, sound level, timing, articulation, vibrato, tone attacks, tone decays, and pauses. Sad emotions were associated with slow tempo, low-sound level, legato articulation, whereas happy expressions were associated with fast tempo, high-sound level, and staccato articulation. Children used the same prosodic cues to express emotions in song—by 4-year olds, they used a fast tempo and high intensity in happy expression, and a low tempo and low intensity in sad expression (Adachi & Trehub, 1998).

Although some studies document listeners' success in choosing the emotion intended in professional performances, they also document individual differences (Gabrielsson & Juslin, 1996; Juslin & Madison, 1999; Kotlyar & Morozov, 1976). Music's emotional connotations are dependent on many factors, including the musical instrument, the particular musical structure, and the particular performance (Gabrielsson & Lindstrom, 2001; Juslin, 2001). Furthermore, different acoustic parameters of music performance interact in emotional judgments. For example, anger judgments, which are influenced by the sharpness of attacks or tone onsets, were expressed well on an electric guitar but not on a flute (Gabrielsson & Juslin, 1996).

There are several models of emotional expression in music, based on Hevner's (1935a,b, 1936, 1937) groundbreaking studies of emotional response to music. This work first documented that music played at a fast tempo tends to be perceived as exciting and happy, whereas music played at a slow tempo is serene and dreamy. Some of these musical features, such as pitch height, are specified by the composition and some, such as tempo, by the performance prosody. Juslin and Laukka (2003) model the expression of emotional states following a functional lens model (Brunswik, 1956) that begins with the encoding of emotional states by certain voice and speech characteristics in the signal. The emotional arousal of the speaker is accompanied by physiological changes that affect respiration, phonation, and articulation in such a way as to produce emotion-specific patterns of acoustic parameters that are understood by listeners (Scherer, 1986; for a detailed description in speech). According to this view, vocal music is physiologically related to vocal expressions of emotion; emotion influences the production of speech and vocal music in the same way (instrumental music is included by association) (Juslin & Laukka, 2003).

Is musical prosody necessary to convey emotion? Peretz et al. (1998) played listeners commercial recordings of music that contained normal expressive features and a computer-generated (prosody-less) version of the same music. Musical pieces that were originally interpreted by the experimenters as happy or sad were classified correctly, even in the absence of prosodic cues. Thus, some information as to emotional content is conveyed through structural features not considered part of performance expression. A second study manipulated the mode (minor or major key signature) and tempo (fast or slow) of the music in versions of the same musical composition. Listeners' emotion judgments were influenced by both tempo (faster tempi evoked happiness judgments) and mode (minor keys evoked sadness judgments). Thus, prosodic features (tempo) conveyed emotion in addition to structural features (mode). Interestingly, listeners were able to discriminate happy/sad musical segments, based primarily on tempo cues, for excerpts as short as 500 ms. This finding is consistent with a view of linguistic prosody as immediate and occurring early in processing (Dogil, 2003), compared with syntactic analysis (such as mode), in which structural cues may occur over larger time-spans (Peretz et al., 1998).

Listener-specific factors, such as musical training or familiarity with the particular music, also influence emotional response (Peretz, Gaudreau, & Bonnel, 1998). Scherer and Zentner (2001) propose that listeners' emotional response to music arises from an interaction of prosodic features (which they label performance features), structural features (such as phrase structure), listener-specific features (such as familiarity), and contextual features (such as location and event of hearing). Thus, this work suggests that prosody may be sufficient, as evidenced in the communication of different emotions for the same musical structure (Juslin, 2001) but not necessary to convey musical emotions.

In sum, musical prosody can serve various functions—segmenting a continuous acoustic stream into its component units, highlighting items of relative importance (prominence), coordination among producers (including turn-taking), and attributing emotional states to performances. Of those, lending prominence may be the single greatest function that prosody serves; without prosody, the ambiguity in musical structure could not easily be resolved. Although there is less research devoted to the role of prosody in coordination or in emotional states, research suggests that prosody is one of several variables that serve those functions.

IV.   Rule-Based Models of Musical Prosody

Is the relationship between musical structure and prosody rule-governed? Can an "appropriate" musical prosody be derived from compositional information without appealing to performer variability or individual interpretation? Several rule-based models have been proposed for mapping music's compositional structure to performed expression (Battel, Bresin, De Poli, & Vidolin, 1994; Clynes, 1995; Sundberg, Askenfelt, & Frydén, 1983; Sundberg & Frydén, 1985; Sundberg, Friberg, & Frydén, 1989; Todd, 1985, 1995), each of which applies to particular types of musical structure. With a few exceptions (Todd, 1992), these systems are composed of rules that take the musical structure notated in a score as input, and generate prosodic manipulations of pitch, duration, and intensity as output. Because performers have flexibility about which prosodic manipulations they use and to what degree, these rules are not meant to be deterministic ones that yield the only correct prosodic structure; instead, they are preference rules that lead to a common or preferred prosodic structure. The distinction between preference rules and well-formed rules was first raised to explain different interpretations of ambiguous musical structure (Lerdahl & Jackendoff, 1983).

Sundberg et al. (1983, 1989; Sundberg & Frydén, 1985) were instrumental in first developing rule-based models with a technique of "analysis-by-synthesis," in which the rules were based on the musical intuitions of a trained performer. The rules can be grouped generally into two classes—those that enhance segmentation by articulating group boundaries or harmonically important events, and those that enhance the prominence of tones by exaggerating pitch or categorical (notated) duration differences. An example of a rule that enhances prominence is to further shorten note durations that are notated as short (such as an eighth-note), and to lengthen note durations that are notated as long (such as a half-note). A rule that marks segmentation is to insert micropauses (of 80 ms) between subphrases and to lengthen note durations at the end of phrases (Sundberg et al., 1983, 1989). These rules can be weighted, and so can be applied moderately or over-expressively. When multiple rules affect the same tone, they are applied additively.

Perceptual tests of the rules were conducted to compare listeners' preferences for the rule-based grammars. Listeners preferred the rule-based performances to the computer-generated performances in which the rules were not applied, and musically trained listeners showed greater sensitivity to the application of the rules than nonmusicians (Sundberg, Friberg, & Frydén, 1991). Breslin, De Poli, and Vidolin (1992) showed that artificial neural networks could learn some of the performance rules specified in Sundberg's

(1983, 1989) grammar. These networks produced performances comparable to those produced by the rule-based systems (Sundberg et al., 1983, 1989), and listeners preferred the network-performances over computer-generated performances that contained no prosodic cues.

Rule-based models of composer-appropriate musical expression have also been proposed as well. Clynes (1983) advocated the incorporation of individual composers' pulses into the musical microstructure—composer-specific differences in the duration and the amplitude of each group of tones within a musical pulse. These pulse manipulations, derived from the author's intuitions and musical experiences, were argued to yield more acceptable interpretations for that composer's music than interpretations with no such manipulations, random manipulations, or the pulses of other composers. Clynes (1995) showed evidence that these pulses were preferred by musically trained listeners, though there is some conflicting evidence from perceptual tests (Repp, 1990), and the composer-specific pulses do not seem to be supported by judgments from untrained listeners, as do Sundberg et al.'s (1983, 1989) rules.

Rule-based models of phrase-final lengthening in music performance have been proposed as well. Based on Lerdahl and Jackendoff's (1983) theory of grouping and meter in Western tonal music, Sundberg and Verillo (1980) proposed a simple model of the final ritard—the deceleration of performance tempo seen at the end of a musical performance. They proposed a linear decrease in tempo to the end of the piece. Todd (1985) predicted the amount of slowing at phrase boundaries from a structural analysis of the musical composition. This model assigned greater lengthening to tones at major structural breaks (higher hierarchical levels in Lerdahl and Jackendoff's (1983) analysis). This approach is similar to Grosjean, Grosjean, and Lane's (1979) model of interword pauses in spoken sentences; Grosjean et al. (1979) found that a large degree of variation in speech pauses was predictable from the hierarchical representation of the utterance's syntactic phrase structure.

Other models have tried to model musical prosody with kinematic laws of physical motion. Feldman, Epstein, and Richards (1992) modeled the timing characteristics of ensemble performances in terms of a cubic polynomial model that smoothly connected sections of constant tempi with those of changing tempi, minimizing abrupt changes in acceleration, a desirable property in physical acceleration. Todd (1992, 1995) proposed a general-purpose algorithm for the timing of phrase-final lengthening, based on kinematic principles of physical motion. This model proposed a linear deceleration in tempo across tones, and treated musical space as continuous (rather than as discrete tone onsets). Based on findings that tempo changes are often coupled with changes in loudness (Gabrielsson, 1987; Palmer, 1996a), so that tempo and intensity increase together, Todd (1992) proposed a model that linked the two, so that intensity is proportional to the square of the number of musical events per unit time, and proposed that musical expression creates the perception of motion in listeners. Although kinematic models of music performance are not universally accepted (Desain & Honing, 1992), they formalize the relationship between music performance and principles of motion.

In sum, rule-governed models focus primarily on notated compositional scores as input and yield prosodic manipulations as output. They reflect general prosodic features related to structural features of the music that can aid listeners in terms of segmentation and prominence. However, it is not clear how well these models generalize; although they are not instrument- or timbre-specific, these potential factors have not been thoroughly investigated. Also, the models do not account for interpretive (performer-specific) variation. Kendall and Carterette (1990) and Palmer (1989a) argued against a rule-governed performance grammar generated solely from compositional structure, based on evidence that performers apply different prosodic cues systematically to the same composition that support different structural intentions. Individual interpretation appears to play a role, as well as compositional structure, and some of these sources of variance can be accounted for by rules that are conceived as preferences, rather than as deterministic outcomes (Lerdahl & Jackendoff, 1983). A deterministic application of these structure-based rules—without any interpretive or individualistic variation—would lead to only one of many appropriate realizations of musical prosody. Empirical measurements of individual performances are necessary to distinguish between structure-based prosodic cues that transcend performers and prosodic features that are specific to performers. A combination of rule-based and measurement-based approaches may be necessary to explicate both the form and function of musical prosody.

V. Acquisition of Musical Prosody

Musical prosody is always present in human performance and appears to have many functions for listeners. What role does prosody play in learning? Prosody may aid perceptual learning of primitive units. Prosodic features in speech can provide low-level cues to aid segmentation and learning of hierarchical relationships (Gleitman & Wanner, 1982; Hirsh-Pasek et al., 1987; Jusczyk & Kemler Nelson, 1996), including delineating word boundaries (Christophe, Doupoux, Bertoncini, & Mehler, 1994; Gout, Christophe, & Morgan, 2004) and marking syntactic relationships (Fisher & Tokura, 1996). Listeners' abilities to identify smaller musical units may likewise bootstrap their ability to perceive higher-order relationship among those units.

Prosodic cues may be especially important in a domain like music that contains structural and emotional ambiguity. In a seminal theory, Meyer (1956) proposed that listeners' expectations, based on the hierarchical structure of the music, are critical to their emotional response. Music creates expectations, which cause listeners to experience tension when unresolved and release upon their resolution; these expectations are based on how the music will continue, as opposed to extramusical ideas. The better the listener can grasp the hierarchical structure of a piece, the more precise the listener's expectations and the more emotion is conveyed. Prosodic cues may help a listener grasp the emotional content of the piece by clarifying the musical structure.

Infants' responses to speech and music offer explanations of why prosody is important. Infant-directed utterances across many cultures contain musical features that are often described as "melodies" (Fernald, 1989; Papoušek, Bornstein, Nuzzo, Papoušek, & Symmes, 1990). According to Fernald (1992), infants are predisposed to selectively attend to the distinctive pitch contours of infant-directed speech, whose primitive emotional meanings can be decoded in the absence of language. Cross-cultural similarities in emotional response to adult speech support this argument (Frick, 1985; Krauss, Curran, & Ferleger, 1983). Intention and affect can be communicated in intonation; caretakers use salient intonational patterns that draw preverbal infants' attention (Fernald, 1985, 1993). Parents use melodic contours in consistent ways to engage babies—infant-directed speech is typically higher in pitch with more exaggerated intonation contours than adult-directed speech (Fernald et al., 1989). Different melodic contours (level, rise, fall, bell-shaped, U-shaped, etc.) can consistently map to different behaviors that parents attempt to elicit, including discouraging unfavorable behavior, encouraging imitation, encouraging play, and contingent rewarding (Papoušek, Papoušek, & Symmes, 1991). Furthermore, adults can successfully discriminate emotional states in both infant-directed and adult-directed speech, but the acoustic correlates of emotional expression are more widely found in infant-directed speech (Trainor, Austin, & Desjardins, 2000). This work suggests that intonation and prosody may aid parent–infant bonding and emotional communication (Trainor et al., 2000), although attempts to relate particular melodic contours to particular emotions have generally failed (Scherer, 1985).

Adults use prosodic features in music as well, to draw the attention of the infant. Caregivers' songs to infants tend to have higher pitch, slower tempo, and more jitter in fundamental frequency and intensity than songs directed at adults (Trainor, Clark, Huntley, & Adams, 1997; Trehub & Trainor, 1998; Trehub et al., 1997), which have been associated with increased emotional expression. These prosodic features appear in songs sung by young children to their infant siblings (Trehub, Unyk, & Henderson, 1994). Parents can adapt their song to the mood and abilities of their listeners. The same song may be sung in a playful way or a soothing way (Trainor & Rock, 1997; Trehub et al., 1997). Mothers can alter their performances of the same song for infants (at a higher pitch level) or for preschool children (in enunciated lyrics).

Prosodic cues in music or speech can draw infants' attention to statistical regularities in the transitional probabilities among sequence items. In a statistical learning paradigm, infants were familiarized with recurring sequences of syllables in brief exposure to an artificial language (Saffran, Aslin, & Newport, 1996). After familiarization, the infants were able to discriminate novel syllable combinations from familiar ones, indicating that they were sensitive to the transitional probabilities between phonemes in strings of speech sounds. Infant-directed speech that contained more prosodic differentiation in pitch height, pitch range, and pitch peaks elicited better statistical learning among infants than did adult-directed speech (Thiessen, Hill, & Saffran, 2005). In a similar experiment, Thiessen, Hill, Emerson, and Saffran (2005) showed that infants learned number sequences that were sung with a unique rhythmic/intonational contour more easily than spoken number sequences. These findings suggest that prosody can benefit statistical learning in music and speech, although several studies demonstrate that statistical learning occurs in the absence of additional prosodic cues (Saffran, Johnson, Aslin, & Newport, 1999; Saffran et al., 1996).

How musical prosody bootstraps learning is likely to be related to the alternatives to be learned. For example, different musical styles and genres permit different degrees of variation in how compositions can be manipulated by performers to make some elements more prominent. In addition, musical instruments differ in how many prosodic features they allow performers to alter; for example, violin permits vibrato but piano does not; most instruments permit change in pitch but drums do not. The musical environment of the infant will shape the space of possible learning alternatives. Because infants' musical environments contain infant-directed music, mostly from their parents' voices, it would not be surprising if the prosodic features of the singing voice are learned first and are then generalized to other nonvocal forms of music, as suggested earlier (Juslin & Laukka, 2003). In this view, it would not be surprising if musical prosody and speech prosody were related. Evolutionary theories of music's origins suggest that musical behavior evolved in conjunction with—or as an adaptation of—vocal communication (Brown, 2000; Dissanayake, 2000). An area for future research is whether prosodic marking of infant-directed song varies across musical styles and across languages. Also of interest is whether musical prosody can aid infants' learning of musical statistical regularities, as in language learning.

VI. How are Musical and Linguistic Prosody Related?

Researchers have sought more direct links between musical and speech prosody. Patel and Daniele (2003) found differences in the amount of durational variation used by French- and English-speaking composers. English, a stress-timed language that alternates in strong and weak stresses, typically shows larger variation in the production of interconsonantal intervals (Ramus, Nespor, & Mehler, 1999) and vowel duration (Grabe & Low, 2002) than French, a syllable-timed language. The amount of rhythmic variation in a corpus of 19th century music compositions, measured by note-to-note changes in notated durations, was smaller in a collection of French musical themes than in the English themes (later confirmed by Huron & Ollen, 2003, in a larger corpus). The rhythmic variability of the music was attributed to the influence of the composers' knowledge of their language on the compositions, even though the instrumental music contained no words. Although these finding are based on analysis of notated musical compositions (which contain no prosodic performance variation), the suggestion of different sensitivity to musical variation related to linguistic knowledge is intriguing.

Some neurological evidence suggests a direct connection between musical and linguistic prosody. Stroke victims who have impairments in musical discrimination and perception often have related impairments in perception of linguistic prosody (Nicholson et al., 2003; Patel, Peretz, Tramo, & Labreque, 1998). Patel et al. (1998) documented two stroke-related cases of amusia—one patient (CN) showing deficits in musical memory, the other (IR) showing perceptual deficits. Perceptual discrimination tasks were created based on sentence pairs, which differed only in linguistic prosody, and musical analogs of the prosodic stimuli were created (only fundamental frequency and duration information were retained from the linguistic stimuli). IR had difficulty on both the linguistic and musical prosody tasks, whereas CN (whose deficits involved long-term memory) performed similarly to control subjects, suggesting shared neural mechanisms between the two domains. Congenitally amusic individuals (with similar music perception deficits but no history of brain damage) did not show deficits in linguistic prosody (Ayotte, Peretz, & Hyde, 2002). The congenitally amusic individuals may have developed different neural mechanisms than the stroke-damage patients to process linguistic prosody.

Music training is associated with increased sensitivity to pitch processing in language tasks. Musicians detect fundamental frequency changes better than nonmusicians; they also show similar ERP responses to small frequency manipulations in music and speech, whereas nonmusicians show similar neural responses in music and speech only for large frequency changes (Schön, Magne, & Besson, 2004). Thompson, Schellenberg, and Husain

(2004) tested whether musical training influenced listeners' ability to detect the emotional connotations in speech. Musically trained and untrained listeners heard semantically neutral utterances spoken with a particular emotional prosody, or musical tone sequences that mimicked the utterances prosody, created in the same way as Patel et al.'s (1998) musical analogs to spoken sentences. Musically trained adults outperformed untrained adults at identifying sadness, fear, and emotionally neutral terms. The influence of music lessons on identifying emotions in speech prosody was extended to children as well; a training study with 6-year olds randomly assigned to 1 year of keyboard, vocal, drama, or no lessons indicated that the keyboard group performed equivalently to the drama group and better than the no-lessons group at identifying anger or fear (Thompson et al., 2004). These studies suggest that musical training facilitates the ability to decode emotional meaning in speech prosody (although motivational differences among groups may play a role as well).

Direct comparisons of musical prosody and speech prosody, both in terms of their functions and their neurological substrates, are beginning to yield areas of overlap. Musical and speech prosody manipulate the same acoustic variables, yield emotional expression, and serve some of the same segmentation and prominence functions. It seems likely that future studies will yield additional similarities in the functions of coordination and how infants acquire prosodic knowledge. Whether these similarities can distinguish a single evolutionary basis or homologous structures for musical and speech prosody is not obvious; perhaps this distinction is not as important as understanding whether the functions served by prosody within each domain imply abilities that transcend domains.

VII.   Conclusions and Caveats

Musical prosody is a complex, rule-governed form of auditory stimulation, and it can move listeners emotionally in systematic ways. The acoustic cues in which musical prosody is instantiated are shared across performers, and performers share with listeners ideas of what constitutes appropriate prosody. Although musical prosody contains individual components of interpretation and prominence, it also reflects constraints based on shared cognitive principles of perceptual organization, emotional response, and even motor production. Thus, it is partially influenced by the structural ambiguity of music that individual interpretation addresses, but it is also determined by cognitive structures that arise from human perceptual and motor biases. Sensitivity to prosodic cues aids listeners in identifying commonalities and differences in sources of musical sound. In sum, this evidence suggests that musical "prosody" captures general principles of musical expression above and beyond individualistic features of musical interpretation.

One important caveat is that not all prosodic variability in music performance is intentional or expressive in nature. Movement demands on performers contribute to the acoustic characteristics of performance; for example, temporal variance in performed event durations has been modeled in terms of an internal timekeeper and motor response delays (Wing & Kristofferson, 1973). Shaffer (1981) applied similar modeling in analyses of timing in piano performance, concluding that the timing variability arose in part from timekeepers that controlled the timing of individual hands. Expressive timing, internal timekeeper variance, and motor response delays are all part of the same measurement of interonset durations, similar to how phrase-final lengthening and the time it takes to produce certain phonetic features are expressed in speech.

Musical prosody appears to be sufficient for signaling segmentation, prominence, and emotional states; there is less known about the role of prosody in how musicians coordinate their performances. Musical prosody may be *necessary* only for signaling prominence, and, it seems, in promoting emotional communication during development. The inherent ambiguity in musical structure may *require* performers to make use of acoustic variability to encode which musical features are more important than others. Prosodic cues, such as tempo, intensity, timbre, and pitch changes, are redundant in music performance; multiple cues reinforce the same segmentation, prominence, etc. Whether musical prosody has a grammar of its own is less obvious. Some rules express well the relation between prominence and acoustic realization, whereas other aspects of performance expression are not well-expressed in rules. Nevertheless, the high degree of consistency in how performers use prosodic features suggests that study of musical prosody, separate from study of musical structure, will inform us about auditory cognition in general.

Two lines of developing research address further the significance of musical prosody: the first is from experiments that manipulate the acoustic parameters of musical prosody, especially in comparison with parameters of linguistic prosody through a continuum from music to speech. The second is neurological evidence from brain-damaged, as well as normal individuals who acquire musical training either early or later in life, mapping the functions of musical prosody to their structural mechanisms. These experimental and neurological techniques allow us to address interesting questions, such as: Is prosody the underpinning of language and music development? Are musical genres, like languages, points on a prosodic continuum that is bounded by general perceptual principles of rhythm, grouping, and prominence? Do individual differences in music or language abilities arise from differences in sensitivity to prosody? A fully-fledged theory of musical prosody, we hope, can address these questions.

ACKNOWLEDGMENTS

Caroline Palmer and Sean Hutchins, Department of Psychology, McGill University, 1205 Dr Penfield Ave, Montreal QC H3A 1B1, Canada. This paper was supported by NSERC 298173 to Caroline Palmer and by the Canada Research Chairs program, and a McGill University Tomlinson Fellowship to Sean Hutchins. The authors thank Shari Baum, Julie Boland, Melissa Jungers, Isabelle Peretz, Peter Pfordresher, Brian Ross, and Jenny Saffran for comments on an earlier draft.

REFERENCES

Adachi, M., & Trehub, S. E. (1998). Children's expression of emotion in song. *Psychology of Music, 26*, 133–153.

American Heritage Dictionary of the English Language® (2004). *Meter* (4th ed.). Houghton Mifflin Company. http://www.bartleby.com/61/17/M0251700.html

Apel, W. (1972). *Harvard dictionary of music*. Cambridge, MA: Harvard University Press.

Ayotte, J., Peretz, I., & Hyde, K. (2002). Congenital amusia: A group study of adults afflicted with a music-specific disorder. *Brain, 238–251.*

Balkwill, L.-L., & Thompson, W. F. (1999). A cross-cultural investigation of the perception of emotion in music: Psychophysical and cultural cues. *Music Perception, 17*, 43–64.

Battel, G. U., Bresin, R., De Poli, G., & Vidolin, A. (1994). Neural networks vs. rules system: Evaluation test of automatic performance of musical scores. In *Proceedings of the 1994 International Computer Music Conference* (pp. 109–113). San Franciso: ICMA.

Beckman, M. E. (1996). The parsing of prosody. *Language and Cognitive Processes, 11*, 17–67.

Bharucha, J. J. (1987). Music cognition and perceptual facilitation: A connectionist framework. *Music Perception, 5*, 1–30.

Bregman, A. S. (1990). *Auditory scene analysis: The perceptual organization of sound.* Cambridge, MA: Bradford Books, MIT Press.

Breslin, R., De Poli, G., & Vidolin, A. (1992). Symbolic and sub-symbolic rules system for real time score performance. In *Proceedings of the 1992 International Computer Music Conference* (pp. 325–327). San Francisco: ICMA.

Brown, S. (2000). The "musilanguage" model of music evolution. In N. L. Wallin, B. Merker, and S. Brown (Eds.), *The origins of music* (pp. 271–300). Cambridge, MA: MIT Press.

Brunswik, E. (1956). *Perception and the representative design of psychological experiments.* Berkeley, CA: University of California Press.

Christophe, A., Dupoux, E., Bertoncini, J., & Mehler, J. (1994). Do infants perceive word boundaries? An empirical study of the bootstrapping of lexical acquisition. *Journal of the Acoustical Society of America, 95*, 1570–1580.

Clarke, E. F. (1993). Imitating and evaluating real and transformed musical performances. *Music Perception, 10*, 317–341.

Clarke, E. F., & Baker-Short, C. (1987). The imitation of perceived rubato: A preliminary study. *Psychology of Music, 15*, 58–75.

Clynes, M. (1983). Expressive microstructure in music, linked to living qualities. In J. Sundberg (Ed.), *Studies of music performance* (Vol. 39, pp. 76–181). Stockholm: Royal Swedish Academy of Music.

Clynes, M. (1995). Microstructural musical linguistics: Composers' pulses are liked most by the best musicians. *Cognition, 55*, 269–310.

Cogan, R. D., & Escot, P. (1976). *Sonic design: The nature of sound and music.* Englewood Cliffs, NJ: Prentice-Hall.

Collier, R., & Hart, J. (1975). The role of intonation in speech perception. In A. Cohen and S. G. Nooteboom (Eds.), *Structure and process in speech perception* (pp. 107–121). Heidelberg: Springer-Verlag.

Cooper, W. E., & Eady, S. J. (1986). Metrical phonology in speech production. *Journal of Memory and Language, 25*, 369–384.

Cooper, G., & Meyer, L. B. (1960). *The rhythmic structure of music.* Chicago: University of Chicago Press.

Cutler, A. (1995). Spoken word recognition and production. In J. Miller and P. Eimas (Eds.), *Speech, language, and communication* (pp. 97–136). New York: Academic Press.

Cutler, A. (1999). Prosody and intonation, processing issues. In R. A. Wilson and F. C. Keil (Eds.), *The MIT encyclopedia of the cognitive sciences* (pp. 682–683). Cambridge: MIT Press.

Cutler, A., Dahan, D., & van Donselaar, W. (1997). Prosody in the comprehension of spoken language: A literature review. *Language and Speech, 40*, 141–201.

Cyr, M. (1992). *Performing baroque music..* Aldershot: Scholar Press.

Davies, S. (2001). Philosophical perspectives on music's expressiveness. In P. Juslin and J. A. Sloboda (Eds.), *Music and emotion: Theory and research* (pp. 23–44). Oxford, England: Oxford University Press.

Desain, P., & Honing, H. (1992). *Music, mind, and machine: Studies in computer music, music cognition, and artificial intelligence.* Amsterdam: Thesis.

De Jong, K. (1995). The supraglottal articulation of prominence in English: Linguistic stress as localized hyperarticulation. *Journal of the Acoustical Society of America, 91*, 491–504.

Deutsch, D., & Feroe, F. (1981). Internal representation of pitch sequence in tonal music. *Psychological Review, 88*, 503–522.

Dissanayake, E. (2000). Antecedents of the temporal arts in early mother-infant interaction. In N. L. Wallin, B. Merker, and S. Brown (Eds.), *The origins of music* (pp. 389–410). Cambridge, MA: MIT Press.

Dogil, G. (2003). Understanding prosody. In G. Rickheit, J. Herrmann, and W. Deutsch (Eds.), *Psycholinguistics: An international handbook* (pp. 544–566). Berlin: Mouton de Gruyter.

Drake, C., & Palmer, C. (1993). Accent structures in music performance. *Music Perception, 10*, 343–378.

Drake, C., Penel, A., & Bigand, E. (2000). Tapping in time with mechanically and expressively performed music. *Music Perception, 18*, 1–23.

Ekman, P. (1973). Darwin and cross-cultural studies of facial expression. In P. Ekman (Ed.), *Darwin and facial expression* (pp. 1–83). New York: Academic Press.

Fais, L. (1994). Conversation as collaboration: Some syntactic evidence. *Speech Communication, 15*, 231–242.

Feldman, J., Epstein, D., & Richards, W. (1992). Force dynamics of tempo change in music. *Music Perception, 10*, 185–204.

Fernald, A. (1985). Four-month-old infants prefer to listen to motherese. *Infant Behavior and Development, 8*, 181–195.

Fernald, A. (1989). Intonation and communicative intent in mothers' speech to infants: Is the melody the message? *Child Development, 60*, 1497–1510.

Fernald, A. (1992). Human maternal vocalizations to infants as biologically relevant signals: An evolutionary perspective. In J. H. Barkow, L. Cosmides, and J. Tooby (Eds.), *The adapted mind: Evolutionary psychology and the generation of culture* (pp. 391–428). Oxford: Oxford University Press.

Fernald, A. (1993). Approval and disapproval: Infant responsiveness to vocal affect in familiar and unfamiliar languages. *Child Development, 64*, 657–674.

Fernald, A., Taeschner, T., Dunn, J., Papoušek, M., de Boysson-Bardies, B., & Fukui, I. (1989). A cross-language study of prosodic modifications in mothers' and fathers' speech to preverbal infants. *Journal of Child Language, 16*, 477–501.

Ferreira, F. (2002). Prosody. In L. Nadel (Ed.), *Encyclopedia of cognitive science* (pp. 258–265). New York: Nature Publishing.

Fisher, C., & Tokura, H. (1996). Acoustic cues to grammatical structure in infant-directed speech: Cross-linguistic evidence. *Child Development, 67*, 3192–3218.

Frick, R. W. (1985). Communicating emotion: The role of prosodic features. *Psychological Bulletin, 97*, 412–429.

Gabrielsson, A. (1974). Performance of rhythm patterns. *Scandanavian Journal of Psychology, 15*, 63–72.

Gabrielsson, A. (1987). Once again: The theme from Mozart's piano Sonata in A Major (k.331). In A. Gabrielsson (Ed.), *Action and perception in rhythm and music* (pp. 81–104). Stockholm: Royal Swedish Academy of Music.

Gabrielsson, A. (1999). The performance of music. In D. Deutsch (Ed.), *The psychology of music* (2nd ed., pp. 501–602). San Diego, CA: Academic Press.

Gabrielsson, A., & Juslin, P. N. (1996). Emotional expression in music performance: Between the performer's intention and the listener's experience. *Psychology of Music, 24*, 68–91.

Gabrielsson, A., & Lindstrom, E. (2001). The influence of musical structure on emotional expression. In P. Juslin and J. A. Sloboda (Eds.), *Music and emotion: Theory and research* (pp. 223–248). Oxford: Oxford University Press.

Gandour, J., Wong, D., & Hutchins, G. (1998). Pitch processing in the human brain is influenced by language experience. *Neuroreport, 9*, 2115–2119.

Gleitman, L. R., & Wanner, E. (1982). Language acquisition: The state of the state of the art. In E. Wanner and L. R. Gleitman (Eds.), *Language acquisition: The state of the art* (pp. 3–48). New York: Cambridge University Press.

Goebl, W. (2001). Melody lead in piano performance: Expressive device or artifact? *The Journal of the Acoustical Society of America, 110*, 563–572.

Gout, A., Christophe, A., & Morgan, J. (2004). Phonological phrase boundaries constrain lexical access: II. Infant data. *Journal of Memory and Language, 51*, 547–567.

Grabe, E., & Low, E. L. (2002). Durational variability in speech and the rhythm class hypothesis. In C. Gussenhoven and N. Warner (Eds.), *Laboratory phonology* (Vol. 7, pp. 515–546). Berlin: Mouton de Gruyter.

Grosjean, F. H., Grosjean, L., & Lane, H. (1979). The patterns of silence: Performance structures in sentence production. *Cognitive Psychology, 11*, 58–81.

Heilman, K. M., Bowers, D., Speedie, L., & Coslett, H. B. (1984). Comprehension of affective and nonaffective prosody. *Neurology, 34*, 917–921.

Henderson, M. T. (1936). Rhythmic organization in artistic piano performance. In C. E. Seashore (Ed.), *Objective analysis of musical performance* (Vol. 4, pp. 281–305). Iowa City: University of Iowa Press.

Hevner, K. (1935a). The affective character of the major and minor modes in music. *American Journal of Psychology, 47*, 103–118.

Hevner, K. (1935b). Expression in music: A discussion of experimental studies and theories. *Psychological Review, 47*, 186–204.

Hevner, K. (1936). Experimental studies of the elements of expression in music. *American Journal of Psychology, 48*, 248–268.

Hevner, K. (1937). The affective value of pitch and tempo in music. *American Journal of Psychology, 49*, 621–630.

Hirsh-Pasek, K., Kemler Nelson, D. G., Jusczyk, P. W., Wright-Cassidy, K., Druss, B., & Kennedy, L. (1987). Clauses are perceptual units for young infants. *Cognition, 26*, 269–286.

Huron, D., & Ollen, J. (2003). Agogic contrast in French and English themes: Further support for Patel and Daniele (2003). *Music Perception, 21*, 267–272.

Johnson-Laird, P. N. (1991). Jazz improvisation: A theory at the computational level. In P. Howell, R. West, and I. Cross (Eds.), *Representing musical structure*. San Diego, CA: Academic Press.

Jungers, M. K., Palmer, C., & Speer, S. R. (2002). Time after time: The coordinating influence of tempo in music and speech. *Cognitive Processing, 1*, 21–35.

Jusczyk, P. W., & Kemler Nelson, D. G. (1996). Syntactic units, prosody, and psychological reality during infancy. In J. L. Morgan and K. Demuth (Eds.), *Signal to syntax* (pp. 389–408). Mahwah, NJ: Erlbaum.

Jusczyk, P. W., & Krumhansl, C. L. (1993). Pitch and rhythmic patterns affecting infants' sensitivity to musical phrase structure. *Journal of Experimental Psychology: Human Perception and Performance, 19*, 1–14.

Jusczyk, P. W., Hirsh-Pasek, K., Kemler Nelson, D. G., Kennedy, L., Woodward, A., & Piwoz, J. (1992). Perception of acoustic correlates of major phrasal units by young infants. *Cognitive Psychology, 24*, 252–293.

Juslin, P. N. (2001). Communicating emotion in music performance: A review and theoretical framework. In P. Juslin and J. A. Sloboda (Eds.), *Music and emotion: Theory and research* (pp. 2309–2337). Oxford: Oxford University Press.

Juslin, P. N., & Laukka, P. (2003). Communication of emotions in vocal expression and music performance: Different channels, same code? *Psychological Bulletin, 129*, 770–814.

Juslin, P. N., & Madison, G. (1999). The role of timing patterns in recognition of emotional expression from musical performance. *Music Perception, 17*, 197–221.

Juslin, P. N., & Sloboda, J. A. (2001). *Music and emotion: Theory and research.* New York: Oxford University Press.

Kelly, M. H., & Bock, J. K. (1988). Stress in time. *Journal of Experimental Psychology: Human Perception & Performance, 14*, 389–403.

Kendall, R. A., & Carterette, E. C. (1990). The communication of musical expression. *Music Perception, 8*, 129–164.

Kotlyar, G. M., & Morozov, V. P. (1976). Acoustic correlates of the emotional content of vocalized speech. *Soviet Physics Acoustics, 22*, 370–376.

Krauss, R. M., Curran, N. M., & Ferleger, N. (1983). Expressive conventions and the cross-cultural expression of emotion. *Basic and Applied Social Psychology, 4*, 295–305.

Kreiman, J. (1982). Perception of sentence and paragraph boundaries in natural conversation. *Journal of Phonetics, 10*, 163–175.

Krumhansl, C. L. (1990). *Cognitive foundations of musical pitch.* New York: Oxford University Press.

Krumhansl, C. L. (1997). An exploratory study of musical emotions and psychophysiology. *Canadian Journal of Experimental Psychology, 51*, 336–353.

Krumhansl, C. L., & Jusczyk, P. W. (1990). Infants' perception of phrase structure in music. *Psychological Science, 1*, 70–73.

La Driere, J. C. (Driere 1993). Prosody. In A. Preminger (Ed.), *Encyclopedia of poetry and poetics*. Princeton: Princeton University Press.

Lehiste, I. (1972). Timing of utterances and linguistic boundaries. *Journal of the Acoustical Society of America, 51*, 2018–2024.

Lerdahl, F., & Jackendoff, R. (1983). *A generative theory of tonal music*. Cambridge, MA: MIT Press.

Levelt, W. P. M. (1989). *Speaking: From intention to articulation*. Cambridge, MA: MIT Press.

Levitin, D. J. (1994). Absolute memory for musical pitch: Evidence from the production of learned melodies. *Perception & Psychophysics, 56*, 414–423.

Levitin, D. J., & Cook, P. R. (1996). Memory for musical tempo: Additional evidence that auditory memory is absolute. *Perception & Psychophysics, 58*, 927–935.

Liberman, M., & Prince, A. (1977). On stress and linguistic rhythm. *Linguistic Inquiry, 8*, 249–336.

Meyer, L. B. (1956). *Emotion and meaning in music*. Chicago: Chicago University Press.

Neumann, F. (1982). *Essays in performance practice*. Ann Arbor: UMI Research Press.

Nicholson, K. G., Baum, S., Kilgour, A., Koh, C. K., Munhall, K. G., & Cuddy, L. L. (2003). Impaired processing of prosodic and musical patters after right hemisphere damage. *Brain and Cognition, 52*, 382–389.

Palmer, C. (1989a). Mapping musical thought to musical performance. *Journal of Experimental Psychology: Human Perception & Performance, 15*, 331–346.

Palmer, C. (1989b). Structural representations of music performance. In *Proceedings of the 11th Annual Conference of the Cognitive Science Society* (pp. 349–356). Hillsdale: Erlbaum.

Palmer, C. (1996a). Anatomy of a performance: Sources of musical expression. *Music Perception, 13*, 433–454.

Palmer, C. (1996b). On the assignment of structure in music performance. *Music Perception, 14*, 21–54.

Palmer, C., Jungers, M., & Jusczyk, P. W. (2001). Episodic memory for musical prosody. *Journal of Memory and Language, 45*, 526–545.

Palmer, C., & Krumhansl, C. L. (1987). Pitch and temporal contributions to musical phrase perception: Effects of harmony, performance timing, and familiarity. *Perception & Psychophysics, 41*, 505–518.

Palmer, C., & van de Sande, C. (1995). Range of planning in music performance. *Journal of Experimental Psychology: Human Perception & Performance, 21*, 947–962.

Papoušek, M., Bornstein, M. H., Nuzzo, C., Papoušek, H., & Symmes, D. (1990). Infant responses to prototypical melodic contours in parental speech. *Infant Behavior and Development, 13*, 539–545.

Papoušek, M., Papoušek, H., & Symmes, D. (1991). The meanings of melodies in motherese in tone and stress language. *Infant Behavior and Development, 14*, 415–440.

Patel, A. D., & Daniele, J. R. (2003). An empirical comparison of rhythm in language and music. *Cognition, 87*, B35–B45.

Patel, A. D., Peretz, I., Tramo, M., & Labreque, R. (1998). Processing prosodic and musical patterns: A neuropsychological investigation. *Brain and Language, 61*, 123–144.

Pell, M. D. (2001). Influence of emotion and focus location on prosody in matched statements and questions. *Journal of the Acoustical Society of America, 109*, 1668–1680.

Pell, M. D., & Baum, S. R. (1997). Unilateral brain damage, prosodic comprehension deficits, and the acoustic cues to prosody. *Brain & Language, 57*, 195–214.

Peretz, I. (2001). Listen to the brain: A biological perspective on musical emotions. In P. Juslin and J. A. Sloboda (Eds.), *Music and emotion: Theory and research* (pp. 105–134). Oxford, England: Oxford University Press.

Peretz, I., & Gagnon, L. (1999). Dissociation between recognition and emotional judgment for melodies. *Neurocase, 5*, 21–30.

Peretz, I., Gagnon, L., & Bouchard, B. (1998). Music and emotion: Perceptual determinants, immediacy, and isolation after brain damage. *Cognition, 68*, 111–141.

Peretz, I., Gaudreau, D., & Bonnel, A.-M. (1998). Exposure effects on music preference and recognition. *Memory and Cognition, 26*, 884–902.

Peretz, I., Belleville, S., & Fontaine, S. (1997). Dissociations entre musique et langage après atteinte cérébrale: Un nouveau cas d'amusie sans aphasie. *Canadian Journal of Experimental Psychology, 51*, 354–368.

Pierrehumbert, J. (1999). Prosody and intonation. In R. A. Wilson and F. C. Keil (Eds.), *MIT encyclopedia of the cognitive sciences* (pp. 679–682). Cambridge, MA: MIT Press.

Pike, K. (1945). *The Intonation of American English*. Ann Arbor, MI: University of Michigan Press.

Pisoni, D. B. (1997). Some thoughts on "normalization" in speech perception. In K. Johnson and J. W. Mullennix (Eds.), *Talker variability in speech processing* (pp. 9–32). San Diego: Academic Press.

Pressing, J. (1988). Improvisation: Methods and models. In J. Sloboda (Ed.), *Generative processes in music: The psychology of performance, improvisation, and composition*. New York: Oxford University Press.

Protopapas, A., & Lieberman, P. (1997). Fundamental frequency of phonation and perceived emotional stress. *Journal of the Acoustical Society of America, 101*, 2267–2277.

Raffman, D. (1993). *Language, music, and mind*. Cambridge, MA: MIT Press.

Ramus, F., Nespor, M., & Mehler, J. (1999). Correlates of linguistic rhythm in the speech signal. *Cognition, 73*, 265–292.

Rasch, R. A. (1978). The perception of simultaneous notes as such in polyphonic music. *Acustica, 40*, 21–33.

Rasch, R. A. (1979). Synchronization in performed ensemble music. *Acustica, 43*, 121–131.

Rasch, R. A. (1988). Timing and synchronization in ensemble performance. In J. A. Sloboda (Ed.), *Generative processes in music: The psychology of performance, improvisation, and composition* (pp. 70–90). Oxford: Clarendon Press.

Repp, B. H. (1990). Patterns of expressive timing in performances of a Beethoven minuet by nineteen famous pianists. *Journal of the Acoustical Society of America, 88*, 622–641.

Repp, B. H. (1992a). A constraint on the expressive timing of a melodic gesture: Evidence from performance and aesthetic judgment. *Music Perception, 10*, 221–241.

Repp, B. H. (1992b). Diversity and commonality in music performance. An analysis of timing microstructure in Schumann's "Träumerei." *Journal of the Acoustical Society of America 92*, 2546–2568.

Repp, B. H. (1992c). Probing the cognitive representation of musical time: Structural constraints on the perception of timing perturbations. *Cognition, 44*, 241–281.

Repp, B. H. (2000). Pattern typicality and dimensional interactions in pianists' imitation of expressive timing and dynamics. *Music Perception, 18*, 173–211.

Ross, E. D., Thompson, R. D., & Yenkosky, J. (1997). Lateralization of affective prosody in brain and the callosal integration of hemispheric language functions. *Brain and Language, 56*, 27–54.

Saffran, J. R., Aslin, R. N., & Newport, E. L. (1996). Statistical learning by 8-month-old infants. *Science, 274*, 1926–1928.

Saffran, J. R., Johnson, E. K., Aslin, R. N., & Newport, E. L. (1999). Statistical learning of tone sequences by human infants and adults. *Cognition, 70*, 27–52.

Schellenberg, E. G., & Trehub, S. E. (2003). Accurate pitch memory is widespread. *Psychological Science, 14*, 262–266.

Scherer, K. R. (1985). Vocal affect signaling: A comparative approach. In J. Rosenblatt, C. Beer, M. Busnel, and P. J. B. Slater (Eds.), *Advances in the study of behavior* (pp. 189–244). New York: Academic Press.

Scherer, K. R. (1986). Vocal affect expression: A review and a model for future research. *Psychological Bulletin, 99,* 143–165.

Scherer, K. R., Ladd, D. R., & Silverman, K. E. A. (1984). Vocal cues to speaker affect: Testing two models. *Journal of the Acoustical Society of America, 76,* 1346–1356.

Scherer, K. R., & Zentner, M. R. (2001). Emotional effects of music: Production rules. In P. Juslin and J. A. Sloboda (Eds.), *Music and emotion: Theory and research* (pp. 361–392). Oxford, England: Oxford University Press.

Schön, D., Magne, C., & Besson, M. (2004). The music of speech: Music training facilitates pitch processing in both music and language. *Psychophysiology, 41,* 341–349.

Seashore, H. G. (1938a). An objective analysis of artistic signing. In C. E. Seashore (Ed.), *University of Iowa studies in the psychology of music: Objective analysis of musical performance* (Vol. 4, pp. 12–157). Iowa City: University of Iowa.

Seashore, C. E. (1938b). *Psychology of music.* New York: McGraw-Hill.

Selkirk, S. (1984). *Phonology and syntax.* Cambridge, MA: MIT Press.

Shackford, C. (1961). Some aspects of perception, Part I. *Journal of Music Theory, 5,* 162–202.

Shackford, C. (1962). Some aspects of perception, Part II. *Journal of Music Theory, 6,* 66–90.

Shaffer, L. H. (1981). Performances of Chopin, Bach, and Bartok: Studies in motor programming. *Cognitive Psychology, 13,* 326–376.

Shaffer, L. H., & Todd, N. P. (1987). The interpretive component in musical performance. In A. Gabrielsson (Ed.), *Action and perception in rhythm and music* (pp. 139–152). Stockholm: Royal Swedish Academy of Music.

Shaffer, L. H. (1992). How to interpret music. In M. R. Jones and S. Holleran (Eds.), *Cognitive bases of musical communication* (pp. 263–278). Washington: APA.

Shattuck-Hufnagel, S., & Turk, A. E. (1996). A prosody tutorial for investigators of auditory sentence processing. *Journal of Psycholinguistic Research, 25,* 193–247.

Sloboda, J. A. (1983). The communication of musical metre in piano performance. *Quarterly Journal of Experimental Psychology A, 35,* 377–396.

Sloboda, J. A. (1985). *The musical mind: The cognitive psychology of music.* Oxford: Clarendon Press.

Sloboda, J. A. (1992). Empirical studies of emotional response to music. In M. R. Jones and S. Holleran (Eds.), *Cognitive bases of musical communication* (pp. 33–46). Washington: APA.

Small, A. M. (1937). An objective analysis of artistic violin performance. In C. E. Seashore (Ed.), *University of Iowa studies in the psychology of music: Objective analysis of musical performance* (Vol. 4, pp. 172–231). Iowa City: University of Iowa.

Sundberg, J., Askenfelt, A., & Frydén, L. (1983). Musical performance: A synthesis-by-rule approach. *Computer Music Journal, 7,* 37–43.

Sundberg, J., & Frydén, L. (1985). Teaching a computer to play melodies musically. In L. Anders and E. Kjellberg (Eds.), *Analytica: Studies in the description and analysis of music* (Vol. 1, pp. 67–76). Uppsala: Aeta University.

Sundberg, J., Friberg, A., & Frydén, L. (1989). Rules for automated performance of ensemble music. *Contemporary Music Review, 3,* 89–109.

Sundberg, J., Friberg, A., & Frydén, L. (1991). Threshold and preference quantities of rules for music performance. *Music Perception, 9,* 71–92.

Sundberg, J., & Verrillo, V. (1980). On the anatomy of the ritard: A study of timing in music. *Journal of the Acoustical Society of America, 68,* 772–779.

Swerts, M., & Geluykens, R. (1994). Prosody as a marker of information flow in spoken discourse. *Language and Speech, 37,* 21–43.

Thiessen, E. D., Hill, E. A., Emerson, D. R., & Saffran, J. R. (2005). Effects of prosodic structure on infants' statistical learning. Paper presented at the Cognitive Development Society, October 2005.

Thiessen, E. D., Hill, E. A., & Saffran, J. R. (2005). Infant-directed speech facilitates word segmentation. *Infancy, 7*, 53–71.

Thompson, W. F., Schellenberg, E. G., & Husain, G. (2004). Decoding speech prosody: Do music lessons help? *Emotion, 4*, 46–64.

Thompson, W. F., & Cuddy, L. L. (1997). Music performance and the perception of key. *Journal of Experimental Psychology: Human Perception & Performance, 23*, 116–135.

Todd, N. P. M. (1985). A model of expressive timing in tonal music. *Music Perception, 3*, 33–58.

Todd, N. P. M. (1989). A computational model of rubato. *Contemporary Music Review, 3*, 69–88.

Todd, N. P. M. (1992). The dynamics of dynamics: A model of musical expression. *Journal of the Acoustical Society of America, 91*, 3540–3550.

Todd, N. P. M. (1995). The kinematics of musical expression. *Journal of the Acousitcal Society of America, 97*, 1940–1949.

Trainor, L. J., Austin, C. M., & Desjardins, R. N. (2000). Is infant-directed speech prosody a result of the vocal expression of emotion? *Psychological Science, 11*, 188–195.

Trainor, L. J., Clark, E. D., Huntley, A., & Adams, B. (1997). The acoustic basis for infant-directed singing. *Infant Behavior and Development, 20*, 383–396.

Trainor, L. J., & Rock, A. M. L. (1997). Distinctive messages in infant-directed lullabies and play songs. Presented at the Biennial Meeting of the Society for Research in Child Development, Washington DC.

Trainor, L. J., Wu, L., & Tsang, C. D. (2004). Long-term memory for music: Infants remember tempo and timbre. *Developmental Science, 7*, 289–296.

Trehub, S. E. (2000). Human processing predispositions and musical universals. In N. L. Wallin, B. Merker, and S. Brown (Eds.), *The origins of music* (pp. 427–448). Cambridge, MA: MIT Press.

Trehub, S. E., & Trainor, L. J. (1998). Singing to infants: Lullabies and play songs. In C. Rovee-Collier and L. Lipsitt (Eds.), *Advances in infancy research* (pp. 43–77). Norwood, NJ: Ablex.

Trehub, S. E., Unyk, A. M., & Henderson, J. L. (1994). Children's songs to infant siblings: Parallels with speech. *Journal of Child Language, 21*, 735–744.

Trehub, S. E., Unyk, A. M., Kamenetsky, S. B., Hill, D. S., Trainor, L. J., Henderson, J. L., & Rasaza, M. (1997). Mothers' and fathers' singing to infants. *Developmental Psychology, 33*, 500–507.

Wennerstrom, A. K. (2001). *The music of everyday speech: Prosody and discourse analysis.* Oxford: Oxford University Press.

Wing, A., & Kristofferson, A. B. (1973). The timing of interresponse intervals. *Perception & Psychophysics, 13*, 455–460.

SUBJECT INDEX

N

O

P

Q

R

CONTENTS OF RECENT VOLUMES

Volume 40

Volume 41

Volume 42

Volume 43

Volume 44

Volume 45